FINANCIAL INSTITUTIONS AND SERVICES

WHO REGULATES WHOM: U.S. FINANCIAL OVERSIGHT

FINANCIAL INSTITUTIONS AND SERVICES

Additional books in this series can be found on Nova's website at:

https://www.novapublishers.com/catalog/index.php?cPath=23_29&seriesp
=Financial%20Institutions%20and%20Services&sort=2a&page=2

Additional E-books in this series can be found on Nova's website at:

https://www.novapublishers.com/catalog/index.php?cPath=23_29&seriespe
=Financial+Institutions+and+Services

FINANCIAL INSTITUTIONS AND SERVICES

WHO REGULATES WHOM: U.S. FINANCIAL OVERSIGHT

MILTON H. LAZARUS
EDITOR

Nova Science Publishers, Inc.
New York

Copyright © 2010 by Nova Science Publishers, Inc.

All rights reserved. No part of this book may be reproduced, stored in a retrieval system or transmitted in any form or by any means: electronic, electrostatic, magnetic, tape, mechanical photocopying, recording or otherwise without the written permission of the Publisher.

For permission to use material from this book please contact us:
Telephone 631-231-7269; Fax 631-231-8175
Web Site: http://www.novapublishers.com

NOTICE TO THE READER

The Publisher has taken reasonable care in the preparation of this book, but makes no expressed or implied warranty of any kind and assumes no responsibility for any errors or omissions. No liability is assumed for incidental or consequential damages in connection with or arising out of information contained in this book. The Publisher shall not be liable for any special, consequential, or exemplary damages resulting, in whole or in part, from the readers' use of, or reliance upon, this material. Any parts of this book based on government reports are so indicated and copyright is claimed for those parts to the extent applicable to compilations of such works.

Independent verification should be sought for any data, advice or recommendations contained in this book. In addition, no responsibility is assumed by the publisher for any injury and/or damage to persons or property arising from any methods, products, instructions, ideas or otherwise contained in this publication.

This publication is designed to provide accurate and authoritative information with regard to the subject matter covered herein. It is sold with the clear understanding that the Publisher is not engaged in rendering legal or any other professional services. If legal or any other expert assistance is required, the services of a competent person should be sought. FROM A DECLARATION OF PARTICIPANTS JOINTLY ADOPTED BY A COMMITTEE OF THE AMERICAN BAR ASSOCIATION AND A COMMITTEE OF PUBLISHERS.

LIBRARY OF CONGRESS CATALOGING-IN-PUBLICATION DATA

Upon Available Request

ISBN : 978-1-60876-981-0

Published by Nova Science Publishers, Inc. ✣ *New York*

CONTENTS

Preface		vii
Chapter 1	**Credit Rating Agencies and Their Regulation** *Gary Shorter and Michael V. Seitzinger*	1
Chapter 2	**Financial Regulatory Reform: Analysis of the Consumer Financial Protection Agency (CFPA) as Proposed by the Obama Administration and H.R. 3126** *David H. Carpenter and Mark Jickling*	23
Chapter 3	**Financial Regulatory Reform A New Foundation: Rebuilding Financial Supervision and Regulation** *Department of the Treasury*	35
Chapter 4	**Hedge Funds: Overview of Regulatory Oversight, Counterparty Risks and Investment Challenges** *Orice M. Williams*	113
Chapter 5	**Hedge Funds: Should They Be Regulated?** *Mark Jickling*	125
Chapter 6	**Macroprudential Oversight: Monitoring the Financial System** *Darryl E. Getter*	133
Chapter 7	**Financial Market Regulation: Financial Crisis Highlights Need to Improve Oversight of Leverage at Financial Institutions and across System** *United States Government Accountability Office*	141
Chapter 8	**Who Regulates Whom? An Overview of U.S. Financial Supervision** *Mark Jickling and Edward V. Murphy*	229
Chapter Sources		265
Index		267

PREFACE

Federal financial regulation in the United States has evolved through a series of piecemeal responses to developments and crises in financial markets. This new book provides an overview of current U.S. financial regulation: which agencies are responsible for which institutions and markets, and what kinds of authority they have. Banking regulation is largely based on a quid pro quo that was adopted in response to widespread bank failures. Federal securities regulation is based on the principle of disclosure, rather than direct regulation. Derivatives trading is supervised by the Commodity Futures Trading Commission (CFTC), which oversees trading on the futures exchanges, which have self-regulatory responsibilities as well. There is also a large over-the-counter (off-exchange) derivatives market that is largely unregulated. The Federal Housing Finance Agency (FHFA) oversees a group of government-sponsored enterprises (GSEs)—public/private hybrid firms that seek both to earn profits and to further the policy objectives set out in their statutory charters. No federal agency has jurisdiction over trading in foreign exchange or U.S. Treasury securities; nonbank lenders fall outside the regulatory umbrella; and hedge funds, private equity firms, and venture capital investors are largely unregulated (although their transactions in securities and derivatives markets may be).

Chapter 1 - Credit rating agencies (CRAs) presumably provide investors with an informed perspective on securities' debt risk (also referred to as credit risk), the risk that issuers will fail to make promised interest or principal payments when they are due. The agencies provide judgments ("opinions") on the creditworthiness of bonds issued by a wide spectrum of entities, including corporations, sovereign nations, nonprofit firms, special purpose entities, and state and municipal governments. The judgments take the form of ratings that are usually displayed in a letter hierarchical format: AAA being the highest and safest, with lower grades representing an increasing scale of risk to the investor. Globally, there are about 100 rating agencies. The three dominant CRAs are Moody's, Standard & Poor's (a subsidiary of McGraw-Hill), and Fitch (a subsidiary of FIMILAC, a French business services conglomerate).

CRAs have been a feature of securities markets since the 19th century; they predate federal regulation of the markets. The Securities and Exchange Commission (SEC) issues a designation of Nationally Recognized Statistical Rating Organization (NRSRO), which is important because a variety of laws and regulations reference their use. (For example, the amount of risk-based capital that banks must hold against a portfolio of securities is linked to ratings; and thrift institutions are not allowed to own bonds rated below investment grade.) In recent years, many assert that the performance of the dominant rating agencies has been marked by a number of spectacular failures. Companies like Enron and WorldCom retained their high credit ratings until a few days before they filed for bankruptcy. More recently, many mortgage-backed securities initially rated AAA have defaulted or have been sharply downgraded. In both situations, investors who relied on the ratings suffered heavy losses. In response, the SEC and other observers have criticized the failings of the three dominant CRAs in their ratings of mortgage-backed securities, which have played a central role in the financial crisis. Subsequently, Moody's, Standard & Poor's, and Fitch have adopted a number of voluntary reforms intended to address their perceived shortcomings, including the installation of corporate ombudsmen.

In June 2008, New York Attorney General Andrew Cuomo reached an agreement with Moody's, Standard & Poor's, and Fitch in which, among other things, they agreed to establish fee-forservice structures under which they will be compensated regardless of whether the investment bank ultimately selects them to rate residential mortgage-backed securities.

In February 2009, the SEC adopted several disclosure and conflict of interest reforms, including a prohibition on a person within an NRSRO with responsibility for determining credit ratings from participating in any fee discussions, negotiations, or arrangements; and a requirement that each NRSRO and NRSRO applicant provide rating change statistics for each asset class of credit ratings for which it is registered or is seeking registration, broken out over 1, 3, and 10 year periods. In April 2009, the European Union (EU) also adopted a number of CRA reforms, including requirements that CRAs will have to disclose the models, methodologies, and key assumptions on which they base their ratings; and CRAs will have to have an internal function to review the quality of their own ratings and have at least two independent directors on their boards who do not receive bonuses that are connected to the CRA's performance.

To date, legislative responses to the perceived CRA failings include S. 927 (Pryor), H.R. 74 (Issa), H.R. 1181 (Ackerman), and H.R. 1445 (McHenry). This report will be updated as events warrant.

Credit rating agencies (CRAs) provide investors with what is presumed to be an informed perspective on securities' debt risk (also referred to as credit risk), the risk that issuers will fail to make promised interest or principal payments when they are due. The agencies provide judgments ("opinions") on the creditworthiness of bonds issued by a wide spectrum of entities, including corporations, nations, nonprofit firms, special purpose entities, and state and municipal governments. The judgments take the form of ratings that are usually displayed in a letter hierarchical format: AAA being the highest and safest, with lower grades representing an increasing scale of risk to the investor. Globally, there are about 100 rating agencies. The three dominant CRAs are Moody's,[1] Standard & Poor's (S&P, a subsidiary of McGraw-Hill), and Fitch (a subsidiary of FIMILAC, a French business services conglomerate). Smaller U.S.-based agencies also exist.

Chapter 2 - In the wake of what many believe is the worst U.S. financial crisis since the Great Depression, the Obama Administration has proposed sweeping reforms of the financial services regulatory system, the broad outline of which has been encompassed in a nearly 90-page document called the President's White Paper (the White Paper or the Proposal). The Proposal seeks to meet five objectives:

(1) "Promote robust supervision and regulation of financial firms";

(2) "Establish comprehensive supervision and regulation of financial markets";
(3) "Protect consumers and investors from financial abuse";
(4) "Improve tools for managing financial crises"; and
(5) "Raise international regulatory standards and improve international cooperation."

The Administration likely will offer specific legislative proposals that would implement each of the five objectives of the White Paper. On June 30, 2009, the Obama Administration made available the first such legislative proposal, called the Consumer Financial Protection Agency Act of 2009 (the CFPA Act or the Act). The Act would establish a new executive agency, the Consumer Financial Protection Agency (the CFPA or the Agency), to protect consumers of financial products and services. On July 8, 2009, Representative Barney Frank, Chairman of the House Financial Services Committee, introduced very similar legislation, H.R. 3126, which also is entitled the CFPA Act of 2009.

This report provides a brief summary of the President's CFPA Act and delineates some of the substantive differences between it and H.R. 3126, as introduced. It then analyzes some of the policy implications of the proposal, focusing on the separation of safety and soundness regulation from consumer protection, financial innovation, and the scope of regulation. The report then raises some questions regarding state law preemption, sources of funding, and rulemaking procedures that the Act does not fully answer.

Chapter 3 - Over the past two years we have faced the most severe financial crisis since the Great Depression. Americans across the nation are struggling with unemployment, failing businesses, falling home prices, and declining savings. These challenges have forced the government to take extraordinary measures to revive our financial system so that people can access loans to buy a car or home, pay for a child's education, or finance a business.

The roots of this crisis go back decades. Years without a serious economic recession bred complacency among financial intermediaries and investors. Financial challenges such as the near-failure of Long-Term Capital Management and the Asian Financial Crisis had minimal impact on economic growth in the U.S., which bred exaggerated expectations about the resilience of our financial markets and firms. Rising asset prices, particularly in housing, hid weak credit underwriting standards and masked the growing leverage throughout the system.

At some of our most sophisticated financial firms, risk management systems did not keep pace with the complexity of new financial products. The lack of transparency and standards in markets for securitized loans helped to weaken underwriting standards. Market discipline broke down as investors relied excessively on credit rating agencies. Compensation practices throughout the financial services industry rewarded short-term profits at the expense of long-term value.

Households saw significant increases in access to credit, but those gains were overshadowed by pervasive failures in consumer protection, leaving many Americans with obligations that they did not understand and could not afford.

While this crisis had many causes, it is clear now that the government could have done more to prevent many of these problems from growing out of control and threatening the stability of our financial system. Gaps and weaknesses in the supervision and regulation of financial firms presented challenges to our government's ability to monitor, prevent, or address risks as they built up in the system. No regulator saw its job as protecting the economy and financial system as a whole. Existing approaches to bank holding company regulation focused on protecting the subsidiary bank, not on comprehensive regulation of the whole firm. Investment banks were permitted to opt for a different regime under a different regulator, and in doing so, escaped adequate constraints on leverage. Other firms, such as AIG, owned insured depositories, but escaped the strictures of serious holding company regulation because the depositories that they owned were technically not "banks" under relevant law.

We must act now to restore confidence in the integrity of our financial system. The lasting economic damage to ordinary families and businesses is a constant reminder of the urgent need to act to reform our financial regulatory system and put our economy on track to a sustainable recovery. We must build a new foundation for financial regulation and supervision that is simpler and more effectively enforced, that protects consumers and investors, that rewards innovation and that is able to adapt and evolve with changes in the financial market.

In the following pages, we propose reforms to meet five key objectives:

(1) *Promote robust supervision and regulation of financial firms.* Financial institutions that are critical to market functioning should be subject to strong oversight. No financial firm that poses a significant risk to the financial system should be unregulated or weakly regulated. We need clear accountability in financial oversight and supervision. We propose:
- A new Financial Services Oversight Council of financial regulators to identify emerging systemic risks and improve interagency cooperation.
- New authority for the Federal Reserve to supervise all firms that could pose a threat to financial stability, even those that do not own banks.
- Stronger capital and other prudential standards for all financial firms, and even higher standards for large, interconnected firms.
- A new National Bank Supervisor to supervise all federally chartered banks.
- Elimination of the federal thrift charter and other loopholes that allowed some depository institutions to avoid bank holding company regulation by the Federal Reserve.
- The registration of advisers of hedge funds and other private pools of capital with the SEC.

(2) *Establish comprehensive supervision of financial markets.* Our major financial markets must be strong enough to withstand both system-wide stress and the failure of one or more large institutions. We propose:
- Enhanced regulation of securitization markets, including new requirements for market transparency, stronger regulation of credit rating agencies, and a requirement that issuers and originators retain a financial interest in securitized loans.
- Comprehensive regulation of all over-the-counter derivatives.
- New authority for the Federal Reserve to oversee payment, clearing, and settlement systems.

(3) *Protect consumers and investors from financial abuse.* To rebuild trust in our markets, we need strong and consistent regulation and supervision of consumer financial services and investment markets. We should base this oversight not on speculation or abstract models, but on actual data about how people make financial decisions. We must promote transparency, simplicity, fairness, accountability, and access. We propose:
- A new Consumer Financial Protection Agency to protect consumers across the financial sector from unfair, deceptive, and abusive practices.
- Stronger regulations to improve the transparency, fairness, and appropriateness of consumer and investor products and services.
- A level playing field and higher standards for providers of consumer financial products and services, whether or not they are part of a bank.

(4) *Provide the government with the tools it needs to manage financial crises.* We need to be sure that the government has the tools it needs to manage crises, if and when they arise, so that we are not left with untenable choices between bailouts and financial collapse. We propose:
- A new regime to resolve nonbank financial institutions whose failure could have serious systemic effects.
- Revisions to the Federal Reserve's emergency lending authority to improve accountability.

(5) *Raise international regulatory standards and improve international cooperation.* The challenges we face are not just American challenges, they are global challenges. So, as we work to set high regulatory standards here in the United States, we must ask the world to do the same. We propose:
- International reforms to support our efforts at home, including strengthening the capital framework; improving oversight of global financial markets; coordinating supervision of internationally active firms; and enhancing crisis management tools.

In addition to substantive reforms of the authorities and practices of regulation and supervision, the proposals contained in this report entail a significant restructuring of our regulatory system. We propose the creation of a Financial Services Oversight Council, chaired by Treasury and including the heads of the principal federal financial regulators as members. We also propose the creation of two new agencies. We propose the creation of the Consumer Financial Protection Agency, which will be an independent entity dedicated to consumer protection in credit, savings, and payments markets. We also propose the creation of the National Bank Supervisor, which will be a single agency with separate status in Treasury with responsibility for federally chartered depository institutions. To promote national coordination in the insurance sector, we propose the creation of an Office of National Insurance within Treasury.

Under our proposal, the Federal Reserve and the Federal Deposit Insurance Corporation (FDIC) would maintain their respective roles in the supervision and regulation of state-chartered banks, and the National Credit Union Administration (NCUA) would maintain its authorities with regard to credit unions. The Securities and Exchange Commission (SEC) and

Commodity Futures Trading Commission (CFTC) would maintain their current responsibilities and authorities as market regulators, though we propose to harmonize the statutory and regulatory frameworks for futures and securities.

The proposals contained in this report do not represent the complete set of potentially desirable reforms in financial regulation. More can and should be done in the future. We focus here on what is essential: to address the causes of the current crisis, to create a more stable financial system that is fair for consumers, and to help prevent and contain potential crises in the future. *(For a detailed list of recommendations, please see Summary of Recommendations following the Introduction.)*

These proposals are the product of broad-ranging individual consultations with members of the President's Working Group on Financial Markets, Members of Congress, academics, consumer and investor advocates, community-based organizations, the business community, and industry and market participants.

Chapter 4 - In 2008, GAO issued two reports on hedge funds—pooled investment vehicles that are privately managed and often engage in active trading of various types of securities and commodity futures and options contracts—highlighting the need for continued regulatory attention and for guidance to better inform pension plans on the risks and challenges of hedge fund investments. Hedge funds generally qualified for exemption from certain securities laws and regulations, including the requirement to register as an investment company. Hedge funds have been deeply affected by the recent financial turmoil. But an industry survey of institutional investors suggests that these investors are still committed to investing in hedge funds in the long term. For the first time hedge funds are allowed to borrow from the Federal Reserve under the Term- Asset Backed Loan Facility. As such, the regulatory oversight issues and investment challenges raised by the 2008 reports still remain relevant.

This testimony discusses: (1) federal regulators' oversight of hedge fund-related activities; (2) potential benefits, risks, and challenges pension plans face in investing in hedge funds; (3) the measures investors, creditors, and counterparties have taken to impose market discipline on hedge funds; and (4) the potential for systemic risk from hedge fund- related activities. To do this work we relied upon our issued reports and updated data where possible.

View GAO-09-677T or key components. For more information, contact Orice M. Williams at (202) 512-8678 or williamso@gao.gov.

Chapter 5 - In an echo of the Robber Baron Era, the late 20th century saw the rise of a new elite class, who made their fortunes not in steel, oil, or railroads, but in financial speculation. These gilded few are the managers of a group of private, unregulated investment partnerships, called hedge funds. Deploying their own capital and that of well-to-do investors, successful hedge fund managers frequently (but not consistently) outperform public mutual funds. Hedge funds use many different investment strategies, but the largest and best-known funds engage in high-risk speculation in markets around the world. Wherever there is financial volatility, the hedge funds will probably be there.

Hedge funds can also lose money very quickly. In 1998, one fund—Long-Term Capital Management—saw its capital shrink from about $4 billion to a few hundred million in a matter of weeks. To prevent default, the Federal Reserve engineered a rescue by 13 large commercial and investment banks. Intervention was thought necessary because the fund's failure might have caused widespread disruption in financial markets. Despite the risks, investors poured money into hedge funds in recent years, until market losses in 2008 prompted a wave of redemption requests.

In view of the growing impact of hedge funds on a variety of financial markets, the Securities and Exchange Commission (SEC) in October 2004 adopted a regulation that required hedge funds to register as investment advisers, disclose basic information about their operations, and open their books for inspection. The regulation took effect in February 2006, but on June 23, 2006, a court challenge was upheld and the rule was vacated. In December 2006, the SEC proposed raising the "accredited investor" standard—to be permitted to invest in hedge funds, an investor would need $2.5 million in assets, instead of $1 million, but has yet to adopt a final rule.

Bills before the 111th Congress would require hedge funds to register with the SEC if their capital exceeded $50 million (S. 344) or $25 million (H.R. 711). S. 1276 would require registration of hedge funds, private equity firms, and venture capital funds, and would authorize the SEC to collect systemic risk data from them. H.R. 712 mandates more disclosure for pension funds that invest in hedge funds, and H.R. 713 directs the President's Working Group on Financial Markets to study the hedge fund industry. S. 506 and H.R. 1265 would change the tax treatment of offshore funds.

Chapter 6 - Recent innovations in finance, while increasing the capacity to borrow and lend, resulted in a large volume of banking transactions occurring outside of traditional banking institutions. Also, even though existing regulatory efforts supervise individual institutions for safety and soundness, there are risks that do not reside with those institutions but may still adversely affect the system as a whole. Macroprudential policy refers to a variety of tasks designed to defend the broad financial system against threats to its stability. Such responsibilities include monitoring the system for systemic risk vulnerabilities; developing early warning systems of financial distress; conducting stress-testing exercises; and advising other regulatory agencies on matters related to financial stability. This report provides background and discusses the benefits and limitations of macroprudential policy.

Chapter 7 - The Emergency Economic Stabilization Act directed GAO to study the role of leverage in the current financial crisis and federal oversight of leverage. GAO's objectives were to review (1) how leveraging and deleveraging by financial institutions may have contributed to the crisis, (2) regulations adopted by federal financial regulators to limit leverage and how regulators oversee compliance with the regulations, and (3) any limitations the current crisis has revealed in regulatory approaches used to restrict leverage and regulatory proposals to address them. To meet these objectives, GAO built on its existing body of work, reviewed relevant laws and regulations and academic and other studies, and interviewed regulators and market participants.

Chapter 8 - Federal financial regulation in the United States has evolved through a series of piecemeal responses to developments and crises in financial markets. This report provides an overview of current U.S. financial regulation: which agencies are responsible for which institutions and markets, and what kinds of authority they have.

Banking regulation is largely based on a quid pro quo that was adopted in response to widespread bank failures. The federal government provides a safety net for some banking operations and in return the banks accept federal regulation of their operations, including the amount of risk they may incur. For example, federal deposit insurance reduces customers' incentive to withdraw their funds at the first sign of trouble. In return for federal deposit insurance, bank regulators can order a stop to "unsafe and unsound" banking practices and can take prompt corrective action with troubled banks, including closing the institution. There are five federal bank regulators, each supervising different (and often overlapping) sets of depository institutions.

Federal securities regulation is based on the principle of disclosure, rather than direct regulation. Firms that sell securities to the public must register with the Securities and Exchange Commission (SEC), but the agency has no authority to prevent excessive risk taking. SEC registration in no way implies that an investment is safe, only that the risks have been fully disclosed. The SEC also registers several classes of securities market participants and firms, but relies more on industry self-regulation than do the banking agencies. Derivatives trading is supervised by the Commodity Futures Trading Commission (CFTC), which oversees trading on the futures exchanges, which have self-regulatory responsibilities as well. There is also a large over-the-counter (off-exchange) derivatives market that is largely unregulated.

The Federal Housing Finance Agency (FHFA) oversees a group of government-sponsored enterprises (GSEs)—public/private hybrid firms that seek both to earn profits and to further the policy objectives set out in their statutory charters. Two GSEs, Fannie Mae and Freddie Mac, were placed in conservatorship by the FHFA in September 2008 after losses in mortgage asset portfolios made them effectively insolvent. A number of financial markets are unregulated, including some of the largest. No federal agency has jurisdiction over trading in foreign exchange or U.S. Treasury securities; nonbank lenders fall outside the regulatory umbrella; and hedge funds, private equity firms, and venture capital investors are largely unregulated (although their transactions in securities and derivatives markets may be).

The United States has never attempted a wholesale reformation of the entire regulatory system comparable to the 1986 "Big Bang" in the UK, which reorganized regulatory agencies across industry lines and sought to implement a consistent philosophy of regulation. In the wake of the current financial turmoil, however, such a reevaluation is possible, and a number of broad restructuring proposals have already come forward.

In the 111th Congress, S. 566, "Financial Product Safety Commission Act of 2009," introduced by Senator Durbin, would create a federal financial regulator whose sole focus is the safety of consumer financial products.

This report does not attempt to analyze the strengths and weaknesses of the U.S. regulatory system. Rather, it provides a description of the current system, to aid in the evaluation of reform proposals. It will be updated as warranted by market events.

Chapter 1

CREDIT RATING AGENCIES AND THEIR REGULATION

Gary Shorter and Michael V. Seitzinger

SUMMARY

Credit rating agencies (CRAs) presumably provide investors with an informed perspective on securities' debt risk (also referred to as credit risk), the risk that issuers will fail to make promised interest or principal payments when they are due. The agencies provide judgments ("opinions") on the creditworthiness of bonds issued by a wide spectrum of entities, including corporations, sovereign nations, nonprofit firms, special purpose entities, and state and municipal governments. The judgments take the form of ratings that are usually displayed in a letter hierarchical format: AAA being the highest and safest, with lower grades representing an increasing scale of risk to the investor. Globally, there are about 100 rating agencies. The three dominant CRAs are Moody's, Standard & Poor's (a subsidiary of McGraw-Hill), and Fitch (a subsidiary of FIMILAC, a French business services conglomerate).

CRAs have been a feature of securities markets since the 19th century; they predate federal regulation of the markets. The Securities and Exchange Commission (SEC) issues a designation of Nationally Recognized Statistical Rating Organization (NRSRO), which is important because a variety of laws and regulations reference their use. (For example, the amount of risk-based capital that banks must hold against a portfolio of securities is linked to ratings; and thrift institutions are not allowed to own bonds rated below investment grade.) In recent years, many assert that the performance of the dominant rating agencies has been marked by a number of spectacular failures. Companies like Enron and WorldCom retained their high credit ratings until a few days before they filed for bankruptcy. More recently, many mortgage-backed securities initially rated AAA have defaulted or have been sharply downgraded. In both situations, investors who relied on the ratings suffered heavy losses. In response, the SEC and other observers have criticized the failings of the three dominant CRAs in their ratings of mortgage-backed securities, which have played a central role in the financial crisis. Subsequently, Moody's, Standard & Poor's, and Fitch have adopted a number of voluntary reforms intended to address their perceived shortcomings, including the installation of corporate ombudsmen.

In June 2008, New York Attorney General Andrew Cuomo reached an agreement with Moody's, Standard & Poor's, and Fitch in which, among other things, they agreed to establish fee-forservice structures under which they will be compensated regardless of whether the investment bank ultimately selects them to rate residential mortgage-backed securities.

In February 2009, the SEC adopted several disclosure and conflict of interest reforms, including a prohibition on a person within an NRSRO with responsibility for determining credit ratings from participating in any fee discussions, negotiations, or arrangements; and a requirement that each NRSRO and NRSRO applicant provide rating change statistics for each asset class of credit ratings for which it is registered or is seeking registration, broken out over 1, 3, and 10 year periods. In April 2009, the European Union (EU) also adopted a number of CRA reforms, including requirements that CRAs will have to disclose the models, methodologies, and key assumptions on which they base their ratings; and CRAs will have to have an internal function to review the quality of their own ratings and have at least two independent directors on their boards who do not receive bonuses that are connected to the CRA's performance.

To date, legislative responses to the perceived CRA failings include S. 927 (Pryor), H.R. 74 (Issa), H.R. 1181 (Ackerman), and H.R. 1445 (McHenry). This report will be updated as events warrant.

Credit rating agencies (CRAs) provide investors with what is presumed to be an informed perspective on securities' debt risk (also referred to as credit risk), the risk that issuers will fail to make promised interest or principal payments when they are due. The agencies provide judgments ("opinions") on the creditworthiness of bonds issued by a wide spectrum of entities, including corporations, nations, nonprofit firms, special purpose entities, and state and municipal governments. The judgments take the form of ratings that are usually displayed in a letter hierarchical format: AAA being the highest and safest, with lower grades representing an increasing scale of risk to the investor. Globally, there are about 100 rating agencies. The three dominant CRAs are Moody's,[1] Standard & Poor's (S&P, a subsidiary of McGraw-Hill), and Fitch (a subsidiary of FIMILAC, a French business services conglomerate). Smaller U.S.-based agencies also exist.

Evolution of the Issuer-Pays Model

At the beginning of the 20th century, John Moody, founder of Moody's, began the practice of selling voluminous rating manuals to bond investors, a business model known as "subscriber- pays." By the 1970s, the three dominant CRAs had changed to an "issuer-pays" model, in which a bond's issuer or arranger pays an agency or agencies for initial ratings and for ongoing ratings. The ratings are then available to the public free of charge.

Several reasons have been advanced for the business change, including (1) the advent of high-speed copying machines in the early 1970s may have sparked concerns among the CRAs that their work would be widely copied by non-payers; (2) the CRAs may have come to the realization that issuers increasingly required certain ratings to sell their bonds to regulated financial institutions and would be willing to pay for a rating; (3) the bond market upheaval brought about by the bankruptcy of the Penn-Central Railroad may have made bond issuers more willing to pay CRAs to confirm their creditworthiness;[2] and (4) the rise of asset-backed securitization in the 1970s.[3]

The subscriber-pays model, however, can still be found among a number of small CRAs. These CRAs are paid by investors or other third parties (e.g., banks, insurance funds, pension funds, large creditors) to rate their securities. Like the issuer-pays agencies, they use publicly available financial data to perform quantitative analysis. Unlike issuer-pays CRAs, they do not receive additional proprietary information from the issuers, and they do not collect qualitative data on the issuer through ongoing interviews. Thus, while issuer-pays CRAs tend to employ both quantitative and qualitative ratings reviews, subscriber-pays CRAs tend to emphasize a quantitative approach involving analytical models and software.[4]

THE NATIONALLY RECOGNIZED STATISTICAL RATING ORGANIZATION DESIGNATION AND ITS POTENTIAL IMPACT

Adopted by the Securities and Exchange Commission (SEC) in 1975, the designation of a nationally recognized statistical rating organization (NRSRO) was originally used as a part of the agency's determination of capital charges on different grades of debt securities under the SEC's net capital rule (Rule 15c3-1 under the Securities Exchange Act of 1934). Under the rule, when broker-dealers compute their net capital amounts, they must deduct from their net worth certain percentages of the market value (haircuts) of their securities positions. The agency applied reduced haircuts to the securities held by broker-dealers that were rated investment grade by a credit rating agency of national repute based on the presumption that such securities typically were more liquid and less volatile in price than securities that were less highly rated.

When it began using ratings to enforce the net capital rule in 1975, the SEC staff, in consultation with agency commissioners, made the determination that the ratings of the three dominant agencies, S&P, Moody's, and Fitch, were nationally used and should thus be considered NRSROs with respect to SEC enforcement of the net capital rule. Between 1975 and 2000, the SEC added four more NRSROs to the original three.

Over time, requiring certain NRSRO-reviewed credit ratings became an integral part of global and national rules. It also was codified in numerous federal and state statutes. For example, Rule 2a-7, an amendment to the Investment Company Act of 1940, requires that money market funds invest in debt that has been rated by an NRSRO. Also, under the Financial Institutions Reform, Recovery, and Enforcement Act of 1989 (FIRREA, P.L. 101-73), savings and loans could no longer purchase bonds with NRSRO-issued below investment grade ratings (i.e., junk bonds). In addition to these and other federal statutes, more than 100 state level statutes make reference to credit ratings issued by NRSROs, by some accounts. Also, under the Basel II agreement of the Basel Committee on Banking Supervision,[5] banking regulators can allow banks to use credit ratings from certain approved CRAs (technically known as External Credit Assessment Institutions), a small group of agencies dominated by Moody's, S&P, and Fitch.

The SEC never defined the term NRSRO or specified how a CRA might become one. Its approach has been described as essentially one of "we know-it-when-we-see-it." The resulting limited growth in the pool of NRSROs was widely believed to have helped to further entrench the three dominant CRAs: by some accounts, they have about 98% of total ratings and collect 90% of total rating revenue.

Earlier in this decade, various firms like the energy behemoth Enron and the telecommunications company Worldcom collapsed soon after having maintained investment grade ratings from the major CRAs. That phenomenon would have enduring regulatory ripple effects. Various congressional hearings ensued and the Sarbanes-Oxley Act of 2002 was adopted. Among other things, it required the SEC to issue a report on the NRSRO determination process.

In January 2003, the SEC issued its congressionally directed report, *Report on the Role and Function of Credit Rating Agencies in the Operation of the Securities Markets*.[6] In June 2003, the agency also issued a 2003 concept release[7] for the purpose of soliciting public comments regarding possible CRA reform, including the possibility of abandoning the use of ratings for regulatory purposes under the federal securities laws and the desirability of a formal process for determining whose ratings should be used and what kind of oversight should be given to the CRAs.[8]

The Credit Rating Agency Reform Act of 2006

With the introduction of H.R. 2990, titled the Credit Rating Agency Duopoly Relief Act of 2005, on June 20, 2005, the 109th Congress began the process of considering legislation to regulate the registration of credit rating agencies. At the end of this legislative process, S. 3850,[9] the Credit Rating Agency Reform Act of 2006, was passed by unanimous consent by the Senate on September 22, 2006, and under suspension of the rules by the House on September 27, 2006. It was signed into law by the President on September 29, 2006, as P.L. 109-291.

Section 2 of P.L. 109-291 sets forth the congressional findings leading to the need for regulation of credit rating agencies. This section, referencing Section 702 of the Sarbanes-Oxley Act and comments on the SEC's concept releases and proposed rules, states the finding that "credit rating agencies are of national importance." Among the reasons provided for the need for legislation to regulate credit rating agencies are that the two largest credit rating agencies [Moody's and Standard & Poor's] serve most of the market and that additional competition is in the public interest and that the SEC has stated that it needs statutory authority to oversee the credit rating industry.

Section 3 adds five new definitions to the Securities Exchange Act of 1934:[10] credit rating, credit rating agency, nationally recognized statistical rating organization, person associated with a nationally recognized statistical rating organization, and qualified institutional buyer.[11] The definition of "nationally recognized statistical rating organization" would appear to resolve uncertainty which might have existed concerning the SEC's somewhat informal recognition of such an organization. Under the new statute a "nationally recognized statistical rating organization" is a credit rating agency that has been in business as a credit rating agency for at least the three consecutive years immediately preceding the date of its application for registration as an NRSRO and which issues credit ratings certified by qualified institutional buyers concerning financial institutions, brokers, or dealers; insurance companies; corporate issuers; issuers of asset-backed securities; issuers of government securities, municipal securities, or securities issued by foreign governments; or a combination of one or more categories of obligors described in any of the aforementioned categories.

To be deemed by the SEC as a nationally recognized statistical rating organization, a credit rating agency must submit in its application to the SEC detailed information, such as the following: (1) credit ratings performance measurement statistics over short-term, mid-term, and long-term periods; (2) the procedures and methodologies that the applicant uses in determining credit ratings; (3) policies or procedures adopted and implemented by the applicant to prevent the misuse of material, nonpublic information; (4) its organizational structure; (5) whether it has in effect a code of ethics and, if not, why not; (6) any conflict of interest relating to its issuance of credit ratings; (7) on a confidential basis a list of the twenty largest issuers and subscribers that use its credit rating services by amount of net revenues received in the fiscal year immediately preceding the date of submission of the application; and (8) any other information and documents which the SEC may by rule prescribe as necessary or appropriate in the public interest or for the protection of investors.[12] The SEC is required to follow a specific time frame and procedure in determining whether to grant the application for treatment as a nationally recognized statistical rating organization.

The legislation makes it unlawful for any nationally recognized statistical rating organization to represent or imply that it has been designated, sponsored, recommended, or approved by the United States or by any U.S. agency, officer, or employee. The legislation requires each nationally recognized statistical rating organization to establish, maintain, and enforce written policies and procedures reasonably designed to address and manage any conflicts of interest that might arise.

P.L. 109-291 fits within the general philosophy of all of the major federal securities laws. This philosophy is premised upon the belief that, so long as there is full and accurate disclosure of all material information by a covered company, the investing public will have sufficient information upon which to make its investment decisions. The Credit Rating Agency Reform Act of 2006 requires a credit agency wishing to have the status of a nationally recognized statistical rating organization to disclose to the SEC significant information about its business and its methods for issuing credit ratings so that the investing public will have information to help determine the likely accuracy of credit ratings that the agency has assigned.

The law took effect in June 2007, with the SEC issuing its first round of final implementation rules that same month. In September 2007, Moody's, S&P, and Fitch were formally registered as NRSROs under the new regime. Currently, there are 10 NRSROs: two are headquartered in Japan; one is based in Canada; and one, A.M. Best, specializes in insurance companies' issues. The others consist of the three dominant and three smaller CRAs.

THE RATING AGENCIES AND STRUCTURED FINANCE

The provision of investment grade ratings by the dominant CRAs was a critical part of the process of structuring the residential mortgage-backed securities (RMBS) and collateralized debt obligations (CDOs) that held subprime housing mortgages. Basically, the

CRAs evaluated the probabilities of default for individual mortgages, analyzed the correlations between individual loans, used this to assess the probability of default for the securitized products, and then rated the different tranches[13] of the structured products[14] accordingly.

Moody's, S&P, and Fitch were all active participants in rating the various structured securities backed by mortgages. However, Moody's structured-finance unit dominated the practice: the unit accounted for about 28% of the firm's revenues in 1998. By 2006, it was pulling about 43%, a year in which it earned more revenue ($881 million) from structured finance than all of its revenues in 2001. By 2007, the company was reportedly rating about 94% of the $190 billion in mortgage-related and other structured-finance CDOs issued in 2007.[15]

Many believe that the three dominant CRAs fundamentally failed in their rating processes when it came to judging the likelihood of a decline in housing prices, the proper weight to be attached to the effect of falling house prices on loan default rates, and the inter-relationship between loan defaults and the prospect of further defaults. In 2006, after several years of the "housing bubble," the subprime mortgage sector began a precipitous collapse, an implosion that helped engender the financial crisis. During the housing boom cycle, the CRAs often gave top tier AAA ratings to many structured securities, only to downgrade many of them later to levels often below investment grade status.

In June 2008, the SEC observed:

> The scope and magnitude of these downgrades has caused a loss of confidence among investors in the reliability of RMBS [residential mortgage-backed securities] and CDO [collateralized debt obligations] credit ratings issued by the NRSROs. This lack of confidence in the accuracy of NRSRO ratings has been a factor in the broader dislocation in the credit markets. For example, the complexity of assessing the risk of structured finance products and the lack of commonly accepted methods for measuring the risk has caused investors to leave the market, including the market for AAA instruments, particularly investors that had relied primarily on NRSRO credit ratings in assessing whether to purchase these instruments. This has had a significant impact on the liquidity of the market for these instruments. In the wake of these events, the NRSROs that rated subprime RMBS and CDOs have come under intense criticism and scrutiny....[16]

A number of key reasons for the CRAs' perceived failings have been advanced. They include

- **Business Model Bias.** The issuer-pays business model is said to create a potential bias toward providing overly favorable ratings and is also said to encourage "ratings shopping." That in turn is said to engender "a race to the bottom" among the competing dominant agencies.[17]

- **The Existence of a Quasi-Regulatory License.** The existence of the aforementioned series of statutes and regulations requiring specific levels of NRSRO ratings is said to further protect and reinforce a rating industry oligopoly in which there is little real competition.[18]

- **Flawed Models and Assumptions.** The agencies used inappropriate models for rating structured finance products. While some observers concede that the modeling exercises posed formidable inherent challenges, CRA models for structured products were reportedly calibrated based on short spans of data over a benign period of economic moderation in financial markets and rising house prices. Scenarios with economic turbulence or falling house prices were not used to gauge the models' reliability under such circumstances. A related issue, noted above, is that they may have failed to (1) correctly calculate underlying house loan defaults because they attached the wrong weights to the effect of falling house prices on loan default rates; and (2) understand the interdependence among loan defaults, and the likelihood of falling house prices occurring.[19]

- **An Inability to Handle a Voluminous Amount of Structured Securities Business.** There are a number of observations that the three CRAs were too undermanned to effectively accommodate the overwhelming volume of structured finance business.[20]

- **Challenges from High Levels of Fraud and Lax Mortgage Underwriting.** A number of observers, including officials of the three top CRAs, have pointed to lax underwriting and outright underwriting fraud for many of the mortgages that backed the structured securities. The pervasiveness of such practices is said to have undermined the integrity of the rating process for the securities.[21]

- **Insufficient CRA Regulation.** As described below, the financial and credit crisis has resulted in an array of newly adopted and proposed rating agency regulations, evidence of a widely held view that the previous regulations were inadequate.

- **The Potential Conflicts of Interest Involved in CRAs both Rating and Helping to Design the Same Securities.** The CRAs were often involved both in rating and providing advice on how to structure the same securities to fetch superior ratings. There are concerns that such a dual role represents a conflict of interest that may have undermined the objectivity of the rating process.

- **The Potential Conflicts of Interest in the CRAs' Provision of Ancillary Services to the Issuers Whose Securities They Rate.** CRAs often charge issuers for advice, which can include pre-rating assessments (providing issuers with a preview of what ratings they are likely to receive under various scenarios) and risk-management consulting. There are concerns that these additional commercial relationships with issuers can undermine their ability to provide unbiased ratings.[22]

- **Limited Liability under the First Amendment.** When CRAs publish ratings for the investing public at large, they often are characterized as having First Amendment privileges similar to those of journalists,[23] which can mean that they are immune from liability absent actual malice; below, this issue is examined in greater detail.

First Amendment Issues and the Rating Agencies

A credit rating agency engaged in the business of publishing ratings concerning the creditworthiness of public companies appears to have limited protection under the First Amendment's guarantee that "Congress shall make no law ... abridging the freedom of speech, or of the press...."

Although no U.S. Supreme Court case was found directly on point, the case *Lowe v. Securities and Exchange Commission*,[24] which concerned an exception to the definition of "investment adviser" as stated in the Investment Advisers Act,[25] stated that publications containing factual information about financial transactions, market trends, and general market conditions were entitled to First Amendment protections.

> The dangers of fraud, deception, or overreaching that motivated the enactment of the statute are present in personalized communications but are not replicated in publications that are advertised and sold in an open market. To the extent that the chart service contains factual information about past transactions and market trends, and the newsletters contain commentary on general market conditions, there can be no doubt about the protected character of the communications, a matter that concerned Congress when the exclusion was drafted. The content of the publications and the audience to which they are directed in this case reveal the specific limits of the exclusion. As long as the communications between petitioners and their subscribers remain entirely impersonal and do not develop into the kind of fiduciary, person-to-person relationships that were discussed at length in the legislative history of the Act and that are characteristic of investment adviser-client relationships, we believe the publications are, at least presumptively, within the exclusion and thus not subject to registration under the Act.[26]

In a more recent case involving Enron litigation, in which credit rating agencies were widely criticized for giving Enron a solid rating until close to the time of the declaration of bankruptcy, a federal district court[27] concluded that, although there is no absolute First Amendment protection for credit rating reports, the courts in general have not precluded First Amendment protection for negligence.

> [W]hile there is no automatic, blanket, absolute *First Amendment* protection for reports from the credit rating agencies based on their status as credit rating agencies, the courts generally have shielded them from liability for allegedly negligent ratings for various reasons.
> The United States Supreme Court has opined, "The liberty of the press is not confined to newspapers and periodicals.... The press in its historic connotation comprehends every sort of publication which affords a vehicle of information and periodicals." As noted by the Rating Agencies, they have been accorded special protections by a few courts when they are characterized as publishers or journalists.[28]

The court goes on to discuss that, nevertheless, the Supreme Court has held that publishers are not entitled to automatic protection under the First Amendment for general violations of laws. However, in the instant case the court found that the credit rating reports concerning Enron were protected by the First Amendment and stated its reasoning as follows:

The credit rating reports regarding Enron by national credit rating agencies were not private or confidential, but distributed "to the world" and were related to the creditworthiness of a powerful public corporation that operated internationally. While not making a per se rule about the level of *First Amendment* protection that should be accorded to such speech, in dicta in *Lowe v. SEC*, the Supreme Court noted that it had previously "held that expression of opinion about a commercial product such as a loudspeaker is protected by the *First Amendment*" and stated, "It is difficult to see why the expression of opinion about a marketable security should not also be protected" [citation omitted]. As noted, credit rating agencies do not profit from the sale of the bonds of any company that they rate for creditworthiness and they perform an essential service for economy and efficiency for the capital markets.[29]

However, it should be noted that, if a credit rating agency issued an opinion with actual malice,[30] the qualified First Amendment protection would likely not be applicable. "Thus a publisher may be liable for a statement of opinion if that statement reasonably implies false facts or relies on stated facts that are provably false."[31]

VARIOUS RESPONSES TO THE PERCEIVED RATING AGENCY FAILINGS

There have been a variety of responses to the perceived failings of the rating agencies with respect to structured mortgage-backed securities. Several important responses are discussed below.

The July 2008 SEC Study on Moody's, S&P, and Fitch

In July 2008, the SEC released a study, Summary Report of Issues Identified in the Commission Staff's Examinations of Select Credit Rating Agencies.[32] Based on a 10-month examination of S&P, Moody's, and Fitch, the report concluded that

- the agencies became overwhelmed by the increase in volume and sophistication of the structured securities they were paid to review, forcing their analysts to short cut the customary and expected due diligence;
- while it was the historical convention for their analysts to be unaware of any of their CRAs' business interests with the arrangers and issuers of the products they rated, the SEC found evidence of instances in which there was no attempt to shield them from e-mails and other communications that spoke of fees and revenue from individual issuers;
- there appeared to be instances in which the CRAs considered adjusting their ratings criteria to make them more competitive; and
- there were instances in which the CRAs did not adequately disclose or document modifications to their ratings criteria.

Voluntary Reforms Adopted by the Rating Agencies

The largest CRAs have acknowledged some failings in their rating of structured securities. For example, S&P has conceded that many of its subprime mortgage-backed structured securities ratings between 2005 and 2007 have "not held up."[33] Also, Raymond W. McDaniel Jr., Moody's chief executive officer, has said that "in hindsight, it is pretty clear that there was a failure in some key assumptions that were supporting our analytics and our models."[34] Likewise, an official at Fitch observed that it was "... clear that many of our structured finance rating opinions have not performed well and have been too volatile. We did not foresee the magnitude or velocity of the decline in the U.S. housing market, nor the dramatic shift in borrower behavior brought on by the changing practices in the market...."[35]

In response to such perceived failings (and as some argue, also perhaps to mitigate the prospect of unwanted regulation), the three top CRAs have instituted a number of internal reforms. These include

- reforming the review of the due diligence process conducted by originators and underwriters;
- improving the effectiveness of their analytical methodologies;
- providing more clarity about the credit characteristics of structured finance ratings;
- promoting objective measurement of ratings performance;
- adopting measures to improve investors' understanding of the attributes and limitations of credit ratings;
- rotating their analysts; and
- establishing an ombudsman to help manage potential conflicts of interest.

The Settlement with the New York Attorney General

In June 2008, after beginning an investigation into S&P's, Moody's, and Fitch's role in the mortgage market failure, New York Attorney General Andrew Cuomo reached a settlement with all three CRAs, agreements that do not appear to be court enforced. Its major provisions are as follows:

- Each agency will establish a fee-for-service structure under which they will be compensated regardless of whether the investment bank ultimately selects them to rate an RMBS. The New York Attorney General's Office explained that the agencies had been paid no fees during their initial reviews of the loan pools underlying the residential mortgage-backed securities or during their discussions and negotiations with the investment banks about the structuring of the loan pools, allowing investment banks to get free previews of assessments of residential mortgage-backed securities from multiple credit rating agencies. This was said to have enabled the investment banks to hire the agency that provided the best rating.
- Each agency will establish criteria for reviewing individual mortgage lenders, as well as the lender's origination processes.

- Each agency will disclose information about all securitizations submitted for their initial review. This Attorney General has said that this will enable investors to determine whether issuers sought, but subsequently decided not to use, ratings from a credit rating agency.
- Each agency will develop criteria for the due diligence information that is collected by investment banks on the mortgages comprising residential mortgage-backed securities. The Attorney General had previously found that the three CRAs were not always privy to pertinent due diligence information that investment banks had about the mortgages underlying the loan pools.
- Each agency will perform an annual review of its residential mortgage-backed securities businesses to identify practices that could compromise its independent ratings. The credit rating agencies will remediate any practices that they find could compromise independence.
- Each agency will require a series of representations and warranties from investment banks and other financially responsible parties about the loans underlying the residential mortgage-backed securities.[36]

At the announcement of the agreement, the New York Attorney General observed: "By increasing the independence of the rating agencies, ensuring they get adequate information to make their ratings, and increasing industry-wide transparency, these reforms will address one of the central causes of that collapse."[37]

However, Lawrence White, a professor of economics at New York University's Stern School of Business, had far less praise for the pact. He observed that "this feels cosmetic to me. Getting paid for just showing up doesn't strike me as a good model or incentive structure." He said that the critical problem is that investors are compelled by a bevy of government regulators to heed the CRAs' ratings.[38]

Reforms Adopted by the SEC

In December 2008, the SEC began a process of adopting a number of NRSRO reforms it had proposed earlier in the year. The process concluded with the final adoption of various reforms in February 2009. According to the agency, the reforms are meant to "address concerns about the integrity of the process by which NRSROs rate structured finance products, particularly mortgage related securities.... " More specifically, the rules, most of which went into effect in April 2009, are intended to (1) increase the transparency of the NRSROs' rating methodologies; (2) strengthen the NRSROs' disclosure of ratings performance; (3) prohibit the NRSROs from engaging in certain practices that create conflicts of interest; and (4) enhance the NRSROs' recordkeeping and reporting requirements obligations for the purpose of aiding the SEC in the performance of its oversight role.[39]

As a group, the reforms generally subject NRSROs to additional disclosure requirements, amend Rule 1 7g-5 of the Securities and Exchange Act of 1934 with respect to NRSRO conflict of interest prohibitions, and amend Rule 17g-2 under the Exchange Act with respect to NRSRO recordkeeping requirements. The key reforms[40]

- prohibits an NRSRO from issuing or maintaining a credit rating if (1) the NRSRO made recommendations to the entity being rated or the issuer, underwriter, or sponsor of the security about the corporate or legal structure, assets, liabilities, or activities of the entity being rated or issuer of the security; or (2) the fee paid for the rating was negotiated, discussed, or arranged by a person within the NRSRO who has responsibility for participating in determining or approving credit ratings, or for developing or approving procedures or methodologies used for determining credit ratings, including qualitative and quantitative models. In its explanation of this "no-advice rule," the SEC explained that it was motivated by its concern that NRSROs occasionally make structural recommendations to securities arrangers and then rate the resulting securities, which the agency described as the NRSROs basically rating their own work. It however, also conceded that the distinction between providing feedback during the rating process and making recommendations could be a potential gray area.
- requires an NRSRO or NRSRO applicant to provide rating change statistics for each asset class of credit ratings for which it is registered or is seeking registration, broken out over 1, 3, and 10 year periods.
- requires an NRSRO to provide all rating change statistics (upgrades as well as downgrades) and disclose default statistics relative to the initial rating, including defaults that occur after a credit rating is withdrawn.
- requires an NRSRO to provide enhanced disclosure in three areas: (1) whether (and, if so, how much) verification performed on assets underlying or referenced by the structured finance transaction is relied on in determining credit ratings; (2) whether (and, if so, how) assessments of the quality of originators of structured finance transactions play a part in the determination of the credit ratings; and (3) more detailed information on the surveillance process, including whether different models or criteria are used for ratings surveillance than for determining initial ratings.
- prohibits a person within an NRSRO who has responsibility in determining credit ratings or for developing or approving procedures or methodologies used for determining credit ratings from participating in any fee discussions, negotiations, or arrangements.
- prohibits an NRSRO from allowing a credit analyst who has participated in determining or monitoring the credit rating to receive gifts, including entertainment, from the obligor being rated or from the issuer, underwriter, or sponsor of the securities being rated, other than items provided in the context of normal business activities, such as meetings, that have an aggregate value of no more than $25.
- requires an NRSRO to make publicly available on its corporate website a random sample of 10% of its issuer-paid credit ratings and their histories for each class of issuer-paid credit rating for which it is registered and has issued 500 or more ratings.
- requires an NRSRO to keep records of all rating actions related to a current rating from the initial rating to the current rating. If a quantitative model is a substantial component of the credit rating process for a structured finance product, a rating agency must keep a record of the rationale for any material difference between the credit rating implied by the model and the final credit rating issued. The agency is to

retain records of any complaints regarding the performance of a credit analyst in determining, maintaining, monitoring, changing, or withdrawing a credit rating.
- requires an NRSRO to disclose ratings history information for 100% of current issuer-paid credit ratings determined after June 26, 2007, in an XBRL format.

While adopting the new NRSRO rules in February 2009, the SEC also published a new policy proposal and re-proposed a modified version of an earlier proposal.

The new proposal would require the public disclosure of credit rating histories for all outstanding credit ratings issued by an NRSRO on or after June 26, 2007, paid for by the obligor being rated or by the issuer. The proposal is limited to issuer-paid credit ratings; the SEC said it "wants to gather more data" before deciding whether or not to extend it to subscriber-paid ratings The SEC suggested that if adopted, the proposal would provide users of credit ratings, investors, and others in the markets with an optimal level of "raw data" for comparing how such NRSROs originally rated an entity or a security with subsequent ratings adjustments. It said that by requiring the disclosure of ratings action histories of each issuer-paid credit rating, opportunities would be created for market participants to utilize the information to develop their own rating performance metrics, supplementing the data that NRSROs are currently required to provide.[41]

Under the SEC's re-proposed amendment: (1) NRSROs that are hired by arrangers to perform credit ratings for structured products would be required to disclose to other NRSROs the deals for which they were in the process of determining such ratings; (2) the arrangers would need to provide the NRSROs they hire with a representation that they will provide information given to the hired NRSROs to other NRSROs; and (3) NRSROs seeking to access information maintained by the NRSROs and the arrangers would be required to annually certify to the SEC that they exclusively access the information to determine credit ratings, and will determine a minimum number of ratings using the data. The SEC explained that a key goal of the proposal is to encourage greater ratings competition by providing a mechanism that would help stimulate more unsolicited ratings.[42]

The aforementioned adopted SEC rules include most of the earlier 2008 SEC NRSRO reform proposals, but two such proposals have not been adopted: (1) a requirement that the rating symbols or the disclosures that are applied to ratings of structured finance products be distinguished from the symbols for non-structured products; and (2) reforms that would reduce the reliance on NRSRO ratings in the SEC's rules.

In February 2009, SEC Commissioner Kathleen Casey urged her fellow SEC commissioners to remove the regulatory reliance on the NRSRO references. She observed that "... it has become evident over time that there are considerable unintended consequences to the regulatory use of ratings. The purpose was not to establish and preserve a valuable franchise for the large rating agencies, while simultaneously inoculating them from market competition. Nor was it intended to serve as a substitute for adequate due diligence on the part of investors, managers, directors, and others, which could have served as a critical check on the rating agencies. Unfortunately, as recent events have demonstrated, it appears to have led to just such results in too many cases.... [I]n my view, ... [removing the reliance] ... is absolutely essential to the commission's efforts to faithfully implement the clear congressional intent of enhancing transparency, accountability, and competition in this industry."[43]

The SEC's newly adopted reforms also do not address what many observers believe to be the fundamental factor behind the CRAs' failings—their issuer-pays business model.

The European Union's Reforms

During the recent global housing boom, numerous European banks were encouraged to buy structured debt because they carried superior ratings from the top CRAs. Many suffered financial losses from such investments, leading to costly financial governmental bailouts by European Union (EU) members.

Reflecting such concerns, EU parliamentary officials have said that the rating agencies "clearly underestimated the risk" that issuers of complex investments would not be able repay debt and had failed to respond to worsening market conditions by lowering ratings.[44]

In April 2009, attempting to address such concerns, the EU parliament adopted a series of CRA reforms:

- The Committee of European Securities Regulators (CESR), a body composed of national regulators, will be placed in temporary charge of registering CRAs, which will be required of all CRAs wanting to do business in the EU. The new rules will require the CESR to manage a database of historical performance information about rating agencies operating in the EU. This is meant to allow users of rating services to quickly verify the accuracy of economic predictions and compare them with rival CRAs. Starting in 2010, this responsibility will shift to a new pan-European authority.
- CRAs will be liable for their rating opinions and could face EU sanctions if they are found guilty of professional misconduct, potentially resulting in the loss of their licenses to rate debt in EU nations.
- CRAs will have to have an internal function to review the quality of their own ratings and have at least two independent directors on their boards who do not receive bonuses that are connected to the CRA's performance. One of the directors will be required to be an expert in securitization and structured finance.
- CRAs will have to issue an annual transparency report.
- CRAs will have to disclose the models, methodologies and key assumptions on which they base their ratings.
- CRAs will have to publish an annual transparency report.
- CRAs will have to disclose the names of rated companies that contribute more than 5% of an agency's revenue. They will also be proscribed from rating companies for which their analysts own shares or financial products. The CRA's consulting and advisory roles would be denied to firms that are themselves subject to ratings. CRA analysts will be forced to rotate in order to avoid becoming too close to the industry sector they rate.
- CRAs will be required to distinguish the ratings of complex securities through the use of distinctive symbols.

- CRAs based outside of the EU will have two years to comply with the new rules, which will require them to show that they have quality information to rate debt and to show regulators the models, methods and key assumptions behind their ratings.
- non-EU based CRAs like S&P and Moody's will have to have their branches in the EU endorse rating done by their parent firms.[45]

European Commission President José Manuel Barroso lauded the reforms, reportedly saying that they "will help give investors the information, integrity and impartiality they need from credit rating agencies if they are to make prudent investment decisions that create growth and jobs, instead of bubbles of excessive risk."[46] The president of S&P also lavished praise on the reform: he predicted that the newly adopted EU oversight along with ongoing market-based scrutiny of credit ratings will provide for more transparency and accountability from the raters and enhanced public confidence in their ratings.[47]

However, as in the case of the SEC rules, the EU's reforms do not address the concerns of those who say that the issuer-pays structure is a fundamental problem and should be eliminated.

The SEC's April 2009 Credit Rating Agency Roundtable

On April 15, 2009, the SEC convened a roundtable on public policy concerns surrounding the CRAs. Convening the roundtable, consisting of panelists representing credit rating agencies, issuers, investors, and academia, SEC Chairman Mary Schapiro reportedly observed:

> The status quo isn't good enough. Rating agency performance in the area of mortgage-backed securities backed by residential subprime loans, and the collateralized debt obligations linked to such securities has shaken investor confidence to its core. Our purpose today is to ask some very basic questions: Should the Commission consider additional rules to better align the raters' interests with those who rely on the ratings—that is, principally, investors? Stated another way, does one form of rating agency business model represent a better way of managing conflicts of interest than another? Is there a way to realign incentives so that rating agencies view investors as the ultimate customer? Do users of ratings—whether they are issuers or investors—have all of the information they need to make the most informed decisions? For example, is there more information about performance, expertise with regard to certain types of securities products, or fees that would be meaningful in restoring investor confidence or would provide investors with the tools to discern the value of the rating? Should we borrow a page from the research analyst conflicts of interest settlement of several years ago and require a mechanism that provides for the issuance of multiple ratings for every security, including one generated independently? Are there additional behaviors—for example, concerning the way that agencies bid for work—that should be examined and modified? Would increased competition in the rating agency space benefit investors and how would we achieve that?[48]

The panelists also proposed several ideas for regulatory improvements in the treatment of NRSROs, and there reportedly was broad agreement that more accountability and transparency and a stronger investor voice were necessary to improve the reliability of ratings. Among the observations made during the roundtable were the following:

- Former SEC commissioner Joseph Grundfest observed that if systemic risk means that a change in one company can have ripple macroeconomic effects on others, then what the CRAs do clearly has systemic consequences. In agreement, Richard Baker, formerly chairman of the House Financial Services Capital Markets Subcommittee, said that the ratings industry presents a systemic risk because of a concentration of information, not assets, but that "the contagion is the same."
- All the rating agencies present reportedly concurred that due to their complexity, a number of products, including collateralized debt obligations, should never have been rated.
- Robert Dobilas, the CEO of Realpoint LLC, the newest NRSRO, said that issuers should be required to provide information to all rating agencies, not just to a favored few. He asserted that the largest problem was that issuers often went "ratings shopping," in which they looked for the agency that would provide the most favorable ratings.
- Moody's Chairman Raymond McDaniel said that underlying information about structured securities should be provided to institutional investors, which would result in a reduction in the reliance on ratings, advances in the quality of the information available to the market, and result in a wider array different opinions and analyses.
- Frank Partnoy, a law professor at the University of San Diego, who has written extensively on the CRAs, observed that the regulatory references to ratings acted as unfair "regulatory licenses" and proposed a separately funded and independent oversight board largely responsible for weaning investors away from such ratings.
- Similarly, Lawrence White, an economics professor at New York University, who has also written extensively on the agencies, advised that the references to credit ratings and NRSROs be completely eliminated, leaving issuers with the burden to validate the safety of their financial products.
- Ethan Berman, CEO of RiskMetrics Group, observed that in establishing the NRSRO designation, the SEC erected regulatory barriers that make it "virtually impossible" for new CRAs to enter the market or gain a competitive foothold.
- In a similar vein, Alex Pollock, a resident fellow at the American Enterprise Institute, recommended that the NRSRO designation be entirely eliminated, noting that it had effectively created a "government cartel" and that "the U.S. government should not enshrine certain agencies as better."
- Greatly at odds with the view that the NRSRO protocol should be abandoned were the views of James Gellert, president of Rapid Ratings International. He suggested that in the interest of boosting rating agency competition, the SEC should consider making it easier for CRAs to receive the NRSRO designation.
- Daniel Curry, president of DBRS Ltd., observed that removing the references to NRSROs was a "good" idea, but it should be done incrementally so the market could gradually adjust to it.

- Alan Fohrer, chairman of Southern California Edison, expressed concerns about the prospect of removing the NRSRO references, noting that any changes that create uncertainty would have a huge impact on his company and its customers.
- Sean Egan, president of Egan-Jones Ratings, claimed that increased CRA competition solves little and that the fundamental public policy need was the removal of the conflict of interest ridden investor-paid model.
- Rebutting the aforementioned critique, a number of panelists, including representatives from S&P, Moody's and Fitch, contended that issuers and investors have varying objectives, and that any kind of product in which there is a client who pays will have potential conflicts of interest.
- In response to a question on making ratings publicly available, a number of smaller subscriber-pays CRAs warned that it would be at odds with their basic business model. They also argued that it could increase their legal liability, which would be much less of a concern with the bigger CRAs who they said could insulate themselves against the threat by being indemnified by their issuer clients.[49]

CRA-RELATED LEGISLATION

Congress has also shared many of the concerns over the perceived failures of the dominant CRAs in the area of structured finance. Several bills involving the CRAs have been introduced, and at least one more is reportedly in draft stage:

- S. 927 (Pryor) would require the SEC to conduct an annual audit of each NRSRO.
- S. 1073 (Reed) would (1) enhance the SEC's oversight of NRSROs through enhanced disclosure and improved oversight of conflicts of interest; (2) allow investors to sue NRSROs that knowingly fail to review factual elements for determining a rating; (3) require the SEC to look at alternative means of NRSRO compensation, and (4) require a Government Accountability Office study on payment methods.
- H.R. 74 (Issa) would establish the Financial Oversight Commission to investigate the financial crisis of 2008, including relevant legislation, Executive Orders, regulations, plans, policies, practices, or procedures that pertain to (1) government sponsored enterprises; (2) the stock market; (3) the housing market; (4) credit rating agencies; (5) the financial services sector, including hedge funds, private equity and the insurance industry; and (6) the role of congressional oversight and resource allocation. It would also require the commission to report to the President and Congress on its findings, conclusions, and recommendations.
- H.R. 1181 (Ackerman) would direct the SEC to establish both a process by which asset-backed instruments can be deemed eligible for NRSRO ratings and an initial list of such eligible asset-backed instruments.
- H.R. 1445 (McHenry) would require NRSROs to provide additional disclosures with respect to the rating of structured securities, including (1) ensuring that issuers and originators are providing NRSROs with adequate information on the assets underlying a structured security; (2) requiring them to institute procedures for getting

data from issuers and originators concerning the procedures employed to attest to the data's veracity and the fraud detection capabilities surrounding the process; and (3) requiring NRSROs to disclose in a central database the historical default rates of all classes of financial products they have rated.

Meanwhile, during a House Financial Services Capital Markets Subcommittee hearing on the rating agencies on May 19, 2009, the subcommittee's chairman Representative Paul Kanjorski, asserted that credit rating agencies must face more rigorous standards of disclosure and transparency and called for the creation of an office at the SEC to regulate them.[50]

End Notes

[1] Moody's was spun off as a public company by the financial publisher Dun & Bradstreet in 2000.
[2] Lawrence J. White, "A New Law for the Bond Rating Industry," *Regulation*, spring 2007.
[3] For example, see "Testimony of Sean J. Egan Managing Director Egan-Jones Rating Co., before the House Committee on Oversight and Government Reform," October 22, 2008. Egan-Jones uses a subscriber-pays model.
[4] According to officials at Egan-Jones, a subscriber-pays firm, the CRA began downgrading Bear Stearns on January 4, 2008, and cut its rating three times before S&P, Moody's, and Fitch started downgrading the company in mid-March of the year. Egan-Jones officials also say that while the three leading issuer-pays CRAs were still giving Lehman Brothers their top ratings a day before it declared bankruptcy, it downgraded the firm to the lower tiered BBB+ rating a half a year before its bankruptcy. Subsequently, Lehman was further downgraded and, by a day before the bankruptcy, Egan- Jones had reportedly given it a below investment grade rating of CCC. Officials at another subscriber-pays firm, Rapid Ratings, say that it began downgrading the retailers Circuit City Stores, Pilgrim's Pride, and Linens 'n Things more than a year before the retailers filed for bankruptcy protection. Officials at Rapid Ratings also say that they started downgrading various home builders in early 2006, well before the equity markets, the dominant rating agencies, and credit market indices began to see material changes in their status. Because of growing disenchantment over the performance of the dominant issuer-pays CRAs, subscriber-pays firms such as Egan-Jones and Rapid Ratings have reportedly been experiencing increased demand for their services from various money managers and large investors. Janet Morrissey, "Disillusioned Advisers Eye Smaller Ratings Firms; Interest in Subscriber-based Raters Grows at the Expense of the Big Three Agencies," *Investment News*, February16, 2009, p. 2. Beat Balzli and Frank Hornig, "Exacerbating the Crisis," *Spiegel International Online*, May 6, 2009.
[5] Basel II is the second of the Basel Accords, which are recommendations on banking laws and regulations issued by the Basel Committee on Banking Supervision. The purpose of Basel II, which was initially published in June 2004, is to create an international standard that banking regulators can use when creating regulations about how much capital banks need to put aside to guard against the types of financial and operational risks banks face.
[6] Available at http://www.sec.gov/news/studies/credratingreport0103.pdf.
[7] U.S. Securities and Exchange Commission, Concept Release: Rating Agencies and the Use of Credit Ratings under the Federal Securities Laws," June 4, 2003, available at http:// http://www.sec.gov/rules/concept/33-8236.htm.
[8] For example, see CRS Report RS22215, *Credit Rating Agencies: Current Federal Oversight and Congressional Concerns*, by Michael V. Seitzinger.
[9] On February 8, 2005, the Senate Committee on Banking, Housing, and Urban Affairs held a hearing titled "Examining the Role of Credit Rating Agencies in the Capital Markets." On March 7, 2006, the committee held a hearing titled "Assessing the Current Oversight and Operations of Credit Rating Agencies." The committee on August 2, 2006, ordered an original measure to be reported. On September 6, 2006, the original measure, with written report No. 109-326, was reported to the Senate.
[10] 15 U.S.C. §§ 78a *et seq.*
[11] Adding sections 3(a)(60)-(64) to the Securities Exchange Act of 1934.
[12] Section 4 of P.L. 109-291, adding section 15E to the Securities Exchange Act of 1934.
[13] A tranche is a "slice," or portion, of a securitized credit portfolio. Tranches are typically organized into classes based on risk (e.g., Class A, Class B). Investors buy portions of a securities portfolio and are paid based on the hierarchy of tranches.

[14] These are securities products that are derived from and/or based on a single security or securities, a basket of stocks, an index, a commodity, debt issuance and/or a foreign currency, etc.

[15] Aaron Lucchetti, "Rating Game: As Housing Boomed, Moody's Opened Up," *Wall Street Journal*, April 11, 2008, p. A1. Some would argue that the dominant CRAs' willingness to sacrifice quality ratings for the enormous amount of structured finance profits may have been illustrated by the following rating agency quotations, which were cited during an October 22, 2008 House Oversight and Government Reform hearing on the rating agencies:

" ... In the September 2007 e-mail made public today, the Moody's employee said that it 'seems to me that we had blinders on and never questioned the information we were given,' according to the congressional investigators. 'It is our job to think of the worst-case scenarios and model them.' The e-mail continued: "Combined, these errors make us look either incompetent at credit analysis, or like we sold our soul to the devil for revenue." '[then House Oversight and Government Reform Chairman Henry] Waxman also cited a transcript of a September 2007 meeting in which Raymond W. McDaniel, chairman and CEO of Moody's Corp. described as a slippery slope of events. 'What happened in '04 and '05 with respect to subordinated tranches is that our competition, Fitch and S&P, went nuts. Everything was investment grade, McDaniel said in the meeting. 'We tried to alert the market. We said 'we're not rating it. This stuff isn't investment grade. No one cared because the machine just kept going.... ' 'In one document, an S&P employee in the structured finance division wrote: 'It could be structured by cows and we would rate it."

Lorraine Woellert and Dawn Kopecki "Moody's, S&P Employees Doubted Ratings," Bloomberg, October 22, 2008.

[16] SEC Proposed Rules, *Federal Register*, June 25, 2008, pp. 36211-36252.

[17] A key response to this kind of concern by issuer-pays CRAs is that they have had to maintain the integrity of their reputational capital to ensure continued demand for their services. The CRAs have also claimed that they have had the proper administrative checks such as (1) ensuring that rating decisions are made by rating committees and not by individual analysts; (2) prohibiting analysts from holding fee discussions with or owning securities in the institutions that they rate (excluding through diversified mutual funds); and (3) not evaluating or compensating analysts on the basis of the revenue associated with the entities they rate. The issuer-pays CRAs have also argued that the subscriber- pays model has its own potential shortcomings, including the fact that investors could press for lower initial ratings because such securities pay higher yields, and possible instances in which short sellers could be motivated to encourage an unexpected negative rating action to the benefit their financial interests. Ultimately, officials at one issuer-pays CRA say that the real issue is not what model one uses, but how transparent its practitioners are regarding their use of models. "S&P Offers Mea Culpa on Ratings," The Bond Buyer, March 5, 2009. Jesse Westbrook, "S&P, Moody's Defend Pay Model Faulted by Regulators," *Bloomberg*, April 14, 2009.

[18] The power of this quasi-regulatory license may be undercut by the fact that S&P and Moody's market domination preceded 1975, the start of NRSRO designation. Interestingly, for years, Moody's has reportedly argued for rescinding the NRSRO designation, claiming that this would allow it to prove that its market dominance is solely related to its expertise. But Jonathan Macey of the Yale School of Finance reportedly thinks that the frequently more accurate subscriber-pays CRA, Egan-Jones, would be equally accurate in an issuer-pays CRA. He reportedly believes that this is because Egan is a relatively new NRSRO and people historically did not hire it for regulatory reasons, but hired it strictly for the quality of its ratings. Chris Nolter, "Redefining the Blob," the Deal.com, December 12, 2008. On the broad issue of federal actions that may help to reinforce the leading CRAs' formidable market share, some have raised concerns that the Federal Reserve's financial firm assistance programs like its commercial-paper facility and the Term Asset-Backed Securities Loan Facility (TALF) accept only collateral that has been appraised by a "major" rating agency, that of one of the three dominant CRAs. They say that this selectivity is a potential setback for the seven other rating firms that have also earned NRSRO status. The Federal Reserve has reportedly spoken of reconsidering expanding the list of eligible raters. In response to an inquiry by the Hon. Keith Ellison, Federal Reserve Chairman Ben Bernanke indicated that the CRAs' role in the current financial crisis has "... led to CRAs to tighten underwriting standards and establish stricter ratings criteria.... [And that] Federal Reserve economists have carefully reviewed the methodologies that the rating agencies are employing to analyze the types of ABS [asset backed securities] that are eligible to be financed in the TALF program.... " Richard Blumenthal, Attorney General for Connecticut, has launched an antitrust probe in which the Federal Reserve is accused of "rewarding the same companies that helped burn down the house." "The Wages of Sin," *The Economist*, April 23, 2009. "Letter to the Hon. Keith Ellison from Ben S. Bernanke, Chairman of the Federal Reserve System," May 12, 2009.

[19] For example, see Paul Mizen, "The Credit Crunch of 2007-2008: A Discussion of the Background, Market Reactions, and Policy Responses," Federal Reserve Bank of St. Louis Review, September-October 2008, p. 531. In addition, others contend that unlike the traditional rating processes for single-named issuers, which primarily relied on empirical analysis, structured-finance rating analysis was basically driven by statistical models. Another criticism is that the data that the agencies used to evaluate mortgage-backed securities, including those backed by subprime mortgages, were significantly biased by an over reliance on conventional 30-year fixed prime mortgage loans, whose behavior would prove to be quite different from the subprime

loans. Joseph R. Mason and Josh Rosner, "Where Did the Risk Go? How Misapplied Bond Ratings Cause Mortgage Backed Securities and Collateralized Debt Obligation Market Disruptions," May 3, 2007, available at http://ssrn.com/abstract=1027475. It has, however, been argued that the CRA's modeling failings did not exist in isolation: many others, including various central bankers, commercial and investment bank analysts, and various financial risk management units also failed to foresee the dramatic housing market price collapse.

[20] In July 2008, the SEC released a study, "Summary Report of Issues Identified in the Commission Staff's Examinations of Select Credit Rating Agencies." Based on a 10-month examination of S&P, Moody's, and Fitch, among the report's findings were (1) the agencies became overwhelmed by the volume and complexity of the structured securities; (2) instances that suggested that there were no attempt to shield analysts from e-mails and other communications that spoke of fees and revenue from individual issuers; (3) the agencies considered adjusting ratings criteria to enhance their competitiveness; and (4) cases in which the CRAs did not adequately document aspects of their ratings criteria. It is available at http://www.sec.gov/news/studies/2008/craexamination070808.pdf.

[21] For example, in late 2007, analysis by Fitch found that "the extraordinarily high level of defaults encountered" by the pool of 2006 subprime mortgages could not be explained only by home price declines but that lax loan underwriting and high instances of fraud also appeared to be significant factors in the declines. "Fitch: Underwriting & Fraud Significant Drivers of Subprime Defaults; New Originator Reviews," *Business Wire*, November 28, 2007.

[22] An argument that has been frequently used to address this charge is that the ancillary services tend to account for a very small portion of CRA revenue.

[23] For example, Floyd Abrams, a visiting professor of First Amendment issues at Columbia University's Graduate School of Journalism and a partner at Cahill Gordon & Reindel LLP who has represented S&P, observed that "What credit rating agencies do in analyzing debt and assessing the likelihood of repayment of the debt and then putting a sort of shorthand label [like triple-A] on it is very similar to what recognized journalists do in covering the market.... As a result, there is a substantial body of law that has developed concluding that rating agencies are protected by the First Amendment in what they do." Lynn Hume, "Can Raters Be Regulated? Lawyer, Cases Cite First Amendment Protection," *The Bond Buyer*, March 30, 2005. By contrast, Richard Blumenthal, the Connecticut attorney general, has indicated that "the very nature of [rating firms'] so-called speech is very different from the classic First Amendment- protected expression .... It's much more akin to an advertisement that misstates the price of an item on sale than a political candidate on a soapbox." Attorney General Blumenthal has a lawsuit pending over some S&P ratings of nonmortgage-backed securities. Ashby Jones, "A First Amendment Defense for the Rating Agencies*, "The Wall Street Journal*, April 21, 2009.

[24] 472 U.S. 181 (1985).

[25] 15 U.S.C. § 80b-2(a)(11). The act defines "investment adviser" in pertinent part as:
any person who, for compensation, engages in the business of advising others, either directly or through publications or writings, as to the value of securities or as to the advisability of investing in, purchasing, or selling securities, or who for compensation and as part of a regular business, issues or promulgates analyses or reports concerning securities; but does not include ... (D) the publisher of any bona fide newspaper, news magazine or business or financial publication of general and regular circulation....

[26] Lowe v. Securities and Exchange Commission, 472 U.S. 181, 210 (1985)(footnotes omitted).

[27] Newby v. Enron Corp., 511 F. Supp. 2d 742 (S.D. Tex. 2005).

[28] *Id.*, at 817-818 (citations omitted).

[29] *Id.*, at 206-207 (citation and quotations omitted).

[30] "Actual malice" has been defined by the Supreme Court as "with knowledge that the statement was false or with reckless disregard for whether or not it was true." Hustler Magazine v. Falwell, 485 U.S. 46, 56 (1988).

[31] Newby v. Enron Corp., at 822, using the reasoning in Milkovich v. Lorain Journal, 497 U.S. 1, 20 (1990).

[32] Available at http://www.sec.gov/news/studies/2008/craexamination070808.pdf.

[33] S&P Official Offers Mea Culpa on Ratings," *The Bond Buyer*, March 5, 2009.

[34] Floyd Norris, "Moody's Official Concedes Failures in Some Ratings," *New York Times*, January 26, 2008.

[35] Lorraine Woellert and Dawn Kopecki, "Moody's, S&P Employees Doubted Ratings," *Bloomberg*, October 22, 2008.

[36] This section derives from: "Attorney General Cuomo Announces Landmark Reform Agreements with the Nation's Principal Credit Rating Agencies," *Release from the Office of the Attorney General, State of New York*, June 5, 2008.

[37] Ibid.

[38] Lawrence White, quoted in: Aaron Elstein "Cuomo Reaches Deal with Ratings Agencies," *Crain's New York Business*, June 5, 2008.

[39] "Amendments to Rules for Nationally Recognized Statistical Rating Organizations," *Federal Register*, vol. 74, no. 25, February 9, 2009, p. 6456.

[40] Ibid.

[41] "Re-Proposed Rules for Nationally Recognized Statistical Rating Organizations," *Federal Register*, vol. 74, no. 25, February 9, 2009, p. 6485.

[42] Ibid.
[43] "Credit Rating Agencies: SEC's Casey Urges Commission To Loosen Reliance on NRSROs," *BNA's Securities Regulation & Law Report*, February 16, 2009.
[44] "EU Approves New Rules for Rating Agencies," *Associated Press*, April 23, 2009.
[45] "Approval of New Regulation will Raise Standards for the issuance of Credit Ratings Used in the Community," press release, April 23, 2009, available at http://europa.eu/rapid/ pressReleasesAction.do? reference=IP/09/629 & format= HTML&aged=0&language=EN&guiLanguage=en.
[46] "Parliament Backs Tighter Rules for Rating Agencies," *Euractiv.com*, April 24, 2009.
[47] "EU Backs New Rules on Rating Agencies," *Associated Press*, April 23, 2009.
[48] "Speech by SEC Chairman: Statement at SEC Roundtable on Credit Rating Agencies," April 15, 2009.
[49] All of these comments come from: "Securities: Panelists Call for More Competition, Accountability, Transparency in Ratings" *BNA's Daily Report for Executives*, April 16, 2009.
[50] Richard Hill, "Kanjorski Calls for More Regulation, SEC Office Devoted to Rating Agencies," *BNA's Securities Regulation & Law Report*, May 25, 2009.

Chapter 2

FINANCIAL REGULATORY REFORM: ANALYSIS OF THE CONSUMER FINANCIAL PROTECTION AGENCY (CFPA) AS PROPOSED BY THE OBAMA ADMINISTRATION AND H.R. 3126

David H. Carpenter and Mark Jickling

SUMMARY

In the wake of what many believe is the worst U.S. financial crisis since the Great Depression, the Obama Administration has proposed sweeping reforms of the financial services regulatory system, the broad outline of which has been encompassed in a nearly 90-page document called the President's White Paper (the White Paper or the Proposal). The Proposal seeks to meet five objectives:

(1) "Promote robust supervision and regulation of financial firms";
(2) "Establish comprehensive supervision and regulation of financial markets";
(3) "Protect consumers and investors from financial abuse";
(4) "Improve tools for managing financial crises"; and
(5) "Raise international regulatory standards and improve international cooperation."

The Administration likely will offer specific legislative proposals that would implement each of the five objectives of the White Paper. On June 30, 2009, the Obama Administration made available the first such legislative proposal, called the Consumer Financial Protection Agency Act of 2009 (the CFPA Act or the Act). The Act would establish a new executive agency, the Consumer Financial Protection Agency (the CFPA or the Agency), to protect consumers of financial products and services. On July 8, 2009, Representative Barney Frank, Chairman of the House Financial Services Committee, introduced very similar legislation, H.R. 3126, which also is entitled the CFPA Act of 2009.

This report provides a brief summary of the President's CFPA Act and delineates some of the substantive differences between it and H.R. 3126, as introduced. It then analyzes some of the policy implications of the proposal, focusing on the separation of safety and soundness regulation from consumer protection, financial innovation, and the scope of regulation. The report then raises some questions regarding state law preemption, sources of funding, and rulemaking procedures that the Act does not fully answer.

INTRODUCTION

In the wake of what many believe is the worst U.S. financial crisis since the Great Depression, the Obama Administration has proposed sweeping reforms of the financial services regulatory system, the broad outline of which has been encompassed in a nearly 90-page document called the President's White Paper (the White Paper or the Proposal).[1] The Proposal seeks to meet five objectives:

(1) "Promote robust supervision and regulation of financial firms" through the creation of an oversight council of the primary federal financial regulators; the provision of systemic risk oversight powers for the Federal Reserve; heightened prudential standards for financial firms; and increased federal oversight of institutions that are unregulated or only lightly regulated under current law;

(2) "Establish comprehensive supervision and regulation of financial markets" by enhancing regulation over credit rating agencies; requiring originators and issuers to retain a long-term interest in securitized loans; regulating over-the-counter (OTC) derivatives; and providing the Federal Reserve with new oversight authority of payment, settlement, and clearing systems;

(3) "Protect consumers and investors from financial abuse" through the creation of a new executive agency devoted exclusively to consumer protection of financial products and services;

(4) "Improve tools for managing financial crises" by establishing an insolvency regime for systemically significant financial institutions and improving the Federal Reserve's emergency lending powers; and

(5) "Raise international regulatory standards and improve international cooperation" by coordinating oversight of international financial firms and other regulatory changes.[2]

The Administration likely will offer specific legislative proposals that would implement each of the five objectives of the White Paper. On June 30, 2009, the Obama Administration made available the first such legislative proposal, called the Consumer Financial Protection Agency Act of 2009 (the CFPA Act or the Act).[3] The Act would establish a new executive agency, the Consumer Financial Protection Agency (the CFPA or the Agency), to protect consumers of financial products and services. On July 8, 2009, Representative Barney Frank, Chairman of the House Financial Services Committee, introduced very similar legislation, H.R. 3126, which also is entitled the CFPA Act of 2009.

This report provides a brief summary of the President's CFPA Act and delineates some of the substantive differences between it and H.R. 3126, as introduced. It then analyzes some of the policy implications of the proposal, focusing on the separation of safety and soundness regulation from consumer protection, financial innovation, and the scope of regulation. The report then raises some questions regarding state law preemption, sources of funding, and rulemaking procedures that the Act does not fully answer.

SUMMARY OF THE CFPA ACT

Under the Act, the CFPA would be headed by a board consisting of four members appointed by the President, subject to the advice and consent of the Senate, for five-year staggered terms and subject to removal only for cause. The board also would have one ex officio member, the Director of the National Bank Supervisor[4] (proposed in the White Paper to be a new government agency, which would be established under subsequent legislation, in charge of prudential regulation of all federally chartered insured depositories).[5] The Agency would be funded through appropriations and potentially through fees assessed by the CFPA against covered entities.[6]

The CFPA would be established to "seek to promote transparency, simplicity, fairness, accountability, and access in the market for consumer financial products and services" to ensure that consumers are able to make educated decisions regarding financial products and services; that they are "protected from abuse, unfairness, deception, and discrimination"; that markets operate efficiently and fairly; and that "traditionally underserved consumers and communities have access to financial services."[7]

To implement these goals, the CFPA would have authority over a vast array of financial activities, including deposit taking, mortgages, credit cards and other extensions of credit, investment advising by entities not subject to registration or regulation by the Securities and Exchange Commission or the Commodity Futures Trading Commission, loan servicing, check- guaranteeing, collection of consumer report data, debt collection, real estate settlement, money transmitting, financial data processing, and others.[8] The CFPA would not have authority over insurance activities other than mortgage, title, and credit insurance.[9] The range of entities engaged in financial activities that would be subject to the CFPA also is expansive under the Act, including banks, credit unions, and mortgage brokers to name a few. The proposed legislation defines those covered by the Act to be

> any person who engages directly or indirectly in a financial activity, in connection with the provision of a consumer financial product or service [used primarily for personal, family, or household purposes]; or any[one who] provides a material service to, or processes a transaction on behalf of, [such] a person.[10]

Additionally, the Act would consolidate in the CFPA consumer protection regulatory and enforcement authority, which is currently shared by a number of federal agencies. The Act would transfer to the CFPA the "consumer financial protection functions"[11] and many of the employees performing those functions from the Board of Governors of the Federal Reserve System (Federal Reserve), the Office of the Comptroller of the Currency (OCC), the Office of Thrift Supervision (OTS), the Federal Deposit Insurance Corporation (FDIC), the Federal Trade Commission (FTC), and the National Credit Union Administration (NCUA).[12] However, according to the guidelines of the White Paper, these agencies, with the exception of the OTS,[13] would retain safety and soundness supervisory and examination powers outside the purview of consumer protection over certain regulated entities.[14]

The CFPA also would be the primary federal regulator, examiner, and rulemaker[15] with enforcement authority under many of the federal consumer protection laws, including

A. the Alternative Mortgage Transaction Parity Act[16];
B. the Community Reinvestment Act[17];
C. the Consumer Leasing Act[18];
D. the Electronic Funds Transfer Act[19];
E. the Equal Credit Opportunity Act[20];
F. the Fair Credit Billing Act[21];
G. the Fair Credit Reporting Act[22] (except with respect to sections 615(e), 624, and 628[23]);
H. the Fair Debt Collection Practices Act[24];
I. the Federal Deposit Insurance Act, subsections 43(c) through (f)[25];
J. the Gramm-Leach-Bliley Act, sections 502 through 509[26];
K. the Home Mortgage Disclosure Act[27];
L. the Home Ownership and Equity Protection Act[28];
M. the Real Estate Settlement Procedures Act (RESPA)[29];
N. the S.A.F.E. Mortgage Licensing Act[30];
O. the Truth in Lending Act (TILA)[31]; and
P. the Truth in Savings Act.[32]

The CFPA would be required to monitor the market and the innovation of new products and services. In order to do so, the Act would provide the Agency the authority to examine covered persons, including national banks, federal credit unions, and federal savings and loan associations.[33] Under current law, examination powers generally rest exclusively in the institutions' primary regulators.

Rather than explicitly imposing new regulation on financial activities and products, the Act primarily (though, not exclusively[34]) leaves such decisions to be made by the CFPA through future rulemaking and guidance. The Agency would have the authority to promulgate rules and issue guidance and orders to meet the objectives of the CFPA Act.[35] The standard rulemaking procedures provided by the Act would require the Agency to weigh the costs and benefits to both consumers and industry, including the potential effect the rule would have on the availability of financial products and services.[36] The Agency also would have to "consult with the Federal banking agencies ... regarding the consistency of a proposed rule with prudential, market, or systemic objectives administered by such agencies."[37] Within three years[38] of any CFPA "significant rule or order" becoming effective and after a public comment period, the Agency must publish a report assessing the effectiveness of the rule or order.[39] The Act does not specify what would be considered "significant," presumably leaving these determinations to the Agency.

The Act imposes additional procedures upon specific types of rulemaking. For instance, the Agency would be authorized to promulgate rules on unfair or deceptive practices in connection with consumer financial services and products. However, the Agency could only promulgate a rule deeming an act unlawfully *unfair* if the Agency has a reasonable basis to conclude that the act or practices causes or is likely to cause substantial injury to consumers which is not reasonably avoidable by consumers and such substantial injury is not outweighed by countervailing benefits to consumers or to competition.[40]

Other examples of specific rulemaking authority for which the CFPA Act would impose requirements in addition to the Act's standard rulemaking procedures outlined above include disclosure requirements;[41] minimum standards for the prevention and detection of "unfair, deceptive, abusive, fraudulent, or illegal transactions";[42] provision of "standard consumer financial products or services" that may serve as a comparison to similar, but less traditional products or services;[43] and imposition of duties, including compensation practices, on covered persons.[44]

All of these steps and restrictions exceed the normal notice and comment procedures of the Administrative Procedure Act, which generally apply to agency rulemaking.[45]

The Act would *not* preempt state consumer protection laws that provide greater protections to consumers, but would preempt otherwise conflicting state laws. The CFPA would decide whether or not particular state laws conflict with the Act,[46] with specific decisions subject to judicial review.[47] Any generally applicable state consumer law would apply to national banks and savings and loans unless it discriminates against them or conflicts with the Act.[48] Additionally, any state consumer law regulating state banks or state savings and loans that was enacted in compliance with federal law also would apply to national banks and savings and loans unless it discriminates against the federally chartered institutions or conflicts with the CFPA Act.[49] Depending on how they are interpreted by the Agency and the courts, these provisions could result in a departure from current federal banking law, which the OCC and other banking regulators interpret as preempting many state consumer laws.[50]

H.R. 3126, CHAIRMAN FRANK'S CFPA ACT OF 2009

There are three major substantive differences between H.R. 3126, as introduced, and the Obama Proposal. One is that H.R. 3126 does not transfer oversight and enforcement authority over the Community Reinvestment Act to the CFPA, as proposed by the Obama Proposal.[51] A second is that H.R. 3126 does not envision the elimination of the thrift charter, and by extension, the Office of Thrift Supervision. The President's White Paper proposes eliminating the thrift charter and converting such entities into state or national banks, while also modifying the regulatory framework to which banks are subject.[52] It is still unclear how (or if) Congress will propose to change the prudential regulation of financial institutions, including banks and thrifts. The fact that H.R. 3126 continues to reference thrifts and the Office of Thrift Supervision is not an indication that changes will not be made to them in the future – just that such changes have yet to be made and are not proposed in H.R. 3126.[53] As a result of their variant treatment of thrifts, the President's CFPA Act and H.R. 3126 divide regulatory authority differently, which is primarily manifested in the two proposals' conforming amendment sections. Similarly, H.R. 3126 does not make reference to a National Bank Supervisor like the President's CFPA Act. Instead, H.R. 3126 refers to "the head of the agency responsible for chartering and regulating national banks."[54]

WOULD THE CFPA BE AN IMPROVEMENT?

The Treasury's White Paper argues that the CFPA is necessary because recent events in financial markets have exposed the inadequacy of the current regulatory framework. As an example, the White Paper cites overly complicated, nontraditional mortgages that were unsuitable for the many borrowers who lost their homes to foreclosure.[55] By creating an agency dedicated exclusively to consumer protection, Treasury hopes to raise standards for financial intermediaries and ultimately foster a culture of consumer protection within financial firms. In the White Paper's analysis, the imperative to protect consumers was simply overwhelmed by profit considerations – by its very existence, the CFPA is intended to right the balance.[56]

There are benefits to having a single agency in charge of virtually all consumer financial products and services and consumer protection laws. But there are also costs, which may fall either on regulated financial institutions or on consumers. The CFPA proposal raises a number of basic questions about the structure and purposes of regulation.

Redundancy?

The powers that CFPA would have are primarily derived from federal banking statutes. This raises the objection that the existing bank regulators already have full authority to do what the new agency would do. What would prevent failures in regulation from being addressed within the existing structure?

One can argue that there is a conflict between safety and soundness regulation and consumer protection. When a banking activity is profitable, regulators tend to look upon it favorably, since it enables the bank to meet capital requirements and withstand financial shocks. According to the White Paper, professional bank examiners are trained "to see the world through the lenses of institutions and markets, not consumers."[57] This conflict may be especially sharp in consumer lending.

Over the past several decades, banks and other financial institutions have expanded the scale and scope of their consumer lending programs. Partly driven by competition from the securities industry (which has largely supplanted banks as a source of funds for large corporations), and partly by the availability of computerized credit scoring models (which dramatically reduce the cost of evaluating borrowers' creditworthiness), mainstream lenders have made credit available to consumers who not long ago would have been viewed as too risky and unqualified.[58]

Credit card and subprime mortgage lending are perhaps the most visible results of this trend. On the one hand, they represent a great expansion in the availability of credit and have allowed many consumers to raise their standard of living. On the other hand, both have been criticized for high costs to borrowers, hidden fees, and/or excessive complexity, to the extent that lending practices have been described as unscrupulous and abusive. If one believes that banks have sought to maintain their profits by offering credit to consumers with limited financial resources and sophistication, many of whom accumulate heavy debt burdens,[59] the case for a CFPA may be strong.

On the other hand, it can be argued that even very expensive forms of credit – such as predatory or payday lending – are welfare-enhancing,[60] that the balance between safety and soundness regulation and consumer protection ought not to be shifted in favor of the latter, and that the CFPA would add a redundant layer of regulation.

Financial Innovation

An argument against CFPA is that it could stifle financial innovation. Innovative practices are by definition less well understood than traditional ones,[61] and financial institutions tend to earn higher margins on new products, at least until their competitors enter the market and compete away excess profits. Both factors might appear problematic to a consumer protection regulator, though not necessarily to a safety and soundness regulator.

The White Paper is explicit about favoring and promoting traditional, "plain-vanilla" financial products. The White Paper stresses the need to achieve simplicity, fairness, and reasonable disclosure;[62] and the Act would provide the CFPA the authority to impose duties of care and suitability requirements on financial firms. Opponents of the CFPA might argue that this attitude could lead to the creation of barriers and hurdles – perhaps in the form of slow approval of disclosure forms – to the introduction of new products.

Treasury officials have made clear their concern that the classical economic model of rational, informed consumers, able to act in their self-interest, is not a sound basis for regulation. For example:

> Michael Barr [Assistant Secretary for Financial Institutions], who is leading the consumer- protection efforts, said the "plain-vanilla" financial products have their roots in behavioral economics and psychology. It isn't enough to provide consumers with more disclosure and more information, since people often get easily overwhelmed and make mistakes, said Mr. Barr, a former academic who studied the financial markets.
> Most people, for example, don't understand the effects of compounding of interest—which leads them to undersave and to overborrow—a basic human failing that some financial institutions have an incentive to exploit.[63]

The debate over strengthened consumer protection, in other words, involves the age-old question of how much government intervention into markets is warranted: should consumers be protected from their mistakes, or trusted to make decisions that will enhance individual and common welfare? The issue of financial innovation can be framed similarly: is development of new and/or exotic financial products to be encouraged, or are they potentially troublesome if they gain wide currency before the risks are fully understood by regulators and market participants?

Jurisdiction

Under the Treasury proposal, the SEC and CFTC would retain their consumer protection role in securities and derivatives markets.[64] This could be viewed as a flaw, which would preserve the existing fragmented federal regulatory structure. The banking and securities industries have for years offered products that compete with each other – money market funds, brokerage checking accounts, investment advice through bank trust departments, etc. – and issues of overly complex products, inadequate disclosure, conflicts of interest, and the extent of fiduciary duties are common to both.

Since the onset of the financial crisis, households' losses in real estate have been exceeded by their losses in securities investments.[65] Not all those losses resulted from fraud or regulatory failure, but the SEC's recent record is not notably better than the bank regulators'. The logic of creating a single agency exclusively concerned with consumer financial protection, and excluding securities (and futures[66]) may not be clear.

For comparison, the Financial Services Authority in the United Kingdom has consumer protection powers over all financial industries, including banking, securities, derivatives, and insurance. Its objectives, as posted on its website, appear to mirror those of the proposed CFPA. The Financial Services and Markets Act gives the FSA four statutory objectives:

- Market confidence: maintaining confidence in the financial system;
- Public awareness: promoting public understanding of the financial system;
- Consumer protection: securing the appropriate degree of protection for consumers; and
- The reduction of financial crime: reducing the extent to which it is possible for a business to be used for a purpose connected with financial crime.[67]

Is there a different regulatory structure, where jurisdiction is split differently among multiple regulators, that could lead to a greater balance of the regulatory costs and benefits? Are there other products and services that should be excepted from the CFPA's jurisdiction?

QUESTIONS LEFT UNANSWERED

Preemption

How narrowly or broadly will the Agency interpret potential conflicts between state and federal law? If interpreted narrowly, then the Act's preemption language could have a detrimental effect on banks and other entities that provide consumer financial products and services in multiple states because they would be working within multiple regulatory regimes, increasing administrative costs that likely would be passed on to consumers.[68] If the Agency interprets conflicts broadly, then interstate actors may only have a single set of rules to follow, but consumers may not be as fully protected from predatory products, services, and practices as they would be otherwise.

Funding

How much funding would come from fees on covered entities? How would the annual fees be tabulated (e.g., based on number of covered transactions or size of company)? If such fees were assessed, would those costs be passed onto the consumer? Would that be more beneficial to the public as a whole than paying for the Agency through normal appropriations? The agencies from which many of the CFPA employees would be transferred are largely self-funded through fees assessed on the companies under their regulatory jurisdiction. Some have argued that this source of funding played a role in lax regulatory enforcement by federal agencies because banks have an incentive to seek the regulator they believe will have the lightest regulatory touch, while the regulators generate more fees with every institution they bring under their jurisdiction.[69] Would funding the CFPA through fees lead to similar problems? On the other hand, running the Agency will be expensive. The ability of the CFPA to generate at least some of its own funding could reduce the Agency's need for general appropriations.

Rulemaking

Are the Act's rulemaking procedures appropriately drawn? As previously mentioned, agency rulemaking generally only requires public notice of proposed rulemaking and a period for public comment on the matter. The Act would require steps in addition to notice and comment. For instance, the CFPA would have to make findings regarding the costs of potential rules on both industry and consumers. Additionally, the Agency would have to review any significant rule within three to five years after its effective date. The Act would impose other restrictions on rulemaking, as well. If rulemaking procedures are too easily met, then the Agency could go too far, promulgating rules that have a deleterious effect on consumers' access to credit and on industry's profitability. If procedures are so restrictive that the Agency is unable to pass rules in a timely fashion, consumers could be harmed by otherwise preventable predatory products and practices, which also could lead to long-term harm to industry. If overly restrictive, the rulemaking process itself could be expensive, increasing costs to taxpayers and potentially to consumers and industry if the Agency imposes fees on products and services.

End Notes

[1] Financial Regulatory Reform, Obama Administration White Paper, available at http://www.financialstability.gov/docs/regs/FinalReport_web.pdf (hereinafter, White Paper).
[2] White Paper at 3-4.
[3] Consumer Financial Protection Agency Act of 2009, available at http://www.financialstability.gov/docs/CFPA-Act.pdf (hereinafter, CFPA Act).
[4] H.R 3126 refers to "the head of the agency responsible for chartering and regulating national banks," rather than a National Bank Supervisor. See the "H.R. 3126: Chairman Frank's CFPA Act of 2009" section of this report.
[5] CFPA Act § 1012. See, also, H.R. 3126 § 112.
[6] CFPA Act § 1018. See, also, H.R. 3126 § 118.
[7] CFPA Act § 1021. See, also, H.R. 3126 § 121.
[8] See definition of "financial activity," CFPA Act § 1002(18). See, also, H.R. 3126 § 101(18).
[9] See definition of "financial activity," CFPA Act § 1002(18). See, also, H.R. 3126 § 101(18).
[10] CFPA Act § 1001(9). See, also, H.R. 3126 § 101(9).
[11] The CFPA Act defines "consumer financial protection functions" as "research, rulemaking, issuance of orders or guidance, supervision, examination, and enforcement activities, powers, and duties relating to the provision of consumer financial products or services, including the authority to assess and collect fees for this purpose." CFPA Act § 1061(d). See, also, H.R. 3126 § 161(d).
[12] CFPA Act §§ 1061-1066. See, also, H.R. 3126 §§ 161-166.

[13] The White Paper proposes the elimination of the thrift charter. White Paper at 32-34.
[14] White Paper at 19-42. The White Paper does propose changes with regards to who regulates whom and the scope of supervision. For a detailed discussion of the current regulatory system, see CRS Report R40249, *Who Regulates Whom? An Overview of U.S. Financial Supervision*, by Mark Jickling and Edward V. Murphy.
[15] CFPA Act § 1022. See, also, H.R. 3126 § 122.
[16] 12 U.S.C. §§ 3801 *et seq.*
[17] 12 U.S.C. §§ 2901 *et seq.* This act is not included as an "Enumerated Consumer Law" in H.R. 3126. See the "H.R. 3126: Chairman Frank's CFPA Act of 2009" section of this report.
[18] 15 U.S.C. §§ 1667 *et seq.* This act is not specifically referenced in H.R. 3126's definition of "Enumerated Consumer Law;" however, the bill does transfer enforcement authority over this act to the CFPA. H.R. 3126 § 184(b)(2).
[19] 15 U.S.C. §§ 1693 *et seq.*
[20] 15 U.S.C. §§ 1691 *et seq.*
[21] 15 U.S.C. §§ 1666-1666j. This act is not specifically referenced in H.R. 3126's definition of "Enumerated Consumer Law;" however, the bill does transfer enforcement authority over this act to the CFPA. H.R. 3126 § 184(b)(2).
[22] 15 U.S.C. §§ 1681 *et seq.*
[23] 15 U.S.C. §§ 1681m(e), 1681s-3, 1681w.
[24] 15 U.S.C. §§ 1692 *et seq.*
[25] 12 U.S.C. § 1831t(c)-(f).
[26] 15 U.S.C. §§ 6802-6809.
[27] 12 U.S.C. §§ 2801 *et seq.*
[28] 15 U.S.C. § 1639.
[29] 12 U.S.C. §§ 2601-2610.
[30] 12 U.S.C. §§ 5101-5116.
[31] 15 U.S.C. §§ 1601 *et seq.*
[32] 12 U.S.C. §§ 4301 *et seq.*
[33] CFPA Act §§ 1022(c) and 1024. See, also, H.R. 3126 §§ 122(c) and 124.
[34] However, the Act would impose some substantive regulations. For example, the Act would require disclosure of new data points under the Home Mortgage Disclosure Act. CFPA Act § 1086(f).
[35] CFPA Act § 1022(a). See, also, H.R. 3126 § 122(a). The CFPA would be expressly prohibited from setting a usury cap without specific authorization by law. CFPA Act § 1022(g). See, also, H.R. 3126 § 122(g). The Act specifically provides the Agency the authority to prohibit or limit arbitration clauses. CFPA Act § 1025. See, also, H.R. 3126 § 125.
[36] CFPA Act § 1022(b). See, also, H.R. 3126 § 122(b).
[37] CFPA Act § 1022(b). See, also, H.R. 3126 § 122(b).
[38] The Agency may delay the report for up to five years after the effective date if it determines that three years is not enough time to adequately review the rule. CFPA Act § 1024. See, also, H.R. 3126 § 124.
[39] CFPA Act § 1024. See, also, H.R. 3126 § 124.
[40] CFPA Act § 1031. See, also, H.R. 3126 § 131.
[41] CFPA Act §§ 1032 and 1034. See, also, H.R. 3126 §§ 132 and 134.
[42] CFPA Act § 1035. See, also, H.R. 3126 § 135.
[43] CFPA Act § 1036. See, also, H.R. 3126 § 136.
[44] CFPA Act § 1037. See, also, H.R. 3126 § 137. The Agency would only be able to enforce violations of duties prescribed under the authority of § 1037 in accordance with an adjudicatory proceeding described in great detail in §§ 1051-1058 of the Act. CFPA Act § 1037. See, also, H.R. 3126 § 137.
[45] 5 U.S.C. § 553. See, also, CRS Report RL32240, *The Federal Rulemaking Process: An Overview*, by Curtis W. Copeland.
[46] CFPA Act § 1041. See, also, H.R. 3126 § 141.
[47] For a description of judicial review of statutory interpretation by agencies, see CRS Report R40595, *Cuomo v. Clearing House Association, L.L. C: National Banks Are Subject to State Lawsuits to Enforce Non-Preempted State Laws*, by M. Maureen Murphy.
[48] CFPA Act §§ 1043(b)-(c) and 1046(b)-(c). See, also, H.R. 3126 §§ 143(b)-(c) and 146(b)-(c).
[49] CFPA Act §§ 1042(d) and 1046(d). See, also, H.R. 3126 §§ 142(c) and 146(d).
[50] See, e.g., 12 C.F.R. §§ 7.4000 et seq. and Part 34. See, also, CRS Report RL32197, *Preemption of State Law for National Banks and Their Subsidiaries by the Office of the Comptroller of the Currency*, by M. Maureen Murphy.
[51] H.R. 3126 § 101(16).
[52] White Paper at 30-31.
[53] However, Chairman Frank has reportedly stated that he does not believe the House Financial Services Committee will pass legislation that would eliminate the thrift charter. Bill Swindell, *Frank: No Need to Scrap Federal Thrift Charter*, CongressDaily, Jul. 15, 2009.

[54] See, e.g., H.R. 3126 § 112(a).
[55] White Paper at 55.
[56] White Paper at 57.
[57] White Paper at 56.
[58] Darryl E. Getter, "Consumer Credit Risk and Pricing," *Journal of Consumer Affairs*, vol. 40, Summer 2006, p. 41.
[59] According to the Federal Reserve's Survey of Consumer Finances, 26.9% of the families in the bottom 20% of the income distribution devoted more than 40% of their incomes to debt repayment in 2007.
[60] There is empirical evidence for this. See, e.g., Paige Marta Skiba and Jeremy Tobacman, "Measuring the Individual- Level Effects of Access to Credit: Evidence from Payday Loans," *The Mixing of Banking and Commerce: Proceedings of the 43rd Annual Conference on Bank Structure and Competition*, Federal Reserve Bank of Chicago, 2007, p. 280; and Jonathan Zinman, "Restricting Consumer Credit Access: Household Survey Evidence on Effects Around the Oregon Rate Cap," Federal Reserve Bank of Philadelphia Working Paper 08-32, December 2008.
[61] This is the case for all financial products, not just those designed for consumers.
[62] White Paper at 63-67.
[63] Jane J. Kim, "Plain-Vanilla Financing Could Melt Bank Profits – U.S.'s Bid to Help Consumers; Mystery of Compound Interest," *Wall Street Journal*, Jun. 26, 2009, p. C1. Behavioral finance posits that consumers are "hardwired" to make bad financial choices, and that education is only a partial remedy.
[64] The White Paper does recommend certain enhancements to the SEC's authority: see, e.g., p. 70.
[65] Between the end of 2006 and the first quarter of 2009, households lost $4.01 trillion of the value of their real estate holdings, while the value of corporate stock and mutual funds held by households (and non-profits) fell by $5.10 trillion. Federal Reserve, Flow of Funds Accounts, Table B. 100.
[66] Although relatively few individuals trade in derivatives markets.
[67] http://www.fsa.gov.uk/Pages/about/aims/statutory/index.shtml.
[68] This potentially could put entities acting only within a single state at a competitive advantage over interstate actors.
[69] See, e.g., Adam Levitin, *Bank Regulatory Arbitrage and Deregulation: The Number of Bank Regulators Matters*, Credit Slips: A Discussion on Credit and Bankruptcy, available at http://www.creditslips.org/creditslips/2009/06/one-of-the-key-points-of-debate-over-financial-institution-regulation-reform-is-how-many-different-bank-regulators-there- shou.html.

Chapter 3

FINANCIAL REGULATORY REFORM A NEW FOUNDATION: REBUILDING FINANCIAL SUPERVISION AND REGULATION

Department of the Treasury

INTRODUCTION

Over the past two years we have faced the most severe financial crisis since the Great Depression. Americans across the nation are struggling with unemployment, failing businesses, falling home prices, and declining savings. These challenges have forced the government to take extraordinary measures to revive our financial system so that people can access loans to buy a car or home, pay for a child's education, or finance a business.

The roots of this crisis go back decades. Years without a serious economic recession bred complacency among financial intermediaries and investors. Financial challenges such as the near-failure of Long-Term Capital Management and the Asian Financial Crisis had minimal impact on economic growth in the U.S., which bred exaggerated expectations about the resilience of our financial markets and firms. Rising asset prices, particularly in housing, hid weak credit underwriting standards and masked the growing leverage throughout the system.

At some of our most sophisticated financial firms, risk management systems did not keep pace with the complexity of new financial products. The lack of transparency and standards in markets for securitized loans helped to weaken underwriting standards. Market discipline broke down as investors relied excessively on credit rating agencies. Compensation practices throughout the financial services industry rewarded short-term profits at the expense of long-term value.

Households saw significant increases in access to credit, but those gains were overshadowed by pervasive failures in consumer protection, leaving many Americans with obligations that they did not understand and could not afford.

While this crisis had many causes, it is clear now that the government could have done more to prevent many of these problems from growing out of control and threatening the stability of our financial system. Gaps and weaknesses in the supervision and regulation of financial firms presented challenges to our government's ability to monitor, prevent, or address risks as they built up in the system. No regulator saw its job as protecting the economy and financial system as a whole. Existing approaches to bank holding company regulation focused on protecting the subsidiary bank, not on comprehensive regulation of the whole firm. Investment banks were permitted to opt for a different regime under a different regulator, and in doing so, escaped adequate constraints on leverage. Other firms, such as AIG, owned insured depositories, but escaped the strictures of serious holding company regulation because the depositories that they owned were technically not "banks" under relevant law.

We must act now to restore confidence in the integrity of our financial system. The lasting economic damage to ordinary families and businesses is a constant reminder of the urgent need to act to reform our financial regulatory system and put our economy on track to a sustainable recovery. We must build a new foundation for financial regulation and supervision that is simpler and more effectively enforced, that protects consumers and investors, that rewards innovation and that is able to adapt and evolve with changes in the financial market.

In the following pages, we propose reforms to meet five key objectives:

(1) *Promote robust supervision and regulation of financial firms.* Financial institutions that are critical to market functioning should be subject to strong oversight. No financial firm that poses a significant risk to the financial system should be unregulated or weakly regulated. We need clear accountability in financial oversight and supervision. We propose:

- A new Financial Services Oversight Council of financial regulators to identify emerging systemic risks and improve interagency cooperation.
- New authority for the Federal Reserve to supervise all firms that could pose a threat to financial stability, even those that do not own banks.
- Stronger capital and other prudential standards for all financial firms, and even higher standards for large, interconnected firms.
- A new National Bank Supervisor to supervise all federally chartered banks.
- Elimination of the federal thrift charter and other loopholes that allowed some depository institutions to avoid bank holding company regulation by the Federal Reserve.
- The registration of advisers of hedge funds and other private pools of capital with the SEC.

(2) *Establish comprehensive supervision of financial markets.* Our major financial markets must be strong enough to withstand both system-wide stress and the failure of one or more large institutions. We propose:

- Enhanced regulation of securitization markets, including new requirements for market transparency, stronger regulation of credit rating agencies, and a

requirement that issuers and originators retain a financial interest in securitized loans.
- Comprehensive regulation of all over-the-counter derivatives.
- New authority for the Federal Reserve to oversee payment, clearing, and settlement systems.

(3) *Protect consumers and investors from financial abuse.* To rebuild trust in our markets, we need strong and consistent regulation and supervision of consumer financial services and investment markets. We should base this oversight not on speculation or abstract models, but on actual data about how people make financial decisions. We must promote transparency, simplicity, fairness, accountability, and access. We propose:

- A new Consumer Financial Protection Agency to protect consumers across the financial sector from unfair, deceptive, and abusive practices.
- Stronger regulations to improve the transparency, fairness, and appropriateness of consumer and investor products and services.
- A level playing field and higher standards for providers of consumer financial products and services, whether or not they are part of a bank.

(4) *Provide the government with the tools it needs to manage financial crises.* We need to be sure that the government has the tools it needs to manage crises, if and when they arise, so that we are not left with untenable choices between bailouts and financial collapse. We propose:

- A new regime to resolve nonbank financial institutions whose failure could have serious systemic effects.
- Revisions to the Federal Reserve's emergency lending authority to improve accountability.

(5) *Raise international regulatory standards and improve international cooperation.* The challenges we face are not just American challenges, they are global challenges. So, as we work to set high regulatory standards here in the United States, we must ask the world to do the same. We propose:

- International reforms to support our efforts at home, including strengthening the capital framework; improving oversight of global financial markets; coordinating supervision of internationally active firms; and enhancing crisis management tools.

In addition to substantive reforms of the authorities and practices of regulation and supervision, the proposals contained in this report entail a significant restructuring of our regulatory system. We propose the creation of a Financial Services Oversight Council, chaired by Treasury and including the heads of the principal federal financial regulators as members. We also propose the creation of two new agencies. We propose the creation of the

Consumer Financial Protection Agency, which will be an independent entity dedicated to consumer protection in credit, savings, and payments markets. We also propose the creation of the National Bank Supervisor, which will be a single agency with separate status in Treasury with responsibility for federally chartered depository institutions. To promote national coordination in the insurance sector, we propose the creation of an Office of National Insurance within Treasury.

Under our proposal, the Federal Reserve and the Federal Deposit Insurance Corporation (FDIC) would maintain their respective roles in the supervision and regulation of state-chartered banks, and the National Credit Union Administration (NCUA) would maintain its authorities with regard to credit unions. The Securities and Exchange Commission (SEC) and Commodity Futures Trading Commission (CFTC) would maintain their current responsibilities and authorities as market regulators, though we propose to harmonize the statutory and regulatory frameworks for futures and securities.

The proposals contained in this report do not represent the complete set of potentially desirable reforms in financial regulation. More can and should be done in the future. We focus here on what is essential: to address the causes of the current crisis, to create a more stable financial system that is fair for consumers, and to help prevent and contain potential crises in the future. *(For a detailed list of recommendations, please see Summary of Recommendations following the Introduction.)*

These proposals are the product of broad-ranging individual consultations with members of the President's Working Group on Financial Markets, Members of Congress, academics, consumer and investor advocates, community-based organizations, the business community, and industry and market participants.

I. Promote Robust Supervision and Regulation of Financial Firms

In the years leading up to the current financial crisis, risks built up dangerously in our financial system. Rising asset prices, particularly in housing, concealed a sharp deterioration of underwriting standards for loans. The nation's largest financial firms, already highly leveraged, became increasingly dependent on unstable sources of short- term funding. In many cases, weaknesses in firms' risk-management systems left them unaware of the aggregate risk exposures on and off their balance sheets. A credit boom accompanied a housing bubble. Taking access to short-term credit for granted, firms did not plan for the potential demands on their liquidity during a crisis. When asset prices started to fall and market liquidity froze, firms were forced to pull back from lending, limiting credit for households and businesses.

Our supervisory framework was not equipped to handle a crisis of this magnitude. To be sure, most of the largest, most interconnected, and most highly leveraged financial firms in the country were subject to some form of supervision and regulation by a federal government agency. But those forms of supervision and regulation proved inadequate and inconsistent.

First, capital and liquidity requirements were simply too low. Regulators did not require firms to hold sufficient capital to cover trading assets, high-risk loans, and off-balance sheet commitments, or to hold increased capital during good times to prepare for bad times.

Regulators did not require firms to plan for a scenario in which the availability of liquidity was sharply curtailed.

Second, on a systemic basis, regulators did not take into account the harm that large, interconnected, and highly leveraged institutions could inflict on the financial system and on the economy if they failed.

Third, the responsibility for supervising the consolidated operations of large financial firms was split among various federal agencies. Fragmentation of supervisory responsibility and loopholes in the legal definition of a "bank" allowed owners of banks and other insured depository institutions to shop for the regulator of their choice.

Fourth, investment banks operated with insufficient government oversight. Money market mutual funds were vulnerable to runs. Hedge funds and other private pools of capital operated completely outside of the supervisory framework.

To create a new foundation for the regulation of financial institutions, we will promote more robust and consistent regulatory standards for all financial institutions. Similar financial institutions should face the same supervisory and regulatory standards, with no gaps, loopholes, or opportunities for arbitrage.

We propose the creation of a Financial Services Oversight Council, chaired by Treasury, to help fill gaps in supervision, facilitate coordination of policy and resolution of disputes, and identify emerging risks in firms and market activities. This Council would include the heads of the principal federal financial regulators and would maintain a permanent staff at Treasury.

We propose an evolution in the Federal Reserve's current supervisory authority for BHCs to create a single point of accountability for the consolidated supervision of all companies that own a bank. All large, interconnected firms whose failure could threaten the stability of the system should be subject to consolidated supervision by the Federal Reserve, regardless of whether they own an insured depository institution. These firms should not be able to escape oversight of their risky activities by manipulating their legal structure.

Under our proposals, the largest, most interconnected, and highly leveraged institutions would face stricter prudential regulation than other regulated firms, including higher capital requirements and more robust consolidated supervision. In effect, our proposals would compel these firms to internalize the costs they could impose on society in the event of failure.

II. Establish Comprehensive Regulation of Financial Markets

The current financial crisis occurred after a long and remarkable period of growth and innovation in our financial markets. New financial instruments allowed credit risks to be spread widely, enabling investors to diversify their portfolios in new ways and enabling banks to shed exposures that had once stayed on their balance sheets. Through securitization, mortgages and other loans could be aggregated with similar loans and sold in tranches to a large and diverse pool of new investors with different risk preferences. Through credit derivatives, banks could transfer much of their credit exposure to third parties without selling the underlying loans. This distribution of risk was widely perceived to reduce systemic risk, to promote efficiency, and to contribute to a better allocation of resources.

However, instead of appropriately distributing risks, this process often concentrated risk in opaque and complex ways. Innovations occurred too rapidly for many financial institutions' risk management systems; for the market infrastructure, which consists of payment, clearing and settlement systems; and for the nation's financial supervisors.

Securitization, by breaking down the traditional relationship between borrowers and lenders, created conflicts of interest that market discipline failed to correct. Loan originators failed to require sufficient documentation of income and ability to pay. Securitizers failed to set high standards for the loans they were willing to buy, encouraging underwriting standards to decline. Investors were overly reliant on credit rating agencies. Credit ratings often failed to accurately describe the risk of rated products. In each case, lack of transparency prevented market participants from understanding the full nature of the risks they were taking.

The build-up of risk in the over-the-counter (OTC) derivatives markets, which were thought to disperse risk to those most able to bear it, became a major source of contagion through the financial sector during the crisis.

We propose to bring the markets for all OTC derivatives and asset-backed securities into a coherent and coordinated regulatory framework that requires transparency and improves market discipline. Our proposal would impose record keeping and reporting requirements on all OTC derivatives. We also propose to strengthen the prudential regulation of all dealers in the OTC derivative markets and to reduce systemic risk in these markets by requiring all standardized OTC derivative transactions to be executed in regulated and transparent venues and cleared through regulated central counterparties.

We propose to enhance the Federal Reserve's authority over market infrastructure to reduce the potential for contagion among financial firms and markets.

Finally, we propose to harmonize the statutory and regulatory regimes for futures and securities. While differences exist between securities and futures markets, many differences in regulation between the markets may no longer be justified. In particular, the growth of derivatives markets and the introduction of new derivative instruments have highlighted the need for addressing gaps and inconsistencies in the regulation of these products by the CFTC and SEC.

III. Protect Consumers and Investors from Financial Abuse

Prior to the current financial crisis, a number of federal and state regulations were in place to protect consumers against fraud and to promote understanding of financial products like credit cards and mortgages. But as abusive practices spread, particularly in the market for subprime and nontraditional mortgages, our regulatory framework proved inadequate in important ways. Multiple agencies have authority over consumer protection in financial products, but for historical reasons, the supervisory framework for enforcing those regulations had significant gaps and weaknesses. Banking regulators at the state and federal level had a potentially conflicting mission to promote safe and sound banking practices, while other agencies had a clear mission but limited tools and jurisdiction. Most critically in the run-up to the financial crisis, mortgage companies and other firms outside of the purview of bank regulation exploited that lack of clear accountability by selling mortgages and other products that were overly complicated and unsuited to borrowers' financial situation. Banks and thrifts followed suit, with disastrous results for consumers and the financial system.

This year, Congress, the Administration, and financial regulators have taken significant measures to address some of the most obvious inadequacies in our consumer protection framework. But these steps have focused on just two, albeit very important, product markets – credit cards and mortgages. We need comprehensive reform.

For that reason, we propose the creation of a single regulatory agency, a Consumer Financial Protection Agency (CFPA), with the authority and accountability to make sure that consumer protection regulations are written fairly and enforced vigorously. The CFPA should reduce gaps in federal supervision and enforcement; improve coordination with the states; set higher standards for financial intermediaries; and promote consistent regulation of similar products.

Consumer protection is a critical foundation for our financial system. It gives the public confidence that financial markets are fair and enables policy makers and regulators to maintain stability in regulation. Stable regulation, in turn, promotes growth, efficiency, and innovation over the long term. We propose legislative, regulatory, and administrative reforms to promote transparency, simplicity, fairness, accountability, and access in the market for consumer financial products and services.

We also propose new authorities and resources for the Federal Trade Commission to protect consumers in a wide range of areas.

Finally, we propose new authorities for the Securities and Exchange Commission to protect investors, improve disclosure, raise standards, and increase enforcement.

IV. Provide the Government with the Tools it Needs to Manage Financial Crises

Over the past two years, the financial system has been threatened by the failure or near failure of some of the largest and most interconnected financial firms. Our current system already has strong procedures and expertise for handling the failure of banks, but when a bank holding company or other nonbank financial firm is in severe distress, there are currently only two options: obtain outside capital or file for bankruptcy. During most economic climates, these are suitable options that will not impact greater financial stability.

However, in stressed conditions it may prove difficult for distressed institutions to raise sufficient private capital. Thus, if a large, interconnected bank holding company or other nonbank financial firm nears failure during a financial crisis, there are only two untenable options: obtain emergency funding from the US government as in the case of AIG, or file for bankruptcy as in the case of Lehman Brothers. Neither of these options is acceptable for managing the resolution of the firm efficiently and effectively in a manner that limits the systemic risk with the least cost to the taxpayer.

We propose a new authority, modeled on the existing authority of the FDIC, that should allow the government to address the potential failure of a bank holding company or other nonbank financial firm when the stability of the financial system is at risk.

In order to improve accountability in the use of other crisis tools, we also propose that the Federal Reserve Board receive prior written approval from the Secretary of the Treasury for emergency lending under its "unusual and exigent circumstances" authority.

V. Raise International Regulatory Standards and Improve International Cooperation

As we have witnessed during this crisis, financial stress can spread easily and quickly across national boundaries. Yet, regulation is still set largely in a national context. Without consistent supervision and regulation, financial institutions will tend to move their activities to jurisdictions with looser standards, creating a race to the bottom and intensifying systemic risk for the entire global financial system.

The United States is playing a strong leadership role in efforts to coordinate international financial policy through the G-20, the Financial Stability Board, and the Basel Committee on Banking Supervision. We will use our leadership position in the international community to promote initiatives compatible with the domestic regulatory reforms described in this report.

We will focus on reaching international consensus on four core issues: regulatory capital standards; oversight of global financial markets; supervision of internationally active financial firms; and crisis prevention and management.

At the April 2009 London Summit, the G-20 Leaders issued an eight-part declaration outlining a comprehensive plan for financial regulatory reform.

The domestic regulatory reform initiatives outlined in this report are consistent with the international commitments the United States has undertaken as part of the G-20 process, and we propose stronger regulatory standards in a number of areas.

SUMMARY OF RECOMMENDATIONS

Please refer to the main text for further details

I. Promote Robust Supervision and Regulation of Financial Firms

A. Create a Financial Services Oversight Council
1. *We propose the creation of a Financial Services Oversight Council to facilitate information sharing and coordination, identify emerging risks, advise the Federal Reserve on the identification of firms whose failure could pose a threat to financial stability due to their combination of size, leverage, and interconnectedness (hereafter referred to as a Tier 1 FHC), and provide a forum for resolving jurisdictional disputes between regulators.*
    a. *The membership of the Council should include (i) the Secretary of the Treasury, who shall serve as the Chairman; (ii) the Chairman of the Board of Governors of the Federal Reserve System; (iii) the Director of the National Bank Supervisor; (iv) the Director of the Consumer Financial*

Protection Agency; (v) the Chairman of the SEC; (vi) the Chairman of the CFTC; (vii) the Chairman of the FDIC; and (viii) the Director of the Federal Housing Finance Agency (FHFA).
    b. *The Council should be supported by a permanent, full-time expert staff at Treasury. The staff should be responsible for providing the Council with the information and resources it needs to fulfill its responsibilities.*
2. *Our legislation will propose to give the Council the authority to gather information from any financial firm and the responsibility for referring emerging risks to the attention of regulators with the authority to respond.*

B. Implement Heightened Consolidated Supervision and Regulation of All Large, Interconnected Financial Firms
1. *Any financial firm whose combination of size, leverage, and interconnectedness could pose a threat to financial stability if it failed (Tier 1 FHC) should be subject to robust consolidated supervision and regulation, regardless of whether the firm owns an insured depository institution.*
2. *The Federal Reserve Board should have the authority and accountability for consolidated supervision and regulation of Tier 1 FHCs.*
3. *Our legislation will propose criteria that the Federal Reserve must consider in identifying Tier 1 FHCs.*
4. *The prudential standards for Tier 1 FHCs – including capital, liquidity and risk management standards – should be stricter and more conservative than those applicable to other financial firms to account for the greater risks that their potential failure would impose on the financial system.*
5. *Consolidated supervision of a Tier 1 FHC should extend to the parent company and to all of its subsidiaries – regulated and unregulated, U.S. and foreign. Functionally regulated and depository institution subsidiaries of a Tier 1 FHC should continue to be supervised and regulated primarily by their functional or bank regulator, as the case may be. The constraints that the Gramm-Leach-Bliley Act (GLB Act) introduced on the Federal Reserve's ability to require reports from, examine, or impose higher prudential requirements or more stringent activity restrictions on the functionally regulated or depository institution subsidiaries of FHCs should be removed.*
6. *Consolidated supervision of a Tier 1 FHC should be macroprudential in focus. That is, it should consider risk to the system as a whole.*
7. *The Federal Reserve, in consultation with Treasury and external experts, should propose recommendations by October 1, 2009 to better align its structure and governance with its authorities and responsibilities.*

C. Strengthen Capital and Other Prudential Standards For All Banks and BHCs
1. *Treasury will lead a working group, with participation by federal financial regulatory agencies and outside experts that will conduct a fundamental reassessment of existing regulatory capital requirements for banks and BHCs, including new Tier 1 FHCs. The working group will issue a report with its conclusions by December 31, 2009.*
2. *Treasury will lead a working group, with participation by federal financial regulatory agencies and outside experts, that will conduct a fundamental reassessment of the supervision of banks and BHCs. The working group will issue a report with its conclusions by October 1, 2009.*

3. *Federal regulators should issue standards and guidelines to better align executive compensation practices of financial firms with long-term shareholder value and to prevent compensation practices from providing incentives that could threaten the safety and soundness of supervised institutions. In addition, we will support legislation requiring all public companies to hold non-binding shareholder resolutions on the compensation packages of senior executive officers, as well as new requirements to make compensation committees more independent.*
4. *Capital and management requirements for FHC status should not be limited to the subsidiary depository institution. All FHCs should be required to meet the capital and management requirements on a consolidated basis as well.*
5. *The accounting standard setters (the FASB, the IASB, and the SEC) should review accounting standards to determine how financial firms should be required to employ more forward-looking loan loss provisioning practices that incorporate a broader range of available credit information. Fair value accounting rules also should be reviewed with the goal of identifying changes that could provide users of financial reports with both fair value information and greater transparency regarding the cash flows management expects to receive by holding investments.*
6. *Firewalls between banks and their affiliates should be strengthened to protect the federal safety net that supports banks and to better prevent spread of the subsidy inherent in the federal safety net to bank affiliates.*

D. Close Loopholes in Bank Regulation
1. *We propose the creation of a new federal government agency, the National Bank Supervisor (NBS), to conduct prudential supervision and regulation of all federally chartered depository institutions, and all federal branches and agencies of foreign banks.*
2. *We propose to eliminate the federal thrift charter, but to preserve its interstate branching rules and apply them to state and national banks.*
3. *All companies that control an insured depository institution, however organized, should be subject to robust consolidated supervision and regulation at the federal level by the Federal Reserve and should be subject to the nonbanking activity restrictions of the BHC Act. The policy of separating banking from commerce should be re-affirmed and strengthened. We must close loopholes in the BHC Act for thrift holding companies, industrial loan companies, credit card banks, trust companies, and grandfathered "nonbank" banks.*

E. Eliminate the SEC's Programs for Consolidated Supervision
The SEC has ended its Consolidated Supervised Entity Program, under which it had been the holding company supervisor for companies such as Lehman Brothers and Bear Stearns. We propose also eliminating the SEC's Supervised Investment Bank Holding Company program. Investment banking firms that seek consolidated supervision by a U.S. regulator should be subject to supervision and regulation by the Federal Reserve.

F. Require Hedge Funds and Other Private Pools of Capital to Register
All advisers to hedge funds (and other private pools of capital, including private equity funds and venture capital funds) whose assets under management exceed some

modest threshold should be required to register with the SEC under the Investment Advisers Act. The advisers should be required to report information on the funds they manage that is sufficient to assess whether any fund poses a threat to financial stability.

G. Reduce the Susceptibility of Money Market Mutual Funds (MMFs) to Runs
The SEC should move forward with its plans to strengthen the regulatory framework around MMFs to reduce the credit and liquidity risk profile of individual MMFs and to make the MMF industry as a whole less susceptible to runs. The President's Working Group on Financial Markets should prepare a report assessing whether more fundamental changes are necessary to further reduce the MMF industry's susceptibility to runs, such as eliminating the ability of a MMF to use a stable net asset value or requiring MMFs to obtain access to reliable emergency liquidity facilities from private sources.

H. Enhance Oversight of the Insurance Sector
Our legislation will propose the establishment of the Office of National Insurance within Treasury to gather information, develop expertise, negotiate international agreements, and coordinate policy in the insurance sector. Treasury will support proposals to modernize and improve our system of insurance regulation in accordance with six principles outlined in the body of the report.

I. Determine the Future Role of the Government Sponsored Enterprises (GSEs)
Treasury and the Department of Housing and Urban Development, in consultation with other government agencies, will engage in a wide-ranging initiative to develop recommendations on the future of Fannie Mae and Freddie Mac, and the Federal Home Loan Bank system. We need to maintain the continued stability and strength of the GSEs during these difficult financial times. We will report to the Congress and the American public at the time of the President's 2011 Budget release.

II. Establish Comprehensive Regulation of Financial Markets

A. Strengthen Supervision and Regulation of Securitization Markets
1. *Federal banking agencies should promulgate regulations that require originators or sponsors to retain an economic interest in a material portion of the credit risk of securitized credit exposures.*
2. *Regulators should promulgate additional regulations to align compensation of market participants with longer term performance of the underlying loans.*
3. *The SEC should continue its efforts to increase the transparency and standardization of securitization markets and be given clear authority to require robust reporting by issuers of asset backed securities (ABS).*
4. *The SEC should continue its efforts to strengthen the regulation of credit rating agencies, including measures to promote robust policies and procedures that manage and disclose conflicts of interest, differentiate between structured and other products, and otherwise strengthen the integrity of the ratings process.*

5. *Regulators should reduce their use of credit ratings in regulations and supervisory practices, wherever possible.*

B. Create Comprehensive Regulation of All OTC Derivatives, Including Credit Default Swaps (CDS)
All OTC derivatives markets, including CDS markets, should be subject to comprehensive regulation that addresses relevant public policy objectives: (1) preventing activities in those markets from posing risk to the financial system; (2) promoting the efficiency and transparency of those markets; (3) preventing market manipulation, fraud, and other market abuses; and (4) ensuring that OTC derivatives are not marketed inappropriately to unsophisticated parties.

C. Harmonize Futures and Securities Regulation
The CFTC and the SEC should make recommendations to Congress for changes to statutes and regulations that would harmonize regulation of futures and securities.

D. Strengthen Oversight of Systemically Important Payment, Clearing, and Settlement Systems and Related Activities
We propose that the Federal Reserve have the responsibility and authority to conduct oversight of systemically important payment, clearing and settlement systems, and activities of financial firms.

E. Strengthen Settlement Capabilities and Liquidity Resources of Systemically Important Payment, Clearing, and Settlement Systems
We propose that the Federal Reserve have authority to provide systemically important payment, clearing, and settlement systems access to Reserve Bank accounts, financial services, and the discount window.

III. Protect Consumers and Investors from Financial Abuse

A. Create a New Consumer Financial Protection Agency
1. *We propose to create a single primary federal consumer protection supervisor to protect consumers of credit, savings, payment, and other consumer financial products and services, and to regulate providers of such products and services.*
2. *The CFPA should have broad jurisdiction to protect consumers in consumer financial products and services such as credit, savings, and payment products.*
3. *The CFPA should be an independent agency with stable, robust funding.*
4. *The CFPA should have sole rule-making authority for consumer financial protection statutes, as well as the ability to fill gaps through rule-making.*
5. *The CFPA should have supervisory and enforcement authority and jurisdiction over all persons covered by the statutes that it implements, including both insured depositories and the range of other firms not previously subject to comprehensive federal supervision, and it should work with the Department of Justice to enforce the statutes under its jurisdiction in federal court.*

6. *The CFPA should pursue measures to promote effective regulation, including conducting periodic reviews of regulations, an outside advisory council, and coordination with the Council.*
7. *The CFPA's strong rules would serve as a floor, not a ceiling. The states should have the ability to adopt and enforce stricter laws for institutions of all types, regardless of charter, and to enforce federal law concurrently with respect to institutions of all types, also regardless of charter.*
8. *The CFPA should coordinate enforcement efforts with the states.*
9. *The CFPA should have a wide variety of tools to enable it to perform its functions effectively.*
10. *The Federal Trade Commission should also be given better tools and additional resources to protect consumers.*

B. Reform Consumer Protection
1. *Transparency. We propose a new proactive approach to disclosure. The CFPA will be authorized to require that all disclosures and other communications with consumers be reasonable: balanced in their presentation of benefits, and clear and conspicuous in their identification of costs, penalties, and risks.*
2. *Simplicity. We propose that the regulator be authorized to define standards for "plain vanilla" products that are simpler and have straightforward pricing. The CFPA should be authorized to require all providers and intermediaries to offer these products prominently, alongside whatever other lawful products they choose to offer.*
3. *Fairness. Where efforts to improve transparency and simplicity prove inadequate to prevent unfair treatment and abuse, we propose that the CFPA be authorized to place tailored restrictions on product terms and provider practices, if the benefits outweigh the costs. Moreover, we propose to authorize the Agency to impose appropriate duties of care on financial intermediaries.*
4. *Access. The Agency should enforce fair lending laws and the Community Reinvestment Act and otherwise seek to ensure that underserved consumers and communities have access to prudent financial services, lending, and investment.*

C. Strengthen Investor Protection
1. *The SEC should be given expanded authority to promote transparency in investor disclosures.*
2. *The SEC should be given new tools to increase fairness for investors by establishing a fiduciary duty for broker-dealers offering investment advice and harmonizing the regulation of investment advisers and broker-dealers.*
3. *Financial firms and public companies should be accountable to their clients and investors by expanding protections for whistleblowers, expanding sanctions available for enforcement, and requiring non-binding shareholder votes on executive pay plans.*
4. *Under the leadership of the Financial Services Oversight Council, we propose the establishment of a Financial Consumer Coordinating Council with a broad membership of federal and state consumer protection agencies, and a permanent role for the SEC's Investor Advisory Committee.*
5. *Promote retirement security for all Americans by strengthening employment-based and private retirement plans and encouraging adequate savings.*

IV. Provide the Government with the Tools it Needs to Manage Financial Crises

    A. Create a Resolution Regime for Failing BHCs, Including Tier 1 FHCs
We recommend the creation of a resolution regime to avoid the disorderly resolution of failing BHCs, including Tier 1 FHCs, if a disorderly resolution would have serious adverse effects on the financial system or the economy. The regime would supplement (rather than replace) and be modeled on to the existing resolution regime for insured depository institutions under the Federal Deposit Insurance Act.

    B. Amend the Federal Reserve's Emergency Lending Authority
We will propose legislation to amend Section 13(3) of the Federal Reserve Act to require the prior written approval of the Secretary of the Treasury for any extensions of credit by the Federal Reserve to individuals, partnerships, or corporations in "unusual and exigent circumstances."

V. Raise International Regulatory Standards and Improve International Cooperation

    A. Strengthen the International Capital Framework
We recommend that the Basel Committee on Banking Supervision (BCBS) continue to modify and improve Basel II by refining the risk weights applicable to the trading book and securitized products, introducing a supplemental leverage ratio, and improving the definition of capital by the end of 2009. We also urge the BCBS to complete an in-depth review of the Basel II framework to mitigate its procyclical effects.

    B. Improve the Oversight of Global Financial Markets
We urge national authorities to promote the standardization and improved oversight of credit derivative and other OTC derivative markets, in particular through the use of central counterparties, along the lines of the G-20 commitment, and to advance these goals through international coordination and cooperation.

    C. Enhance Supervision of Internationally Active Financial Firms
We recommend that the Financial Stability Board (FSB) and national authorities implement G-20 commitments to strengthen arrangements for international cooperation on supervision of global financial firms through establishment and continued operational development of supervisory colleges.

    D. Reform Crisis Prevention and Management Authorities and Procedures
We recommend that the BCBS expedite its work to improve cross-border resolution of global financial firms and develop recommendations by the end of 2009. We further urge national authorities to improve information-sharing arrangements and implement the FSB principles for cross-border crisis management.

E. Strengthen the Financial Stability Board
   We recommend that the FSB complete its restructuring and institutionalize its new mandate to promote global financial stability by September 2009.

F. Strengthen Prudential Regulations
   We recommend that the BCBS take steps to improve liquidity risk management standards for financial firms and that the FSB work with the Bank for International Settlements (BIS) and standard setters to develop macroprudential tools.

G. Expand the Scope of Regulation
   1. *Determine the appropriate Tier 1 FHC definition and application of requirements for foreign financial firms.*
   2. *We urge national authorities to implement by the end of 2009 the G-20 commitment to require hedge funds or their managers to register and disclose appropriate information necessary to assess the systemic risk they pose individually or collectively*

H. Introduce Better Compensation Practices
   In line with G-20 commitments, we urge each national authority to put guidelines in place to align compensation with long-term shareholder value and to promote compensation structures do not provide incentives for excessive risk taking. We recommend that the BCBS expediently integrate the FSB principles on compensation into its risk management guidance by the end of 2009.

I. Promote Stronger Standards in the Prudential Regulation, Money Laundering/Terrorist Financing, and Tax Information Exchange Areas
   1. *We urge the FSB to expeditiously establish and coordinate peer reviews to assess compliance and implementation of international regulatory standards, with priority attention on the international cooperation elements of prudential regulatory standards.*
   2. *The United States will work to implement the updated International Cooperation Review Group (ICRG) peer review process and work with partners in the Financial Action Task Force (FATF) to address jurisdictions not complying with international anti-money laundering/terrorist financing (AML/CFT) standards.*

J. Improve Accounting Standards
   1. *We recommend that the accounting standard setters clarify and make consistent the application of fair value accounting standards, including the impairment of financial instruments, by the end of 2009.*
   2. *We recommend that the accounting standard setters improve accounting standards for loan loss provisioning by the end of 2009 that would make it more forward looking, as long as the transparency of financial statements is not compromised.*
   3. *We recommend that the accounting standard setters make substantial progress by the end of 2009 toward development of a single set of high quality global accounting standards.*

K. Tighten Oversight of Credit Rating Agencies
We urge national authorities to enhance their regulatory regimes to effectively oversee credit rating agencies (CRAs), consistent with international standards and the G-20 Leaders' recommendations.

I. Promote Robust Supervision and Regulation of Financial Firms

In the years leading up to the current financial crisis, risks built up dangerously in our financial system. Rising asset prices, particularly in housing, concealed a sharp deterioration of underwriting standards for loans. The nation's largest financial firms, already highly leveraged, became increasingly dependent on unstable sources of short- term funding. In many cases, weaknesses in firms' risk-management systems left them unaware of the aggregate risk exposures on and off their balance sheets. A credit boom accompanied a housing bubble. Taking access to short-term credit for granted, firms did not plan for the potential demands on their liquidity during a crisis. When asset prices started to fall and market liquidity froze, firms were forced to pull back from lending, limiting credit for households and businesses.

Our supervisory framework was not equipped to handle a crisis of this magnitude. To be sure, most of the largest, most interconnected, and most highly leveraged financial firms in the country were subject to some form of supervision and regulation by a federal government agency. But those forms of supervision and regulation proved inadequate and inconsistent.

First, capital and liquidity requirements were simply too low. Regulators did not require firms to hold sufficient capital to cover trading assets, high-risk loans, and off-balance sheet commitments, or to hold increased capital during good times to prepare for bad times. Regulators did not require firms to plan for a scenario in which the availability of liquidity was sharply curtailed.

Second, on a systemic basis, regulators did not take into account the harm that large, interconnected, and highly leveraged institutions could inflict on the financial system and on the economy if they failed.

Third, the responsibility for supervising the consolidated operations of large financial firms was split among various federal agencies. Fragmentation of supervisory responsibility and loopholes in the legal definition of a "bank" allowed owners of banks and other insured depository institutions to shop for the regulator of their choice.

Fourth, investment banks operated with insufficient government oversight. Money market mutual funds were vulnerable to runs. Hedge funds and other private pools of capital operated completely outside of the supervisory framework.

To create a new foundation for the regulation of financial institutions, we will promote more robust and consistent regulatory standards for all financial institutions. Similar financial institutions should face the same supervisory and regulatory standards, with no gaps, loopholes, or opportunities for arbitrage.

We propose the creation of a Financial Services Oversight Council, chaired by Treasury, to help fill gaps in supervision, facilitate coordination of policy and resolution of disputes, and identify emerging risks in firms and market activities. This Council would include the heads of the principal federal financial regulators and would maintain a permanent staff at Treasury.

We propose an evolution in the Federal Reserve's current supervisory authority for BHCs to create a single point of accountability for the consolidated supervision of all companies that own a bank. All large, interconnected firms whose failure could threaten the stability of the system should be subject to consolidated supervision by the Federal Reserve, regardless of whether they own an insured depository institution. These firms should not be able to escape oversight of their risky activities by manipulating their legal structure.

Under our proposals, the largest, most interconnected, and highly leveraged institutions would face stricter prudential regulation than other regulated firms, including higher capital requirements and more robust consolidated supervision. In effect, our proposals would compel these firms to internalize the costs they could impose on society in the event of failure.

A. Create a Financial Services Oversight Council

1. *We propose the creation of a Financial Services Oversight Council to facilitate information sharing and coordination, identify emerging risks, advise the Federal Reserve on the identification of firms whose failure could pose a threat to financial stability due to their combination of size, leverage, and interconnectedness (hereafter referred to as a Tier 1 FHC), and provide a forum for discussion of cross-cutting issues among regulators.*

We propose the creation of a permanent Financial Services Oversight Council (Council) to facilitate interagency discussion and analysis of financial regulatory policy issues to support a consistent well-informed response to emerging trends, potential regulatory gaps, and issues that cut across jurisdictions.

The membership of the Council should include (i) the Secretary of the Treasury, who shall serve as the Chairman; (ii) the Chairman of the Board of Governors of the Federal Reserve System; (iii) the Director of the National Bank Supervisor (NBS) (described below in Section I.D.); (iv) the Director of the Consumer Financial Protection Agency (described below in Section III.A.); (v) the Chairman of the Securities and Exchange Commission (SEC); (vi) the Chairman of the Commodity Futures Trading Commission (CFTC); (vii) the Chairman of the Federal Deposit Insurance Corporation (FDIC); and (viii) the Director of the Federal Housing Finance Agency (FHFA). To fulfill its mission, we propose to create an office within Treasury that will provide full-time, expert staff support to the missions of the Council.

The Council should replace the President's Working Group on Financial Markets and have additional authorities and responsibilities with respect to systemic risk and coordination of financial regulation. We propose that the Council should:
- facilitate information sharing and coordination among the principal federal financial regulatory agencies regarding policy development, rulemakings, examinations, reporting requirements, and enforcement actions;
- provide a forum for discussion of cross-cutting issues among the principal federal financial regulatory agencies; and
- identify gaps in regulation and prepare an annual report to Congress on market developments and potential emerging risks.

The Council should have authority to recommend firms that will be subject to Tier 1 FHC supervision and regulation. The Federal Reserve should also be required to consult with the Council in setting material prudential standards for Tier 1 FHCs and in setting risk-management standards for systemically important payment, clearing, and settlement systems and activities. As described below, a subset of the Council's membership should be responsible for determining whether to invoke resolution authority with respect to large, interconnected firms.

2. *Our legislation will propose to give the Council the authority to gather information from any financial firm and the responsibility for referring emerging risks to the attention of regulators with the authority to respond.*

The jurisdictional boundaries among new and existing federal financial regulatory agencies should be drawn carefully to prevent mission overlap, and each of the federal financial regulatory agencies generally should have exclusive jurisdiction to issue and enforce rules to achieve its mission. Nevertheless, many emerging financial products and practices will raise issues relating to systemic risk, prudential regulation of financial firms, and consumer or investor protection.

To enable the monitoring of emerging threats that activities in financial markets may pose to financial stability, we propose that the Council have the authority, through its permanent secretariat in Treasury, to require periodic and other reports from any U.S. financial firm solely for the purpose of assessing the extent to which a financial activity or financial market in which the firm participates poses a threat to financial stability. In the case of federally regulated firms, the Council should, wherever possible, rely upon information that is already being collected by members of the Council in their role as regulators.

B. Implement Heightened Consolidated Supervision and Regulation of All Large, Interconnected Financial Firms

1. *Any financial firm whose combination of size, leverage, and interconnectedness could pose a threat to financial stability if it failed (Tier 1 FHC) should be subject to robust consolidated supervision and regulation, regardless of whether the firm owns an insured depository institution.*

The sudden failures of large U.S.-based investment banks and of American International Group (AIG) were among the most destabilizing events of the financial crisis. These companies were large, highly leveraged, and had significant financial connections to the other major players in our financial system, yet they were ineffectively supervised and regulated. As a consequence, they did not have sufficient capital or liquidity buffers to withstand the deterioration in financial conditions that occurred during 2008. Although most of these firms owned federally insured depository institutions, they chose to own depository institutions that are not considered "banks" under the Bank Holding Company (BHC) Act. This allowed them to avoid the more rigorous oversight regime applicable to BHCs.

We propose a new, more robust supervisory regime for any firm whose combination of size, leverage, and interconnectedness could pose a threat to financial stability if it failed. Such firms, which we identify as Tier 1 Financial Holding Companies (Tier 1 FHCs), should be subject to robust consolidated supervision and regulation, regardless of whether they are currently supervised as BHCs.

2. ***The Federal Reserve Board should have the authority and accountability for consolidated supervision and regulation of Tier 1 FHCs.***

We propose that authority for supervision and regulation of Tier 1 FHCs be vested in the Federal Reserve Board, which is by statute the consolidated supervisor and regulator of all bank holding companies today. As a result of changes in corporate structure during the current crisis, the Federal Reserve already supervises and regulates all major U.S. commercial and investment banks on a firm-wide basis. The Federal Reserve has by far the most experience and resources to handle consolidated supervision and regulation of Tier 1 FHCs.

The Council should play an important role in recommending the identification of firms that will be subject to regulation as Tier 1 FHCs. The Federal Reserve should also be required to consult with the Council in setting material prudential standards for Tier 1 FHCs.

The ultimate responsibility for prudential standard-setting and supervision for Tier 1 FHCs must rest with a single regulator. The public has a right to expect that a clearly identifiable entity, not a committee of multiple agencies, will be answerable for setting standards that will protect the financial system and the public from risks posed by the potential failure of Tier 1 FHCs. Moreover, a committee that included regulators of specific types of financial institutions such as commercial banks or broker-dealers (functional regulators) may be less focused on systemic needs and more focused on the needs of the financial firms they regulate. For example, to promote financial stability, the supervisor of a Tier 1 FHC may hold that firm's subsidiaries to stricter prudential standards than would be required by the functional regulator, whose focus is only on keeping that particular subsidiary safe.

Diffusing responsibility among several regulators would weaken incentives for effective regulation in other ways. For example, it would weaken both the incentive for and the ability of the relevant agencies to act in a timely fashion – creating the risk that clearly ineffective standards remain in place for long periods.

The Federal Reserve should fundamentally adjust its current framework for supervising all BHCs in order to carry out its new responsibilities effectively with respect to Tier 1 FHCs. For example, the focus of BHC regulation would need to expand beyond the safety and soundness of the bank subsidiary to include the activities of the firm as a whole and the risks the firm might pose to the financial system. The Federal Reserve would also need to develop new supervisory approaches for activities that to date have not been significant activities for most BHCs.

3. ***Our legislation will propose criteria that the Federal Reserve must consider in identifying Tier 1 FHCs.***

We recommend that legislation specify factors that the Federal Reserve must consider when determining whether an individual financial firm poses a threat to financial stability. Those factors should include:
- the impact the firm's failure would have on the financial system and the economy;
- the firm's combination of size, leverage (including off-balance sheet exposures), and degree of reliance on short-term funding; and
- the firm's criticality as a source of credit for households, businesses, and state and local governments and as a source of liquidity for the financial system.

We propose that the Federal Reserve establish rules, in consultation with Treasury, to guide the identification of Tier 1 FHCs. The Federal Reserve, however, should be allowed to consider other relevant factors and exercise discretion in applying the specified factors to individual financial firms. Treasury would have no role in determining the application of these rules to individual financial firms. This discretion would allow the regulatory system to adapt to inevitable innovations in financial activity and in the organizational structure of financial firms. In addition, without this discretion, large, highly leveraged, and interconnected firms that should be subject to consolidated supervision and regulation as Tier 1 FHCs might be able to escape the regime. For instance, if the Federal Reserve were to treat as a Tier 1 FHC only those firms with balance-sheet assets above a certain amount, firms would have incentives to conduct activities through off-balance sheet transactions and in off-balance sheet vehicles. Flexibility is essential to minimizing the risk that an "AIG-like" firm could grow outside the regulated system.

In identifying Tier 1 FHCs, the Federal Reserve should analyze the systemic importance of a firm under stressed economic conditions. This analysis should consider the impact the firm's failure would have on other large financial institutions, on payment, clearing and settlement systems, and on the availability of credit in the economy. In the case of a firm that has one or more subsidiaries subject to prudential regulation by other federal regulators, the Federal Reserve should be required to consult with those regulators before requiring the firm to be regulated as a Tier 1 FHC. The Federal Reserve should regularly review the classification of firms as Tier 1 FHCs. The Council should have the authority to receive information from its members and to recommend to the Federal Reserve that a firm be designated as a Tier 1 FHC, as described above.

To enable the Federal Reserve to identify financial firms other than BHCs that require supervision and regulation as Tier 1 FHCs, we recommend that the Federal Reserve should have the authority to collect periodic and other reports from all U.S. financial firms that meet certain minimum size thresholds. The Federal Reserve's authority to require reports from a financial firm would be limited to reports that contain information reasonably necessary to determine whether the firm is a Tier 1 FHC. In the case of firms that are subject to federal regulation, the Federal Reserve should have access to relevant reports submitted to other regulators, and its authority to require reports should be limited to information that cannot be obtained from reports to other regulators.

The Federal Reserve also should have the ability to examine any U.S. financial firm that meets certain minimum size thresholds if the Federal Reserve is unable to determine whether the firm's financial activities pose a threat to financial stability based on regulatory reports, discussions with management, and publicly available information. The scope of the Federal Reserve's examination authority over a financial firm would be strictly limited to examinations reasonably necessary to enable the Federal Reserve to determine whether the firm is a Tier 1 FHC.

4. *The prudential standards for Tier 1 FHCs – including capital, liquidity and risk management standards – should be stricter and more conservative than those applicable to other financial firms to account for the greater risks that their potential failure would impose on the financial system.*

Tier 1 FHCs should be subject to heightened supervision and regulation because of the greater risks their potential failure would pose to the financial system. At the same time, given the important role of Tier 1 FHCs in the financial system and the economy, setting their prudential standards too high could constrain long-term financial and economic growth. Therefore, the Federal Reserve, in consultation with the Council, should set prudential standards for Tier 1 FHCs to maximize financial stability at the lowest cost to long-term financial and economic growth.

Tier 1 FHCs should, at a minimum, be required to meet the qualification requirements for FHC status (as revised in this proposal and discussed in more detail below).

Capital Requirements. Capital requirements for Tier 1 FHCs should reflect the large negative externalities associated with the financial distress, rapid deleveraging, or disorderly failure of each firm and should, therefore, be strict enough to be effective under extremely stressful economic and financial conditions. Tier 1 FHCs should be required to have enough high-quality capital during good economic times to keep them above prudential minimum capital requirements during stressed economic times. In addition to regulatory capital ratios, the Federal Reserve should evaluate a Tier 1 FHC's capital strength using supervisory assessments, including assessments of capital adequacy under severe stress scenarios and assessments of the firm's capital planning practices, and market-based indicators of the firm's credit quality.

Prompt Corrective Action. Tier 1 FHCs should be subject to a prompt corrective action regime that would require the firm or its supervisor to take corrective actions as the firm's regulatory capital levels decline, similar to the existing prompt corrective action regime for insured depository institutions established under the Federal Deposit Insurance Corporation Improvement Act (FDICIA).

Liquidity Standards. The Federal Reserve should impose rigorous liquidity risk requirements on Tier 1 FHCs that recognize the potential negative impact that the financial distress, rapid deleveraging, or disorderly failure of each firm would have on the financial system. The Federal Reserve should put in place a robust process for continuously monitoring the liquidity risk profiles of these institutions and their liquidity risk management processes.

Federal Reserve supervision should promote the full integration of liquidity risk management of Tier 1 FHCs into the overall risk management of the institution. The Federal Reserve should also establish explicit internal liquidity risk exposure limits and risk management policies. Tier 1 FHCs should have sound processes for monitoring and controlling the full range of their liquidity risks. They should regularly conduct stress tests across a variety of liquidity stress scenarios, including short-term and protracted scenarios and institution-specific and market-wide scenarios. The stress tests should incorporate both on- and off-balance sheet exposures, including non-contractual off- balance sheet obligations.

Overall Risk Management. Supervisory expectations regarding Tier 1 FHCs' risk-management practices must be in proportion to the risk, complexity, and scope of their operations. These firms should be able to identify firm-wide risk concentrations (credit, business lines, liquidity, and other) and establish appropriate limits and controls around these concentrations. In order to credibly measure and monitor risk concentrations, Tier 1 FHCs must be able to identify aggregate exposures quickly on a firm-wide basis.

Market Discipline and Disclosure. To support market evaluation of a Tier 1 FHC's risk profile, capital adequacy, and risk management capabilities, such firms should be required to make enhanced public disclosures.

Restrictions on Nonfinancial Activities. Tier 1 FHCs that do not control insured depository institutions should be subject to the full range of prudential regulations and supervisory guidance applicable to BHCs. In addition, the long-standing wall between banking and commerce – which has served our economy well – should be extended to apply to this new class of financial firm. Accordingly, each Tier 1 FHC also should be required to comply with the nonfinancial activity restrictions of the BHC Act, regardless of whether it controls an insured depository institution. We propose that a Tier 1 FHC that has not been previously subject to the BHC Act should be given five years to conform to the existing activity restrictions imposed on FHCs by the BHC Act.

Rapid Resolution Plans. The Federal Reserve also should require each Tier 1 FHC to prepare and continuously update a credible plan for the rapid resolution of the firm in the event of severe financial distress. Such a requirement would create incentives for the firm to better monitor and simplify its organizational structure and would better prepare the government, as well as the firm's investors, creditors, and counterparties, in the event that the firm collapsed. The Federal Reserve should review the adequacy of each firm's plan regularly.

5. ***Consolidated supervision of a Tier 1 FHC should extend to the parent company and to all of its subsidiaries – regulated and unregulated, U.S. and foreign. Functionally regulated and depository institution subsidiaries of a Tier 1 FHC should continue to be supervised and regulated primarily by their functional or bank regulator, as the case may be. The constraints that the Gramm-Leach-Bliley Act (GLB Act) introduced on the Federal Reserve's ability to require reports from, examine, or impose higher prudential requirements or more stringent activity restrictions on the functionally regulated or depository institution subsidiaries of FHCs should be removed.***

The financial crisis has demonstrated the crucial importance of having a consolidated supervisor and regulator for all Tier 1 FHCs with a deep understanding of the operations of each firm. The crisis has made clear that threats to a consolidated financial firm and threats to financial stability can emerge from any business line and any subsidiary. It is not reasonable to hold the functional regulator of a single subsidiary responsible for identifying or managing risks that cut across many different subsidiaries and business lines.

The GLB Act impedes the Federal Reserve's ability, as a consolidated supervisor, to obtain information from or impose prudential restrictions on subsidiaries of a BHC that already have a primary supervisor, including banks and other insured depository institutions; SEC-registered broker-dealers, investment advisers and investment companies; entities regulated by the CFTC; and insurance companies subject to supervision by state insurance supervisors. By relying solely on other supervisors for information and for ensuring that the activities of the regulated subsidiary do not cause excessive risk to the financial system, these restrictions also make it difficult to take a truly firm-wide perspective on a BHC and to execute its responsibility to protect the system as a whole.

To promote accountability in supervision and regulation, the Federal Reserve should have authority to require reports from and conduct examinations of a Tier 1 FHC and all its subsidiaries, including those that have a primary supervisor. To the extent possible, information should be gathered from reports required or exams conducted by other supervisors. The Federal Reserve should also have the authority to impose and enforce more stringent prudential requirements on the regulated subsidiary of a Tier 1 FHC to address systemic risk concerns, but only after consulting with that subsidiary's primary federal or state supervisor and Treasury.

6. ***Consolidated supervision of a Tier 1 FHC should be macroprudential in focus. That is, it should consider risk to the system as a whole.***

Prudential supervision has historically focused on the safety and soundness of individual financial firms, or, in the case of BHCs, on the risks that an organization's non- depository subsidiaries pose to its depository institution subsidiaries. The financial crisis has demonstrated that a narrow supervisory focus on the safety and soundness of individual financial firms can result in a failure to detect and thwart emerging threats to financial stability that cut across many institutions or have other systemic implications. Going forward, the consolidated supervisor of Tier 1 FHCs should continue to employ enhanced forms of its normal supervisory tools, but should supplement those tools with rigorous assessments of the potential impact of the activities and risk exposures of these companies on each other, on critical markets, and on the broader financial system.

The Federal Reserve should continuously analyze the connections among the major financial firms and the dependence of the major financial markets on such firms, in order to track potential impact on the broader financial system. To conduct this analysis, the Federal Reserve should require each Tier 1 FHC to regularly report the nature and extent to which other major financial firms are exposed to it. In addition, the Federal Reserve should constantly monitor the build-up of concentrations of risk across all Tier 1 FHCs that may collectively threaten financial stability – even though no single firm, viewed in isolation, may appear at risk.

7. ***The Federal Reserve, in consultation with Treasury and external experts, should propose recommendations by October 1, 2009 to better align its structure and governance with its authorities and responsibilities.***

This report proposes a number of major changes to the formal powers and duties of the Federal Reserve System, including the addition of several new financial stability responsibilities and a reduction in its consumer protection role. These proposals would put into effect the biggest changes to the Federal Reserve's authority in decades.

For that reason, we propose a comprehensive review of the ways in which the structure and governance of the Federal Reserve System affect its ability to accomplish its existing and proposed functions. This review should include, among other things, the governance of the Federal Reserve Banks and the role of Reserve Bank boards in supervision and regulation. This review should be led by the Federal Reserve Board, but to promote a diversity of views within and without government, Treasury and a wide range of external experts should have substantial input into the review and resulting report. Once the report is issued, Treasury will consider the recommendations in the report and will propose any changes to the governance and structure of the Federal Reserve that are appropriate to improve its accountability and its capacity to achieve its statutory responsibilities.

C. Strengthen Capital and Other Prudential Standards Applicable to All Banks and BHCs

1. *Treasury will lead a working group, with participation by federal financial regulatory agencies and outside experts, that will conduct a fundamental reassessment of existing regulatory capital requirements for banks and BHCs, including new Tier 1 FHCs. The working group will issue a report with its conclusions by December 31, 2009.*

Capital requirements have long been the principal regulatory tool to promote the safety and soundness of banking firms and the stability of the banking system. The capital rules in place at the inception of the financial crisis, however, simply did not require banking firms to hold enough capital in light of the risks the firms faced. Most banks that failed during this crisis were considered well-capitalized just prior to their failure.

The financial crisis highlighted a number of problems with our existing regulatory capital rules. Our capital rules do not require institutions to hold sufficient capital against implicit exposures to off-balance sheet vehicles, as was made clear by the actions many institutions took to support their structured investment vehicles, asset-backed commercial paper programs, and advised money market mutual funds. The capital rules provide insufficient coverage for the risks of trading assets and certain structured credit products.

In addition, many of the capital instruments that comprised the capital base of banks and BHCs did not have the loss-absorption capacity expected of them.

The financial crisis has demonstrated the need for a fundamental review of the regulatory capital framework for banks and BHCs. This review should be comprehensive and should cover all elements of the framework, including composition of capital, scope of risk coverage, relative risk weights, and calibration. In particular, the review should include:

- proposed changes to the capital rules to reduce procyclicality, for example, by requiring all banks and BHCs to hold enough high-quality capital during good economic times to keep them above prudential minimum capital requirements during stressed times;
- analysis of the costs, benefits, and feasibility of allowing banks and BHCs to satisfy a portion of their regulatory capital requirements through the issuance of contingent capital instruments (such as debt securities that automatically convert into common equity in stressed economic circumstances) or through the purchase of tail insurance against macroeconomic risks;
- proposed increases in regulatory capital requirements on investments and exposures that pose high levels of risk under stressed market conditions, including in particular: (i) trading positions; (ii) equity investments; (iii) credit exposures to low-credit-quality firms and persons; (iv) highly rated asset-backed securities (ABS) and mortgage-backed securities (MBS); (v) explicit and implicit exposures to sponsored off-balance sheet vehicles; and (vi) OTC derivatives that are not centrally cleared; and
- recognition of the importance of a simpler, more transparent measure of leverage for banks and BHCs to supplement the risk-based capital measures.

As a general rule, banks and BHCs should be subject to a risk-based capital rule that covers all lines of business, assesses capital adequacy relative to appropriate measures of the relative risk of various types of exposures, is transparent and comparable across firms, and is credible and enforceable.

We also support the Basel Committee's efforts to improve the Basel II Capital Accord, as discussed in Section V.

2. *Treasury will lead a working group, with participation by federal financial regulatory agencies and outside experts, that will conduct a fundamental reassessment of the supervision of banks and BHCs. The working group will issue a report with its conclusions by October 1, 2009.*

As noted above, many of the large and complex financial firms that failed or approached the brink of failure in the recent financial crisis were subject to supervision and regulation by a federal government agency. Ensuring that financial firms do not take excessive risks requires the establishment and enforcement of strong prudential rules. Financial firms, however, often can navigate around generally applicable rules. A strong supervisor is needed to enforce rules and to monitor individual firms' risk taking and risk management practices.

The working group will undertake a review and analysis of lessons learned about banking supervision and regulation from the recent financial crisis, addressing issues such as:

- how to effectively conduct continuous, on-site supervision of large, complex banking firms;
- what information supervisors must obtain from regulated firms on a regular basis;
- how functional and bank supervisors should interact with consolidated holding company supervisors;
- how federal and state supervisors should coordinate with foreign supervisors in the supervision of multi-national banking firms;
- the extent to which supervision of smaller, simpler banking firms should differ from supervision of larger, more complex firms;
- how supervisory agencies should be funded and structured, keeping in mind that the funding structure can seriously impact regulatory competition and potentially lead to regulatory capture; and
- the costs and benefits of having supervisory agencies that also conduct other governmental functions, such as deposit insurance, consumer protection, or monetary policy.

3. *Federal regulators should issue standards and guidelines to better align executive compensation practices of financial firms with long-term shareholder value and to prevent compensation practices from providing incentives that could threaten the safety and soundness of supervised institutions. In addition, we will support legislation requiring all public companies to hold non-binding shareholder resolutions on the compensation packages of senior executive officers, as well as new requirements to make compensation committees more independent.*

Among the many significant causes of the financial crisis were compensation practices. In particular, incentives for short-term gains overwhelmed the checks and balances meant to mitigate against the risk of excess leverage. We will seek to better align compensation practices with the interests of shareholders and the stability of firms and the financial system through the following five principles. First, compensation plans should properly measure and reward performance. Second, compensation should be structured to account for the time horizon of risks. Third, compensation practices should be aligned with sound risk management. Fourth, golden parachutes and supplemental retirement packages should be reexamined to determine whether they align the interests of executives and shareholders. Finally, transparency and accountability should be promoted in the process of setting compensation.

As part of this effort, Treasury will support federal regulators, including the Federal Reserve, the SEC, and the federal banking regulators in laying out standards on compensation for financial firms that will be fully integrated into the supervisory process. These efforts recognize that an important component of risk management involves properly aligning incentives, and that properly designed compensation practices for both executives and employees are a necessary part of ensuring safety and soundness in the financial sector. We will also ask the President's Working Group on Financial Markets (and the Council when it is established to replace the PWG) to perform a review of compensation practices to monitor their impact on risk-taking, with a focus on identifying whether new trends might be creating risks that would otherwise go unseen.

These standards will be supplemented by increased disclosure requirements from the SEC as well as proposed legislation in two areas to increase transparency and accountability in setting executive compensation.

First, we will work with Congress to pass "say on pay" legislation – further discussed in a later section – that will require all public companies to offer an annual non-binding vote on compensation packages for senior executive officers.

Additionally, we will propose legislation giving the SEC the power to require that compensation committees are more independent. Under this legislation, compensation committees would be given the responsibility and the resources to hire their own independent compensation consultants and outside counsel. The legislation would also direct the SEC to create standards for ensuring the independence of compensation consultants, providing shareholders with the confidence that the compensation committee is receiving objective, expert advice.

4. ***Capital and management requirements for FHC status should not be limited to the subsidiary depository institution. All FHCs should be required to meet the capital and management requirements on a consolidated basis as well.***

The GLB Act currently requires a BHC to keep its subsidiary depository institutions "well-capitalized" and "well-managed" in order to qualify as a financial holding company (FHC) and thereby engage in riskier financial activities such as merchant banking, insurance underwriting, and securities underwriting and dealing. The GLB Act does not, however, require an FHC to be "well-capitalized" or "well-managed" on a consolidated basis. As a result, many of the BHCs that were most active in volatile capital markets activities were not held to the highest consolidated regulatory capital standard available.

We propose that, in addition to the current FHC eligibility requirements, all FHCs should be required to achieve and maintain well-capitalized and well-managed status on a consolidated basis. The specific capital standards should be determined in line with the results of the capital review recommended previously in this report.

5. *The accounting standard setters – the Financial Accounting Standards Board (FASB), the International Accounting Standards Board (IASB), and the SEC – should review accounting standards to determine how financial firms should be required to employ more forward-looking loan loss provisioning practices that incorporate a broader range of available credit information. Fair value accounting rules also should be reviewed with the goal of identifying changes that could provide users of financial reports with both fair value information and greater transparency regarding the cash flows management expects to receive by holding investments.*

Certain aspects of accounting standards have had procyclical tendencies, meaning that they have tended to amplify business cycles. For example, during good times, loan loss reserves tend to decline because recent historical losses are low. In determining their loan loss reserves, firms should be required to be more forward-looking and consider factors that would cause loan losses to differ from recent historical experience. This would likely result in recognition of higher provisions earlier in the credit cycle. During the current crisis, such earlier loss recognition could have reduced procyclicality, while still providing necessary transparency to users of financial reports on changes in credit trends. Similarly, the interpretation and application of fair value accounting standards during the crisis raised significant procyclicality concerns.

6. *Firewalls between banks and their affiliates should be strengthened to protect the federal safety net that supports banks and to better prevent spread of the subsidy inherent in the federal safety net to bank affiliates.*

Sections 23A and 23B of the Federal Reserve Act are designed to protect a depository institution from suffering losses in its transactions with affiliates. These provisions also limit the ability of a depository institution to transfer to its affiliates the subsidy arising from the institution's access to the federal safety net, which includes FDIC deposit insurance, access to Federal Reserve liquidity, and access to Federal Reserve payment systems. Sections 23A and 23B accomplish these purposes by placing quantitative limits and collateral requirements on certain covered transactions between a bank and an affiliate and by requiring all financial transactions between a bank and an affiliate to be performed on market terms. The Federal Reserve administers these statutory provisions for all depository institutions and has the power to provide exemptions from these provisions.

The recent financial crisis has highlighted, more clearly than ever, the value of the federal subsidy associated with the banking charter, as well as the related value to a consolidated financial firm of owning a bank. Although the existing set of firewalls in sections 23A and 23B are strong, the framework can and should be strengthened further.

Holes in the existing set of federal restrictions on transactions between banks and their affiliates should be closed. Specifically, we propose that regulators should place more effective constraints on the ability of banks to engage in over-the-counter (OTC) derivatives and securities financing transactions with affiliates. In addition, covered transactions between banks and their affiliates should be required to be fully collateralized throughout the life of the transactions. Moreover, the existing federal restrictions on transactions between banks and affiliates should be applied to transactions between a bank and all private investment vehicles sponsored or advised by the bank. The Federal Reserve's discretion to provide exemptions from the bank/affiliate firewalls also should be limited.

Finally, the Federal Reserve and the federal banking agencies should tighten the supervision and regulation of potential conflicts of interest generated by the affiliation of banks and other financial firms, such as proprietary trading units and hedge funds.

D. Close Loopholes in Bank Regulation

1. *We propose the creation of a new federal government agency, the National Bank Supervisor (NBS), to conduct prudential supervision and regulation of all federally chartered depository institutions, and all federal branches and agencies of foreign banks.*

One clear lesson learned from the recent crisis was that competition among different government agencies responsible for regulating similar financial firms led to reduced regulation in important parts of the financial system. The presence of multiple federal supervisors of firms that could easily change their charter led to weaker regulation and became a serious structural problem within our supervisory system.

We propose to establish a single federal agency dedicated to the chartering and prudential supervision and regulation of national banks and federal branches and agencies of foreign banks. This agency would take over the prudential responsibilities of the Office of the Comptroller of the Currency, which currently charters and supervises nationally chartered banks and federal branches and agencies of foreign banks, and responsibility for the institutions currently supervised by the Office of Thrift Supervision, which supervises federally chartered thrifts and thrift holding companies. As described below, we propose to eliminate the thrift charter. The nature and extent of prudential supervision and regulation of a federally chartered depository institution should no longer be a function of whether a firm conducts its business as a national bank or a federal thrift.

To accomplish its mission effectively, the NBS should inherit the OCC's and OTS's authorities to require reports, conduct examinations, impose and enforce prudential requirements, and conduct overall supervision. The new agency should be given all the tools, authorities, and financial, technical, and human resources needed to ensure that our federally chartered banks, branches, and agencies are subject to the strongest possible supervision and regulation.

The NBS should be an agency with separate status within Treasury and should be led by a single executive.

Under our proposal, the Federal Reserve and the FDIC would maintain their respective roles in the supervision and regulation of state-chartered banks, and the National Credit Union Administration (NCUA) would maintain its authorities for credit unions.

2. *We propose to eliminate the federal thrift charter, but to preserve its interstate branching rules and apply them to state and national banks.*

Federal Thrift Charter

Congress created the federal thrift charter in the Home Owners' Loan Act of 1933 in response to the extensive failures of state-chartered thrifts and the collapse of the broader financial system during the Great Depression. The rationale for federal thrifts as a specialized class of depository institutions focused on residential mortgage lending made sense at the time but the case for such specialized institutions has weakened considerably in recent years. Moreover, over the past few decades, the powers of thrifts and banks have substantially converged.

As securitization markets for residential mortgages have grown, commercial banks have increased their appetite for mortgage lending, and the Federal Home Loan Bank System has expanded its membership base. Accordingly, the need for a special class of mortgage-focused depository institutions has fallen. Moreover, the fragility of thrifts has become readily apparent during the financial crisis. In part because thrifts are required by law to focus more of their lending on residential mortgages, thrifts were more vulnerable to the housing downturn that the United States has been experiencing since 2007. The availability of the federal thrift charter has created opportunities for private sector arbitrage of our financial regulatory system. We propose to eliminate the charter going forward, subject to reasonable transition arrangements.

Supervision and Regulation of National and State Banks

Our efforts to simplify and strengthen weak spots in our system of federal bank supervision and regulation will not end with the elimination of the federal thrift charter. Although FDICIA and other work by the federal banking agencies over the past few decades have substantially improved the uniformity of the regulatory framework for national banks, state member banks, and state nonmember banks, more work can and should be done in this area. To further minimize arbitrage opportunities associated with the multiple remaining bank charters and supervisors, we propose to further reduce the differences in the substantive regulations and supervisory policies applicable to national banks, state member banks, and state nonmember banks. We also propose to restrict the ability of troubled banks to switch charters and supervisors.

Interstate Branching

Federal thrifts enjoyed the unrestricted ability to branch across state lines. Banks do not always have that ability. Although many states have enacted legislation permitting interstate branching, many other states continue to require interstate entry only through the acquisition of an existing bank. This limitation on interstate branching is an obstacle to interstate operations for all banks and creates special problems for community banks seeking to operate across state lines.

We propose the elimination of the remaining restrictions on interstate branching by national and state banks. Interstate banking and branching is good for consumers, good for banks, and good for the broader economy. Permitting banks to expand across state lines improves their geographical diversification and, consequently, their resilience in the face of local economic shocks. Competition through interstate branching also makes the banking system more efficient – improving consumer and business access to banking services in under-served markets, and increasing convenience for customers who live or work near state borders.

We propose that states should not be allowed to prevent de novo branching into their states, or to impose a minimum requirement on the age of in-state banks that can be acquired by an out-of-state banking firm. All consumer protections and deposit concentration caps with respect to interstate banking should remain.

3. *All companies that control an insured depository institution, however organized, should be subject to robust consolidated supervision and regulation at the federal level by the Federal Reserve and should be subject to the nonbanking activity restrictions of the BHC Act. The policy of separating banking from commerce should be re-affirmed and strengthened. We must close loopholes in the BHC Act for thrift holding companies, industrial loan companies, credit card banks, trust companies, and grandfathered "nonbank" banks.*

The BHC Act currently requires, as a general matter, that any company that owns an insured depository institution must register as a BHC. BHCs are subject to consolidated supervision and regulation by the Federal Reserve and are subject to the nonbanking activity restrictions of the BHC Act. However, companies that own an FDIC-insured thrift, industrial loan company (ILC), credit card bank, trust company, or grandfathered depository institution are not required to become BHCs.

Companies that own a thrift are required to submit to a more limited form of supervision and regulation by the OTS; companies that own an ILC, special-purpose credit card bank, trust company, or grandfathered depository institution are not required to submit to consolidated supervision and regulation of any kind.

As a result, by owning depository institutions that are not considered "banks" under the BHC Act, some investment banks (including the now defunct Bear Stearns and Lehman Brothers), insurance companies (including AIG), finance companies, commercial companies, and other firms have been able to obtain access to the federal safety net, while avoiding activity restrictions and more stringent consolidated supervision and regulation by the Federal Reserve under the BHC Act.

By escaping the BHC Act, these firms generally were able to evade effective, consolidated supervision and the long-standing federal policy of separating banking from commerce. Federal law has long prevented commercial banks from affiliating with commercial companies because of the conflicts of interest, biases in credit allocation, risks to the safety net, concentrations of economic power, and regulatory and supervisory difficulties generated by such affiliations. This policy has served our country well, and the wall between banking and commerce should be retained and strengthened. Such firms should be given five years to conform to the existing activity restrictions imposed by the BHC Act

In addition, these firms were able to build up excessive balance-sheet leverage and to take off-balance sheet risks with insufficient capital buffers because of the limited consolidated supervision and weaker or non-existent consolidated capital requirements at the holding company level. Their complex structures made them hard to supervise. Some of the very largest of these firms failed during the current crisis or avoided failure during the crisis only as a result of receiving extraordinary government support. In fact, some of these firms voluntarily chose to become BHCs, subject to Federal Reserve supervision, in part to address concerns by creditors regarding the effectiveness of the alternative regulatory frameworks.

Thrift Holding Companies

Elimination of the thrift charter will eliminate the separate regime of supervision and regulation of thrift holding companies. Significant differences between thrift holding company and BHC supervision and regulation have created material arbitrage opportunities. For example, although the Federal Reserve imposes leverage and risk- based capital requirements on BHCs, the OTS does not impose any capital requirements on thrift holding companies, such as AIG. The intensity of supervision also has been greater for BHCs than thrift holding companies. Finally, although BHCs generally are prohibited from engaging in commercial activities, many thrift holding companies established before the GLB Act in 1999 qualify as unitary thrift holding companies and are permitted to engage freely in commercial activities. Under our plan, all thrift holding companies would become BHCs and would be fully regulated on a consolidated basis.

Industrial Loan Companies

Congress added the ILC exception to the BHC Act in 1987. At that time, ILCs were small, special-purpose banks that primarily engaged in the business of making small loans to industrial workers and had limited deposit-taking powers. Today, however, ILCs are FDIC-insured depository institutions that have authority to offer a full range of commercial banking services. Although ILCs closely resemble commercial banks, their holding companies can avoid the restrictions of the BHC Act – including consolidated supervision and regulation by the Federal Reserve – by complying with a BHC exception. Formation of an ILC has been a common way for commercial companies and financial firms (including large investment banks) to get access to the federal bank safety net but avoid the robust governmental supervision and activity restrictions of the BHC Act. Under our plan, holding companies of ILCs would become BHCs.

Credit Card Banks

Congress also added the special-purpose credit card bank exception to the BHC Act in 1987. Companies that own a credit card bank can avoid the restrictions of the BHC Act, engage in any commercial activity, and completely avoid consolidated supervision and regulation. Many of these companies use their bank to offer private-label cards to retail customers. They use their bank charter primarily to access payment systems and avoid state usury laws.

The credit card bank exception in the BHC Act provides significant competitive advantages to its beneficiaries. Credit card banks are also more vulnerable to conflicts of interest than most other banks because of their common status as captive financing units of commercial firms. A substantial proportion of the credit card loans made by such a bank provide direct benefits to its parent company. As with ILCs, the loophole for special-purpose credit card banks creates an unwarranted gap in the separation of banking and commerce and creates a supervisory "blind spot" because Federal Reserve supervision does not extend to the credit card bank holding company. Under our plan, holding companies of credit card banks would become BHCs.

Trust Companies

The BHC Act also exempts from the definition of "bank" an institution that functions solely in a trust or fiduciary capacity if: (i) all or substantially all of the institution's deposits are in trust funds and are received in a bona fide fiduciary capacity; (ii) the institution does not accept demand deposits or transaction accounts or make commercial loans; and (iii) the institution does not obtain payment services or borrowing privileges from the Federal Reserve. Although these FDIC-insured trust companies enjoy less of the federal bank subsidy than full-service commercial banks, they do obtain material benefits from their status as

FDIC-insured depository institutions. As a result, they should be treated as banks for purposes of the BHC Act, and their parent holding companies should be supervised and regulated as BHCs. Under our plan, holding companies of trust companies would become BHCs.

"Nonbank Banks"

When Congress amended the definition of "bank" in the BHC Act in 1987, it grandfathered a number of companies that controlled depository institutions that became a "bank" solely as a result of the 1987 amendments. As a result, the holding companies of these so-called "nonbank banks" are not treated as BHCs for purposes of the BHC Act. Although few of these companies remain today, there is no economic justification for allowing these companies to continue to escape the activity restrictions and consolidated supervision and regulation requirements of the BHC Act. Under our plan, holding companies of "nonbank banks" would become BHCs.

E. Eliminate the SEC's Programs for Consolidated Supervision

The SEC has ended its Consolidated Supervised Entity Program, under which it had been the holding company supervisor for companies such as Lehman Brothers and Bear Stearns. We propose also eliminating the SEC's Supervised Investment Bank Holding Company program. Investment banking firms that seek consolidated supervision by a U.S. regulator should be subject to supervision and regulation by the Federal Reserve.

Section 17(i) of the Securities Exchange Act of 1934 (Exchange Act), enacted as part of the GLB Act, requires the SEC to permit investment bank holding companies to elect for consolidated supervision by the SEC. In 2004, the SEC adopted two consolidated supervision regimes for companies that own an SEC-registered securities broker or dealer – one for "consolidated supervised entities" (CSEs) and the other for "supervised investment bank holding companies" (SIBHCs). The major stand-alone investment banks (and several large commercial banking organizations) opted into either the CSE regime or the SIBHC regime. The stand-alone investment banks that opted into one of these regimes generally did so to demonstrate to European regulators that they were subject to consolidated supervision by a U.S. federal regulator.

The two regimes were substantially the same, although the CSE structure was designed for the largest securities firms. Under both regimes, supervised entities are required to submit to SEC examinations and to comply with SEC requirements on reporting, regulatory capital calculation, internal risk management systems, and recordkeeping.

In light of the failure or acquisition of three of the major stand-alone investment banks supervised as CSEs, and the transformation of the remaining major investment banks into BHCs supervised by the Federal Reserve, the SEC abandoned its voluntary CSE regime in the fall of 2008. The SIBHC regime, required by section 17(i) of the Exchange Act, remains in place, with only one entity currently subject to supervision under that regime.

The SEC's remaining consolidated supervision program for investment bank holding companies should be eliminated. Investment banking firms that seek consolidated supervision by a U.S. regulator should be subject to comprehensive supervision and regulation by the Federal Reserve.

F. Require Hedge Funds and Other Private Pools of Capital to Register

All advisers to hedge funds (and other private pools of capital, including private equity funds and venture capital funds) whose assets under management exceed some modest threshold should be required to register with the SEC under the Investment Advisers Act. The advisers should be required to report information on the funds they manage that is sufficient to assess whether any fund poses a threat to financial stability.

In recent years, the United States has seen explosive growth in a variety of privately-owned investment funds, including hedge funds, private equity funds, and venture capital funds. Although some private investment funds that trade commodity derivatives must register with the CFTC, and many funds register voluntarily with the SEC, U.S. law generally does not require such funds to register with a federal financial regulator. At various points in the financial crisis, de-leveraging by hedge funds contributed to the strain on financial markets. Since these funds were not required to register with regulators, however, the government lacked reliable, comprehensive data with which to assess this sort of market activity. In addition to the need to gather information in order to assess potential systemic implications of the activity of hedge funds and other private pools of capital, it has also become clear that there is a compelling investor protection rationale to fill the gaps in the regulation of investment advisors and the funds that they manage.

Requiring the SEC registration of investment advisers to hedge funds and other private pools of capital would allow data to be collected that would permit an informed assessment of how such funds are changing over time and whether any such funds have become so large, leveraged, or interconnected that they require regulation for financial stability purposes.

We further propose that all investment funds advised by an SEC-registered investment adviser should be subject to recordkeeping requirements; requirements with respect to disclosures to investors, creditors, and counterparties; and regulatory reporting requirements. The SEC should conduct regular, periodic examinations of such funds to monitor compliance with these requirements. Some of those requirements may vary across the different types of private pools. The regulatory reporting requirements for such funds should require reporting on a confidential basis of the amount of assets under management, borrowings, off-balance sheet exposures, and other information necessary to assess whether the fund or fund family is so large, highly leveraged, or interconnected that it poses a threat to financial stability. The SEC should share the reports that it receives from the funds with the Federal Reserve. The Federal Reserve should determine whether any of the funds or fund families meets the Tier 1 FHC criteria. If so, those funds should be supervised and regulated as Tier 1 FHCs.

G. Reduce the Susceptibility of Money Market Mutual Funds (MMFs) to Runs

The SEC should move forward with its plans to strengthen the regulatory framework around MMFs to reduce the credit and liquidity risk profile of individual MMFs and to make the MMF industry as a whole less susceptible to runs. The President's Working Group on Financial Markets should prepare a report assessing whether more fundamental changes are necessary to further reduce the MMF industry's susceptibility to runs, such as eliminating the ability of a MMF to use a stable net asset value or requiring MMFs to obtain access to reliable emergency liquidity facilities from private sources.

When the aggressive pursuit of higher yield left one MMF vulnerable to the failure of Lehman Brothers and the fund "broke the buck," it sparked a run on the entire MMF industry. This run resulted in severe liquidity pressures, not only on prime MMFs but also on banks and other financial institutions that relied significantly on MMFs for funding and on private money market participants generally. The run on MMFs was stopped only by introduction of Treasury's Temporary Guarantee Program for MMFs and new Federal Reserve liquidity facilities targeted at MMFs.

Even after the run stopped, for some time MMFs and other money market investors were unwilling to lend other than at very short maturities, which greatly increased liquidity risks for businesses, banks, and other institutions. The vulnerability of MMFs to breaking the buck and the susceptibility of the entire prime MMF industry to a run in such circumstances remains a significant source of systemic risk.

The SEC should move forward with its plans to strengthen the regulatory framework around MMFs. In doing so, the SEC should consider: (i) requiring MMFs to maintain substantial liquidity buffers; (ii) reducing the maximum weighted average maturity of MMF assets; (iii) tightening the credit concentration limits applicable to MMFs; (iv) improving the credit risk analysis and management of MMFs; and (v) empowering MMF boards of directors to suspend redemptions in extraordinary circumstances to protect the interests of fund shareholders.

These measures should be helpful, as they should enhance investor protection and mitigate the risk of runs. However, these measures should not, by themselves, be expected to prevent a run on MMFs of the scale experienced in September 2008. We propose that the President's Working Group on Financial Markets (PWG) should prepare a report considering fundamental changes to address systemic risk more directly. Those changes could include, for example, moving away from a stable net asset value for MMFs or requiring MMFs to obtain access to reliable emergency liquidity facilities from private sources. For liquidity facilities to provide MMFs with meaningful protection against runs, the facilities should be reliable, scalable, and designed in such a way that drawing on the facilities to meet redemptions would not disadvantage remaining MMF shareholders. The PWG should complete the report by September 15, 2009. Due to the short time-frame and the work that is currently on-going, we believe that this report should be conducted by the PWG, rather than the proposed Council, which we propose to be created through legislation.

The SEC and the PWG should carefully consider ways to mitigate any potential adverse effects of such a stronger regulatory framework for MMFs, such as investor flight from MMFs into unregulated or less regulated money market investment vehicles or reductions in the term of money market liabilities issued by major financial and non-financial firms.

H. Enhance Oversight of the Insurance Sector

Our legislation will propose the establishment of the Office of National Insurance within Treasury to gather information, develop expertise, negotiate international agreements, and coordinate policy in the insurance sector. Treasury will support proposals to modernize and improve our system of insurance regulation in accordance with six principles outlined in the body of the report.

Insurance plays a vital role in the smooth and efficient functioning of our economy. By insulating households and businesses against unforeseen loss, insurance facilitates the efficient deployment of resources and provides stability, certainty and peace of mind. The current crisis highlighted the lack of expertise within the federal government regarding the insurance industry. While AIG's main problems were created outside of its traditional insurance business, significant losses arose inside its state-regulated insurance companies as well.

Insurance is a major component of the financial system. In 2008, the insurance industry had $5.7 trillion in assets, compared with $15.8 trillion in the banking sector. There are 2.3 million jobs in the insurance industry, making up almost a third of all financial sector jobs. For over 135 years, insurance has primarily been regulated by the states, which has led to a lack of uniformity and reduced competition across state and international boundaries, resulting in inefficiency, reduced product innovation, and higher costs to consumers. Beyond a few specific areas where the federal government has a statutory responsibility, such as employee benefits, terrorism risk insurance, flood insurance, or anti-money laundering, there is no standing federal entity that is accountable for understanding and monitoring the insurance industry. Given the importance of a healthy insurance industry to the well functioning of our economy, it is important that we establish a federal Office of National Insurance (ONI) within Treasury, and that we develop a modern regulatory framework for insurance.

The ONI should be responsible for monitoring all aspects of the insurance industry. It should gather information and be responsible for identifying the emergence of any problems or gaps in regulation that could contribute to a future crisis. The ONI should also recommend to the Federal Reserve any insurance companies that the Office believes should be supervised as Tier 1 FHCs. The ONI should also carry out the government's existing responsibilities under the Terrorism Risk Insurance Act.

In the international context, the lack of a federal entity with responsibility and expertise for insurance has hampered our nation's effectiveness in engaging internationally with other nations on issues related to insurance. The United States is the only country in the International Association of Insurance Supervisors (IAIS – whose membership includes insurance regulators and supervisors of over 190 jurisdictions) that is not represented by a federal insurance regulatory entity able to speak with one voice. In addition, the European Union has recently passed legislation that will require a foreign insurance company operating in its member states to be subject to supervision in the company's home country comparable to the supervision required in the EU. Accordingly, the ONI will be empowered to work with other nations and within the IAIS to better represent American interests, have the authority to enter into international agreements, and increase international cooperation on insurance regulation.

Treasury will support proposals to modernize and improve our system of insurance regulation. Treasury supports the following six principles for insurance regulation:

1. *Effective systemic risk regulation with respect to insurance.* The steps proposed in this report, if enacted, will address systemic risks posed to the financial system by the insurance industry. However, if additional insurance regulation would help to further reduce systemic risk or would increase integration into the new regulatory regime, we will consider those changes.
2. *Strong capital standards and an appropriate match between capital allocation and liabilities for all insurance companies.* Although the current crisis did not

stem from widespread problems in the insurance industry, the crisis did make clear the importance of adequate capital standards and a strong capital position for all financial firms. Any insurance regulatory regime should include strong capital standards and appropriate risk management, including the management of liquidity and duration risk.

3. *Meaningful and consistent consumer protection for insurance products and practices.* While many states have enacted strong consumer protections in the insurance marketplace, protections vary widely among states. Any new insurance regulatory regime should enhance consumer protections and address any gaps and problems that exist under the current system, including the regulation of producers of insurance. Further, any changes to the insurance regulatory system that would weaken or undermine important consumer protections are unacceptable.

4. *Increased national uniformity through either a federal charter or effective action by the states.* Our current insurance regulatory system is highly fragmented, inconsistent, and inefficient. While some steps have been taken to increase uniformity, they have been insufficient. As a result there remain tremendous differences in regulatory adequacy and consumer protection among the states. Increased consistency in the regulatory treatment of insurance – including strong capital standards and consumer protections – should enhance financial stability, increase economic efficiency and result in real improvements for consumers.

5. *Improve and broaden the regulation of insurance companies and affiliates on a consolidated basis, including those affiliates outside of the traditional insurance business.* As we saw with respect to AIG, the problems of associated affiliates outside of a consolidated insurance company's traditional insurance business can grow to threaten the solvency of the underlying insurance company and the economy. Any new regulatory regime must address the current gaps in insurance holding company regulation.

6. *International coordination.* Improvements to our system of insurance regulation should satisfy existing international frameworks, enhance the international competitiveness of the American insurance industry, and expand opportunities for the insurance industry to export its services.

I. Determine the Future Role of the Government Sponsored Enterprises (GSEs)

Treasury and the Department of Housing and Urban Development, in consultation with other government agencies, will engage in a wide-ranging initiative to develop recommendations on the future of Fannie Mae and Freddie Mac, and the Federal Home Loan Bank system. We need to maintain the continued stability and strength of the GSEs during these difficult financial times. We will report to the Congress and the American public at the time of the President's 2011 Budget release.

The 2008 Housing and Economic Recovery Act (HERA) reformed and strengthened the GSEs' safety and soundness regulation by creating the Federal Housing Finance Agency

(FHFA), a new independent regulator for Fannie Mae, Freddie Mac, and the Federal Home Loan Banks.

HERA provided FHFA with authority to develop regulations on the size and composition of the Fannie Mae and Freddie Mac investment portfolios, set capital requirements, and place the companies into receivership. FHFA is also required to issue housing goals for each of the regulated enterprises with respect to single-family and multi-family mortgages. In addition, HERA provided temporary authority for Treasury to purchase securities or other obligations of Fannie Mae, Freddie Mac, and the Federal Home Loan Banks through December 31, 2009. The purpose of this authority is to preserve the stability of the financial market, prevent disruption to the availability of mortgage finance, and protect taxpayers.

The growing stress in the mortgage markets over the last two years reduced the capital positions of Fannie Mae and Freddie Mac. In September 2008, FHFA placed Fannie Mae and Freddie Mac under conservatorship, and Treasury began to exercise its GSE assistance authorities in order to promote the stability and strength of the GSEs during these difficult financial times.

Treasury and the Department of Housing and Urban Development, together with other government agencies, will engage in a wide-ranging process and seek public input to explore options regarding the future of the GSEs, and will report to the Congress and the American public at the time of the President's 2011 budget.

There are a number of options for the reform of the GSEs, including: (i) returning them to their previous status as GSEs with the paired interests of maximizing returns for private shareholders and pursuing public policy home ownership goals; (ii) gradual wind-down of their operations and liquidation of their assets; (iii) incorporating the GSEs' functions into a federal agency; (iv) a public utility model where the government regulates the GSEs' profit margin, sets guarantee fees, and provides explicit backing for GSE commitments; (v) a conversion to providing insurance for covered bonds; (vi) and the dissolution of Fannie Mae and Freddie Mac into many smaller companies.

II. Establish Comprehensive Regulation of Financial Markets

The current financial crisis occurred after a long and remarkable period of growth and innovation in our financial markets. New financial instruments allowed credit risks to be spread widely, enabling investors to diversify their portfolios in new ways and enabling banks to shed exposures that had once stayed on their balance sheets. Through securitization, mortgages and other loans could be aggregated with similar loans and sold in tranches to a large and diverse pool of new investors with different risk preferences. Through credit derivatives, banks could transfer much of their credit exposure to third parties without selling the underlying loans. This distribution of risk was widely perceived to reduce systemic risk, to promote efficiency, and to contribute to a better allocation of resources.

However, instead of appropriately distributing risks, this process often concentrated risk in opaque and complex ways. Innovations occurred too rapidly for many financial institutions' risk management systems; for the market infrastructure, which consists of payment, clearing and settlement systems; and for the nation's financial supervisors.

Securitization, by breaking down the traditional relationship between borrowers and lenders, created conflicts of interest that market discipline failed to correct. Loan originators failed to require sufficient documentation of income and ability to pay. Securitizers failed to set high standards for the loans they were willing to buy, encouraging underwriting standards to decline. Investors were overly reliant on credit rating agencies. Credit ratings often failed to accurately describe the risk of rated products. In each case, lack of transparency prevented market participants from understanding the full nature of the risks they were taking.

The build-up of risk in the over-the-counter (OTC) derivatives markets, which were thought to disperse risk to those most able to bear it, became a major source of contagion through the financial sector during the crisis.

We propose to bring the markets for all OTC derivatives and asset-backed securities into a coherent and coordinated regulatory framework that requires transparency and improves market discipline. Our proposal would impose record keeping and reporting requirements on all OTC derivatives. We also propose to strengthen the prudential regulation of all dealers in the OTC derivative markets and to reduce systemic risk in these markets by requiring all standardized OTC derivative transactions to be executed in regulated and transparent venues and cleared through regulated central counterparties.

We propose to enhance the Federal Reserve's authority over market infrastructure to reduce the potential for contagion among financial firms and markets.

Finally, we propose to harmonize the statutory and regulatory regimes for futures and securities. While differences exist between securities and futures markets, many differences in regulation between the markets may no longer be justified. In particular, the growth of derivatives markets and the introduction of new derivative instruments have highlighted the need for addressing gaps and inconsistencies in the regulation of these products by the CFTC and SEC.

A. Strengthen Supervision and Regulation of Securitization Markets

The financial crisis was triggered by a breakdown in credit underwriting standards in subprime and other residential mortgage markets. That breakdown was enabled by lax or nonexistent regulation of nonbank mortgage originators and brokers. But the breakdown also reflected a broad relaxation in market discipline on the credit quality of loans that originators intended to distribute to investors through securitizations rather than hold in their own loan portfolios.

We propose several initiatives to address this breakdown in market discipline: changing the incentive structure of market participants; increasing transparency to allow for better due diligence; strengthening credit rating agency performance; and reducing the incentives for over-reliance on credit ratings.

1. ***Federal banking agencies should promulgate regulations that require originators or sponsors to retain an economic interest in a material portion of the credit risk of securitized credit exposures.***

One of the most significant problems in the securitization markets was the lack of sufficient incentives for lenders and securitizers to consider the performance of the underlying loans after asset backed securities (ABS) were issued. Lenders and securitizers had weak incentives to conduct due diligence regarding the quality of the underlying assets being securitized. This problem was exacerbated as the structure of ABS became more complex and opaque. Inadequate disclosure regimes exacerbated the gap in incentives between lenders, securitizers and investors.

The federal banking agencies should promulgate regulations that require loan originators or sponsors to retain five percent of the credit risk of securitized exposures. The regulations should prohibit the originator from directly or indirectly hedging or otherwise transferring the risk it is required to retain under these regulations. This is critical to prevent gaming of the system to undermine the economic tie between the originator and the issued ABS.

The federal banking agencies should have authority to specify the permissible forms of required risk retention (for example, first loss position or pro rata vertical slice) and the minimum duration of the required risk retention. The agencies also should have authority to provide exceptions or adjustments to these requirements as needed in certain cases, including authority to raise or lower the five percent threshold and to provide exemptions from the "no hedging" requirement that are consistent with safety and soundness. The agencies should also have authority to apply the requirements to securitization sponsors rather than loan originators in order to achieve the appropriate alignment of incentives contemplated by this proposal.

2. ***Regulators should promulgate additional regulations to align compensation of market participants with longer term performance of the underlying loans.***

The securitization process should provide appropriate incentives for participants to best serve the interests of their clients, the borrowers and investors. To do that, the compensation of brokers, originators, sponsors, underwriters, and others involved in the securitization process should be linked to the longer-term performance of the securitized assets, rather than only to the production, creation or inception of those products.

For example, as proposed by Financial Accounting Standards Board (FASB), Generally Accepted Accounting Principles (GAAP) should be changed to eliminate the immediate recognition of gain on sale by originators at the inception of a securitization transaction and instead require originators to recognize income over time. The proposed changes should also require many securitizations to be consolidated on the originator's balance sheet and their asset performance to be reflected in the originator's consolidated financial statements.

Similar performance-based, medium-to-long term approaches to securitization fees should enhance incentives for market participants to focus on underwriting standards. For example, the fees and commissions received by loan brokers and loan officers, who otherwise have no ongoing relationship with the loans they generate, should be disbursed over time and should be reduced if underwriting or asset quality problems emerge over time.

Sponsors of securitizations should be required to provide assurances to investors, in the form of strong, standardized representations and warranties, regarding the risk associated with the origination and underwriting practices for the securitized loans underlying ABS.

3. ***The SEC should continue its efforts to increase the transparency and standardization of securitization markets and be given clear authority to require robust reporting by issuers of asset backed securities (ABS).***

The SEC is currently working to improve and standardize disclosure practices by originators, underwriters, and credit rating agencies involved in the securitization process. Those efforts should continue. To strengthen those efforts, the SEC should be given clear authority to require robust ongoing reporting by ABS issuers.

Investors and credit rating agencies should have access to the information necessary to assess the credit quality of the assets underlying a securitization transaction at inception and over the life of the transaction, as well as the information necessary to assess the credit, market, liquidity, and other risks of ABS. In particular, the issuers of ABS should be required to disclose loan-level data (broken down by loan broker or originator). Issuers should also be required to disclose the nature and extent of broker, originator and sponsor compensation and risk retention for each securitization.

We urge the industry to complete its initiatives to standardize and make transparent the legal documentation for securitization transactions to make it easier for market participants to make informed investment decisions. With respect to residential mortgage-backed securities, the standards should include clear and uniform rules for servicers to modify home mortgage loans under appropriate circumstances, if such modifications would benefit the securitization trust as a whole.

Finally, the SEC and the Financial Industry Regulatory Authority (FINRA) should expand the Trade Reporting and Compliance Engine (TRACE), the standard electronic trade reporting database for corporate bonds, to include asset-backed securities.

4. *The SEC should continue its efforts to strengthen the regulation of credit rating agencies, including measures to require that firms have robust policies and procedures that manage and disclose conflicts of interest, differentiate between structured and other products, and otherwise promote the integrity of the ratings process.*

Credit rating agencies should be required to maintain robust policies and procedures for managing and disclosing conflicts of interest and otherwise ensuring the integrity of the ratings process.

Credit rating agencies should differentiate the credit ratings that they assign to structured credit products from those they assign to unstructured debt. Credit Rating Agencies should also publicly disclose credit rating performance measures for structured credit products in a manner that facilitates comparisons across products and credit ratings and that provides meaningful measures of the uncertainty and potential volatility associated with credit ratings.

Credit rating agencies should also publicly disclose, in a manner comprehensible to the investing public, precisely what risks their credit ratings are designed to assess (for example, likelihood of default and/or loss severity in event of default), as well as material risks not reflected in the ratings. Such disclosure should highlight how the risks of structured products, which rely on diversification across a large number of individual loans to protect the more senior investors, differ fundamentally from the risks of unstructured corporate debt.

Credit rating agencies should disclose sufficient information about their methodologies for rating structured finance products, including qualitative reviews of originators, to allow users of credit ratings and market observers to reach their own conclusions about the efficacy of the methodologies. Credit rating agencies should also disclose to the SEC any unpublished rating agency data and methodologies.

5. *Regulators should reduce their use of credit ratings in regulations and supervisory practices, wherever possible.*

Where regulators use credit ratings in regulations and supervisory practices, they should recognize the potential differences in performance between structured and unstructured credit products with the same credit rating.

Risk-based regulatory capital requirements should appropriately reflect the risk of structured credit products, including the concentrated systematic risk of senior tranches and re-securitizations and the risk of exposures held in highly leveraged off-balance sheet vehicles. They should also minimize opportunities for firms to use securitization to reduce their regulatory capital requirements without a commensurate reduction in risk.

B. Create Comprehensive Regulation of All OTC Derivatives, Including Credit Default Swaps (CDS)

OTC derivatives markets, including CDS markets, should be subject to comprehensive regulation that addresses relevant public policy objectives: (1) preventing activities in those markets from posing risk to the financial system; (2) promoting the efficiency and transparency of those markets; (3) preventing market manipulation, fraud, and other market abuses; and (4) ensuring that OTC derivatives are not marketed inappropriately to unsophisticated parties.

One of the most significant changes in the world of finance in recent decades has been the explosive growth and rapid innovation in the market for financial derivatives. Much of this development has occurred in the market for OTC derivatives, which are not executed on regulated exchanges. In 2000, the Commodity Futures Modernization Act (CFMA) explicitly exempted OTC derivatives, to a large extent, from regulation by the Commodity Futures Trading Commission. In addition, the law limited the SEC's authority to regulate certain types of OTC derivatives. As a result, the market for OTC derivatives has largely gone unregulated.

The downside of this lax regulatory regime for OTC derivatives – and, in particular, for credit default swaps (CDS) – became disastrously clear during the recent financial crisis. In the years prior to the crisis, many institutions and investors had substantial positions in CDS – particularly CDS that were tied to asset backed securities (ABS), complex instruments whose risk characteristics proved to be poorly understood even by the most sophisticated of market participants. At the same time, excessive risk taking by AIG and certain monoline insurance companies that provided protection against declines in the value of such ABS, as well as poor counterparty credit risk management by many banks, saddled our financial system with an enormous – and largely unrecognized – level of risk.

When the value of the ABS fell, the danger became clear. Individual institutions believed that these derivatives would protect their investments and provide return, even if the market went down. But, during the crisis, the sheer volume of these contracts overwhelmed some firms that had promised to provide payment on the CDS and left institutions with losses that they believed they had been protected against. Lacking authority to regulate the OTC derivatives market, regulators were unable to identify or mitigate the enormous systemic threat that had developed.

Government regulation of the OTC derivatives markets should be designed to achieve four broad objectives: (1) preventing activities in those markets from posing risk to the financial system; (2) promoting the efficiency and transparency of those markets; (3) preventing market manipulation, fraud, and other market abuses; and (4) ensuring that OTC derivatives are not marketed inappropriately to unsophisticated parties. To achieve these goals, it is critical that similar products and activities be subject to similar regulations and oversight.

To contain systemic risks, the Commodities Exchange Act (CEA) and the securities laws should be amended to require clearing of all standardized OTC derivatives through regulated central counterparties (CCPs). To make these measures effective, regulators will need to require that CCPs impose robust margin requirements as well as other necessary risk controls and that customized OTC derivatives are not used solely as a means to avoid using a CCP. For example, if an OTC derivative is accepted for clearing by one or more fully regulated CCPs, it should create a presumption that it is a standardized contract and thus required to be cleared.

All OTC derivatives dealers and all other firms whose activities in those markets create large exposures to counterparties should be subject to a robust and appropriate regime of prudential supervision and regulation. Key elements of that robust regulatory regime must include conservative capital requirements (more conservative than the existing bank regulatory capital requirements for OTC derivatives), business conduct standards, reporting requirements, and conservative requirements relating to initial margins on counterparty credit exposures. Counterparty risks associated with customized bilateral OTC derivatives transactions that should not be accepted by a CCP would be addressed by this robust regime covering derivative dealers. As noted above, regulatory capital requirements on OTC derivatives that are not centrally cleared also should be increased for all banks and BHCs.

The OTC derivatives markets should be made more transparent by amending the CEA and the securities laws to authorize the CFTC and the SEC, consistent with their respective missions, to impose recordkeeping and reporting requirements (including an audit trail) on all OTC derivatives. Certain of those requirements should be deemed to be satisfied by either clearing standardized transactions through a CCP or by reporting customized transactions to a regulated trade repository. CCPs and trade repositories should be required to, among other things, make aggregate data on open positions and trading volumes available to the public and make data on any individual counterparty's trades and positions available on a confidential basis to the CFTC, SEC, and the institution's primary regulators.

Market efficiency and price transparency should be improved in derivatives markets by requiring the clearing of standardized contracts through regulated CCPs as discussed earlier and by moving the standardized part of these markets onto regulated exchanges and regulated transparent electronic trade execution systems for OTC derivatives and by requiring development of a system for timely reporting of trades and prompt dissemination of prices and other trade information. Furthermore, regulated financial institutions should be encouraged to make greater use of regulated exchange-traded derivatives. Competition between appropriately regulated OTC derivatives markets and regulated exchanges would make both sets of markets more efficient and thereby better serve end-users of derivatives.

Market integrity concerns should be addressed by making whatever amendments to the CEA and the securities laws which are necessary to ensure that the CFTC and the SEC, consistent with their respective missions, have clear, unimpeded authority to police and prevent fraud, market manipulation, and other market abuses involving all OTC derivatives. The CFTC also should have authority to set position limits on OTC derivatives that perform or affect a significant price discovery function with respect to regulated markets. Requiring CCPs, trade repositories, and other market participants to provide the CFTC, SEC, and institutions' primary regulators with a complete picture of activity in the OTC derivatives markets will assist those regulators in detecting and deterring all such market abuses.

Current law seeks to protect unsophisticated parties from entering into inappropriate derivatives transactions by limiting the types of counterparties that could participate in those markets. But the limits are not sufficiently stringent. The CFTC and SEC are reviewing the participation limits in current law to recommend how the CEA and the securities laws should be amended to tighten the limits or to impose additional disclosure requirements or standards of care with respect to the marketing of derivatives to less sophisticated counterparties such as small municipalities.

C. Harmonize Futures and Securities Regulation

The CFTC and the SEC should make recommendations to Congress for changes to statutes and regulations that would harmonize regulation of futures and securities.

The broad public policy objectives of futures regulation and securities regulation are the same: protecting investors, ensuring market integrity, and promoting price transparency. While differences exist between securities and futures markets, many differences in regulation between the markets are no longer justified. In particular, the growth of derivatives markets and the introduction of new derivative instruments have highlighted the need for addressing gaps and inconsistencies in the regulation of these products by the CFTC and SEC.

Many of the instruments traded on the commodity and securities exchanges and in the over-the-counter markets have attributes that may place the instrument within the purview of both regulatory agencies. One result of this jurisdictional overlap has been that economically equivalent instruments may be regulated by two agencies operating under different and sometimes conflicting regulatory philosophies and statutes. For example, many financial options and futures products are similar (and, indeed, the returns to one often can be replicated with the other). Under the current federal regulatory structure, however, options on a security are regulated by the SEC, whereas futures contracts on the same underlying security are regulated jointly by the CFTC and SEC.

In many instances the result of these overlapping yet different regulatory authorities has been numerous and protracted legal disputes about whether particular products should be regulated as futures or securities. These disputes have consumed significant agency resources that otherwise could have been devoted to the furtherance of the agency's mission. Uncertainty regarding how an instrument will be regulated has impeded and delayed the launch of exchange-traded equity, equity index, and credit event products, as litigation sorted out whether a particular product should be regulated as a futures contract or as a security. Eliminating jurisdictional uncertainties and ensuring that economically equivalent instruments are regulated in the same manner, regardless of which agency has jurisdiction, would remove impediments to product innovation.

Arbitrary jurisdictional distinctions also have unnecessarily limited competition between markets and exchanges. Under existing law, financial instruments with similar characteristics may be forced to trade on different exchanges that are subject to different regulatory regimes. Harmonizing the regulatory regimes would remove such distinctions and permit a broader range of instruments to trade on any regulated exchange. Permitting direct competition between exchanges also would help ensure that plans to bring OTC derivatives trading onto regulated exchanges or regulated transparent electronic trading systems would promote rather than retard competition. Greater competition would make these markets more efficient, which would benefit users of the markets, including investors and risk managers.

We also will need greater coordination and harmonization between these agencies as we move forward. The CEA currently provides that funds trading in the futures markets register as Commodity Pool Operators (CPO) and file annual financials with the CFTC. Over 1300 CPOs, including many of the largest hedge funds, are currently registered with and make annual filings with the CFTC. It will be important that the CFTC be able to maintain its enforcement authority over these entities as the SEC takes on important new responsibilities in this area.

Pursuant to the CEA, the CFTC currently employs a "principles-based approach" to regulation of exchanges, clearing organizations, and intermediaries, while pursuant to the securities laws; the SEC employs a "rules-based approach." Efforts at harmonization should seek to build a common foundation for market regulation through agreement by the two agencies on principles of regulation that are significantly more precise than the CEA's current "core principles." The new principles need to be sufficiently precise so that market practices that violate those principles can be readily identified and subjected to enforcement actions by regulators. At the same time, they should be sufficiently flexible to allow for innovations by market participants that are consistent with the principles. For example, the CFTC has indicated that it is willing to recommend adopting as core principles for clearing organizations key elements of international standards for central counterparty clearing organizations (the CPSS-IOSCO standards), which are considerably more precise than the current CEA core principles for CFTC regulated clearing organizations.

Harmonization of substantive futures and securities regulation for economically equivalent instruments also should require the development of consistent procedures for reviewing and approving proposals for new products and rulemakings by self-regulatory organizations (SROs). Here again, the agencies should strike a balance between their existing approaches. The SEC should recommend requirements to respond more expeditiously to proposals for new products and SRO rule changes and should recommend expansion of the types of filings that should be deemed effective upon filing, while the CFTC should recommend requiring prior approval for more types of rules and allowing it appropriate and reasonable time for approving rules that require prior approval.

The harmonization of futures and securities laws for economically equivalent instruments would not require eliminating or modifying provisions relating to futures and options contracts on agricultural, energy, and other physical commodity products. There are important protections related to these markets which must be maintained and in certain circumstances enhanced in applicable law and regulation.

We recommend that the CFTC and the SEC complete a report to Congress by September 30, 2009 that identifies all existing conflicts in statutes and regulations with respect to similar types of financial instruments and either explains why those differences are essential to achieve underlying policy objectives with respect to investor protection, market integrity, and price transparency or makes recommendations for changes to statutes and regulations that would eliminate the differences. If the two agencies cannot reach agreement on such explanations and recommendations by September 30, 2009, their differences should be referred to the new Financial Services Oversight Council. The Council should be required to address such differences and report its recommendations to Congress within six months of its formation.

D. Strengthen Oversight and Functioning of Systemically Important Payment, Clearing, and Settlement Systems and Related Activities

We propose that the Federal Reserve have the responsibility and authority to conduct oversight of systemically important payment, clearing and settlement systems, and activities of financial firms.

A key determinant of the risk posed by the interconnectedness of financial institutions is the strength or weakness of arrangements for settling payment obligations and financial transactions between banks and other financial institutions. Where such arrangements are strong they can help guard against instability in times of crisis. Where they are weak they can be a major source of financial contagion, transmitting a financial shock from one firm or market to many other firms and markets.

When major financial institutions came under significant financial stress during 2008, policymakers were extremely concerned that weaknesses in settlement arrangements for certain financial transactions, notably tri-party repurchase agreements and OTC derivatives, would be a source of contagion. For several years prior to 2008, the Federal Reserve had worked with other regulators and market participants to strengthen those arrangements. In the case of CDS and other OTC derivatives, significant progress was achieved, notably the cessation of unauthorized assignments of trades, reductions of backlogs of unconfirmed trades, and efforts to compress portfolios of outstanding trades. Still, progress was slow and insufficient.

Progress in strengthening payment and settlement arrangements is inherently difficult because improvements in such arrangements require collective action by market participants. Existing federal authority over such arrangements is incomplete and fragmented. In such circumstances, the Federal Reserve and other regulators have been forced to rely heavily on moral suasion to encourage market participants to take such collective actions. The criticality of such arrangements and the slow progress in strengthening certain key infrastructure arrangements indicates a need for clear and comprehensive federal authority for oversight focused on the risk management of systemically important payment, clearing, and settlement systems and of systemically important payment, clearing, and settlement activities of financial firms.

Responsibility and authority for ensuring consistent oversight of all systemically important payment, clearing, and settlement systems and activities should be assigned to the Federal Reserve. The Federal Reserve has long played a role in the supervision, oversight, development, and operation of payment, clearing, and settlement systems. It also has played a leading role in developing international standards for payment, clearing, and settlement systems. As the central bank, it inherently has a special interest in promoting the safety and efficiency of such systems, because they are important to the liquidity of financial institutions and the implementation of monetary policy. The authority we propose to give to the Federal Reserve should supplement rather than replace the existing authority of regulators of clearing and settlement systems and prudential regulators of financial firms.

Systemically Important Systems

We will propose legislation that broadly defines the characteristics of systemically important payment, clearing, and settlement systems (covered systems) and sets objectives and principles for their oversight. We propose that the Federal Reserve, in consultation with the Council, to identify covered systems and to set risk management standards for their operation. We will propose legislation that defines a covered system as a payment, clearing, or settlement system the failure or disruption of which could create or increase the risk of significant liquidity or credit problems spreading among financial institutions or markets and thereby threatening the stability of the financial system.

The Federal Reserve should have authority to collect information from any payment, clearing, or settlement system for the purpose of assessing whether the system is systemically important. In the case of a system that is subject to comprehensive regulation by a federal market regulator (the CFTC or the SEC), the market regulator will remain the primary regulator of the system. The Federal Reserve should first seek to obtain the information it needs from the primary regulator, but may request additional information directly from the system if it is determined that the information is not currently collected by or available to the primary regulator.

The risk management standards imposed by the Federal Reserve on covered systems should require such systems to have consistent and robust policies and practices for ensuring timely settlement by the systems across a range of extreme but plausible scenarios. The standards for such systems should be reviewed periodically by the Federal Reserve, in consultation with the Council, and should take into account relevant international standards.

A covered system should be subject to regular, consistent, and rigorous on-site safety and soundness examinations as well as prior reviews of changes to its rules and operations in order to ensure that the amended rules and operations meet the applicable risk management standards. If a system is subject to comprehensive regulation by a federal market regulator (CFTC or SEC), the market regulator should lead those exams and reviews. The Federal Reserve should have the right to participate in the exams, including in the determination of their scope and methodology, and should be consulted on rule changes that affect the system's risk management. The Federal Reserve and the market regulator should regularly conduct joint assessments of the system's adherence to the applicable risk management standards.

If a covered system's risk management policies and practices do not meet the applicable standards, the Federal Reserve should have adequate authority to compel corrective actions by the system. If a covered system is subject to comprehensive regulation by a federal market regulator (CFTC or SEC), the market regulator should have primary authority for enforcement. If the Federal Reserve concludes that corrective actions are necessary, it should recommend those actions to the market regulator. If the Federal Reserve and the market regulator cannot agree on the need for enforcement action, the Federal Reserve should have emergency authority to take enforcement action but only after consultation with the Council, which should attempt to mediate the agencies' differences.

The Federal Reserve should have authority to require a covered system to submit reports for the purpose of enabling the Federal Reserve to assess the risk that the system's operations pose to the financial system and to assess the safety and soundness of the system. In the case of a covered system that is subject to comprehensive regulation by a federal market regulator, the Federal Reserve should have access to relevant reports submitted to that regulator, but its authority to require reports should be limited to information that cannot be obtained from reports to the other regulator.

Systemically Important Activities

We will propose legislation that broadly defines the characteristics of systemically important payment, clearing, and settlement activities of financial firms (covered activities) and sets objectives and principles for their conduct. We propose that the Federal Reserve, in consultation with the Council, to identify covered activities and to set risk management standards for their conduct by financial firms. We propose to define a covered activity as a payment, clearing, or settlement activity of financial firms the failure or disruption of which could create or increase the risk of significant liquidity or credit problems spreading among financial institutions or markets and thereby threatening the stability of the financial system.

If the Federal Reserve has reason to believe that a payment, clearing, or settlement activity is systemically important, it should have authority to collect information from any financial firm engaged in that activity for the purpose of assessing whether the activity is systemically important. In the case of a firm that is subject to federal regulation, the Federal Reserve should have access to relevant reports submitted to other regulators and its authority to require reports should be limited to information that cannot be obtained from reports to other regulators.

Compliance by financial firms with standards established by the Federal Reserve with respect to a systemically important activity will be administratively enforceable by the firm's primary federal regulator (if applicable). The Federal Reserve, however, will have back-up examination and administrative enforcement authority with respect to such standards.

The Federal Reserve should have authority to require financial firms engaged in a covered activity to submit reports with respect to the firm's conduct of such activity. In the case of a firm that is subject to federal regulation, the Federal Reserve should have access to relevant reports submitted to other regulators, and its authority to require reports should be limited to information that cannot be obtained from reports to other regulators.

E. Strengthen Settlement Capabilities and Liquidity Resources of Systemically Important Payment, Clearing, and Settlement Systems

We propose that the Federal Reserve have authority to provide systemically important payment, clearing, and settlement systems access to Reserve Bank accounts, financial services, and the discount window.

The safety and efficiency of financial institutions and markets depend critically on the strength of the infrastructure of the financial system—the payment, clearing, and settlement systems that are used to clear and settle financial transactions. In particular, confidence in financial markets and financial market participants depends critically on the ability of the payment, clearing, and settlement systems used by the markets to meet their financial obligations to participants without delay. Many systemically important payment, clearing, and settlement systems currently depend on commercial banks to perform critical payment and other financial services and to provide them with the liquidity necessary to convert margin and other collateral into funds when necessary to complete settlement. These dependencies create the risk that a systemically important system may be unable to meet its obligations to participants when due because the bank on which it relies for such services (or another market participant) is unable or unwilling to provide the liquidity the system needs. During the recent financial crisis some systemically important settlement systems have encountered performance and other issues with their banks. At the same time, many market participants have had trouble obtaining liquidity by pledging or selling collateral, even the forms that are most liquid under normal circumstances.

The risk posed by such impediments to timely settlement would be eliminated by providing (where not already available under other authorities) direct access to Reserve Bank accounts and financial services and to the discount window for payment, clearing, and settlement systems that the Federal Reserve, in consultation with the Council, has identified as systemically significant. Discount window access for such systems should be for emergency purposes, such as enabling the system to convert noncash margin and collateral assets to liquid settlement funds in the event that one of the system's participants fails to settle its obligations to the system and the system's contingency plans for converting collateral into cash fail to perform as expected on the day of a participant default. Systemically important systems would be expected to meet applicable standards for liquidity risk management for such systems, which generally require systemically important systems to maintain sufficient liquid financial resources to make timely payments, notwithstanding a default by the participant to which the system has the largest exposure under extreme but plausible market conditions.

III. Protect Consumers and Investors from Financial Abuse

Prior to the current financial crisis, a number of federal and state regulations were in place to protect consumers against fraud and to promote understanding of financial products like credit cards and mortgages. But as abusive practices spread, particularly in the market for subprime and nontraditional mortgages, our regulatory framework proved inadequate in important ways. Multiple agencies have authority over consumer protection in financial products, but for historical reasons, the supervisory framework for enforcing those regulations had significant gaps and weaknesses. Banking regulators at the state and federal level had a potentially conflicting mission to promote safe and sound banking practices, while other agencies had a clear mission but limited tools and jurisdiction. Most critically in the run-up to the financial crisis, mortgage companies and other firms outside of the purview of bank regulation exploited that lack of clear accountability by selling mortgages and other products that were overly complicated and unsuited to borrowers' financial situation. Banks and thrifts followed suit, with disastrous results for consumers and the financial system.

This year, Congress, the Administration, and financial regulators have taken significant measures to address some of the most obvious inadequacies in our consumer protection framework. But these steps have focused on just two, albeit very important, product markets – credit cards and mortgages. We need comprehensive reform.

For that reason, we propose the creation of a single regulatory agency, a Consumer Financial Protection Agency (CFPA), with the authority and accountability to make sure that consumer protection regulations are written fairly and enforced vigorously. The CFPA should reduce gaps in federal supervision and enforcement; improve coordination with the states; set higher standards for financial intermediaries; and promote consistent regulation of similar products.

Consumer protection is a critical foundation for our financial system. It gives the public confidence that financial markets are fair and enables policy makers and regulators to maintain stability in regulation. Stable regulation, in turn, promotes growth, efficiency, and innovation over the long term. We propose legislative, regulatory, and administrative reforms to promote transparency, simplicity, fairness, accountability, and access in the market for consumer financial products and services.

We also propose new authorities and resources for the Federal Trade Commission to protect consumers in a wide range of areas.

Finally, we propose new authorities for the Securities and Exchange Commission to protect investors, improve disclosure, raise standards, and increase enforcement.

A. Create a New Consumer Financial Protection Agency

We propose the creation of a single federal agency, the Consumer Financial Protection Agency, dedicated to protecting consumers in the financial products and services markets, except for investment products and services already regulated by the SEC or CFTC. We recommend that the CFPA be granted consolidated authority over the closely related functions of writing rules, supervising and examining institutions' compliance, and administratively enforcing violations. The CFPA should reduce gaps in federal supervision; improve coordination among the states; set higher standards for financial intermediaries; and promote consistent regulation of similar products. Nothing in this proposal is intended to constrain the Attorney General's current authorities to enforce the law or direct litigation on behalf of the United States.

The CFPA should give consumer protection an independent seat at the table in our financial regulatory system. Consumer protection is a critical foundation for our financial system. It gives the public confidence that financial markets are fair and enables policy makers and regulators to maintain stability in regulation. Stable regulation, in turn, promotes growth, efficiency, and innovation over the long term. Consumer protection cannot live up to this role, however, unless the financial system develops and sustains a culture that places a high value on helping responsible consumers thrive and treating all consumers fairly.

The spread of unsustainable subprime mortgages and abusive credit card contracts highlighted a serious shortcoming of our present regulatory infrastructure. It too easily allows consumer protection values to be overwhelmed by other imperatives – whether short-term gain, innovation for its own sake, or keeping up with the competition. To instill a genuine culture of consumer protection and not merely of legal compliance in our financial institutions, we need first to instill that culture in the federal regulatory structure. For the public to have confidence that consumer protection is important to regulators, there must be clear accountability in government for this task.

The current system of regulation does not meet these needs. Oversight of federally supervised institutions for compliance with consumer protection, fair lending, and community reinvestment laws is fragmented among four agencies. This makes coordination of supervisory policies difficult, slows responses to emerging consumer protection threats, and creates opportunities for regulatory arbitrage, where firms choose their regulator according to which entity will be least restrictive.

The Federal Trade Commission has a clear mission to protect consumers but generally lacks jurisdiction over the banking sector and has limited tools and resources to promote robust compliance of nonbank institutions. Mortgage companies not owned by banks fall into a regulatory "no man's land" where no regulator exercises leadership and state attorneys general are left to try to fill the gap. State and federal bank supervisory agencies' primary mission is to ensure that financial institutions act prudently, a mission that, in appearance if not always in practice, often conflicts with their consumer protection responsibilities.

In addition, the systems, expertise, and culture necessary for the federal banking agencies to perform their core missions and functions are not conducive to sustaining over the long term a federal consumer protection program that is vigorous, balanced, and creative. These agencies are designed, and their professional staff is trained, to see the world through the lenses of institutions and markets, not consumers. Recent Federal Reserve regulations have been strong, but quite late in coming. Moreover, they do not ensure that the federal banking agencies will remain committed to consumer protection.

We do not propose a new regulatory agency because we seek more regulation, but because we seek better regulation. The very existence of an agency devoted to consumer protection in financial services will be a strong incentive for institutions to develop strong cultures of consumer protection. The core of such an agency can be assembled reasonably quickly from discrete operations of other agencies. Most rule writing authority is concentrated in a single division of the Federal Reserve, and three of the four federal banking agencies have mostly or entirely separated consumer compliance supervision from prudential supervision. Combining staff from different agencies is not simple, to be sure, but it will bring significant benefits for responsible consumers and institutions, as well as for the market for consumer financial services and products.

1. *We propose to create a single primary federal consumer protection supervisor to protect consumers of credit, savings, payment, and other consumer financial products and services, and to regulate providers of such products and services.*

Creating a single federal agency (the CFPA) with supervisory, examination, and enforcement authority for protecting consumers would better promote accountability and help prevent regulatory arbitrage. A federally supervised institution would no longer be able to choose its supervisor based on any consideration of real or perceived differences in agencies' approaches to consumer protection supervision and enforcement.

The CFPA should also have the ability to act comprehensively to address emerging consumer protection concerns. For example, under the current fragmented structure, the federal banking agencies took until December 2005 to propose, and then until June 2007 to finalize, supervisory guidance on consumer protection concerns about subprime and nontraditional mortgages; the worst of these mortgages were originated in 2005 and 2006. A single agency, such as the CFPA, could have acted much more quickly and potentially saved many more consumers, communities, and institutions from significant losses.

2. *The CFPA should have broad jurisdiction to protect consumers in consumer financial products and services such as credit, savings, and payment products.*

We propose that the CFPA's jurisdiction should cover consumer financial services and products such as credit, savings and payment products and related services, as well as the

institutions that issue, provide, or service these products and provide services to the entities that provide the financial products. The mission of the CFPA would be to help ensure that:
- consumers have the information they need to make responsible financial decisions;
- consumers are protected from abuse, unfairness, deception, or discrimination;
- consumer financial services markets operate fairly and efficiently with ample room for sustainable growth and innovation; and
- traditionally underserved consumers and communities have access to lending, investment and financial services.

3. *The CFPA should be an independent agency with stable and robust funding.*

The CFPA should be structured to promote its independence and accountability. The CFPA will have a Director and a Board. The Board should represent a diverse set of viewpoints and experiences. At least one seat on the Board should be reserved for the head of a prudential regulator.

The CFPA should have a stable funding stream, which could come in part from fees assessed on entities and transactions across the financial sector, including bank and non- bank institutions and other providers of covered products and services. We look forward to working with Congress to create an agency that is strong, robust, and accountable.

The CFPA should be allowed to appoint and compensate officers and professional, financial and technical staff on terms commensurate with those currently used by other independent financial regulatory agencies.

4. *The CFPA should have sole rule-making authority for consumer financial protection statutes, as well as the ability to fill gaps through rule-making.*

The CFPA should have sole authority to promulgate and interpret regulations under existing consumer financial services and fair lending statutes, such as the Truth in Lending Act (TILA), Home Ownership and Equity Protection Act (HOEPA), Real Estate Settlement and Procedures Act (RE SPA), Community Reinvestment Act (CRA), Equal Credit Opportunity Act (ECOA), and Home Mortgage Disclosure Act (HMDA), and the Fair Debt Collection Practices Act (FDCPA). The CFPA should be given similar rulemaking authority under any future consumer protection laws addressing the consumer credit, savings, collection, or payment markets.

These laws generally contain broad grants of authority to adopt and enforce rules. But questionable practices may arise in the gaps between these laws or just beyond their boundaries. To promote consistent protection, we propose to vest in the CFPA broad authority to adopt tailored protections – such as disclosures or restrictions on contract terms or sales practices – against unfairness, abuse, or deception, subject to the notice and comment procedures of the Administrative Procedure Act. These protections would apply to any entity that engages in providing a covered financial product or service, including intermediaries such as mortgage brokers, as well as entities that provide services related to consumer debt, such as debt collectors and debt buyers. We also propose that the CFPA should have authority to craft appropriate exemptions from its regulations.

Many of the existing consumer protection statutes contain private rights of action. We do not propose disturbing these longstanding arrangements. In some cases we may seek legislation to increase statutory damages.

Various measures would help ensure that the CFPA's rulemaking reflects an appropriate and balanced array of considerations. Promoting access to financial services is a core part of the CFPA's mission. Therefore, our proposed legislation requires the CFPA to consider the costs to consumers of existing or new regulations, including any potential reduction in consumers' access to financial services, as well as the benefits. It also requires the CFPA to review regulations periodically to assess whether they should be strengthened, adjusted, or scaled back. The CFPA would be required to consult with other federal regulators to promote consistency with prudential, market, and systemic objectives. Our proposal to allocate one of the CFPA's five board seats to a prudential regulator would facilitate appropriate coordination.

5. ***The CFPA should have supervisory and enforcement authority and jurisdiction over all persons covered by the statutes that it implements, including both insured depositories and the range of other firms not previously subject to comprehensive federal supervision, and it should work with the Department of Justice to enforce the statutes under its jurisdiction in federal court.***

We propose that the CFPA have supervisory, examination, and enforcement authority over all entities subject to its regulations, including regulations implementing consumer protection, fair lending, and community reinvestment laws, as well as entities subject to selected statutes for which existing rule-writing authority does not exist or is limited (e.g., Fair Housing Act to the extent it covers mortgages, the Credit Repair Organization Act, the Fair Debt Collection Practices Act, and provisions of the Fair Credit Reporting Act).

The CFPA should assume from the federal prudential regulators all responsibilities for supervising banking institutions for compliance with consumer regulations, whether federally chartered or state chartered and supervised by a federal banking regulator. The CFPA's jurisdiction should extend to bank affiliates that are not currently supervised by a federal regulator. The CFPA should also be required to notify prudential regulators of major matters and share confidential examination reports with them. These agencies, in turn, should be required to refer potential compliance matters to the CFPA and should be authorized to take action if the CFPA fails to act; the same should hold for state supervisors of state-chartered institutions.

The Community Reinvestment Act (CRA) is unique among the panoply of consumer protection and fair lending laws. The CFPA should maintain a group of examiners specially trained and certified in community development to conduct CRA examinations of larger institutions.

The CFPA should also have supervisory and enforcement authority over nonbanking institutions, although the states should be the first line of defense. In its discretion, the CFPA should exercise the full range of supervisory authorities over nonbanking institutions within its jurisdiction, including supervision, information collection and on- site examination. The CFPA should also have the full range of enforcement powers over such institutions, including subpoena authority for documents and testimony, with capacity to compel production by court order. If a state enforcement agency brings an action against an institution within the CFPA's jurisdiction for a violation of one of the CFPA's regulations, the CFPA should have the ability to intervene in the action for all purposes, including appeals. The CFPA, moreover, should also be able to request that the U.S. Attorney General bring any action necessary to enforce its subpoena authority or to bring any other enforcement action on its behalf in the appropriate court.

The CFPA should be able to promote compliance by publishing supervisory guidance indicating how it intends to administer the laws it implements. The CFPA should also be able to use other creative tools to promote compliance, such as publishing best and worst practices based on surveys, mystery shopping, and information collected from supervision and investigations.

With respect to enforcement, the CFPA will cooperate closely with the Department of Justice. As in other areas of the law, the Department of Justice will also have independent authority to enforce violations of the statutes administered by the CFPA. In addition, the CFPA shall be authorized to share data with the Department of Justice to support enforcement of statutes administered by the CFPA as well as other statutes, such as civil rights statutes, enforced by the Department.

6. ***The CFPA should pursue measures to promote effective regulation, including conducting periodic reviews of regulations, an outside advisory council, and coordination with the Council.***

To promote accountability, the CFPA should be required to complete a regulatory study of each newly enacted regulation at least every three years after the effective date. The study will assess the effectiveness of the enacted regulation in meeting its stated goals, and will allow for public comment on recommendations for expanding, modifying, or eliminating the regulation. For example, these reviews should include mandatory assessments of consumers' ability to understand and use current disclosures and the adequacy of these disclosures to communicate key information that consumers need about the costs and risks of new products. The CFPA should also review existing regulations (such as those implementing TILA), as time and priorities allow, for the same purpose.

Second, we propose the establishment of an outside advisory panel, akin to the Federal Reserve's Consumer Advisory Council, to promote the CFPA's accountability and provide useful information on emerging industry practices. Members of this Council should have deep experience in financial services and community development and be selected to promote a diversity of views on the Council.

Third, the CFPA should work with other agencies through the Council to promote consistent treatment of similar products and to help ensure that no product goes unregulated merely because of uncertainty over jurisdiction. Through this Council, the CFPA should coordinate its efforts with the SEC, the CFTC, and other state and federal regulators to promote consistent, gap-free coverage of consumer and investor products and services. These agencies will report to Congress on their work and will be responsible for joint initiatives where appropriate.

7. ***The CFPA's strong rules would serve as a floor, not a ceiling. The states should have the ability to adopt and enforce stricter laws for institutions of***

Today, states typically retain authority under federal consumer protection and fair lending statutes to adopt stricter laws, so long as they do not conflict with federal law. We do not propose disturbing these long-standing arrangements. Federal rules promulgated by the CFPA under a pre-existing statute or its own organic rulemaking authority should override weaker state laws, but states should be free to adopt stricter laws. In addition, we propose that states should have concurrent authority to enforce regulations of the CFPA.

We propose that federally chartered institutions be subject to nondiscriminatory state consumer protection and civil rights laws to the same extent as other financial institutions. This would restore a fairer and more measured approach to the roles of the states with respect to federally chartered institutions. We also propose that states should be able to enforce these laws, as well as regulations of the CFPA, with respect to federally chartered institutions, subject to appropriate arrangements with prudential supervisors. With respect to state banks supervised by a federal prudential regulator, the CFPA will be the primary consumer compliance supervisor at the federal level.

8. *The CFPA should coordinate enforcement efforts with the states.*

Maintaining consistency among fifty states' supervisory and enforcement efforts will always remain a significant challenge, but the CFPA's concurrent supervisory and enforcement powers should place it in a position to help. The CFPA should assume responsibility for federal efforts to help the states unify and strengthen standards for registering and improving the quality of providers and intermediaries.

For example, the CFPA should administer the SAFE Act, under which it would set standards for registering and licensing any type of institution that originates mortgages. At present, the authority to administer the act is splintered among many federal agencies. Among other things, the CFPA should be authorized to set higher minimum net worth requirements for originators so that they will have resources to stand behind the strong representations and warranties we are proposing they be required to make.

We further propose that the CFPA be authorized to establish or facilitate registration and licensing regimes for other financial service providers and intermediaries, such as debt collectors, debt counselors or mortgage modification outfits. The CFPA and state enforcement agencies should be able to use registration systems to help weed out bad actors wherever they may operate.

Insufficient resources were devoted to enforcement during the mortgage boom. Periods of rapid market growth are precisely the time when government needs to be more vigilant. Resources have been increased significantly to address the inevitable fraudulent activities that are associated with the fallout of the mortgage crisis. When financial services markets begin to grow again, it is critical that funding at the federal and state levels be adequate to meet the challenge.

9. *The CFPA should have a wide variety of tools to enable it to perform its functions effectively.*

Research and Data. Empirical evidence is critical to a well designed regulatory structure. The CFPA should have authority to collect information through the supervisory process as well as through specific data collection statutes, such as the Home Mortgage Disclosure Act. The CFPA should use this information to improve regulations, promote compliance, and encourage community development. The CFPA should also establish a robust research and statistics department to conduct and promote research across the full range of consumer protection, fair lending, and community development finance issues. The CFPA would need the resources to acquire proprietary databases and collect and process its own data.

Complaints. Complaint data are an important barometer of consumer protection concerns and must be continuously communicated to the persons responsible for consumer regulation, enforcement, and supervision. Currently, however, many consumers do not know where to file a complaint about financial services because of the balkanized regulatory structure. The CFPA should have responsibility for collecting and tracking complaints about consumer financial services and facilitating complaint resolution with respect to federally-supervised institutions. Other federal supervisory agencies should refer any complaints they receive on consumer issues to the CFPA; complaint data should be shared across agencies. The states should retain primary responsibility for tracking and facilitating resolution of complaints against other institutions, and the CFPA should seek to coordinate exchanges of complaint data with state regulators.

Financial education. The CFPA should play a leading role in efforts to educate consumers about financial matters, to improve their ability to manage their own financial affairs, and to make their own judgments about the appropriateness of certain financial products. Additionally, the CFPA should review and streamline existing financial literacy and education initiatives government-wide.

Community Affairs. The CFPA's community affairs function should promote community development investment and fair and impartial access to credit. It should engage in a wide variety of activities to help financial institutions, community-based organizations, government entities, and the public understand and address financial services issues that affect low and middle-income people across various geographic regions.

10. **To improve incentives for compliance, the CFPA should have authority to restrict or ban mandatory arbitration clauses.**

Many consumers do not know that they often waive their rights to trial when signing form contracts in taking out a loan, and that a private party dependent on large firms for their business will decide the case without offering the right to appeal or a public review of decisions. The CFPA should be directed to gather information and study mandatory arbitration clauses in consumer financial services and products contracts to determine to what extent, and in what contexts, they promote fair adjudication and effective redress. If the CFPA determines that mandatory arbitration fails to achieve these goals, it should be required to establish conditions for fair arbitration, or, if necessary, to ban mandatory arbitration clauses in particular contexts, such as mortgage loans.

11. **The Federal Trade Commission should be given better tools to protect consumers.**

The Federal Trade Commission (FTC) plays a critical role in protecting consumers across the full range of products and services. While the FTC's primary authority for financial product and services protections should be transferred to the CFPA, the FTC should retain backup authority with the CFPA for the statutes for which the FTC currently has jurisdiction. We propose that the FTC should retain authority for dealing with fraud in the financial marketplace, including the sale of services like advance fee loans, credit repair, debt negotiation, and foreclosure rescue/loan modification fraud, but also provide such authority to the CFPA.

The FTC should also remain the lead federal consumer protection agency on matters of data security, with front-end privacy protection on financial issues moved to the CFPA.

We also propose to give the FTC the tools and human, financial, and technical resources it needs to do its job effectively by substantially increasing its capacity to protect consumers in all areas of commerce that remain under its authority. For example, the FTC should be authorized to conduct rulemakings for unfair and deceptive practices under standard notice and comment procedures, and to obtain civil penalties for unfair and deceptive practices.

B. Reform Consumer Protection

We propose a series of recommendations for legislation, regulations, and administrative measures by the CFPA to reform consumer protection based on principles of transparency, simplicity, fairness, accountability, and access for all.

1. *Transparency. We propose a new proactive approach to disclosure. The CFPA will be authorized to require that all disclosures and other communications with consumers be reasonable: balanced in their presentation of benefits, and clear and conspicuous in their identification of costs, penalties, and risks.*

We propose the following initiatives to improve the transparency of consumer product and service disclosures.

Make all mandatory disclosure forms clear, simple, and concise, and test them regularly.

Mandatory disclosure forms should be clear, simple, and concise. This means the CFPA should make judgments about which risks and costs should be highlighted and which need not be. Consumers should verify their ability to understand and use disclosure forms with qualitative and statistical tests.

A regulator is typically limited to testing disclosures in a "laboratory" environment. A product provider, however, has the capacity to test disclosures in the field, which can produce more robust and relevant results. For example, a credit card provider can try two different methods to disclose the same product risk and determine which was more effective by surveying consumers and evaluating their behaviors. We propose that the CFPA should be authorized to establish standards and procedures, including appropriate immunity from liability, for providers to conduct field tests of disclosures.

In particular, mortgage disclosures are due for significant reform. The Department of Housing and Urban Development (HUD) and the Federal Reserve have made progress in this regard. HUD, for example, recently developed new RESPA disclosures, and the Federal Reserve is testing new TILA disclosures. The CFPA, having authority over both TILA and RESPA, should have the responsibility to develop and test a single, integrated federal mortgage disclosure that provides consumers with the simplicity they deserve, and reduces regulatory burdens on providers. This provision should not, however, delay or affect current efforts to achieve a single federal disclosure for TILA and RESPA.

Require that disclosures and other communications with consumers be reasonable.

Disclosure mandates for consumer credit and other financial products are typically very technical and detailed. This approach lets the regulator determine which information must be emphasized and helps ensure that disclosures are standard and comparable. Flaws in this approach, however, were made clear by the spread of new and complex credit card plans and mortgages that preceded the credit crisis. The growth in the types of risks stemming from these products far outpaced the ability of disclosure regulations to keep up. Indeed, a regulator must take time to update mandatory disclosures because of the need for consumer testing and public input, and it is unduly burdensome to require the entire industry to update its disclosures too frequently. In addition to detailed rules, we propose a principles-based approach to disclosure.

We propose a regime strict enough to keep disclosures standard throughout the marketplace, yet flexible enough to adapt to new products. Our proposed legislation authorizes the CFPA to impose a duty on providers and intermediaries to require that communications with the consumer are reasonable, not merely technically compliant and non-deceptive.

Reasonableness includes balance in the presentation of risks and benefits, as well as clarity and conspicuousness in the description of significant product costs and risks. This is a higher standard than merely refraining from deception. Moreover, reasonableness does not mean a litany of every conceivable risk, which effectively obscures significant risks. It means identifying conspicuously the more significant risks. It means providing consumers with disclosures that help them to understand the consequences of their financial decisions.

The CFPA should be authorized to apply the duty of reasonableness to communications with or to the consumer, as appropriate, including marketing materials and solicitations. The CFPA should determine the appropriate scope of this duty. A provider or intermediary should be subject to administrative action, but not civil liability, if its communications violate this duty.

The CFPA also should be authorized to apply the duty of reasonableness to mandatory disclosures. The regulator typically sets requirements for disclosure for mainstream products and services. If a new product emerges that the regulator did not anticipate, the mandatory disclosure may not adequately disclose a major risk of the product. A deficient but compliant mandatory disclosure may lull the consumer into a false sense of security, undermining the very purpose of a disclosure mandate. It is not fair or efficient to make the consumer bear the cost of disclosures that are out of date. Nor is it reasonable to expect that the regulator will have the capacity to update disclosures on a real-time basis. Therefore, we propose that providers should share with the regulator the burden of updating mandatory disclosures when they introduce new products.

The CFPA should be authorized to implement a process under which a provider, acting reasonably and in good faith, could obtain the equivalent of a "no action" letter for disclosure and other communications for a new product. For example, the CFPA could adopt a procedure under which a provider petitions the CFPA for a determination that its product's risks were adequately disclosed by the mandatory model disclosure or marketing materials. The CFPA could approve use of the mandatory model or marketing materials, or provide a waiver, admissible in court to defend against a claim, for varying the model disclosure. As a further example, if the CFPA failed to respond in a timely fashion, the provider could proceed to market without fear of administrative sanction on that basis. The provider could potentially shorten the mandatory waiting period if it submitted empirical evidence, according to prescribed standards, that its marketing materials and the mandatory disclosure adequately disclosed relevant risks. The CFPA should have authority to adapt and adjust its standards and procedures to seek to maximize the benefits of product innovation while minimizing the costs.

Harness technology to make disclosures more dynamic and relevant to the individual consumer.

Disclosure rules today assume disclosures are on paper and follow a prescribed content, format, and timing; the consumer has no ability to adapt content, timing, or format to her needs. The CFPA should harness technology to make disclosures more dynamic and adaptable to the needs of the individual consumer. New technology can be costly, and the CFPA should consider those costs, but it should also consider that spinoff benefits from new technology can be hard to quantify and could be substantial.

Disclosures should show consumers the consequences of their financial decisions. For example, the recently enacted Credit CARD Act of 2009 requires issuers to show the total cost and time for repayment if a consumer paid only the minimum due each month, and it further requires issuers to show the amount a consumer would have to pay in order to pay off the balance in three years. Technology enhances the ability to tailor this disclosure, and an internet calculator would permit the consumer to select a different period, or input a payment amount above the minimum. Such calculators are common on the internet. The CFPA should mandate a calculator disclosure in circumstances where the CFPA determines the benefits to consumers outweigh the costs. It should also mandate or encourage calculator disclosures for mortgages to assist with comparison shopping. For example, a calculator that shows the costs of a mortgage based on the consumer's expectations for how long she will stay in the home may reveal a more significant difference between two products than appears on standard paper disclosures.

Technology can also help consumers better manage their use of credit by providing information and options at the most relevant times to them. For example, the CFPA should have authority, after considering the costs and benefits of such a measure, to require issuers to warn consumers who use a debit card at the point of sale or ATM machines that doing so would overdraft their account. The CFPA should also promote adoption of innovations in point-of-sale technology, such as allowing consumers who use a credit card to choose a payment plan for the purchase.

2. *Simplicity. We propose that the regulator be authorized to define standards for "plain vanilla" products that are simpler and have straightforward pricing. The CFPA should be authorized to require all providers and intermediaries to offer these products prominently, alongside whatever other lawful products they choose to offer.*

Even if disclosures are fully tested and all communications are properly balanced, product complexity itself can lead consumers to make costly errors. A careful regulatory approach can tilt the scales in favor of simpler, less risky products while preserving choice and innovation.

"Plain vanilla" mortgages, whether they have fixed or adjustable interest rates, should be easy for consumers to understand. They should not include prepayment penalties and should be underwritten to fully document income, collect escrow for taxes and insurance, and have predictable payments. These products are also easy to compare because they can be differentiated by a single, simple characteristic, the interest rate. We propose that the government do more to promote "plain vanilla" products. The CFPA should be authorized to define standards for such products and require firms to offer them alongside whatever other lawful products a firm chooses to offer.

The Federal Reserve Board issued final regulations last year, which take effect in October, that impose extra protections and higher penalties on "alternative" or "higher cost" loans, that is, mortgages that are not "plain vanilla". The CFPA should assume responsibility for this regulation. The CFPA should consider whether to add other types of mortgages to the class that receive additional scrutiny and higher penalties, considering the complexity of the mortgage itself, such as negative amortization features, and the performance of the loan type. It should leave in the class that doesn't have these extra protections only products that meet a plain vanilla test. The CFPA should use survey methods to determine whether consumers who obtained the product type in the marketplace demonstrated awareness and understanding of the product and its risks, such as the risk of payment shock and of the balance exceeding the value of the house. The CFPA should also consider access to credit and costs to consumers of stricter regulations.

The CFPA should be authorized to use a variety of measures to help ensure alternative mortgages were obtained only by consumers who understood the risks and could manage them. For example, the CFPA could impose a strong warning label on all alternative products; require providers to have applicants fill out financial experience questionnaires; or require providers to obtain the applicant's written "opt-in" to such products. Originators and purchasers of "plain vanilla" mortgages should enjoy a strong presumption that the products are suitable and affordable for the borrower. Originators and purchasers of alternative products should not enjoy such a presumption, and they should be subject to significantly higher penalties for violations.

3. *Fairness. Where efforts to improve transparency and simplicity prove inadequate to prevent unfair treatment and abuse, we propose that the CFPA be authorized to place tailored restrictions on product terms and provider practices, if the benefits outweigh the costs. Moreover, we propose to authorize the CFPA to impose appropriate duties of care on financial intermediaries.*

In recent years, the principle that product and service providers should treat consumers fairly has been too often honored only in the breach. The mortgage and credit card markets have demonstrated convincingly the need for rules that require fair contracts and practices and remove or reduce perverse and hidden incentives to take advantage of consumers.

The excessive complexity of many mortgage products created an opportunity to take advantage of consumers' lack of awareness and understanding of product risks. Mortgage originators received direct incentives to exploit this opportunity. They were paid for loan volume rather than loan performance and paid more for loans with higher interest rates and riskier terms. As noted in Section II, the securitization model, without appropriate regulation or transparency, exacerbated these problems by eroding the capacity and incentives for originators, securitizers, and investors to ensure that loans were viable.

In the credit card market, the opacity of increasingly complicated products led major card issuers to migrate almost uniformly to unfavorable methods for assessing fees and interest that could easily trap a responsible consumer in debt. Competition did not force these methods out, because consumers were not aware of them or could not understand them, and issuers did not find it profitable to offer contract terms that were transparent to consumers. For a variety of reasons, regulators have not brought enforcement actions under existing law.

We propose the following measures to promote fair treatment of consumers:

Give the CFPA authority to regulate unfair, deceptive, or abusive acts or practices.

As mortgages and credit cards illustrate, even seemingly "simple" financial products remain complicated to large numbers of Americans. As a result, in addition to meaningful disclosure, there must also be standards for appropriate business conduct and regulations that help ensure providers do not have undue incentives to undermine those standards. Accordingly, the Federal Reserve recently responded to unfair mortgage practices with regulations imposing affordability requirements on subprime loans, and the House recently passed a strong, comprehensive predatory lending bill. Congress, moreover, recently improved credit card contract regulation by passing the Credit CARD Act of 2009.

As described above, the CFPA should assume the statutory authorities to regulate unfair, deceptive, and abusive acts or practices for all credit, savings, and payment products.

The legal standards for these authorities are generally well-established and would require the CFPA to develop a record and weigh costs and benefits before exercising these authorities. The mortgage and credit card cases demonstrate clearly that properly tailored restrictions not only benefit individual consumers, but also institutions and markets by increasing consumer confidence and promoting more effective competition.

The CFPA should also have authority to address overly complex financial contracts. For example, the CFPA should be authorized to consider whether mortgage regulations require strengthening. The CFPA could determine that prepayment penalties should be banned for certain types of products, such as subprime or nontraditional mortgages, or for all products, because the penalties make loans too complex for the least sophisticated consumers or those least able to shop effectively. The CFPA could adopt a "life of loan" approach to regulating mortgages that provides a consumer adequate protections through servicing and loss mitigation stages. The CFPA should also be authorized to ban often- invisible side payments to mortgage originators – so called yield spread premiums or overages – that are tied to the borrower receiving worse terms than she qualifies for, if the CFPA finds that disclosure is not an adequate remedy. These payments incentivize originators to steer consumers to higher-priced or inappropriate mortgages. In addition, the CFPA could consider requiring that originators receive a portion of their compensation over time, contingent on loan performance, rather than in a lump sum at origination.

Give the CFPA authority to impose empirically justified and appropriately tailored duties of care on financial intermediaries.

Impartial advice represents one of the most important financial services consumers can receive. Currently, debt counselors advise distressed and vulnerable borrowers on how to manage and reduce their debts. Mortgage brokers often advertise their trustworthiness as advisors on difficult mortgage decisions. When these intermediaries accept side payments from product providers, they can compromise their ability to be impartial. Consumers, however, may retain faith that the intermediary is working for them and placing their interests above his or her own, even if the conflict of interest is disclosed. Accordingly, in some cases consumers may reasonably but mistakenly rely on advice from conflicted intermediaries. It is unfair for intermediaries to take advantage of that trust.

To address this problem, we propose granting the CFPA authority to impose carefully crafted duties of care on financial intermediaries. For example, the CFPA could impose a duty of care to counteract an intermediary's patent conflict of interest, or to align an intermediary's conduct with consumers' reasonable expectations as demonstrated by empirical evidence. The CFPA could also consider imposing on originators a requirement to disclose material information such as the consumer's likely ability to qualify for a lower interest rate based on her risk profile. In that regard, the CFPA could impose on mortgage brokers a duty of best execution with respect to available mortgage loans and a duty to determine affordability for borrowers.

The CFPA should apply consistent regulation to similar products.

Fairness, effective competition, and efficient markets require consistent regulatory treatment for similar products. For example, similar disclosure treatment for similar products enables consumers to make informed choices based on a full appreciation of the nature and risks of the product and enables providers to compete fairly and vigorously. Ensuring consistency will require judgment on the part of the CFPA because products often have hybrid features and could fall under different statutes that call for different treatment. The CFPA should assess consumers' understanding and perception of such products. In some cases, it may be appropriate to align the regulation of the products more closely with consumers' perceptions. In other cases, however, consumers' perceptions may reflect a failure of existing regulations to properly inform consumers about a product. In that case, regulations should be revised to frame the presentation of the product more appropriately.

One example is overdraft protection plans. These are a form of consumer credit, and consumers often use them as substitutes for other forms of credit such as payday loans, credit card cash advances, and traditional overdraft lines of credit. However, overdraft protection plans have not been regulated as credit, and, as a result, consumers may not overtly think of the plans as credit. Consumers may not, therefore, take the same care in their use of overdrafts that they take with other, more overt credit products. The CFPA would be authorized by existing statutes to regulate overdraft protection more like a credit product, with Truth in Lending disclosures as appropriate. The CFPA could also prohibit charging for overdraft coverage under a plan unless the consumer has "opted in" to the plan, just as the Credit CARD Act prohibits over-the-limit fees unless the consumer has "opted in" to over-the-limit coverage. It could also require affirmative consent at point of sale with debit transactions or at an ATM machine before collecting an "overdraft fee".

4. *Access. The Agency should enforce fair lending laws and the Community Reinvestment Act and otherwise seek to ensure that underserved consumers and communities have access to prudent financial services, lending, and investment.*

A critical part of the CFPA's mission should be to promote access to financial services, especially for households and communities that traditionally have had limited access. This focus will also help ensure that the CFPA fully internalizes the value of preserving access to financial services and weighs that value against other values when it considers new consumer protection regulations.

Rigorous application of the Community Reinvestment Act (CRA) should be a core function of the CFPA. Some have attempted to blame the subprime meltdown and financial crisis on the CRA and have argued that the CRA must be weakened in order to restore financial stability. These claims and arguments are without any logical or evidentiary basis. It is not tenable that the CRA could suddenly have caused an explosion in bad subprime loans more than 25 years after its enactment. In fact, enforcement of CRA was weakened during the boom and the worst abuses were made by firms not covered by CRA. Moreover, the Federal Reserve has reported that only six percent of all the higher-priced loans were extended by the CRA-covered lenders to lower income borrowers or neighborhoods in the local areas that are the focus of CRA evaluations.

The appropriate response to the crisis is not to weaken the CRA; it is rather to promote robust application of the CRA so that low-income households and communities have access to responsible financial services that truly meet their needs. To that end, we propose that the CFPA should have sole authority to evaluate institutions under the CRA. While the prudential regulators should have the authority to decide applications for institutions to merge, the CFPA should be responsible for determining the institution's record of meeting the lending, investment, and services needs of its community under the CRA, which would be part of the merger application.

The CFPA should also vigorously enforce fair lending laws to promote access to credit. Furthermore, the CFPA should maintain a fair lending unit with attorneys, compliance specialists, economists, and statisticians. The CFPA should have primary fair lending jurisdiction over federally supervised institutions and concurrent authority with the states over other institutions. Its comprehensive jurisdiction should enable it to develop a holistic, integrated approach to fair lending that targets resources to the areas of greatest risk for discrimination.

To promote fair lending enforcement, as well as community investment objectives, the CFPA should have authority to collect data on mortgage and small business lending. Critical new fields should be added to HMDA data such as a universal loan identifier that permits tying HMDA data to property databases and proprietary loan performance databases, a flag for loans originated by mortgage brokers, information about the type of interest rate (e.g., fixed vs. variable), and other fields that the mortgage crisis has shown to be of critical importance.

C. Strengthen the framework for investor protection by focusing on principles of transparency, fairness, and accountability

In the Securities and Exchange Commission (SEC), we already have an experienced federal supervisor with comprehensive responsibilities for protecting investors against fraud and abuse. In the wake of the scandals associated with the current financial crisis, including Ponzi schemes such as the Madoff affair, the SEC has already begun to strengthen and streamline its enforcement process and to expand resources for enforcement in the FY2010 budget. It has streamlined the process of obtaining formal orders that grant the staff subpoena power and begun a review of its technology and processes to assess risk and manage leads for potential fraud and abuse. The SEC is also using its existing authority to make improvements in investor protections.

We propose the following measures to modernize the financial regulatory structure and improve the SEC's ability to protect investors, focusing on principles of transparency, fairness, and accountability.

1. ***The SEC should be given expanded authority to promote transparency in disclosures to investors.***

To promote transparency, we propose revisions in the federal securities laws to enable the SEC to improve the timing and quality of disclosures to investors.

The SEC should be authorized to require that certain disclosures (including a summary prospectus) be provided to investors at or before the point of sale, if it finds that such disclosures would improve investor understanding of the particular financial products, and their costs and risks. Currently, most prospectuses (including the mutual fund summary prospectus) are delivered with the confirmation of sale, *after* the sale has taken place. Without slowing the pace of transactions in modern capital markets, the SEC should require that adequate information is given to investor to make informed investment decisions.

The SEC can better evaluate the effectiveness of investor disclosures if it can meaningfully engage in consumer testing of those disclosures. The SEC should be better enabled to engage in field testing, consumer outreach and testing of disclosures to individual investors, including by providing budgetary support for those activities.

2. ***The SEC should be given new tools to promote fair treatment of investors.***

We propose the following initiatives to empower the SEC to increase fairness for investors:

Establish a fiduciary duty for broker-dealers offering investment advice and harmonize the regulation of investment advisers and broker-dealers.

Retail investors face a large array of investment products and often turn to financial intermediaries – whether investment advisors or brokers-dealers – to help them manage their investments. However, investment advisers and broker-dealers are regulated under different statutory and regulatory frameworks, even though the services they provide often are virtually identical from a retail investor's perspective.

Retail investors are often confused about the differences between investment advisers and broker-dealers. Meanwhile, the distinction is no longer meaningful between a disinterested investment advisor and a broker who acts as an agent for an investor; the current laws and regulations are based on antiquated distinctions between the two types of financial professionals that date back to the early 20th century. Brokers are allowed to give "incidental advice" in the course of their business, and yet retail investors rely on a trusted relationship that is often not matched by the legal responsibility of the securities broker. In general, a broker-dealer's relationship with a customer is not legally a fiduciary relationship, while an investment adviser is legally its customer's fiduciary.

From the vantage point of the retail customer, however, an investment adviser and a broker-dealer providing "incidental advice" appear in all respects identical. In the retail context, the legal distinction between the two is no longer meaningful. Retail customers repose the same degree of trust in their brokers as they do in investment advisers, but the legal responsibilities of the intermediaries may not be the same

The SEC should be permitted to align duties for intermediaries across financial products. Standards of care for all broker-dealers when providing investment advice about securities to retail investors should be raised to the fiduciary standard to align the legal framework with investment advisers. In addition, the SEC should be empowered to examine and ban forms of compensation that encourage intermediaries to put investors into products that are profitable to the intermediary, but are not in the investors' best interest.

New legislation should bolster investor protections and bring important consistency to the regulation of these two types of financial professionals by:

- requiring that broker-dealers who provide investment advice about securities to investors have the same fiduciary obligations as registered investment advisers;
- providing simple and clear disclosure to investors regarding the scope of the terms of their relationships with investment professionals; and
- prohibiting certain conflict of interests and sales practices that are contrary to the interests of investors.

The SEC should study the use of mandatory arbitration clauses in investor contracts.

Broker-dealers generally require their customers to contract at account opening to arbitrate all disputes. Although arbitration may be a reasonable option for many consumers to accept after a dispute arises, mandating a particular venue and up-front method of adjudicating disputes – and eliminating access to courts – may unjustifiably undermine investor interests. We recommend legislation that would give the SEC clear authority to prohibit mandatory arbitration clauses in broker-dealer and investment advisory accounts with retail customers. The legislation should also provide that, before using such authority, the SEC would need to conduct a study on the use of mandatory arbitration clauses in these contracts. The study shall consider whether investors are harmed by being unable to obtain effective redress of legitimate grievances, as well as whether changes to arbitration are appropriate.

3. **Financial firms and public companies should be accountable to their clients and investors.**

Expand protections for whistleblowers.

The SEC should gain the authority to establish a fund to pay whistleblowers for information that leads to enforcement actions resulting in significant financial awards. Currently, the SEC has the authority to compensate sources in insider trading cases; that authority should be extended to compensate whistleblowers that bring well-documented evidence of fraudulent activity. We support the creation of this fund using monies that the SEC collects from enforcement actions that are not otherwise distributed to investors.

Expand sanctions available in enforcement actions and harmonize liability standards.

Improved sanctions would better enable the SEC to enforce the federal securities laws. We support the SEC in pursuing authority to impose collateral bars against regulated persons across all aspects of the industry rather than in a specific segment of the industry. The interrelationship among the securities activities under the SEC's jurisdiction, the similar grounds for exclusion from each, and the SEC's overarching responsibility to regulate these activities support the imposition of collateral bars.

The SEC also proposes amending the federal securities laws to provide a single explicit standard for primary liability to replace various circuits' formulations of different "tests" for primary liability.

Require non-binding shareholder votes on executive compensation packages.

Public companies should be required to implement "say on pay" rules, which require shareholder votes on executive compensation packages. While such votes are nonbinding, they provide a strong message to management and boards and serve to support a culture of performance, transparency, and accountability in executive compensation. Shareholders are often concerned about large corporate bonus plans in situations in which they, as the company's owners, have experienced losses. Currently, these decisions are often not directly reviewed by shareholders – leaving shareholders with limited rights to voice their concerns about compensation through an advisory vote.

To facilitate greater communication between shareholders and management over executive compensation, public companies should include on their proxies a nonbinding shareholder vote on executive compensation. Legislation that would authorize SEC "say on pay" rules for all public companies could help restore investor trust by promoting increased shareholder participation and increasing accountability of board members and corporate management. It would provide shareholders of all public U.S. companies with the same rights that are accorded to shareholders in many other countries.

4. ***Under the leadership of the Financial Services Oversight Council, we propose the establishment of a Financial Consumer Coordinating Council and a permanent role for the SEC's Investor Advisory Committee.***

To address potential gaps in consumer and investor protection and to promote best practices across different markets, we propose to create a coordinating council of the heads of the SEC, Federal Trade Commission, the Department of Justice, and the Consumer Financial Protection Agency or their designees, and other state and federal agencies. The Coordinating Council should meet at least quarterly to identify gaps in consumer protection across financial products and facilitate coordination of consumer protection efforts. Our proposal will help ensure the effectiveness of the Coordinating Council for the benefit of consumers by:

- empowering the Council to establish mechanisms for state attorneys general, consumer advocates, and others to make recommendations to the Council on issues to be considered or gaps to be filled;
- requiring the Council to report to Congress and the member agencies semiannually with recommendations for legislative and regulatory changes to improve consumer and investor protection, and with updates on progress made on prior recommendations; and
- empowering the Council to sponsor studies or engage in consumer testing to identify gaps, share information and find solutions for improving consumer protection across a range of financial products.

The SEC has recently established an Investor Advisory Committee, made up of a diverse group of well-respected investors, to advise on the SEC's regulatory priorities, including issues concerning new products, trading strategies, fee structures, and the effectiveness of disclosure. The Investor Advisory Committee should be made permanent by statute.

5. ***Promote retirement security for all Americans by strengthening employment-based and private retirement plans and encouraging adequate savings.***
We propose the enactment of the "Automatic IRA" and a strengthened saver's credit.

For many years, until the current recession, the personal saving rate in the United States has been exceedingly low. In addition, tens of millions of U.S. households have not placed themselves on a path to become financially prepared for retirement. In order to address this problem, the President has proposed two innovative initiatives in his 2010 Budget: (1) introducing an "Automatic IRA" (with opt-out) for employees whose employers do not offer a plan; and (2) increasing tax incentives for retirement savings for families that earn less than $65,000 by modifying the "saver's credit" and making it refundable. Together these initiatives will expand plan coverage, combat inertia, and increase incentives to save.

Under the "Automatic IRA" plan, employers in business for at least two years that have 10 or more employees would be required to offer an automatic IRA option (with opt-out), under which regular payroll-deduction contributions would be made to an IRA. Employers would not have to choose or arrange default investments. Instead, a low-cost, standard type of default investment and a handful of standard, low-cost investment alternatives would be prescribed by statute or regulation.

The modified saver's credit would be fully refundable and deposited automatically in the individual's qualified retirement plan account or IRA. These changes make the saver's credit more like a matching contribution, enhancing the likelihood that the credit would be saved. The proposal would offer a meaningful saving incentive to tens of millions of additional households while simplifying the current complex structure of the credit and raising the eligibility income threshold to cover millions of additional moderate-income taxpayers.

Improve retirement security through employee-directed workplace retirement plans, automatic IRAs and other measures.

Employee-directed workplace retirement plans (such as 401(k)s) and Automatic IRAs should be governed by the same core principles that inform our comprehensive approach to consumer and investor protection in the retail marketplace. Plans should be *transparent*, providing information about the risks, returns, and costs of different investment choices in terms that real people can use to make decisions. They should be as *simple* as possible, designed to make savings and investment decisions easy, such as by offering the convenience of automation. They should be *fair* and free from conflicts of interest (such as those that can affect third party providers) that could harm employees. Plan sponsors and others who provide services to the plan or to individual employees (such as the management of employee investments) should be *accountable* and subject to appropriate oversight. Finally, high-quality plans that make savings and investment easy should be *accessible* to all workers.

There are a number of other critical issues in the area of retirement security that need to be addressed. We should explore ways to encourage the use of automatic features to increase participation and improve saving and investment behavior in 401(k) plans, and restore more lifetime income throughout the retirement system – in defined benefit plans, defined contribution plans, and IRAs. We should aim to reduce costs, such as investment fees. We should investigate how to better preserve savings for retirement, reducing "leakage" from retirement plans. Finally, we should explore means of strengthening the defined benefit plan system.

IV. Provide the Government with the Tools it Needs To Manage Financial Crises

Over the past two years, the financial system has been threatened by the failure or near failure of some of the largest and most interconnected financial firms. Our current system already has strong procedures and expertise for handling the failure of banks, but when a bank holding company or other nonbank financial firm is in severe distress, there are currently only two options: obtain outside capital or file for bankruptcy. During most economic climates, these are suitable options that will not impact greater financial stability.

However, in stressed conditions it may prove difficult for distressed institutions to raise sufficient private capital. Thus, if a large, interconnected bank holding company or other nonbank financial firm nears failure during a financial crisis, there are only two untenable options: obtain emergency funding from the US government as in the case of AIG, or file for bankruptcy as in the case of Lehman Brothers. Neither of these options is acceptable for managing the resolution of the firm efficiently and effectively in a manner that limits the systemic risk with the least cost to the taxpayer.

We propose a new authority, modeled on the existing authority of the FDIC, that should allow the government to address the potential failure of a bank holding company or other nonbank financial firm when the stability of the financial system is at risk.

In order to improve accountability in the use of other crisis tools, we also propose that the Federal Reserve Board receive prior written approval from the Secretary of the Treasury for emergency lending under its "unusual and exigent circumstances" authority.

A. Create a resolution regime for failing BHCs, Including Tier 1 FHCs

We recommend the creation of a resolution regime to avoid the disorderly resolution of failing BHCs, including Tier 1 FHCs, if a disorderly resolution would have serious adverse effects on the financial system or the economy. The regime would supplement (rather than replace) and be modeled on to the existing resolution regime for insured depository institutions under the Federal Deposit Insurance Act.

The federal government's responses to the impending bankruptcy of Bear Stearns, Lehman Brothers, and AIG were complicated by the lack of a statutory framework for avoiding the disorderly failure of nonbank financial firms, including affiliates of banks or other insured depository institutions. In the absence of such a framework, the government's only avenue to avoid the disorderly failures of Bear Stearns and AIG was the use of the Federal Reserve's lending authority. And this mechanism was insufficient to prevent the bankruptcy of Lehman Brothers, an event which served to demonstrate how disruptive the disorderly failure of a nonbank financial firm can be to the financial system and the economy.

For these reasons, we propose the creation of a resolution regime to allow for the orderly resolution of failing BHCs, including Tier 1 FHCs, in situations where the stability of the financial system is at risk.

This resolution regime should not replace bankruptcy procedures in the normal course of business. Bankruptcy is and will remain the dominant tool for handling the failure of a BHC, unless the special resolution regime is triggered because of concerns about financial stability.

The proposed resolution regime is modeled on the "systemic risk exception" contained within the existing FDIC resolution regime. This exception allows the FDIC to depart from the least cost resolution standard, when financial stability is at risk. Like that authority, the authority that we propose here would be only for extraordinary times and would be subject to very strict governance and control procedures.

We propose a formal process for deciding whether use of this special resolution regime is necessary for a particular firm and determining the form that the resolution process for the firm should take. The process could be initiated by Treasury or the Federal Reserve. In addition, the process could be initiated by the FDIC, or, by the SEC, when the largest subsidiary of the failing firm is a broker-dealer or securities firm.

The authority to decide whether to resolve a failing firm under the special resolution regime should be vested in Treasury, which could invoke the authority only after consulting with the President and only upon the written recommendation of two-thirds of the members of the Federal Reserve Board and two-thirds of the members of the FDIC Board. But, if the largest subsidiary of the firm (measured by total assets) is a broker- dealer, then FDIC Board approval is not required and two-thirds of the commissioners of the SEC must approve. If the failing firm includes an insurance company, the Office of National Insurance within Treasury will provide consultation to the Federal Reserve and FDIC Boards on insurance specific matters.

To invoke this authority, Treasury should have to determine that: (1) the firm is in default or in danger of defaulting; (2) the failure of the firm and its resolution under otherwise applicable law would have serious adverse effects on the financial system or the economy; and (3) use by the government of the special resolution regime would avoid or mitigate these adverse effects.

The authority to decide how to resolve a failing firm under the special resolution regime should also be vested in Treasury. The tools available to Treasury should include the ability to establish conservatorship or receivership for a failing firm. The regime also should provide for the ability to stabilize a failing institution (including one that is in conservatorship or receivership) by providing loans to the firm, purchasing assets from the firm, guaranteeing the liabilities of the firm, or making equity investments in the firm. We propose that, in choosing among available tools, Treasury should consider the effectiveness of an action for mitigating potential adverse effects on the financial system or the economy, the action's cost to the taxpayers, and the action's potential for increasing moral hazard.

Treasury generally should appoint the FDIC to act as conservator or receiver, in cases where it has decided to establish conservatorship or receivership. Treasury should have the authority to appoint the SEC as conservator or receiver when the largest subsidiary of the failing firm, measured by total assets, is a broker-dealer or securities firm. The conservator or receiver should coordinate with foreign authorities that may be involved in the resolution of subsidiaries of the firm located in foreign jurisdictions. The existing customer protections provided to insured depositors, customers of broker-dealers and futures commission merchants, and insurance policyholders under federal or state law should be maintained.

The conservator or receiver of the firm should have broad powers to take action with respect to the financial firm. For example, it should have the authority to take control of the operations of the firm or to sell or transfer all or any part of the assets of the firm in receivership to a bridge institution or other entity. That should include the authority to transfer the firm's derivatives contracts to a bridge institution and thereby avoid termination of the contracts by the firm's counterparties (notwithstanding any contractual rights of counterparties to terminate the contracts if a receiver is appointed). The conservator or receiver should also have the power to renegotiate or repudiate the firm's contracts, including contracts with its employees.

The entity acting as conservator or receiver should be authorized to borrow from Treasury when necessary to finance exercise of the authorities under the resolution regime, and Treasury should be authorized to issue public debt to finance any such loans. The costs of any such loans should be paid from the proceeds of assessments on BHCs. Such assessments should be based on the total liabilities (other than liabilities that are assessed to fund other federal or state insurance schemes).

In addition, in light of the FDIC's role in the proposed special resolution regime for BHCs, the FDIC should have the authority to obtain any examination report prepared by the Federal Reserve with respect to any BHC, and should have back-up examination authority over BHCs.

B. Amend the Federal Reserve's Emergency Lending Authority

We will propose legislation to amend Section 13(3) of the Federal Reserve Act to require the prior written approval of the Secretary of the Treasury for any extensions of credit by the Federal Reserve to individuals, partnerships, or corporations in "unusual and exigent circumstances."

Section 13(3) of the Federal Reserve Act provides that in "unusual and exigent circumstances" the Federal Reserve Board, upon a vote of five or more members, may authorize a Federal Reserve Bank to lend to any individual, partnership, or corporation. The only constraints on such lending are that any such loans must be guaranteed or secured to the satisfaction of the Reserve Bank and that the Reserve Bank must obtain evidence that the borrower is unable to obtain "adequate credit accommodations" from banks.

During the recent financial crisis, the Federal Reserve Board has used this authority on several occasions to protect the financial system and the economy. It has lent to individual financial institutions to avoid their disorderly failure (e.g. AIG). It has created liquidity facilities to bolster confidence and liquidity in numerous sectors (e.g., investment banks, MMFs, commercial paper issuers). Further, it has created liquidity facilities designed to revive the securitization markets and thereby restore lending to consumers and businesses whose access to credit was dependent on those markets.

The Federal Reserve Board currently has authority to make such loans without the approval of the Secretary of the Treasury. In practice, in each instance during the crisis in which it has used its Section 13(3) authority it has sought and received the approval of the Secretary. Indeed, the liquidity facilities designed to revive the securitization markets have involved use of TARP funds to secure the 13(3) loans and the facilities were jointly designed by the Federal Reserve and Treasury.

The Federal Reserve's Section 13(3) authority should be subject to prior written approval of the Secretary of Treasury for lending under Section 13(3) to provide appropriate accountability going forward.

V. Raise International Regulatory Standards and Improve International Cooperation

As we have witnessed during this crisis, financial stress can spread easily and quickly across national boundaries. Yet, regulation is still set largely in a national context. Without consistent supervision and regulation, financial institutions will tend to move their activities to jurisdictions with looser standards, creating a race to the bottom and intensifying systemic risk for the entire global financial system.

The United States is playing a strong leadership role in efforts to coordinate international financial policy through the G-20, the Financial Stability Board, and the Basel Committee on Banking Supervision. We will use our leadership position in the international community to promote initiatives compatible with the domestic regulatory reforms described in this report.

We will focus on reaching international consensus on four core issues: regulatory capital standards; oversight of global financial markets; supervision of internationally active financial firms; and crisis prevention and management.

At the April 2009 London Summit, the G-20 Leaders issued an eight-part declaration outlining a comprehensive plan for financial regulatory reform.

The domestic regulatory reform initiatives outlined in this report are consistent with the international commitments the United States has undertaken as part of the G-20 process, and we propose stronger regulatory standards in a number of areas.

A. Strengthen the International Capital Framework

We recommend that the Basel Committee on Banking Supervision (BCBS) continue to modify and improve Basel II by refining the risk weights applicable to the trading book and securitized products, introducing a supplemental leverage ratio, and improving the definition of capital by the end of 2009. We also urge the BCBS to complete an in-depth review of the Basel II framework to mitigate its procyclical effects.

In 1988, the BCBS developed the Basel Accord to provide a framework to strengthen banking system safety and soundness through internationally consistent bank regulatory capital requirements. As weaknesses in the original Basel Accord became increasingly apparent, the BCBS developed a new accord, known as Basel II. The United States has not fully implemented Basel II, but the international financial crisis has already demonstrated weaknesses in the Basel II framework.

We support the BCBS's efforts to address these weaknesses. In particular, we support the BCBS's efforts to improve the regulatory capital framework for trading book and securitization exposures by 2010.

Second, we urge the BCBS to strengthen the definition of regulatory capital to improve the quality, quantity, and international consistency of capital. We urge the BCB S to issue guidelines to harmonize the definition of capital by the end of 2009, and develop recommendations on minimum capital levels in 2010.

Third, we urge the BCBS to develop a simple, transparent, non-model based measure of leverage, as recommended by the G-20 Leaders.

Fourth, we urge the Financial Stability Board (FSB), BCBS, and the Committee on the Global Financial System (CGFS), in coordination with accounting standard setters, to implement by the end of 2009 the G-20's recommendations to mitigate procyclicality, including a requirement for banks to build capital buffers in good times that they can draw down when conditions deteriorate. This is consistent with our proposal in Section I that banks and BHCs should have enough high-quality capital during good economic times to keep them above prudential minimum capital requirements during stressed economic circumstances.

B. Improve the Oversight of Global Financial Markets

We urge national authorities to promote the standardization and improved oversight of credit derivative and other OTC derivative markets, in particular through the use of central counterparties, along the lines of the G-20 commitment, and to advance these goals through international coordination and cooperation.

The G-20 Leaders agreed to promote the standardization and central clearing of credit derivatives and called on industry to develop an action plan in that regard by autumn 2009. Market participants within the United States have already created standardized contracts for use in North America that meet the G-20 commitment. Several central counterparties have also been established globally to clear credit derivatives.

In Section II, we propose regulations for the Over-the-Counter (OTC) derivatives market that go beyond G-20 commitments. Given the global nature of financial markets, the United States must continue to work with our international counterparts to raise international standards for OTC derivatives markets, further integrate our financial market infrastructures, and avoid measures that may result in market fragmentation.

C. Enhance Supervision of Internationally Active Financial Firms

We recommend that the Financial Stability Board (FSB) and national authorities implement G-20 commitments to strengthen arrangements for international cooperation on supervision of global financial firms through establishment and continued operational development of supervisory colleges.

The financial crisis highlighted the need for an ongoing mechanism for cross-border information sharing and collaboration among international regulators of significant global financial institutions.

At the recommendation of the G-20 Leaders, supervisors have established "supervisory colleges" for the thirty most significant global financial institutions. The supervisory colleges for all thirty firms have met at least once. Supervisors will establish additional colleges for other significant cross-border firms. The FSB will review the colleges' activities for lessons learned once the colleges have garnered sufficient experience.

D. Reform Crisis Prevention and Management Authorities and Procedures

We recommend that the BCBS expedite its work to improve cross-border resolution of global financial firms and develop recommendations by the end of 2009. We further urge national authorities to improve information-sharing arrangements and implement the FSB principles for cross-border crisis management.

Cross-Border Resolution of Financial Firms

The current financial crisis has affected banks and nonbank financial firms without regard to their legal structure, domicile, or location of customers. Many of the ailing financial institutions are large, have complex internal structures and activities, and operate in multiple nations. The global financial system is more interconnected than it has ever been.

Currently, neither a common procedure nor a complete understanding exists of how countries can intervene in the failure of a large financial firm and how those actions might interact with resolution efforts of other countries. For instance, countries differ on close-out netting rules for financial transactions or deposits. National regulatory authorities are inclined to protect the assets within their own jurisdictions, even when doing so can have spillover effects for other countries.

Many countries do not have effective systems for resolving bank failures, which has forced policy makers to employ sub-optimal, ad hoc responses to failing financial firms.

As discussed above, the United States already has in place a robust resolution regime for insured depository institutions. Moreover, we are proposing to create a resolution regime that provides sufficient authority to avoid the disorderly resolution of any firm whose failure would have systemic implications.

The G-20 welcomed continued efforts by the International Monetary Fund (IMF), FSB, World Bank, and BCBS to develop an international framework for cross-border bank resolutions.

The United States and its international counterparts should work together to improve mechanisms for the cross-border resolution of financial firms by:

- creating a flexible set of powers for resolution authorities to provide for continuity of systemically significant functions, such as the ability to transfer assets, contracts, and operations to other firms or a bridge institution; the ability to create and operate short-term bridge institutions; the immediate authority to resolve a failed institution; and more predictable and consistent closure thresholds;
- furthering the development of mechanisms for cross-border information sharing among relevant regulatory authorities and increasing the understanding of how the various national resolution regimes for cross-border bank and nonbank financial firms interact with each other;
- implementing reforms to enhance the effectiveness and efficiency of crisis management and resolutions under the currently prevailing 'separate entity' approach. The BCBS should initiate further work on the feasibility and desirability of moving towards the development of methods for allocating the financial burden associated with the failure of large, multinational financial firms to maximize resolution options; and

- further enhancing the effectiveness of existing rules for the clearing and settlement of cross-border financial contracts and large value payments transactions, including by providing options for the maintenance of contractual relationships during insolvency, such as through the bridge institution option available in U.S. bank receivership law.

Crisis Management Principles

National regulators, including U.S. regulators, are implementing the FSB principles for cross-border crisis management endorsed by the G-20 Leaders. The home country regulators for each major international financial institution will be responsible for ensuring that the group of authorities with a common interest in a particular financial institution will meet at least annually.

In addition to the four above-mentioned core priorities, the United States is committed to implementing the rest of the regulatory reform agenda that the G-20 Leaders adopted at their Summit in April. The United States will host the third leaders' summit in Pittsburgh in September 2009, and would like to see progress made on the rest of the issues addressed in the G-20 *Declaration on Strengthening the Financial System,* outlined below.

E. Strengthen the Financial Stability Board

We recommend that the FSB complete its restructuring and institutionalize its new mandate to promote global financial stability by September 2009.

At the London Summit, the G-20 Leaders called for the reconstitution of the FSF, originally created in 1999. The FSF, now called the FSB, expanded its membership to include all G-20 members, and the G-20 Leaders strengthened the FSB's mandate to promote financial stability. Under its strengthened mandate, the FSB will assess financial system vulnerabilities, promote coordination and information exchange among authorities, advise and monitor best practices to meet regulatory standards, set guidelines for and support the establishment of supervisory colleges, and support cross-border crisis management and contingency planning.

F. Strengthen Prudential Regulations

We recommend that the BCBS improve liquidity risk management standards for financial firms and that the FSB work with the Bank for International Settlements (BIS) and standard setters to develop macroprudential tools.

The BCBS and national authorities should develop, by 2010, a global framework for promoting stronger liquidity buffers at financial institutions, including cross-border institutions.

The FSB should work with the BIS and international standard setters to develop macroprudential tools and provide a report to the G-20 by autumn 2009.

G. Expand the Scope of Regulation

1. *Identify Foreign Financial Firms that are Tier 1 FHCs. Determine the appropriate Tier 1 FHC definition and application of requirements for foreign financial firms.*

As discussed above in Section I, we propose that a stricter regime of supervision and regulation apply to Tier 1 FHCs than to other BHCs. This regime should include, among other things, stronger capital, liquidity and risk management standards for Tier 1 FHCs than for other BHCs. Similarly, the G-20 Leaders agreed in April that "all systemically important financial institutions, markets, and instruments should be subject to an appropriate degree of regulation and oversight."

In consultation with Treasury, the Federal Reserve should develop rules to guide the identification of foreign financial firms as Tier 1 FHCs based on whether their U.S. operations pose a threat to financial stability. This evaluation should be similar to that used to identify domestic Tier 1 FHCs. The Federal Reserve could consider applying the criteria to the world-wide operations of the foreign firm. The Federal Reserve could also choose to apply the criteria only to the U.S. operations of the foreign firm or to those operations of the foreign firm that affect the U.S. financial markets. Several options are available for foreign financial firms.

In determining which foreign firms are subject to the Tier 1 FHC regime, the Federal Reserve should give due regard to the principle of national treatment and equality of competitive opportunity between foreign-based firms operating in the United States and U.S.-based firms. The Federal Reserve should also consider the implications of these determinations for international agreements negotiated by the executive branch. Under our proposal, Treasury would not play a role in the application of these rules to specific firms.

In addition, the new "well-capitalized" and "well-managed" tests for FHC status proposed in this report should apply to foreign financial institutions operating in the United States in a manner comparable to that of U.S. owned financial institutions, while taking into account the difference in their legal forms (such as branch) from their U.S. counterparts.

Under the current Gramm Leach Bliley (GLB) Act regime, a foreign bank that owns or controls a U.S. bank must comply with the same requirements as a domestic BHC to achieve FHC status, namely, all the U.S. subsidiary banks of the BHC or foreign bank must be "well-capitalized" and "well-managed." A foreign bank that does not own or control a U.S. bank, but instead operates through a branch, agency, or commercial lending company located in the United States must itself be "well-capitalized" and "well managed" if it elects to become an FHC. If a foreign bank operates in the United States through branches and subsidiary banks, both the foreign parent bank and its U.S. subsidiary bank must be "well-capitalized" and "well-managed" if the foreign bank elects to become an FHC.

Although we propose to change the FHC eligibility requirements in this report, we do not propose to dictate the manner in which those requirements are applied to foreign financial firms with U.S. operations. We propose to permit the Federal Reserve, in consultation with Treasury, to determine how to apply these new requirements to foreign banks that seek FHC status. The Federal Reserve should also make its determination giving due regard to the principle of national treatment and equality of competitive opportunity.

2. *Expand Regulation of Hedge Funds. We urge national authorities to implement by the end of 2009 the G-20 commitment to require hedge funds or their managers to register and disclose appropriate information necessary to assess the systemic risk they pose individually or collectively.*

The G-20 Leaders agreed to require registration of hedge funds or their managers subject to threshold limits and to require hedge funds to disclose appropriate information on an ongoing basis to allow supervisors to assess the systemic risk they pose individually or collectively. Our regulatory reform proposal expands upon the G-20's recommendations to include registration of advisors to other private pools of capital, along with recordkeeping and additional disclosure requirements to investors, creditors and counterparties.

H. Introduce Better Compensation Practices

In line with G-20 commitments, we urge each national authority to put guidelines in place to align compensation with long-term shareholder value and to promote compensation structures do not provide incentives for excessive risk taking. We recommend that the BCBS expediently integrate the FSB principles on compensation into its risk management guidance by the end of 2009.

The financial crisis highlighted the problems associated with compensation structures that do not take into consideration risk and firms' goals over the longer term. In April, the G20 Leaders endorsed the principles on compensation in significant financial institutions developed by the FSB to align compensation structures with firms' long-term goals and prudent risk taking.

Consistent with that commitment, we propose in this report that federal regulators issue standards for compensation practices by banks and BHCs.

I. Promote Stronger Standards in the Prudential Regulation, Money Laundering/Terrorist Financing, and Tax Information Exchange Areas

The United States is committed to working diligently to raise both U.S. and global regulatory standards, improving and coordinating implementation of those standards, and thereby closing geographic regulatory gaps.

In advance of the G-20 London Summit, Secretary Geithner put forward the U.S. "Trifecta" initiative to raise international standards in areas of prudential supervision, tax information exchange, and anti-money laundering/terrorist financing (AML/CFT) through greater use of objective assessments, due diligence, and objective peer reviews. The G-20 London Summit Declaration endorsed the U.S. initiative.

1. *We urge the FSB to expeditiously establish and coordinate peer reviews to assess compliance and implementation of international regulatory standards, with priority attention on the international cooperation elements of prudential regulatory standards.*

    As part of the U.S. initiative, the FSB began joint work with international standard setters (the BCBS, the International Association of Insurance Supervisors, and the International Organization of Securities Commissions—IOSCO) and with the IMF to expand the use of assessments and peer reviews. The FSB and standard setters should build upon existing applicable processes already in use by standard setters in order to assess compliance. The FSB is focusing particular attention on assessing compliance with those standards related to information exchange and international cooperation.

2. *The United States will work to implement the updated International Cooperation Review Group (ICRG) peer review process and work with partners in the Financial*

Action Task Force (FA TF) to address jurisdictions not complying with international anti-money laundering/terrorist financing (AML/CFT) standards.

The International Cooperation Review Group (ICRG) of the Financial Action Task Force (FATF) is responsible for engaging with non-compliant jurisdictions and recommending application of countermeasures by the FATF. The United States is co-chair, with Italy, of the ICRG and is leading efforts to revise and strengthen the procedures used to select jurisdictions for further scrutiny. FATF will finalize the revision of ICRG assessment procedures at its upcoming plenary meeting at the end of June.

J. Improve Accounting Standards

1. *We recommend that the accounting standard setters clarify and make consistent the application of fair value accounting standards, including the impairment of financial instruments, by the end of 2009.*

The G-20 Leaders directed the accounting standard setters to improve the standards for the valuation of financial instruments and to reduce the complexity of financial instrument accounting. The International Accounting Standards Board (IASB) undertook a project to develop by July 2009 a new financial measurement standard that would replace International Accounting Standard (IAS) 39, *Financial Instruments: Recognition and Measurement*, the fair value measurement standard under International Financial Reporting Standards (IFRS), and reduce the complexity of accounting standards.

In addition, the Financial Accounting Standards Board (FASB) and IASB have provided additional guidance on fair value measurement. The standard setters are also evaluating the recommendations provided by the Financial Crisis Advisory Group ("FCAG"), a high level advisory group that standard setters established in December 2008.

In response to FASB's recent changes to its impairment standard for debt securities, the IASB has committed to making improvements to its own impairment requirements as part of its comprehensive financial instrument project, slated for an exposure draft by October 2009. Moreover, the IASB has also committed to work with FASB as part of its comprehensive financial instrument project to promote global consistency in impairment approaches.

2. *We recommend that the accounting standard setters improve accounting standards for loan loss provisioning by the end of 2009 that would make it more forward looking, as long as the transparency of financial statements is not compromised.*

In its April 2009 report addressing procyclicality in the financial system, the FSB determined that earlier recognition of loan losses by financial firms could have reduced the procyclical effect of write-downs in the current crisis. The FSB recommended that the accounting standard setters issue a statement that the current incurred loss approach to loan loss provisions allows for more judgment than banks currently exercise.

The FSB also recommended that the accounting standard setters give consideration to alternative conceptual approaches to loan loss recognition, such as a fair value model, an expected loss model, and dynamic provisioning.

As directed by the FSB and G-20 Leaders, accounting standard setters continue to evaluate the issue of loan loss provisioning, including developing an expected loss model to replace the current incurred loss model.

3. *We recommend that the accounting standard setters make substantial progress by the end of 2009 toward development of a single set of high quality global accounting standards.*

The G-20 Leaders agreed that the accounting standard setters should make substantial progress toward a single set of high quality global accounting standards by the end of 2009. The IASB and FASB have engaged in extensive efforts to converge IFRS and U.S. Generally Accepted Accounting Principles (GAAP) to minimize or eliminate differences in the two sets of accounting standards. Last year, the IASB and FASB reiterated their objective of achieving broad convergence of IFRS and U.S. GAAP by the end of 2010, which is a necessary precondition under the SEC's proposed roadmap to adopt IFRS. Currently, the SEC is considering comments submitted on its proposed roadmap that sets forth several milestones that could lead to the eventual use of IFRS by all U.S. issuers.

K. Tighten Oversight of Credit Rating Agencies

We urge national authorities to enhance their regulatory regimes to effectively oversee credit rating agencies (CRAs), consistent with international standards and the G-20 Leaders' recommendations.

As discussed above, the performance of CRAs, particularly their ratings of mortgage-backed securities and other asset-backed securities, contributed significantly to the financial crisis.

The G-20 Leaders pledged to undertake more effective oversight of the activities of CRAs. Specifically, national authorities should register and oversee all CRAs whose ratings are used for regulatory purposes consistent with the IOSCO Code of Conduct Fundamentals for CRAs by the end of 2009.

Moreover, all national authorities should enforce compliance with their oversight regime to promote adequate practices and procedures for managing conflicts of interest in CRAs and to maintain the transparency and quality of the ratings process. The G-20 Leaders also called for the CRAs to differentiate ratings for structured products and provide full disclosure on performance measures and ratings methodologies.

The U.S. regulatory regime for CRAs is consistent with IOSCO's Code of Conduct for CRAs. Moreover, Treasury proposed, consistent with the G-20's recommendations, that the SEC continue its efforts to tighten the regulation of CRAs along a number of dimensions, including through public disclosures of performance measures and methodologies and better differentiation of structured credit from other credit products.

Given the important role played by CRAs in our financial markets, the United States will continue to work with our international counterparts to promote consistency of national oversight regimes across jurisdictions and that national authorities engage in appropriate information sharing, as called for by the G-20 Leaders.

In: Who Regulates Whom: U.S. Financial Oversight
Editor: Milton H. Lazarus

ISBN: 978-1-60876-981-0
© 2010 Nova Science Publishers, Inc.

Chapter 4

HEDGE FUNDS: OVERVIEW OF REGULATORY OVERSIGHT, COUNTERPARTY RISKS AND INVESTMENT CHALLENGES

Orice M. Williams

WHY GAO DID THIS STUDY

In 2008, GAO issued two reports on hedge funds—pooled investment vehicles that are privately managed and often engage in active trading of various types of securities and commodity futures and options contracts—highlighting the need for continued regulatory attention and for guidance to better inform pension plans on the risks and challenges of hedge fund investments. Hedge funds generally qualified for exemption from certain securities laws and regulations, including the requirement to register as an investment company. Hedge funds have been deeply affected by the recent financial turmoil. But an industry survey of institutional investors suggests that these investors are still committed to investing in hedge funds in the long term. For the first time hedge funds are allowed to borrow from the Federal Reserve under the Term- Asset Backed Loan Facility. As such, the regulatory oversight issues and investment challenges raised by the 2008 reports still remain relevant.

This testimony discusses: (1) federal regulators' oversight of hedge fund-related activities; (2) potential benefits, risks, and challenges pension plans face in investing in hedge funds; (3) the measures investors, creditors, and counterparties have taken to impose market discipline on hedge funds; and (4) the potential for systemic risk from hedge fund- related activities. To do this work we relied upon our issued reports and updated data where possible.

View GAO-09-677T or key components. For more information, contact Orice M. Williams at (202) 512-8678 or williamso@gao.gov.

WHAT GAO FOUND

Under the existing regulatory structure, the Securities and Exchange Commission and Commodity Futures Trading Commission can provide direct oversight of registered hedge fund advisers, and along with federal bank regulators, they monitor hedge fund-related activities conducted at their regulated entities. Although some examinations found that banks generally have strengthened practices for managing risk exposures to hedge funds, regulators recommended that they enhance firmwide risk management systems and practices, including expanded stress testing. The federal government does not specifically limit or monitor private sector plan investment in hedge funds. Under federal law, fiduciaries must comply with a standard of prudence, but no explicit restrictions on hedge funds exist.

Pension plans invest in hedge funds to obtain a number of potential benefits, such as returns greater than the stock market and stable returns on investment. However, hedge funds also pose challenges and risks beyond those posed by traditional investments. For example, some investors may have little information on funds' underlying assets and their values, which limits the opportunity for oversight. Plan representatives said they take steps to mitigate these and other challenges, but doing so requires resources beyond the means of some plans.

According to market participants, hedge fund advisers have improved disclosures and transparency about their operations as a result of industry guidance issued and pressure from investors and creditors and counterparties. Regulators and market participants said that creditors and counterparties have generally conducted more due diligence and tightened their credit standards for hedge funds. However, several factors may limit the effectiveness of market discipline or illustrate failures to properly exercise it. Further, if the risk controls of creditors and counterparties are inadequate, their actions may not prevent hedge funds from taking excessive risk and can contribute to conditions that create systemic risk if breakdowns in market discipline and risk controls are sufficiently severe that losses by hedge funds in turn cause significant losses at key intermediaries or in financial markets.

Financial regulators and industry observers remain concerned about the adequacy of counterparty credit risk management at major financial institutions because it is a key factor in controlling the potential for hedge funds to become a source of systemic risk. Although hedge funds generally add liquidity to many markets, including distressed asset markets, in some circumstances hedge funds' activities can strain liquidity and contribute to financial distress. In response to their concerns regarding the adequacy of counterparty credit risk, a group of regulators had collaborated to examine particular hedge fund-related activities across entities they regulate, and the President's Working Group on Financial Markets (PWG). The PWG also established two private sector committees that recently released guidelines to address systemic risk and investor protection.

Mr. Chairman and Members of the Subcommittee:

I am pleased to be here to participate in today's hearing on hedge funds. A hedge fund is a pooled investment vehicle that is privately managed and often engages in active trading of various types of securities and commodity futures and options. In general, hedge funds qualify for exemption from certain securities laws and regulations, including the requirement to register as an investment company.[1] When we conducted the two studies on hedge funds in

2007, the hedge fund sector was growing in importance and continuing to evolve within the financial system. Hedge funds, largely driven by investments from institutional investors, such as endowments, foundations, insurance companies, and pension plans, seeking to diversify their risks and increase returns, have grown dramatically over the last decade. From 1998 to early 2007, the estimated number of funds grew from more than 3,000 to more than 9,000 and assets under management from $200 billion to more than $2 trillion globally.[2] An estimated $1.5 trillion of these assets is managed by U.S. hedge fund advisers. Hedge funds have significant business relationships with the largest regulated banking organizations. Hedge funds act as trading counterparties for a wide range of over-the-counter derivatives and other financing transactions. They also act as clients through their purchase of clearing and other services and as borrowers through their use of margin loans from prime brokers.

Much has happened in the financial markets since we issued our reports. Hedge funds have been deeply affected in the financial turmoil. According to an industry survey, most hedge fund strategies produced double-digit losses in 2008 and hedge funds saw approximately $70 billion in redemptions between June and November 2008.[3] Some observers blamed hedge funds for dramatic volatility in the stock and commodity markets last year and some funds of hedge funds were heavily invested in the alleged Madoff fraud. Nevertheless, an industry survey of institutional investors suggests that these investors are still committed to investing in hedge funds in the long term.[4] Financial regulators' views on hedge funds appear to be shifting as well, perhaps signaling recognition that hedge funds have become an integral part of the financial markets. For example, hedge funds are allowed to borrow from the Federal Reserve for the first time under the Term Asset-Backed Securities Loan Facility (TALF) intended to support consumer credit. While the Federal Reserve Chairman and Treasury Secretary have supported the position of enhanced market discipline over stricter regulation of hedge funds in 2007, Treasury has recently called for greater regulatory oversight of hedge funds. Despite changes surrounding the hedge fund sector, the issues and concerns related to regulatory oversight of hedge funds and challenges posed by hedge fund investing that were raised in our 2008 reports remain relevant today.

This statement is based on our January 24, 2008 and August 14, 2008 reports.[5] Specifically, I will discuss: (1) the oversight of hedge fund-related activities provided by federal financial regulators under their existing authorities; (2) the potential benefits, risks, and challenges pension plans face in investing in hedge funds; (3) the measures investors, creditors, and counterparties have taken to impose market discipline on hedge funds; and (4) the potential for systemic risk from hedge fund-related activities and actions regulators have taken to address this risk.

To do this work, we reviewed and analyzed relevant regulatory examination documentation and enforcement cases from federal financial regulators. We also analyzed relevant laws and regulations, survey data, speeches, testimonies, studies, and industry protocols and guidelines about private pools of capital. In addition, we interviewed officials representing various U.S. regulators, as well as representatives from market participants such as commercial and investment banks, large hedge funds, pension industry participants, credit rating agencies, a risk management firm, trade groups representing hedge funds and institutional investors, and academics. We conducted these performance audits from September 2006 to August 2008 in accordance with generally accepted government auditing standards. Those standards require that we plan and perform the audit to obtain sufficient, appropriate evidence to provide a reasonable basis for our findings and conclusions based on our audit objectives. We believe that the evidence obtained provides a reasonable basis for our findings and conclusions based on our audit objectives.

SUMMARY

Under the existing regulatory structure, the Securities and Exchange Commission's (SEC) ability to directly oversee hedge fund advisers is limited to those that are required to register or voluntarily register with SEC as an investment advisor. Examinations of registered advisers raised concerns in areas such as disclosure, reporting and filing, personal trading, and asset valuation. SEC also oversees some of the securities firms that engage in significant hedge fund-related activities. The Commodity Futures Trading Commission (CFTC) regulates those hedge fund advisers who are registered as registered as commodity pool operators (CPO) or commodity trading advisors (CTA). Federal banking regulators monitor hedge fund-related activities conducted at their regulated entities.[6] Although some examinations found that banks generally have strengthened practices for managing risk exposures to hedge funds since the 1998 near collapse of Long-Term Capital Management (LTCM), a large highly leveraged hedge fund, regulators recommended that they enhance firmwide risk management systems and practices, including expanded stress testing.[7] Regulated entities have the responsibility to practice prudent risk management standards, but prudent standards do not guarantee prudent practices. As such, it will be important for regulators to show continued vigilance in overseeing the hedge fund-related activities of regulated institutions. The federal government does not specifically limit or monitor private sector plan investment in hedge funds, and state approaches to public plans vary. Under federal law, fiduciaries must comply with a standard of prudence, but no explicit restrictions on hedge funds exist.

Pension plans invest in hedge funds in order to achieve one or more of several goals, including steadier, less volatile returns, obtaining returns greater than those expected in the stock market, or diversification of portfolio investments. Nonetheless, hedge fund investments pose investment challenges beyond those posed by traditional investments in stocks and bonds. For example, some investors may have little information on funds' underlying assets and their values, which limits the opportunity for oversight. Plan officials and others described steps plans can take to address these challenges. However, they said that some of these steps require considerably greater effort and expertise from fiduciaries than is required for more traditional investments, and such steps may be beyond the capabilities of some pension plans, particularly smaller ones.

According to market participants, hedge fund advisers had improved disclosures and transparency about their operations since LTCM as a result of industry guidance issued and pressure from investors and creditors and counterparties (such as prime brokers), but noted limitations. Regulators and market participants also said that creditors and counterparties had generally conducted more due diligence and tightened their credit standards for hedge funds. However, several factors may limit the effectiveness of market discipline or illustrate failures to properly exercise it. For example, because most large hedge funds use multiple prime brokers as service providers, no one broker may have all the data necessary to assess the total leverage of a hedge fund client. Further, if the risk controls of creditors and counterparties are inadequate, their actions may not prevent hedge funds from taking excessive risk. These factors can contribute to conditions that create systemic risk if breakdowns in market discipline and risk controls are sufficiently severe that losses by hedge funds in turn cause significant losses at key intermediaries or instability in financial markets.

Financial regulators and industry observers remained concerned about the adequacy of counterparty credit risk management at major financial institutions because it is a key factor in controlling the potential for hedge funds to become a source of systemic risk. Although hedge funds generally add liquidity to many markets, including distressed asset markets, in some circumstances hedge funds' activities can strain liquidity and contribute to financial distress. For example, the concentration created by numerous market participants establishing large positions on the same side of a trade, especially in combination with a high degree of leverage, can contribute to a liquidity crisis if market conditions compel traders to simultaneously unwind their positions. In response to their concerns regarding the adequacy of counterparty credit risk, a group of regulators had collaborated to examine particular hedge fund-related activities across entities they regulate, mainly through international multilateral efforts and the President's Working Group on Financial Markets (PWG).[8] The PWG also has established two private sector committees to identify best practices to address systemic risk and investor protection, which released reports for comments in 2008 and issued final reports in 2009 respectively.

HEDGE FUNDS GENERALLY ARE SUBJECT TO LIMITED DIRECT OVERSIGHT AND THE FEDERAL GOVERNMENT DOES NOT SPECIFICALLY LIMIT OR MONITOR PRIVATE SECTOR PLANS' INVESTMENTS IN HEDGE FUNDS

SEC's ability to directly oversee hedge fund advisers is limited to those that are required to register or voluntarily register with SEC as investment advisers. Registered hedge fund advisers are subject to the same disclosure requirements as all other registered investment advisers. These advisers must provide current information to both SEC and investors about their business practices and disciplinary history. Advisers also must maintain required books and records, and are subject to periodic examinations by SEC staff. Meanwhile, hedge funds, like other investors in publicly traded securities, are subject to various regulatory reporting requirements. For example, upon acquiring a 5 percent beneficial ownership position of a particular publicly traded security, a hedge fund may be required to file a report disclosing its holdings with SEC.[9]

In December 2004, SEC adopted an amendment to Rule 203(b)(3)-1, which had the effect of requiring certain hedge fund advisers that previously enjoyed the private adviser exemption from registration to register with SEC as investment advisers. In June 2006, a federal court vacated the 2004 amendment to Rule 203(b)(3)-1.[10] According to SEC, when the rule was in effect (from February 1, 2006, through August 21, 2006), SEC was better able to identify hedge fund advisers. In August 2006, SEC estimated that 2,534 advisers that sponsored at least one hedge fund were registered with the agency. Since August 2006, SEC's ability to identify an adviser that manages a hedge fund has been further limited due to changes in filing requirements and to advisers that chose to retain registered status. As of

April 2007, 488, or about 19 percent of the 2,534 advisers, had withdrawn their registrations. At the same time, 76 new registrants were added and some others changed their filing status, leaving an estimated 1,991 hedge fund advisers registered. While the list of registered hedge fund advisers is not all-inclusive, many of the largest hedge fund advisers—including 49 of the largest 78 U.S. hedge fund advisers—are registered. These 49 hedge fund advisers account for approximately $492 billion of assets under management, or about 33 percent of the estimated $1.5 trillion in hedge fund assets under management in the United States. In an April 2009 speech, Chairman Schapiro stated that there are approximately 150 active hedge fund investigations at SEC, some of which include possible Ponzi schemes, misappropriations, and performance smoothing. In a separate speech in April, Chairman Schapiro renewed SEC's call for greater oversight of hedge funds, including the registration of hedge fund advisers and potentially the hedge funds themselves.

SEC uses a risk-based examination approach to select investment advisers for inspections. Under this approach, higher-risk investment advisers are examined every 3 years. One of the variables in determining risk level is the amount of assets under management. SEC officials told us that most hedge funds, even the larger ones, do not meet the dollar threshold to be automatically considered higher-risk. In fiscal year 2006, SEC examined 321 hedge fund advisers and identified issues (such as information disclosure, reporting and filing, personal trading, and asset valuation) that are not exclusive to hedge funds. Also, from 2004 to 2008, SEC oversaw the large internationally active securities firms on a consolidated basis.[11] These securities firms have significant interaction with hedge funds through affiliates previously not overseen by SEC. One aspect of this program was to examine how the securities firms manage various risk exposures, including those from hedge fund-related activities such as providing prime brokerage services and acting as creditors and counterparties. SEC found areas where capital computation methodology and risk management practices can be improved.

Similarly, CFTC regulates those hedge fund advisers registered as CPOs or CTAs. CFTC has authorized the National Futures Association (NFA), a self-regulatory organization for the U.S. futures industry, to conduct day- to-day monitoring of registered CPOs and CTAs. In fiscal year 2006, NFA examinations of CPOs included six of the largest U.S. hedge fund advisers. In addition, SEC, CFTC, and bank regulators can use their existing authorities—to establish capital standards and reporting requirements, conduct risk-based examinations, and take enforcement actions—to oversee activities, including those involving hedge funds, of broker- dealers, of futures commission merchants, and of banks, respectively.

While none of the regulators we interviewed specifically monitored hedge fund activities on an ongoing basis, generally regulators had increased reviews—by such means as targeted examinations—of systems and policies to mitigate counterparty credit risk at the large regulated entities. For instance, from 2004 to 2007, the Federal Reserve Bank of New York (FRBNY) had conducted various reviews—including horizontal reviews— of credit risk management practices that involved hedge fund-related activities at several large banks.[12] On the basis of the results, FRBNY noted that the banks generally had strengthened practices for managing risk exposures to hedge funds, but the banks could further enhance firmwide risk management systems and practices, including expanded stress testing.

The federal government does not specifically limit or monitor private sector pension investment in hedge funds and, while some states do so for public plans, their approaches vary. Although the Employee Retirement and Income Security Act (ERISA) governs the investment practices of private sector pension plans, neither federal law nor regulation specifically limit pension investment in hedge funds or private equity. Instead, ERISA requires that plan fiduciaries apply a "prudent man" standard, including diversifying assets and minimizing the risk of large losses. The prudent man standard does not explicitly prohibit investment in any specific category of investment. The standard focuses on the process for making investment decisions, requiring documentation of the investment decisions, due diligence, and ongoing monitoring of any managers hired to invest plan assets. Plan fiduciaries are expected to meet general standards of prudent investing and no specific restrictions on investments in hedge funds or private equity have been established. The Department of Labor is tasked with helping to ensure plan sponsors meet their fiduciary duties; however, it does not currently provide any guidance specific to pension plan investments in hedge funds or private equity.

Conversely, some states specifically regulate and monitor public sector pension investment in hedge funds, but these approaches vary from state to state. While states generally have adopted a "prudent man" standard similar to that in ERISA, some states also explicitly restrict or prohibit pension plan investment in hedge funds or private equity. For instance, in Massachusetts, the agency overseeing public plans will not permit plans with less than $250 million in total assets to invest directly in hedge funds. Some states have detailed lists of authorized investments that exclude hedge funds and/or private equity. Other states may limit investment in certain investment vehicles or trading strategies employed by hedge fund or private equity fund managers. While some guidance exists for hedge fund investors, specific guidance aimed at pension plans could serve as an additional tool for plan fiduciaries when assessing whether and to what degree hedge funds would be a prudent investment.

PENSION PLANS SEEK VARIOUS INVESTMENT OBJECTIVES THROUGH HEDGE FUNDS, AND SUCH INVESTMENTS POSE CHALLENGES THAT REQUIRE CONSIDERABLE EFFORT AND EXPERTISE TO ADDRESS

According to several 2006 and 2007 surveys of private and public sector plans, investments in hedge funds are typically a small portion of total plan assets—about 4 to 5 percent on average—but a considerable and growing number of plans invest in them.[13] Updates to the surveys indicated that institutional investors plan to continue to invest in hedge funds. One 2008 survey reported that nearly half of over 200 plans surveyed had hedge funds and hedge-fund-type strategies. This was a large increase when compared to the previous survey when 80 percent of the funds had no hedge fund exposure.[14] Pension plans' investments in hedge funds n part were a response to stock market declines and disenchantment with traditional investment management in recent years. Officials with most of the plans we contacted indicated that they invested in hedge funds, at least in part, to reduce the volatility of returns. Several pension plan officials told us that they sought to obtain returns greater than the returns of the overall stock market through at least some of their hedge fund investments. Officials of pension plans that we contacted also stated that hedge funds are used to help diversify their overall portfolio and provide a vehicle that will, to some degree, be uncorrelated with the other investments in their portfolio. This reduced correlation was viewed as having a number of benefits, including reduction in overall portfolio volatility and risk.

While any plan investment may fail to deliver expected returns over time, hedge fund investments pose investment challenges beyond those posed by traditional investments in stocks and bonds. These include the reliance on the skill of hedge fund managers, who often have broad latitude to engage in complex investment techniques that can involve various financial instruments in various financial markets; use of leverage, which amplifies both potential gains and losses; and higher fees, which require a plan to earn a higher gross return to achieve a higher net return. In addition to investment challenges, hedge funds pose additional challenges, including: (1) limited information on a hedge fund's underlying assets and valuation (limited transparency); (2) contract provisions which limit an investor's ability to redeem an investment in a hedge fund for a defined period of time (limited liquidity); and (3) the possibility that a hedge fund's active or risky trading activity will result in losses due to operational failure such as trading errors or outright fraud (operational risk).

Pension plans that invest in hedge funds take various steps to mitigate the risks and challenges posed by hedge fund investing, including developing a specific investment purpose and strategy, negotiating important investment terms, conducting due diligence, and investing through funds of funds. Such steps require greater effort, expertise and expense than required for more traditional investments. As a result, according to plan officials, state and federal regulators, and others, some pension plans, especially smaller plans, may not be equipped to address the various demands of hedge fund investing.

INVESTORS, CREDITORS, AND COUNTERPARTIES HAVE INCREASED EFFORTS TO IMPOSE DISCIPLINE ON HEDGE FUND ADVISERS, BUT SOME LIMITATIONS REMAIN

Investors, creditors, and counterparties have the power to impose market discipline—rewarding well-managed hedge funds and reducing their exposure to risky, poorly managed hedge funds—during due diligence exercises and through ongoing monitoring. Creditors and counterparties also can impose market discipline through ongoing management of credit terms (such as collateral requirements). According to market participants doing business with larger hedge funds, hedge fund advisers have improved disclosure and become more transparent about their operations, including risk management practices, partly as a result of recent increases in investments by institutional investors with fiduciary responsibilities, such as pension plans, and guidance provided by regulators and industry groups.

Despite the requirement that fund investors be sophisticated, some market participants suggested that not all prospective investors have the capacity or retain the expertise to analyze the information they receive from hedge funds, and some may choose to invest in a hedge fund largely as a result of its prior returns and may fail to fully evaluate its risks. Since the near collapse of LTCM in 1998, investors, creditors, and counterparties have increased their efforts to impose market discipline on hedge funds. Regulators and market participants also said creditors and counterparties have been conducting more extensive due diligence and monitoring risk exposures to their hedge fund clients since LTCM. The creditors and counterparties we interviewed said that they have exercised market discipline by tightening their credit standards for hedge funds and demanding greater disclosure.

However, regulators and market participants also identified issues that limit the effectiveness of market discipline or illustrate failures to properly exercise it. For example, most large hedge funds use multiple prime brokers as service providers. Thus, no one broker may have all the data necessary to assess the total leverage used by a hedge fund client. In addition, the actions of creditors and counterparties may not fully prevent hedge funds from taking excessive risk if these creditors' and counterparties' risk controls are inadequate. For example, the risk controls may not keep pace with the increasing complexity of financial instruments and investment strategies that hedge funds employ. Similarly, regulators have been concerned that in competing for hedge fund clients, creditors sometimes relaxed credit standards. These factors can contribute to conditions that create the potential for systemic risk if breakdowns in market discipline and the risk controls of creditors and counterparties are sufficiently severe that losses by hedge funds in turn cause significant losses at key intermediaries or instability in financial markets.

REGULATORS VIEW HEDGE FUND ACTIVITIES AS POTENTIAL SOURCES OF SYSTEMIC RISK AND ARE TAKING MEASURES TO ENHANCE MARKET DISCIPLINE AND PREPARE FOR FINANCIAL DISRUPTIONS

Although financial regulators and market participants recognize that the enhanced efforts by investors, creditors, and counterparties since LTCM impose greater market discipline on hedge funds, some remain concerned that hedge funds' activities are a potential source of systemic risk. Counterparty credit risk arises when hedge funds enter into transactions, including derivatives contracts, with regulated financial institutions.[15] Some regulators regard counterparty credit risk as the primary channel for potentially creating systemic risk. At the time of our work in 2007, financial regulators said that the market discipline imposed by investors, creditors, and counterparties is the most effective mechanism for limiting the systemic risk from the activities of hedge funds (and other private pools of capital). The most important providers of market discipline are the large, global commercial and investment banks that are hedge funds' principal creditors and counterparties. As part of the credit extension process, creditors and counterparties typically require hedge funds to post collateral that can be sold in the event of default. OCC officials told us that losses at their supervised banks due to the extension of credit to hedge funds were rare. Similarly, several prime brokers told us that losses from hedge fund clients were extremely rare due to the asset-based lending they provided such funds. While regulators and others recognize that counterparty credit risk management has improved since LTCM, the ability of financial institutions to maintain the adequacy of these management processes in light of the dramatic growth in hedge fund activities remained a particular focus of concern.

In addition to counterparty credit risk, other factors such as trading behavior can create conditions that contribute to systemic risk. Given certain market conditions, the simultaneous liquidation of similar positions by hedge funds that hold large positions on the same side of a trade could lead to losses or a liquidity crisis that might aggravate financial distress.

Recognizing that market discipline cannot eliminate the potential systemic risk posed by hedge funds and others, regulators have been taking steps to better understand the potential for systemic risk and respond more effectively to financial disruptions that can spread across markets. For instance, they have examined particular hedge fund activities across regulated entities, mainly through international multilateral efforts. The PWG has issued guidelines that provide a framework for addressing risks associated with hedge funds and implemented protocols to respond to market turmoil. Finally, in September 2007, the PWG formed two private sector committees comprising hedge fund advisers and investors to address investor protection and systemic risk concerns, including counterparty credit risk management issues. On January 15, 2009, these two committees, the Asset Managers' Committee and the Investors' Committee, released their final best practices reports to hedge fund managers and investors. The final best practices for the asset managers establishes a framework on five aspects of the hedge fund business— disclosure, valuation of assets, risk management, business operations, compliance and conflicts of interest—to help hedge fund managers take a comprehensive approach to adopting best practices and serve as the foundation upon which those best practices are established. The final best practices for investors include a Fiduciary's Guide, which provides recommendations to individuals charged with evaluating the appropriateness of hedge funds as a component of an investment portfolio, and an Investor's Guide, which provides recommendations to those charged with executing and administering a hedge fund program if one is added to the investment portfolio.

In closing, I would like to include a final thought. It is likely that hedge funds will continue to be a source of capital and liquidity in financial markets, by providing financing to new companies, industries and markets, as well as a source of investments for institutional investors. Given our recent experience with the financial crisis, it is important that regulators have the information to monitor the activities of market participants that play a prominent role in the financial system, such as hedge funds, to protect investors and manage systemic risk.

Mr. Chairman, this completes my prepared statement. I would be happy to respond to any questions you or other Members of the Subcommittee may have at this time.

End Notes

[1] To avoid being required to register as an investment company under the Investment Company Act of 1940 (Investment Company Act), hedge funds typically rely on sections 3(c)(1) or 3(c)(7) of that act. Hedge fund advisers also typically satisfy the "private manager" exemption from registration under section 203(b)(3) of the Investments Advisers Act of 1940 (Advisers Act).

[2] By comparison, assets under management in the mutual fund industry grew from about $5.5 trillion in 1998 to about $10.4 trillion in 2006.

[3] Greenwich Associates and SEI Knowledge Partnership, *Hedge Funds Under the Microscope: Examining Institutional Commitment in Challenging Times* (January 2009).

[4] SEI Knowledge Partnership and Greenwich Associates, *Hedge Funds Under the Microscope.*

[5] GAO, *Hedge Funds: Regulators and Market Participants Are Taking Steps to Strengthen Market Discipline, but Continued Attention Is Needed,* GAO-08-200 (Washington, D.C. Jan. 24, 2008) and *Defined Benefit Pension Plans: Guidance Needed to Better Inform Plans of the Challenges and Risks of Investing in Hedge Funds and Private Equity,* GAO-08-692 (Washington, D.C. Aug. 14, 2008)

[6] Banking regulators include the Office of the Comptroller of the Currency (OCC), Board of Governors of the Federal Reserve System (Federal Reserve), and Federal Deposit Insurance Corporation (FDIC).

[7] Inadequate market discipline is often cited as a contributing factor to the near collapse in 1998 of LTCM.

[8] The PWG was established by Executive Order 12631, signed on March 18, 1988. The Secretary of the Treasury chairs the PWG, the other members of which are the chairpersons of the Board of Governors of the Federal

Reserve System, Securities and Exchange Commission, and Commodity Futures Trading Commission. The group was formed in 1988 to enhance the integrity, efficiency, orderliness, and competitiveness of the U.S. financial markets and maintain the public's confidence in those markets.

[9] Under the Securities Act of 1933, a public offering or sale of securities must be registered with SEC, unless otherwise exempted. In order to exempt an offering or sale of hedge fund shares (ownership interests) to investors from registration under the Securities Act of 1933, most hedge funds restrict their sales to accredited investors in compliance with the safe harbor requirements of Rule 506 of Regulation D. See 15 U.S.C. § 77d and § 77e; 17 C.F.R. § 230.506 (2007). Such investors must meet certain wealth and income thresholds. SEC generally has proposed a rule that would raise the accredited investor qualification standards for individual investors (natural persons) from $1 million in net worth to $2.5 million in investments. See *Revisions to Limited Offering Exemptions in Regulation D*, 72 Fed. Reg. 45116 (Aug. 10, 2007) (proposed rules and request for additional comments). In addition, hedge funds typically limit the number of investors to fewer than 500, so as not to fall within the purview of Section 12(g) of the Securities Exchange Act of 1934, which requires the registration of any class of equity securities (other than exempted securities) held of record by 500 or more persons. 15 U.S.C. § 78l(g).

[10] See *Goldstein v. Securities and Exchange Commission*, 451 F.3d 873 (D.C. Cir. 2006). In Goldstein, the U.S. Circuit Court of Appeals for the District of Columbia held that SEC's hedge fund rule was arbitrary because it departed, without reasonable justification, from SEC's long-standing interpretation of the term "client" in the private adviser exemption as referring to the hedge fund itself, and not to the individual investors in the fund. See footnote 19, supra, for a description of the private adviser exemption from registration under the Advisers Act.

[11] In September 2008, SEC ended the Consolidated Supervised Entities program, created in 2004 as a way for global investment bank conglomerates that lack a supervisor under law to voluntarily submit to regulation. The agency plans for enhancing SEC oversight of the broker-dealer subsidiaries of bank holding companies regulated by the Federal Reserve, based on a Memorandum of Understanding between the two agencies.

[12] A horizontal review is a coordinated supervisory review of a specific activity, business line, or risk management practice conducted across a group of peer institutions.

[13] We reviewed data from surveys of defined benefit pension plans conducted by three organizations—Greenwich Associates (covering mid- to large-size pension plans, with $250 million or more in total assets), Pyramis Global Advisors (covering mid- to large-size pension plans, with $200 million or more in total assets), and *Pensions & Investments* (limited to large plans, which generally had $1 billion or more in total assets). Greenwich Associates is an institutional financial services consulting and research firm; Pyramis Global Advisors, a division of Fidelity Investments, is an institutional asset management firm; and *Pensions & Investments* is a money management industry publication. These data cannot be generalized to all plans.

[14] Pyramis Global Advisers. *Pyramis Defined Benefit Survey Shows Institutional Investors Seek Balance in a Volatile World*, October, 2008

[15] Counterparty credit risk is the risk that a loss will be incurred if a counterparty to a transaction does not fulfill its financial obligations in a timely manner.

In: Who Regulates Whom: U.S. Financial Oversight
Editor: Milton H. Lazarus

ISBN: 978-1-60876-981-0
© 2010 Nova Science Publishers, Inc.

Chapter 5

HEDGE FUNDS: SHOULD THEY BE REGULATED?

Mark Jickling

SUMMARY

In an echo of the Robber Baron Era, the late 20th century saw the rise of a new elite class, who made their fortunes not in steel, oil, or railroads, but in financial speculation. These gilded few are the managers of a group of private, unregulated investment partnerships, called hedge funds. Deploying their own capital and that of well-to-do investors, successful hedge fund managers frequently (but not consistently) outperform public mutual funds. Hedge funds use many different investment strategies, but the largest and best-known funds engage in high-risk speculation in markets around the world. Wherever there is financial volatility, the hedge funds will probably be there.

Hedge funds can also lose money very quickly. In 1998, one fund—Long-Term Capital Management—saw its capital shrink from about $4 billion to a few hundred million in a matter of weeks. To prevent default, the Federal Reserve engineered a rescue by 13 large commercial and investment banks. Intervention was thought necessary because the fund's failure might have caused widespread disruption in financial markets. Despite the risks, investors poured money into hedge funds in recent years, until market losses in 2008 prompted a wave of redemption requests.

In view of the growing impact of hedge funds on a variety of financial markets, the Securities and Exchange Commission (SEC) in October 2004 adopted a regulation that required hedge funds to register as investment advisers, disclose basic information about their operations, and open their books for inspection. The regulation took effect in February 2006, but on June 23, 2006, a court challenge was upheld and the rule was vacated. In December 2006, the SEC proposed raising the "accredited investor" standard—to be permitted to invest in hedge funds, an investor would need $2.5 million in assets, instead of $1 million, but has yet to adopt a final rule.

Bills before the 111th Congress would require hedge funds to register with the SEC if their capital exceeded $50 million (S. 344) or $25 million (H.R. 711). S. 1276 would require registration of hedge funds, private equity firms, and venture capital funds, and would authorize the SEC to collect systemic risk data from them. H.R. 712 mandates more disclosure for pension funds that invest in hedge funds, and H.R. 713 directs the President's Working Group on Financial Markets to study the hedge fund industry. S. 506 and H.R. 1265 would change the tax treatment of offshore funds.

INTRODUCTION

Hedge funds are essentially unregulated mutual funds. They are pools of invested money that buy and sell stocks and bonds and many other assets, including foreign currencies, precious metals, commodities, and derivatives. Some funds follow narrowly-defined investment strategies (e.g., investing only in mortgage bonds, or East Asian stock markets), while others, the so-called macro funds, invest their capital in any market in the world where the fund managers see opportunities for profit.

Hedge funds are structured to avoid SEC regulation. To avoid becoming public issuers of securities, subject to extensive disclosure requirements, they accept funds only from "accredited investors," defined by SEC regulations as persons with assets of $1 million or more.

Hedge funds also avail themselves of statutory exemptions in the Investment Company Act of 1940, which governs public mutual funds. Mutual funds must comply with a comprehensive set of regulations designed to protect small, unsophisticated investors. These regulations include limits on the use of borrowed money, strict record keeping and reporting rules, capital structure requirements, mandated adherence to specified investment goals and strategies, bonding requirements, and a requirement that shareholder approval be obtained (through proxy solicitation) for certain fund business. An investment company becomes subject to this regulation only if it has 100 or more shareholders; hedge funds therefore generally limit themselves to 99 investors. (The National Securities Market Improvement Act of 1996 (P.L. 104-290) broadened this exemption by permitting hedge funds to have an unlimited number of partners, provided that each is a "qualified purchaser" with at least $5 million in total invested assets.)

Most hedge funds are structured as limited partnerships, with a few general partners who also serve as investment managers. Hedge fund managers are often ex-employees of large securities firms, who strike out on their own in search perhaps of greater entrepreneurial freedom and certainly in search of greater financial rewards. Those rewards, even by Wall Street standards, can be extremely high. In addition to the return on his or her own capital, the typical hedge fund manager takes 1 5%-25% of all profits earned by the fund *plus* an annual management fee of 1%- 2% of total fund assets.

Data on hedge funds are available from several private sources, but estimates as to the size of the hedge fund universe vary considerably. Before the financial crisis that began in 2007, estimates were in the range of 8,000-9,000 funds, with about $2 trillion in assets under management. Large numbers of funds have closed as a result of severe losses in the bear markets of 2008; George Soros, one of the best-known hedge fund managers, has estimated that the value of capital under management may shrink by 75%.[1]

Starting a hedge fund is relatively simple, and, with a few quarters of good results, new hedge fund managers can attract capital and thrive on performance and management fees.

Because many of them make risky investments in search of high returns, hedge funds also have a high mortality rate. Studies find that the rate of attrition for funds is about 20% per year, and that the average life span is about three years.[2]

PERFORMANCE: CAN HEDGE FUNDS BEAT THE MARKET?

Estimates of the average annual return earned by hedge funds differ. Some studies find that they generally outperform common benchmarks such as the Standard & Poor's 500, but others conclude that they have lagged. The short life span of many funds creates obvious difficulties for measurement, including a strong survivorship bias: the many funds that shut down each year are not included in return calculations. Annual return figures of course conceal a wide variation from year to year and from fund to fund. In any period, the law of averages dictates that at least a few funds will do extremely well. These success stories may explain the continued popularity of hedge funds with investors, despite the high fees that they charge, and the high risk of loss.

THE LONG-TERM CAPITAL MANAGEMENT CASE

Hedge funds are understood to be high risk/high return operations, where investors must be prepared for losses. Investors who accept the risks are seeking high returns or a means to diversify their portfolio risk. As long as these investors are sophisticated and wealthy, as current law requires, hedge fund losses or even failures should not be a public policy concern. However, a 1998 case provided an exception to this rule.

Long-Term Capital Management (LTCM), a fund headquartered in Connecticut and chartered in the Cayman Islands, opened in 1994 and produced annual returns of over 40% through 1996. It was billed as a "market-neutral" fund, that is, its positions were based not on predictions of the direction of interest rates or other variables, but on the persistence of historical price relationships, or spreads, among different types of bonds. In 1998, however, turmoil in world markets, stemming from financial crises in Asia and Russia, proved to be too much for its computer models: during the month of August 1998 alone, the fund lost almost $2 billion, or about half its capital. By late September, LTCM was on the verge of collapse, whereupon the New York Fed stepped in and "facilitated" a rescue package of $3.6 billion cash contributed by 13 private financial institutions, who became 90% owners of the fund's portfolio.

Why was government intervention needed? The Fed cited concerns about systemic risk to the world's financial markets—while LTCM's capital was a relatively modest $3-4 billion (during the first half of 1998), it had borrowed extensively from a broad range of financial institutions, domestic and foreign, so that the total value of its securities holdings was estimated to be about $80-$100 billion. In addition, the fund supplemented its holdings of stocks and bonds with complex and extensive derivatives positions, magnifying the total exposure of the fund's creditors and counterparties, and making the effect of a general collapse and default difficult to gauge. If the fund (or its creditors) had tried to liquidate its assets and unwind its derivative positions in the troubled market conditions that prevailed, the result might have been extreme price drops and high volatility, with a negative impact on firms not directly involved with LTCM.

Critics of the Fed's action expressed concerns about moral hazard—if market participants believe they will be rescued from their mistakes (because they are "too big to fail"), they may take imprudent risks. To the Fed, however, the immediate dangers of system-wide damage to financial markets, and possibly to the real economy as well, clearly outweighed the risks of creating perceptions of an expanded federal safety net.

POLICY CONCERNS

In the wake of the Long-Term Capital Management episode, systemic risk emerged as the major policy issue raised by hedge funds. The funds had demonstrated an ability to raise large sums of money from wealthy individuals and institutions, and to leverage those sums, by borrowing and through the use of derivatives, until they become so large that even U.S. financial markets may be at risk if they fail. Not all hedge funds borrow heavily and not all follow high-risk strategies. But many do, and there is no reason to think that other hedge funds will not amass positions as large and complex as LTCM's. In time, some of them can be expected to suffer equally spectacular losses. The systemic risk concerns may be summarized as follows:

- failing funds may sell billions of dollars of securities at a time when the liquidity to absorb them is not present, causing markets to "seize up";
- lenders to hedge funds, including federally insured banks, may suffer serious losses when funds default—LTCM raised questions about their ability to evaluate the risks lending to hedge funds;
- default on derivatives contracts may disrupt markets and may threaten hedge fund counterparties in ways that are hard to predict, given the lack of comprehensive regulatory supervision over derivative instruments; and
- since little information about hedge fund portfolios and trading strategies is publicly available, uncertainty regarding the solvency of hedge funds or their lenders and trading partners may exacerbate panic in the markets.

LTCM illustrates the dangers of hedge fund failure. However, the funds' successes can also worry policymakers and regulators. Particularly in foreign exchange markets, manipulation by hedge funds has been blamed as a cause of instability (e.g., the European currency crises in the early 1990s and the Asian devaluations of 1997-1998). Hedge funds and other speculators can borrow a currency and sell it, hoping to profit if the currency is devalued (allowing them to repay with cheaper money). If the size of these sales or short positions is significant in relation to the target country's foreign currency reserves, pressure to devalue can become intense. To defend the currency's value may call for painful steps such as sharp increases in domestic interest rates, which have negative effects on the stock market and economic growth.

In the United States, which has not been the target of such speculative raids, many argue that blaming hedge funds for crises is like shooting the messenger who brings bad news, and that speculators' profit opportunities are often created by bad economic policies. The effect of speculation on price volatility is an unresolved question in finance. While there has never been a conclusive demonstration that speculation *causes* volatility, the two are frequently observed together. Hedge funds, as the most visible agents of speculation in today's global markets, are looked upon by some regulators and market participants with a fair amount of suspicion.

POLICY RESPONSES AND PROPOSALS

In April 1999, the President's Working Group on Financial Markets, which includes the Fed, the SEC, the CFTC, and Treasury, issued a report on hedge funds.[3] The report cites the LTCM case as demonstrating that a single excessively-leveraged institution can pose a threat to other institutions and to the financial system, and found that the proprietary trading operations of commercial and investment banks follow the same strategies in the same markets as the hedge funds, and they are much larger and often more highly-leveraged. The general issue, then, is how to constrain excessive leverage.

The Working Group concluded that more disclosure of financial information by hedge funds was desirable. The report recommended that large funds be required to publish annual disclosure statements containing a "snapshot" of their portfolios and a comprehensive estimate of the riskiness of the fund's position, and that public companies and financial institutions should include in their quarterly and annual reports a statement of their financial exposure to hedge funds and other highly-leveraged entities.

In 2003, in response to continued rapid growth in hedge fund investment, an SEC staff report recommended that hedge funds be required to register as investment advisers.[4] The staff set out several benefits to mandatory registration:

- funds registered as investment advisers would become subject to regular examinations, permitting early detection and deterrence of fraud;
- the SEC would gain basic information about hedge fund investments and strategies in markets where they may have a significant impact; and
- the SEC could require registered hedge funds to adopt uniform standards and improve disclosures they make to their investors.

On October 26, 2004, the SEC adopted (by a 3-2 vote) a rule to require hedge funds to register under the Investment Advisers Act.[5] The rule was controversial: opponents argued that hedge fund investors are sophisticated and know the risks, that the SEC already has authority to pursue hedge fund fraud, that systemic risk concerns are overstated, and that instead of trying to circumscribe hedge funds, the SEC ought to be encouraging registered mutual funds to adopt hedge fund investment techniques.

The regulation fell short of what some critics of hedge fund behavior would have liked to see. The SEC would still not be able to monitor hedge fund trading in real time, and the possibility of another LTCM remains. However, the SEC explicitly decided against this course—the 2003 staff report found "no justification for direct regulation" and the adopted rule had "no interest in impeding the manner in which a hedge fund invests or placing restrictions on a hedge fund's ability to trade securities, use leverage, sell securities short or enter into derivatives transactions."[6]

The rule took effect on February 1, 2006, and some basic information on registering hedge funds appeared on the SEC website. However, on June 23, 2006, an appeals court found that the rule was arbitrary and not compatible with the plain language of the Investment Advisers Act, vacated it, and returned it to the SEC for reconsideration. SEC Chairman Cox instructed the SEC's professional staff to provide the Commission with a set of alternatives for consideration.

Another issue involves the "retailization" of hedge funds.[7] As noted above, all fund investors must meet an "accredited investor" standard: they must have incomes of at least $200,000 and assets of $1 million. This threshold was established in the 1 980s, and a much larger fraction of the population now meets the test, particularly since the $1 million includes the value of the investor's residence. The SEC has been concerned that relatively unsophisticated households may be putting their money in hedge funds, encouraged by market developments such as the introduction of funds-of-hedge funds, which accept smaller investments than traditional funds.

A related investor protection issue arises from the fact that pension funds and other institutional investors are placing more of their money with hedge funds, meaning that unsophisticated beneficiaries may be unwittingly at risk of significant hedge fund-related losses, if the plan fiduciaries are not prudent and cautious.

On December 13, 2006, the SEC proposed a regulation that would raise the accredited investor threshold from $1 million to $2.5 million in assets (excluding the value of the investor's home). If adopted, the rule would significantly reduce the pool of potential hedge fund investors, but would not be expected to have a strong impact on the largest funds, which do not depend on "mere" millionaires. The SEC received many unfavorable comments from investors who meet the current standard but would be excluded under the new limits: these investors do not wish to be protected from risks that the SEC might view as excessive. The SEC has yet to adopt a final rule raising the accredited investor standard.

In February 2007, the President's Working Group issued an "Agreement Among PWG and U.S. Agency Principals on Principles and Guidelines Regarding Private Pools of Capital."[8] The document expresses the view that policies that support market discipline, participant awareness of risk, and prudent risk management are the best means of protecting investors and limiting systemic risk. The Agreement does not call for legislation to give regulators new powers or authorities to regulate hedge funds.

In December 2008, the revelation that a firm registered as both a broker/dealer and an investment adviser with the SEC, Bernard L. Madoff Investment Securities, had operated a multi-billion dollar Ponzi scheme raised new questions about the efficacy of market self-regulation. A number of hedge funds and funds-of-funds had placed billions of their clients' money with Madoff, but failed to detect the fraud.[9] The Madoff case prompted calls for more stringent regulation of investment advisers, including hedge funds.

The Obama Administration's 2009 white paper, *Financial Regulatory Reform: A New Foundation*, recommends that advisers to hedge funds (and other private pools of capital, including private equity funds and venture capital funds) whose assets under management exceed some modest threshold should be required to register with the SEC under the Investment Advisers Act. The advisers should be required to report information on the funds they manage that is sufficient to assess whether any fund poses a threat to financial stability.[10]

LEGISLATIVE PROPOSALS

In the 109th Congress, the House passed H.R. 6079 (Representative Castle), which directed the President's Working Group to study the growth of hedge funds, the risks they pose, their use of leverage, and the benefits they confer. The Senate did not act on the bill.

In the 111th Congress, H.R. 711 (Representatives Capuano and Castle) would remove the exemption in the Investment Advisers Act for firms with fewer than 15 clients, which was the figure at the center of the 2006 *Goldstein* decision. This would require hedge funds with more than $25 million in client funds to register as investment advisers with the SEC.

H.R. 712 (Representative Castle) would require defined benefit pension plans to disclose their investments in hedge funds.

H.R. 713 (Representative Castle) directs the President's Working Group on Financial Markets to conduct a study of the hedge fund industry, and report to Congress with any recommendations regarding hedge fund regulation.

S. 344 (Senator Grassley) would limit the exemptions available under the Investment Company Act, requiring hedge funds with more than $50 million under management to register with the SEC.

S. 506 and H.R. 1265 would change the tax treatment of offshore funds.

S. 1276 would require managers of hedge funds to register as investment advisers, private equity firms, and venture capital funds, and would authorize the SEC to collect systemic risk data from them.

End Notes

[1] Imogen Rose-Smith, "The Credit Pandemic and the New World Order," *Alpha*, December 2008/January 2009, p. 26. See also Lawrence C Strauss, "Hedge Funds Meet Their Match," *Barron's*., January 5, 2009, p. 18.

[2] Many hedge funds bill themselves as low-risk, or "market-neutral," but these appear no less likely to fail. Stephen J. Brown, William N. Goetzmann, and Roger G. Ibbotson, *Offshore Hedge Funds: Survival and Performance, 1989- 1995*, NYU Stern School of Business, Working Paper FIN 98-011, January 1998, pp. 2 and 12.

[3] *Hedge Funds, Leverage, and the Lessons of Long-Term Capital Management*, Washington, April 28, 1999.

[4] U.S. Securities and Exchange Commission, *Implications of the Growth of Hedge Funds: Staff Report to the U.S. SEC*, September 2003, at http://www.sec.gov/news/studies/hedgefunds0903.pdf.

[5] See http://www.sec.gov/news/press/2004-95.htm.

[6] Ibid.

[7] Instead of the traditional minimum investment of several hundred thousand, some funds now allow investors to put in as little as $10- or $20,000. Hedge funds-of-funds are increasingly marketed not just to the "super-rich" but to the merely "mass affluent."

[8] See http://www.treasury.gov/press/releases/reports/hp272_principles.pdf.

[9] Assuming they were not accomplices.

[10] Available online at http://www.financialstability.gov/docs/regs/FinalReport_web

In: Who Regulates Whom: U.S. Financial Oversight
Editor: Milton H. Lazarus

ISBN: 978-1-60876-981-0
© 2010 Nova Science Publishers, Inc.

Chapter 6

MACROPRUDENTIAL OVERSIGHT: MONITORING THE FINANCIAL SYSTEM

Darryl E. Getter

SUMMARY

Recent innovations in finance, while increasing the capacity to borrow and lend, resulted in a large volume of banking transactions occurring outside of traditional banking institutions. Also, even though existing regulatory efforts supervise individual institutions for safety and soundness, there are risks that do not reside with those institutions but may still adversely affect the system as a whole. Macroprudential policy refers to a variety of tasks designed to defend the broad financial system against threats to its stability. Such responsibilities include monitoring the system for systemic risk vulnerabilities; developing early warning systems of financial distress; conducting stress-testing exercises; and advising other regulatory agencies on matters related to financial stability. This report provides background and discusses the benefits and limitations of macroprudential policy.

INTRODUCTION

On August 22, 2008, Federal Reserve Board Chairman Ben S. Bernanke spoke about systemic risk and raised the issue of having the authority to conduct macroprudential oversight.[1] Similarly, Timothy F. Geithner, while president of the Federal Reserve Bank of New York, also spoke about the need for expanding current prudential supervision of individual financial institutions.[2] Both Federal Reserve officials spoke in the context of growing discussions among academics and central bankers concerning the adoption of a macroprudential policy perspective.

Macroprudential policy refers to the monitoring of the entire financial system and its vulnerability to systemic risk. Systemic risk may be defined as risk that can not be avoided through diversification. Systemic risk may also be defined in a similar manner to contagion, in which liquidity and payment problems that affect one or a few financial entities will spread and disrupt financial activity more widely in the system.[3] Systemic risk can arise as a result of financial innovation, which makes it possible to increase capital mobility and access additional sources of capital. Financial innovation has also made it possible for many financial transactions to occur outside of the confines of financial institutions that are regulated for safety and soundness. If a panic, liquidity disruption, or decline in asset prices were to affect the financial markets, regulated financial institutions may still be affected despite having sound risk management practices. Consequently, macroprudential oversight of risks that can affect the overall financial system may be desirable to complement the current regulatory structure for individual financial institutions.

In addition to monitoring for systemic risk, other tasks fall under the scope of macroprudential oversight. Administrators would be responsible for the development of early warning systems of financial distress, such as a composite index of leading indicators. Stress-testing exercises, which involve introducing some extreme financial disruption into a model of the financial system to evaluate the impact on asset portfolios, would be conducted. Finally, macroprudential policy administrators would also be able to provide advice to other regulatory agencies on matters related to financial stability.

This report begins by briefly summarizing how recent innovations in finance, while increasing the capacity to borrower and lend, resulted in a large volume of banking transactions occurring outside of traditional banking institutions. Monitoring these institutions for safety and soundness, which is referred as microprudential oversight, does not directly address the challenges posed by systemic risk. Hence, the benefits and limitations of macroprudential policy will be discussed.

INTERMEDIATION AND FINANCIAL INNOVATION

Financial intermediation is the process of matching borrowers with lenders. The typical intermediation transaction made by banks consists of providing loans to borrowers at higher rates than it costs banks to borrow the funds from savers, who are the ultimate lenders. In other words, long-term loans that banks originate to borrowers are funded by short term loans made to banks, usually in the form of savings deposits. Banks profit from the spread between the rates they receive and the rates they pay. Banks also earn income from various fees and service charges.

The intermediation transaction carries a variety of risks. Banks face the risk of borrower default on the long-term loans. Banks face liquidity and interest rate risks on the short term funding side of the transaction. Until the long-term loan is fully repaid, banks must continue to attract short term savers. A bank must continuously be able to roll over or renew its short term funding (loans) because the funds used to originate the long-term loan have been disbursed to the borrower. It is possible that banks could find themselves low on deposits, perhaps due to a sudden demand for cash or changes in economic conditions. Financial market conditions could also change such that short term rates rise higher than long term rates, and continued funding of long term loans becomes costly. Given the default and funding liquidity risks associated with the intermediation transaction, banks and other financial institutions are always looking for innovative ways to reduce risk, which ultimately facilitates the expansion of intermediation and credit availability.[4]

Although the intermediation transaction remains the same conceptually over time, its means of execution has evolved and diversified, which is considered financial innovation. Financial innovations include securitization, growth of the commercial paper market, automated underwriting, derivative markets, and non-traditional mortgage products, which allow the longterm borrower and lender to share the risk of fluctuating long rates. These developments arguably facilitated intermediation in terms of reducing or managing the risks associated with supplying credit, which increased lending capacity. In fact, financial innovation in the mortgage market during the 1990s arguably enhanced homeownership by reducing loan origination costs and increasing the array of mortgage products that could be better paired to fit the demographic characteristics and financial needs of borrowers.[5]

Such financial innovation also allowed aspects of the intermediation transactions to occur outside of what is considered traditional banking institutions. For example, some businesses, rather than obtaining traditional short term loans from depository institutions, may issue their own debt in the form of commercial paper. Commercial paper issuances are typically unsecured, short-term promissory notes or bonds that investors (savers) can hold in their portfolios and, upon maturity, roll the proceeds into newer commercial paper issuances. Hedge funds, pension funds, and other financial entities may decide to purchase long-term, less liquid assets with funds obtained from their issuances of commercial paper. The commercial paper is the liability of the issuing firms, and the long-term assets (loans) acquired were not funded by liabilities (deposits) of a traditional depository institution. Securitization is another example of a financial innovation that allowed aspects of the intermediation transaction to occur off bank balance sheets. Securitizers are entities that purchase long-term loans, then use the payment streams to create short term securities (similar in nature to commercial paper with a variety of risk-return options) to investors, which fund the loan purchases. During the 2000s, many subprime loans were originated by non-bank lenders that did not hold deposits. These loans were then funded via the securitization process with funds raised from commercial paper or similar issuances.[6] Consequently, intermediation transactions were no longer limited to taking place inside traditional banks; they could now occur in the broader financial markets.

MICROPRUDENTIAL OVERSIGHT AND LIMITATIONS

A microprudential regulatory approach focuses on the safety and soundness of individual financial institutions. This regulatory approach monitors lending by supervised institutions and attempts to encourage prudent behavior.[7] Microprudential regulators evaluate bank data against Basel I and II capital ratios and CAMELS rating criteria.[8] The objective of microprudential oversight is to increase the protection of the deposits in these institutions.[9]

The microprudential approach to regulation, however, can not completely prevent bank failures. The market value of bank assets or loans can suddenly decline with sudden increases in unemployment, which is indicative of future repayment problems, even though the loans were prudently originated before the shift in local financial conditions. This vulnerability applies especially to small banks whose loans are tied to the local economy.

Larger banks may be less susceptible to regional economic conditions if they are geographically diversified, but they remain vulnerable to systemic risk, which falls outside the scope of microprudential regulation. Financial innovation may expand the financial system such that more intermediation transactions can take place outside of more traditional banking institutions, but the risks have not disappeared. The risks, rather than being borne by a particular institution, are spread among a multitude of financial market participants. Furthermore, the transfer of risk to financial markets may increase the interconnectivity among all financial market participants, causing the entire financial system to be vulnerable to unanticipated payments disruptions or sudden declines in asset values.

For example, suppose banking institutions used derivatives instruments to reduce the default and interest rate risks associated with the intermediation transaction. These instruments would have transferred these risks to another counterparty, perhaps outside of the banking system, willing to sell protection against such risks. If, however, the counterparty finds itself having to make *higher than anticipated* payments following some unforeseen event, all financial market participants may question the ability of other market participants to repay commitments. Such erosion of confidence may be considered systemic and have harmful consequences on other participants even though only one counterparty was late or completely defaulted on a payment.[10] Hence, the transfer of risk led to an increase in the interconnectivity of financial market participants. Moreover, microprudential oversight, which is limited to the regulation of the risk management practices of individual institutions, would not eliminate the systemic risk in this scenario largely because financial market expectations are impossible to regulate.

MACROPRUDENTIAL OVERSIGHT AND LIMITATIONS

Central banks are generally tasked with "lender-of-last-resort" responsibilities to ensure that regulated depository institutions reliably have access to short-term loans. This access ensures that healthy but illiquid banks continue funding long-term loans without disruption. Under a traditional banking model where regulated institutions originate long term loans and fund them with short term deposits, a central bank may assist banks in a short-term funding crunch, perhaps due to a bank run, as part of its normal course of activities. Consequently, central banks may be considered systemic risk managers for supervised banks, and they have typically been involved in macroprudential policy oversight, even if that role has not been formalized by legislation.[11] Macroprudential oversight structures have typically been set up inside of central banks.[12] The following discussion, however, refers to a designated regulator with explicit authority to conduct macroprudential oversight without necessarily having to rely upon any central bank policy tools.[13]

A formal approach to macroprudential oversight arguably complements existing microprudential oversight to reduce systemic risks. Suppose an agency conducting macroprudential oversight were to ask microprudential supervisors to require increased transparency for a specific intermediation activity from their supervised institutions. Disclosure of such information to the entire financial system may increase overall confidence.[14] Furthermore, if such policy actions were taken under normal conditions when financial markets are not in distress, then implementation may be more likely to boost rather than erode the confidence of financial market participants.

A regulatory body specifically tasked with macroprudential oversight would try to guard against bubbles and over-leveraging. The regulator would also monitor stress-testing activities as well as the extent to which financial market participants are becoming more interconnected by risks.

When asset values are rising, the balance sheets of financial institutions are likely to appear healthier. Financial institutions may decide to increase their lending in such an environment.[15] As long as financial institutions maintain capital risk ratios at or above safety thresholds, the increase in lending activity would still fall within the guidelines of safety and soundness set by microprudential oversight. A rise in asset market prices, however, may be indicative of a speculative bubble. An agency responsible for macroprudential oversight may warn or even attempt to curtail the level of risk taking activity when related asset prices appear to rise rapidly at what may be considered an unsustainable pace. The macroprudential objective would be to build up safety buffers during good times that can be used as a cushion during unstable times.

A limitation or drawback of macroprudential policy is its counter cyclical nature, which means the policy impact will dampen current business cycle activity.[16] As stated in the previous example, procyclical microprudential policy would be less likely to curtail lending activities for banking institutions when collateral asset values are rising. Macroprudential administrators, however, may perceive rising asset prices as evidence of a bubble and call for banks to raise capital or reduce lending. Although this macroprudential response may reduce systemic risk, it may possibly restrain short run banking profits, economic activity, and economic growth.

Consider the debate about the existence of a housing market bubble. The substantial decline in mortgage interest rates during the 1990s, resulting in part from securitization reducing the funding costs of lending, helped lower the cost of homeownership relative to renting.[17] Changing demographic trends also affected changes in housing demand.[18] On the other hand, the rise in house prices and use of mortgage credit levels was interpreted by some as evidence of a bubble in the housing market. Consequently, it would have been problematic to determine with certainty whether the rise in the demand for homes, which would be reflected in house price increases, was due to a rise in underlying fundamentals or speculative behavior, since both occurred simultaneously. Even if the market is characterized by speculation, speculative trading provides liquidity for assets. Speculation increases the number of transactions, which makes it easier to price and sell assets. Hence, identifying bubbles would still present a challenge for macroprudential oversight. Not only would it be difficult to determine how much financial market activity would be the result of speculation, but it would also be difficult to determine how much speculation to reduce without compromising overall asset market liquidity.

Despite the problems of identifying and managing speculative behavior, macroprudential regulators would be tasked with responding to conditions that suggest the presence of a bubble given the systemic risks to financial markets when it deflates. A macroprudential response, however, may be at odds with other policy goals in which the primary focus is not safety and soundness. Some policy goals are aimed at increasing credit access to low and moderate income households and households living in underserved areas.[19] It may be easier for financial institutions to facilitate more lending to those individuals covered by policy goals at times when collateral assets are rising and there is expanded lending capacity. Macroprudential oversight, however, might encourage a reduction of lending at a time when asset values are rising and financial conditions would be better suited to facilitate the achievement of other policy goals.

A macroprudential oversight regulator may also find itself in the middle of occasional conflicts between regulators. For example, consider a case that occurred in the mid-1990s.[20] A regulator concerned with the adequate capitalization of banks preferred that banks adopt conservative accounting practices that would result in the reporting of higher loan loss allowances. Higher loan loss allowances would indicate the ability of banks to avoid severe financial distress when unexpected loan losses occur. Another regulator, concerned with the accurate reporting of income to investors, preferred adoption of accounting practices that would reduce the reported amount of loan-loss allowances. Overstatement of loan loss allowances reduce bank net income and retained earnings on paper. Investors may interpret large loan loss allowances as evidence of high risk lending practices, which may reduce bank profitability, and that could translate into a decline in the bank's value or stock price. In addition, a reporting of higher loan loss allowances may result in an initial understatement of assets and overstatement of bank income in future periods, which would translate into overly optimistic information being reported to investors in subsequent periods. A macroprudential regulator may be more inclined to support regulations that foster increased safety and soundness. Given that regulators can always require banks to provide any critical information, disputes of this nature may be settled in favor of investor needs. If, in this particular case, a regulator responsible for macroprudential oversight combined efforts with the regulator in favor of more conservative accounting practices, the collective efforts possibly may have had a greater influence on the outcome.

End Notes

[1] See speech by Chairman Ben S. Bernanke entitled *Reducing Systemic Risk* at http://www.federalreserve.gov/newsevents/speech/bernanke20080822a.htm.

[2] See speech by Timothy F. Geithner entitled *Reducing Systemic Risk in a Dynamic Financial System* at http://www.newyorkfed.org/newsevents/speeches/2008/tfg080609.html

[3] See Steven L. Schwarcz, "Systemic Risk," *Georgetown Law Journal*, vol. 97, no. 1 (November 2008), pp. 193-249.

[4] For a more in-depth understanding of intermediation theory, see Franklin Allen and Anthony M. Santomero, *The Theory of Financial Intermediation*, Wharton School, University of Pennsylvania, Financial Institutions Center 96-32, Philadelphia, PA, August 31, 1996, http://fic.wharton.upenn.edu/fic/papers/96/9632.pdf.

[5] See Mark Doms and John Krainer, *Innovations in Mortgage Markets and Increased Spending on Housing*, Federal Reserve Bank of San Francisco, Working Paper 2007-05, San Francisco, CA, July 2007, http://www.frbsf.org/publications/economics/papers/2007/wp07-05bk.pdf.

[6] Many subprime originations were not subject to federal safety and soundness banking guidances. These loans were not originated by depository institutions that would have a federal charter or federal deposit insurance; these loans were insured by FHA or sold directly to GSEs. Hence, these loans were not covered by any federal guidance. See CRS Report RS22722, *Securitization and Federal Regulation of Mortgages for Safety and Soundness*, by Edward V. Murphy.

[7] For information on the U.S. regulators of financial institutions, see CRS Report RL33036, *Federal Financial Services Regulatory Consolidation: An Overview*, by Walter W. Eubanks.

[8] Basel I and II refer to recommendations for banking laws and regulations with the objective of achieving uniform international standards with respect to capitalization. CAMELS refers to the uniform rating standards adopted to monitor the safety and soundness of regulated banks. See CRS Report R40249, *Who Regulates Whom? An Overview of U.S. Financial Supervision*, by Mark Jickling and Edward V. Murphy; CRS Report RL34485,

Basel II in the United States: Progress Toward a Workable Framework, by Walter W. Eubanks; and CRS Report RL33036, *Federal Financial Services Regulatory Consolidation: An Overview*, by Walter W. Eubanks.

[9] See Claudio Borio, *The Macroprudential Approach to Regulation and Supervision: Where Do We Stand?*, Kredittilsynet, Kapittel 7, Norway, September 13, 2006, pp. 108-120, http://www.kredittilsynet.no/archive/stab_pdf/01/ 03/7Kapi013.pdf.

[10] See CRS Report RL34427, *Financial Turmoil: Federal Reserve Policy Responses*, by Marc Labonte.

[11] After drawing upon its emergency powers in the lender-of-last-resort clause, the Federal Reserve assumed the responsibility for managing the disruption in the financial system. See CRS Report RL34427, *Financial Turmoil: Federal Reserve Policy Responses*, by Marc Labonte. The Federal Reserve does not officially have authority to take preventative actions to reduce systemic risk, and it may only respond to systemic risk problems, in particular those that impact non-supervised institutions, only after such disruptions have occurred.

[12] For some descriptions of various macroprudential oversight structures, see http://www.bof.fi/en/rahoitusmarkkinat/vakausvalvonta/index.htm, http://www.snb.ch/en/iabout/finstab/id/finstab_report, and http://www.bankofengland.co.uk/financialstability/overseeing_fs/.

[13] The Federal Financial Institutions Examination Council (FFIEC) in the United States, for example, is an interagency body that promotes uniform regulations among the various regulators of financial institutions. This agency has some rule-making powers, but it typically makes recommendations and allows other regulators to implement final rules.

[14] See Sebastian Schich, "Financial Crisis: Deposit Insurance and Related Financial Safety Net," *Financial Market Trends*, vol. 2, no. 95 (November 2008).

[15] See David Greeenlaw, Jan Hatzius, and Anil K. Kashyap, et al., *Leveraged Losses: Lessons from the Mortgage Market Meltdown*, Rosenberg Institute, Brandeis International Business School and Initiative on Global Markets, University of Chicago Graduate School of Business, U.S. Monetary Policy Forum Report No. 2, 2008, http://research.chicagogsb.edu/igm/events/docs/USMPF-final.pdf.

[16] See Sharon K. Blei, "If Fed Becomes Super Regulator, Politicians Would Be Its Kryptonite," *The Regional Economist*, January 2009 at http://www.stlouisfed.org/publications/re/2009/a/pages/super_regulator.html.

[17] See Moorad Choudhry, *The Bond and Money Markets: Strategy, Trading, Analysis* (Butterworth-Heinemann, 2001), p. 545.

[18] See the discussion of various demographic trends and possible impact on housing demand at http://www.fdic.gov/bank/analytical/regional/ro20061q/na/2006_spring03.html.

[19] See CRS Report RL34049, *Community Reinvestment Act: Regulation and Legislation*, by Walter W. Eubanks.

[20] See Larry D. Wall and Timothy W. Koch, "Bank Loan-Loss Accounting: A Review of Theoretical and Empirical Evidence," *Economic Review, Federal Reserve Bank of Atlanta*, Second Quarter 2000, at http://www.frbatlanta.org/ filelegacydocs/wallkoch.pdf.

In: Who Regulates Whom: U.S. Financial Oversight
Editor: Milton H. Lazarus

ISBN: 978-1-60876-981-0
© 2010 Nova Science Publishers, Inc.

Chapter 7

FINANCIAL MARKET REGULATION: FINANCIAL CRISIS HIGHLIGHTS NEED TO IMPROVE OVERSIGHT OF LEVERAGE AT FINANCIAL INSTITUTIONS AND ACROSS SYSTEM

United States Government Accountability Office

WHY GAO DID THIS STUDY

The Emergency Economic Stabilization Act directed GAO to study the role of leverage in the current financial crisis and federal oversight of leverage. GAO's objectives were to review (1) how leveraging and deleveraging by financial institutions may have contributed to the crisis, (2) regulations adopted by federal financial regulators to limit leverage and how regulators oversee compliance with the regulations, and (3) any limitations the current crisis has revealed in regulatory approaches used to restrict leverage and regulatory proposals to address them. To meet these objectives, GAO built on its existing body of work, reviewed relevant laws and regulations and academic and other studies, and interviewed regulators and market participants.

WHAT GAO RECOMMENDS

As Congress considers establishing a systemic risk regulator, it should consider the merits of assigning such a regulator with responsibility for overseeing systemwide leverage. As U.S. regulators continue to consider reforms to strengthen oversight of leverage, we recommend that they assess the extent to which reforms under Basel II, a new risk-based capital framework, will address risk evaluation and regulatory oversight concerns associated with advanced modeling approaches used for capital adequacy purposes. In their written comments, the regulators generally agreed with our conclusions and recommendation.

View GAO-09-739 or key components. For more information, contact Orice Williams Brown at (202) 512-8678 or williamso@gao.gov.

WHAT GAO FOUND

Some studies suggested that leverage steadily increased in the financial sector before the crisis, and deleveraging by financial institutions may have contributed to the crisis. First, the studies suggested that deleveraging by selling financial assets could cause prices to spiral downward during times of market stress. Second, the studies suggested that deleveraging by restricting new lending could slow economic growth. However, other theories also provide possible explanations for the sharp price declines observed in certain assets. As the crisis is complex, no single theory is likely to fully explain what occurred or rule out other explanations. Regulators and market participants we interviewed had mixed views about the effects of deleveraging. Some officials told us that they generally have not seen asset sales leading to downward price spirals, but others said that asset sales have led to such spirals.

Federal regulators impose capital and other requirements on their regulated institutions to limit leverage and ensure financial stability. Federal bank regulators impose minimum risk-based capital and leverage ratios on banks and thrifts and supervise the capital adequacy of such firms through on-site examinations and off-site monitoring. Bank holding companies are subject to similar capital requirements as banks, but thrift holding companies are not. The Securities and Exchange Commission uses its net capital rule to limit broker-dealer leverage and used to require certain broker-dealer holding companies to report risk-based capital ratios and meet certain liquidity requirements. Other important market participants, such as hedge funds, use leverage. Hedge funds typically are not subject to regulatory capital requirements, but market discipline, supplemented by regulatory oversight of institutions that transact with them, can serve to constrain their leverage.

The crisis has revealed limitations in regulatory approaches used to restrict leverage. First, regulatory capital measures did not always fully capture certain risks. For example, many financial institutions applied risk models in ways that significantly underestimated certain risk exposures. As a result, these institutions did not hold capital commensurate with their risks and some faced capital shortfalls when the crisis began. Federal regulators have called for reforms, including through international efforts to revise the Basel II capital framework. The planned U.S. implementation of Basel II would increase reliance on risk models for determining capital needs for certain large institutions. Although the crisis underscored concerns about the use of such models for determining capital adequacy, regulators have not assessed whether proposed Basel II reforms will address these concerns. However, such an assessment is critical to ensure that changes to the regulatory framework address the limitations revealed by the crisis. Second, regulators face challenges in counteracting cyclical leverage trends and are working on reform proposals. Finally, the crisis has reinforced the need to focus greater attention on systemic risk. With multiple regulators responsible for individual markets or institutions, none has clear responsibility to assess the potential effects of the buildup of systemwide leverage or the collective activities of institutions to deleverage.

ABBREVIATIONS

CAMELS	capital, asset quality, management, earnings, liquidity, sensitivity to market risk
CDO	collateralized debt obligations
CORE	capital, organizational structure, risk management, and earnings
CSE	Consolidated Supervised Entity
CFTC	Commodity Futures Trading Commission
FDIC	Federal Deposit Insurance Corporation
FINRA	Financial Industry Regulatory Authority
FSOC	Financial Services Oversight Council
GAAP	Generally Accepted Accounting Principles
GDP	gross domestic product
IG	inspector general
MRA	Market Risk Amendment
NYSE	New York Stock Exchange
OCC	Office of the Comptroller of the Currency
OTC	over the counter
OTS	Office of Thrift Supervision
PCA	Prompt Corrective Action
SEC	Securities and Exchange Commission
SPE	special purpose entity
SRC	systemic risk council
SRO	self-regulatory organization
VaR	value-at-risk

> This is a work of the U.S. government and is not subject to copyright protection in the United States. The published product may be reproduced and distributed in its entirety without further permission from GAO. However, because this work may contain copyrighted images or other material, permission from the copyright holder may be necessary if you wish to reproduce this material separately.

July 22, 2009
Congressional Committees

The United States is in the midst of the worst financial crisis in more than 75 years. To date, federal regulators and authorities have taken unprecedented steps to stem the unraveling of the financial services sector by committing trillions of dollars of taxpayer funds to rescue financial institutions and restore order to credit markets. Although the current crisis has spread across a broad range of financial instruments, it was initially triggered by defaults on U.S. subprime mortgage loans, many of which had been packaged and sold as securities to buyers in the United States and around the world. With financial institutions from many countries participating in these activities, the resulting turmoil has afflicted financial markets globally and has spurred coordinated action by world leaders in an attempt to protect savings and restore the health of the markets.

The buildup of leverage during a market expansion and the rush to reduce leverage, or "deleverage," when market conditions deteriorated was common to this and other financial crises. Leverage traditionally has referred to the use of debt, instead of equity, to fund an asset and been measured by the ratio of total assets to equity on the balance sheet. But as witnessed in the current crisis, leverage also can be used to increase an exposure to a financial asset without using debt, such as by using derivatives.[1] In that regard, leverage can be defined broadly as the ratio between some measure of risk exposure and capital that can be used to absorb unexpected losses from the exposure.[2] However, because leverage can be achieved through many different strategies, no single measure can capture all aspects of leverage. Federal financial regulators are responsible for establishing regulations that restrict the use of leverage by financial institutions under their authority and supervising their institutions' compliance with such regulations.

On October 3, 2008, the Emergency Economic Stabilization Act of 2008 (the act) was signed into law.[3] The act's purpose is to provide the Secretary of the Department of the Treasury (Treasury) with the authority to restore liquidity and stability to the U.S. financial system and to ensure the economic well-being of Americans. To that end, the act established the Office of Financial Stability within Treasury and authorized the Troubled Asset Relief Program. The act provided Treasury with broad, flexible authorities to buy or guarantee up to $700 billion in "troubled assets," which include mortgages and mortgage-related instruments, and any other financial instrument the purchase of which Treasury determines is needed to stabilize the financial markets.[4]

The act also established several reporting requirements for GAO. One of these requires the U.S. Comptroller General to "undertake a study to determine the extent to which leverage and sudden deleveraging of financial institutions was a factor behind the current financial crisis."[5] Additionally, the study is to include an analysis of the roles and responsibilities of federal financial regulators for monitoring leverage and the authority of the Board of Governors of the Federal Reserve System (Federal Reserve) to regulate leverage.[6] To address this mandate, we sought to answer the following questions:

1. How have leveraging and deleveraging by financial institutions contributed to the current financial crisis, according to primarily academic and other studies?
2. What regulations have federal financial regulators adopted to try to limit the use of leverage by financial institutions, and how do the regulators oversee the institutions' compliance with the regulations?
3. What, if any, limitations has the current financial crisis revealed about the regulatory framework used to restrict leverage, and what changes have regulators and others proposed to address these limitations?

To satisfy our responsibility under the act's mandate to report the results of this work by June 1, 2009, we provided an interim report on the results of this work in the form of a briefing to the committees' staffs on May 27, 2009. Appendix II contains the full briefing. This letter represents the final report.

To address our objectives, we reviewed and analyzed academic and other studies assessing the buildup of leverage prior to the current financial crisis and the economic mechanisms that possibly helped the mortgage- related losses spread to other markets and expand into the current crisis. We reviewed and analyzed relevant laws and regulations, and other regulatory guidance and materials, related to the oversight of financial institutions' use of leverage by the Federal Reserve, Federal Deposit Insurance Corporation (FDIC), Office of the Comptroller of the Currency (OCC), Office of Thrift Supervision (OTS), and Securities and Exchange Commission (SEC). We also collected and analyzed various data to illustrate leverage and other relevant trends. We assessed the reliability of the data and found that they were sufficiently reliable for our purposes. In addition, we interviewed staff from these federal financial regulators and officials from two securities firms, a bank, and a credit rating agency. We also reviewed and analyzed studies done by U.S. and international regulators and others identifying limitations in the regulatory framework used to restrict leverage and proposals to address such limitations. Finally, we reviewed prior GAO work on the financial regulatory system.

The work upon which this report is based was conducted in accordance with generally accepted government auditing standards. Those standards require that we plan and perform the audit to obtain sufficient, appropriate evidence to provide a reasonable basis for our findings and conclusions based on our audit objectives. We believe that the evidence obtained provides a reasonable basis for our findings and conclusions based on our audit objectives. This work was conducted between February and July 2009. A more extensive discussion of our scope and methodology appears in appendix I.

RESULTS IN BRIEF

According to studies we reviewed, leverage steadily increased within the financial sector before the crisis began around mid-2007, and banks, securities firms, hedge funds, and other financial institutions have sought to deleverage and reduce their risk since the onset of the crisis. Some studies suggested that the efforts taken by financial institutions to deleverage by selling financial assets and restricting new lending could have contributed to the current crisis. First, some studies we reviewed suggested that deleveraging through asset sales could trigger downward spirals in financial asset prices. In times of market crisis, a sharp drop in an asset's price can lead investors to sell the asset, which could push the asset's price even lower. For leveraged institutions holding the asset, the impact of their losses on capital will be magnified. The subsequent price decline could induce additional sales that cause the asset's price to fall further. In the extreme, this downward asset spiral could cause the asset's price to be set below its fundamental value, or at a "fire sale" price. In addition, a decline in a financial asset's price could trigger sales, when the asset is used as collateral for a loan. In such a case, the borrower could be required to post additional collateral for its loan, but if the borrower could not do so, the lender could take ownership of the collateral and then sell it, which could cause the asset's price to decline further. However, other theories, such as that the current market prices are the result of asset prices reverting to their fundamental values after a period of overvaluation, provide possible explanations for the sharp price declines in mortgage-related securities and other financial instruments. As the crisis is complex, no single theory likely is to explain in full what occurred. Second, some studies we reviewed suggested that deleveraging by restricting new lending could contribute to the crisis by slowing economic growth. In short, the concern is that banks, because of their leverage, will need to cut back their lending by a multiple of their credit losses. Moreover, rapidly declining asset prices can inhibit the ability of borrowers to raise money in the securities markets. Financial regulators and market participants we interviewed had mixed views about the effects of deleveraging by financial institutions in the current crisis. Some regulatory officials and market participants told us that they generally have not seen asset sales leading to downward price spirals, but others said that asset sales involving a variety of debt instruments have contributed to such spirals. Regulatory and credit rating agency officials told us that banks have tightened their lending standards for some loans, such as ones with less favorable risk-adjusted returns. They also said that some banks rely on the securities markets to help them fund loans and, thus, need conditions in the securities markets to improve. As we have discussed in our prior work, since the crisis began, federal regulators and authorities have undertaken a number of steps to facilitate financial intermediation by banks and the securities markets.[7]

Federal financial regulators generally impose capital and other requirements on their regulated institutions as a way to limit the use of leverage and ensure the stability of the financial system and markets. Specifically, federal banking and thrift regulators have imposed minimum risk-based capital and leverage ratios on their regulated institutions. The risk-based capital ratios generally are designed to require banks and thrifts to hold more capital for more risky assets. Although regulators have imposed minimum leverage ratios on regulated institutions, some regulators told us that they primarily focus on the risk-based capital ratios to limit the use of leverage. In addition, they supervise the capital adequacy of their regulated institutions through on-site examinations and off-site monitoring. Bank holding companies are subject to capital and leverage ratio requirements similar to those imposed on banks, but thrift holding companies are not subject to such requirements. Instead, capital levels of thrift holding companies are individually evaluated based on each company's risk profile. SEC primarily uses its net capital rule to limit the use of leverage by broker-dealers. The rule serves to protect market participants from broker-dealer failures and to enable broker-dealers that fail to meet the rule's minimum requirements to be liquidated in an orderly fashion. For the holding companies of broker-dealers that participated in SEC's discontinued Consolidated Supervised Entity (CSE) program, they calculated their risk-based capital ratios in a manner designed to be consistent with the method used by banks.[8] In addition to the capital ratio, SEC imposed a liquidity requirement on CSE holding companies. Other financial institutions, such as hedge funds, have become important participants in the financial markets, and many use leverage. But, unlike banks and broker-dealers, hedge funds typically are not subject to regulatory capital requirements that limit their use of leverage. Rather, their use of leverage is to be constrained primarily through market discipline, supplemented by regulatory oversight of banks and broker- dealers that transact with hedge funds as creditors and counterparties. Finally, the Federal Reserve regulates the use of securities as collateral to finance security purchases, but federal financial regulators told us that such credit did not play a significant role in the buildup of leverage in the current crisis.

The financial crisis has revealed limitations in existing regulatory approaches that serve to restrict leverage. Federal financial regulators have proposed reforms, but have not yet fully evaluated the extent to which these proposals would address these limitations. First, although large banks and broker-dealers generally held capital above the minimum regulatory capital requirements prior to the crisis, regulatory capital measures did not always fully capture certain risks, particularly those associated with some mortgage-related securities held on and off their balance sheets. As a result, a number of these institutions did not hold capital commensurate with their risks and some lacked adequate capital or liquidity to withstand the market stresses of the crisis. Federal financial regulators have acknowledged the need to improve the risk coverage of the regulatory capital framework and are considering reforms to better align capital requirements with risk. Furthermore, the crisis highlighted past concerns about the approach to be taken under Basel II, a new risk- based capital framework based on an international accord, such as the ability of banks' models to adequately measure risks for regulatory capital purposes and the regulators' ability to oversee them. Federal financial regulators have not formally assessed the extent to which Basel II reforms proposed by U.S. and international regulators may address these concerns. Such an assessment is critical to ensure that Basel II reforms, particularly those that would increase reliance on complex risk models for determining capital needs, do not exacerbate regulatory limitations revealed by the crisis. Second, the crisis illustrated how the existing regulatory framework, along with other factors, might have contributed to cyclical leverage trends that potentially exacerbated the current crisis. For example, minimum regulatory capital requirements may not provide adequate incentives for banks to build loss-absorbing capital buffers in benign markets when it is relatively less expensive to do so. When market conditions deteriorated, minimum capital requirements became binding for many institutions that lacked adequate buffers to absorb losses and faced sudden pressures to deleverage. As discussed, actions taken by individual institutions to deleverage by selling assets in stressed markets may exacerbate a financial crisis. Regulators are considering several options to counteract potentially harmful cyclical leverage trends, but implementation of these proposals presents challenges. Finally, the financial crisis has illustrated the potential for financial market disruptions, not just firm failures, to be a source of systemic risk. As some studies we reviewed suggested, ensuring the solvency of individual institutions may not be sufficient to protect the stability of the financial system, in part because of the potential for deleveraging by institutions to have negative spillover effects. In our prior work, we have noted that a regulatory system should focus on risk to the financial system, not just institutions.[9] With multiple regulators primarily responsible for individual markets or institutions, none of the financial regulators has clear responsibility to assess the potential effects of the buildup of leverage and deleveraging by a few institutions or by the collective activities of the industry for the financial system. As a result, regulators may be limited in their ability to prevent or mitigate future financial crises.

To ensure that there is a systemwide approach to addressing leverage- related issues across the financial system, we are providing a matter for congressional consideration. In particular, as Congress moves toward the creation of a systemic risk regulator, it should consider the merits of tasking this entity with the responsibility for measuring and monitoring systemwide leverage and evaluating options to limit procyclical leverage trends. Furthermore, to address concerns about the Basel II approach highlighted by the current financial crisis, we are making one recommendation to the heads of the Federal Reserve, FDIC, OCC, and OTS. Specifically, these regulators should assess the extent to which Basel II reforms may address risk evaluation and regulatory oversight concerns associated with advanced modeling approaches used for capital adequacy purposes.

We provided the heads of the Federal Reserve, FDIC, OCC, OTS, SEC, and Treasury with a draft of this report for their review and comment. We received written comments from the Federal Reserve, FDIC, OCC, and SEC, which are reprinted in appendices V through VIII, respectively. The regulators generally agreed with our conclusions and recommendation. We did not receive written comments from OTS and Treasury. Except for

Treasury, the agencies also provided technical comments that we incorporated in the report where appropriate.

BACKGROUND

The financial services industry comprises a broad range of financial institutions—including broker-dealers, banks, government-sponsored enterprises, hedge funds, insurance companies, and thrifts. Moreover, many of these financial institutions are part of a holding company structure, such as a bank or financial holding company.[10] In the United States, large parts of the financial services industry are regulated under a complex system of multiple federal and state regulators, and self- regulatory organizations (SRO) that operate largely along functional lines (see figure 1).[11] Such oversight serves, in part, to help ensure that the financial institutions do not take on excessive risk that could undermine their safety and soundness. Primary bank supervisors—the Federal Reserve, FDIC, OCC, and OTS—oversee banks and thrifts according to their charters. Functional supervisors—primarily SEC, the Commodity Futures Trading Commission (CFTC), SROs, and state insurance regulators—oversee entities engaged in the securities and insurance industries as appropriate. Consolidated supervisors oversee holding companies that contain subsidiaries that have primary bank or functional supervisors—the Federal Reserve oversees bank holding companies and OTS oversees thrift holding companies.[12] In the last few decades, nonbank lenders, hedge funds, and other firms have become important participants in the financial services industry but are unregulated or less regulated.

To varying degrees, all financial institutions are exposed to a variety of risks that create the potential for financial loss associated with

- failure of a borrower or counterparty to perform on an obligation—credit risk;
- broad movements in financial prices—interest rates or stock prices— market risk;
- failure to meet obligations because of inability to liquidate assets or obtain funding—liquidity risk;
- inadequate information systems, operational problems, and breaches in internal controls—operational risk;
- negative publicity regarding an institution's business practices and subsequent decline in customers, costly litigation, or revenue reductions— reputation risk;
- breaches of law or regulation that may result in heavy penalties or other costs—legal risk;
- risks that an insurance underwriter takes in exchange for premiums— insurance risk; and
- events not covered above, such as credit rating downgrades or factors beyond the control of the firm, such as major shocks in the firm's markets—business/event risk

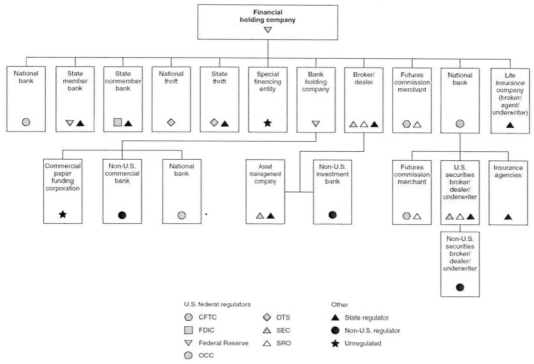

Source: GAO

Figure 1. Supervisors for a Hypothetical Financial Holding Company

In addition, the industry as a whole is exposed to systemic risk, the risk that a disruption could cause widespread difficulties in the financial system as a whole.

Many financial institutions use leverage to expand their ability to invest or trade in financial assets and to increase their return on equity. A firm can use leverage through a number of strategies, including by using debt to finance an asset or entering into derivatives. Greater financial leverage, as measured by lower proportions of capital relative to assets, can increase the firm's market risk, because leverage magnifies gains and losses relative to equity. Leverage also can increase a firm's liquidity risk, because a leveraged firm may be forced to sell assets under adverse market conditions to reduce its exposure. As illustrated in figure 2, a 10 percent decline in the value of assets of an institution with an assets-to-equity ratio of 5-to-1 would deplete the institution's equity by 50 percent. Although commonly used as a leverage measure, the ratio of assets to equity captures only on-balance sheet assets and treats all assets as equally risky. Moreover, the ratio of assets to equity helps to measure the extent to which a change in total assets would affect equity but provides no information on the probability of such a change occurring. Finally, a leveraged position may not be more risky than a non-leveraged position, when other aspects of the position are not equal. For example, a non-leveraged position in a highly risky asset could be more risky than a leveraged position in a low risk asset.

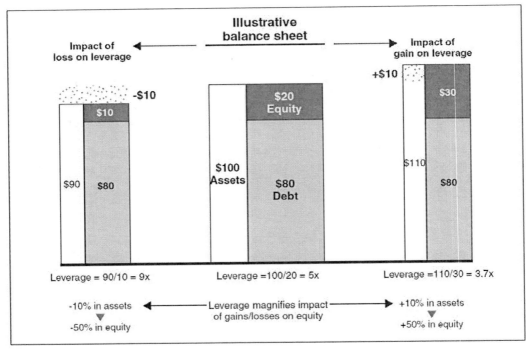

Source: GAO.

Figure 2. Effect of a Gain or Loss on a Leveraged Institution's Balance Sheet

During the 1980s, banking regulators became concerned that simple leverage measures—such as the ratio of assets to equity or debt to equity—required too much capital for less-risky assets and not enough for riskier assets. Another concern was that such measures did not require capital for growing portfolios of off-balance sheet items. In response to these concerns, the Basel Committee on Banking Supervision adopted Basel I, an international framework for risk-based capital that required banks to meet minimum risk-based capital ratios, in 1988.[13] By 1992, U.S. regulators had fully implemented Basel I; and in 1996, they and supervisors from other Basel Committee member countries amended the framework to include explicit capital requirements for market risk from trading activity (called the Market Risk Amendment).[14] In response to the views of bankers and many regulators that innovation in financial markets and advances in risk management have revealed limitations in the existing Basel I risk-based capital framework, especially for large, complex banks, the Basel Committee released the Basel II international accord in 2004. (App. III discusses limitations of Basel I, and app. IV describes the three pillars of Basel II.) Since then, individual countries have been implementing national rules based on the principles and detailed framework. In a prior report, we discussed the status of efforts by U.S. regulators to implement the Basel II accord.[15]

The dramatic decline in the U.S. housing market precipitated a decline in the price of financial assets around mid-2007 that were associated with housing, in particular mortgage assets based on subprime loans that lost value as the housing boom ended and the market underwent a dramatic correction. Some institutions found themselves so exposed that they were threatened with failure—and some failed—because they were unable to raise the necessary capital as the value of their portfolios declined. Other institutions, ranging from government-sponsored enterprises such as Fannie Mae and Freddie Mac to large securities firms, were left holding "toxic" mortgages or mortgage-related assets that became increasingly difficult to value, were illiquid, and potentially had little worth. Moreover, investors not only stopped buying securities backed by mortgages but also became reluctant to buy securities backed by many types of assets. Because of uncertainty about the financial condition and solvency of financial entities, the prices banks charged each other for funds rose dramatically, and interbank lending effectively came to a halt. The resulting liquidity and credit crunch made the financing on which businesses and individuals depend increasingly difficult to obtain as cash-strapped banks held on to their assets. By late summer of 2008, the potential ramifications of the financial crisis ranged from the continued failure of financial institutions to increased losses of individual savings and corporate investments and further tightening of credit that would exacerbate the emerging global economic slowdown that was beginning to take shape.

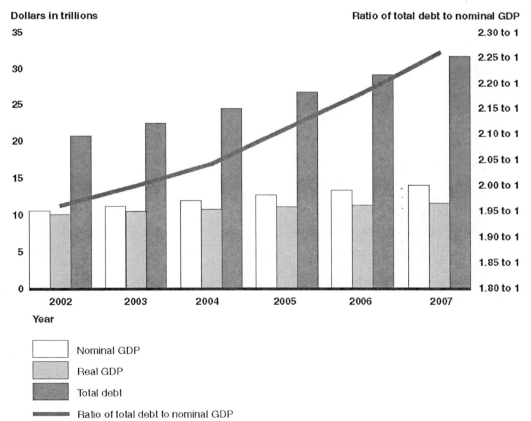

Source: GAO analysis of the Federal Reserve's Flow of Funds data and the Bureau of Economic Analysis's GDP data.

Figure 3. Nominal GDP, Real GDP, Total Debt, and Ratio of Total Debt to Nominal GDP, 2002 to 2007

RESEARCH SUGGESTS LEVERAGE INCREASED BEFORE THE CRISIS AND SUBSEQUENT DELEVERAGING COULD HAVE CONTRIBUTED TO THE CRISIS

The current financial crisis is complex and multifaceted; and likewise, so are its causes, which remain subject to debate and ongoing research. Before the current crisis, leverage broadly increased across the economy. For example, as shown in figure 3, total debt in the United States increased from $20.7 trillion to $31.7 trillion, or by nearly 53 percent, from year-end 2002 to year-end 2007, and the ratio of total debt to gross domestic product (GDP) increased from 1.96 to 1 to 2.26 to 1, or by 15 percent, during the same period. In general, the more leveraged an economy, the more prone it is to crisis generated by moderate economic shocks.

According to many researchers, the crisis initially was triggered by defaults on U.S. subprime mortgages around mid-2007. Academics and others have identified a number of factors that possibly helped fuel the housing boom, which helped set the stage for the subsequent problems in the subprime mortgage market. These factors include

- imprudent mortgage lending that permitted people to buy houses they could not afford;
- securitization of mortgages that reduced originators' incentives to be prudent;
- imprudent business and risk management decisions based on the expectation of continued housing price appreciation;
- faulty assumptions in the models used by credit rating agencies to rate mortgage-related securities;
- establishment of off-balance sheet entities by banks to hold mortgages or mortgage-related securities that allowed banks to make more loans during the expansion; and
- economic conditions, characterized by permissive monetary policies, ample liquidity and availability of credit, and low interest rates that spurred housing investment.[16]

Around mid-2007, the losses in the subprime mortgage market triggered a reassessment of financial risk in other debt instruments and sparked the current financial crisis. Academics and others have identified a number of economic mechanisms that possibly helped to cause the relatively small subprime mortgage-related losses to become a financial crisis. However, given our mandate, our review of the economic literature focused narrowly on deleveraging by financial institutions as one of the potential mechanisms.[17] (See the bibliography for the studies included in our literature review.) The studies we reviewed do not provide definitive findings about the role of deleveraging relative to other mechanisms, and we relied on our interpretation and reasoning to develop insights from the studies reviewed. Other theories that do not involve deleveraging may provide possible explanations for the sharp price declines in mortgage- related securities and other financial instruments. Because such theories are largely beyond the scope of our work, we discuss them only in brief.

Leverage within the Financial Sector Increased before the Financial Crisis, and Financial Institutions Have Sought to Deleverage Since the Crisis Began

Leverage steadily increased in the financial sector during the prolonged rise in housing and other asset prices and created vulnerabilities that have increased the severity of the crisis, according to studies we reviewed.[18] Leverage can take many different forms, and no single measure of leverage exists; in that regard, the studies generally identified a range of sources that aided in the buildup of leverage before the crisis. One such source was the use of short-term debt, such as repurchase agreements, by financial institutions to help fund their assets.[19] The reliance on short-term funding made the institutions vulnerable to a decline in the availability of such credit.[20] Another source of leverage was special purpose entities (SPE), which some banks created to buy and hold mortgage-related and other assets that the banks did not want to hold on their balance sheets.[21]

To obtain the funds to purchase their assets, SPEs often borrowed by issuing shorter-term instruments, such as commercial paper and medium- term notes, but this strategy exposed the SPEs to the risk of not being able to renew their debt. Similarly, to expand their funding sources or provide additional capacity on their balance sheets, financial institutions securitized mortgage-backed securities, among other assets, to form collateralized debt obligations (CDO). In a basic CDO, a group of debt securities are pooled, and securities are then issued in different tranches (or slices) that vary in risk and return. Through pooling and slicing, CDOs can give investors an embedded leveraged exposure.[22] Finally, the growth in credit default swaps, a type of OTC derivative, was another source of leverage. Credit default swaps aided the securitization process by providing credit enhancements to CDO issuers and provided financial institutions with another way to leverage their exposure to the mortgage market.

For securities firms, hedge funds, and other financial intermediaries that operate mainly through the capital markets, their balance sheet leverage, or ratio of total assets to equity, tends to be procyclical.[23] Historically, such institutions tended to increase their leverage when asset prices rose and decrease their leverage when asset prices fell.[24] One explanation for this behavior is that they actively measure and manage the risk exposure of their portfolios by adjusting their balance sheets. For a given amount of equity, an increase in asset prices will lower a firm's measured risk exposure and allow it to expand its balance sheet, such as by increasing its debt to buy more assets. Because measured risk typically is low during booms and high during busts, the firm's efforts to control its risk will lead to procyclical leverage. Another possible factor leading financial institutions to manage their leverage procyclically is their use of fair value accounting to revalue their trading assets periodically at current market values.[25] When asset prices rise, financial institutions holding the assets recognize a gain that increases their equity and decreases their leverage ratio. In turn, the institutions will seek profitable ways to use their increase in equity by expanding their balance sheets and thereby increasing their leverage. Consistent with this research, the ratio of assets to equity for five large broker-dealer holding companies, in aggregate, increased from an average ratio of around 22 to 1 in 2002 to around 30 to 1 in 2007 (see figure 4).[26] In contrast, the ratio of assets to equity for five large bank holding companies, in aggregate, was relatively flat during this period (see figure 5). As discussed in the background, the ratio of assets to equity treats all assets as equally risky and does not capture off-balance sheet risks.

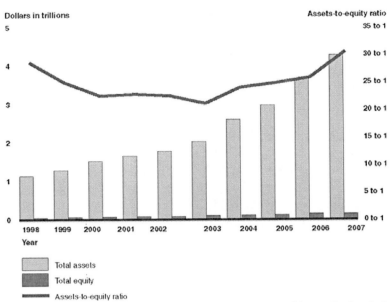

Source: GAO analysis of annual report data for Bear Stearns, Goldman Sachs, Lehman Brothers, Merrill Lynch, and Morgan Stanley.

Figure 4. Total Assets, Total Equity, and Leverage (Assets-to-Equity) Ratio in Aggregate for Five Large U.S. Broker-Dealer Holding Companies, 1998 to 2007

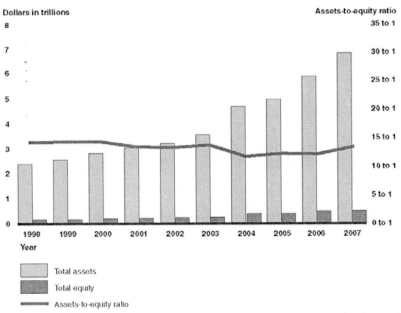

Source: GAO analysis of annual report and Federal Reserve Y-9C data for Bank of America, Citigroup, JPMorgan Chase, Wachovia, and Wells Fargo.

Figure 5. Total Assets, Total Equity, and Assets-to-Equity Ratio in Aggregate for Five Large U.S. Bank Holding Companies, 1998 to 2007

The securitization of subprime mortgages and other loans can enable banks and securities firms to transfer credit risk from their balance sheets to parties more willing or able to manage that risk. However, the current crisis has revealed that much of the subprime mortgage exposure and losses have been concentrated among leveraged financial institutions, including banks, securities firms, and hedge funds.[27] For example, some banks and securities firms ended up with large exposures because they (1) were holding mortgages or mortgage-related securities for trading or investment purposes, (2) were holding mortgages or mortgage-related securities in inventory, or warehouses, that they planned to securitize but could not do so after the crisis began, or (3) brought onto their balance sheets mortgage-related securities held by SPEs. According to an equity analyst report, 10 large banks and securities firms had over $24 billion and $64 billion in writedowns in the third and fourth quarters of 2007, respectively.[28] Importantly, higher leverage magnifies market risk and can magnify liquidity risk if leveraged firms experiencing losses are forced to sell assets under adverse market conditions.

As their mortgage-related and other losses grew after the onset of the crisis, banks, securities firms, hedge funds, and other financial institutions have attempted to deleverage and reduce their risk. Deleveraging can cover a range of strategies, including raising new equity, reducing dividend payouts, diversifying sources of funds, selling assets, and reducing lending. After the crisis began, U.S. banks and securities firms initially deleveraged by raising more than $200 billion in new capital from private sources and sovereign wealth funds.[29] However, raising capital began to be increasingly difficult in the subsequent period, and financial institutions have deleveraged by selling assets, including financial instruments and noncore businesses. For example, in the fourth quarter of 2008, broker-dealers reduced assets by nearly $785 billion and banks reduced bank credit by nearly $84 billion.

Some Studies Suggested That Deleveraging Could Have Led to Downward Spirals in Asset Prices, but Other Theories also May Explain Price Declines

Some studies we reviewed highlighted the possibility that deleveraging through asset sales by financial institutions could trigger downward spirals in asset prices and contribute to a financial crisis.[30] These studies generally build on a broader theory that holds a market disruption, such as a sharp drop in asset prices, can be a source of systemic risk under certain circumstances.[31] Today, the securities markets, rather than banks, are the primary source of financial intermediation—the channeling of capital to investment opportunities. For example, in 1975, banks and thrifts held 56 percent of the total credit to households and businesses; by 2007, they held less than 30 percent.[32] To function efficiently, the securities markets need market liquidity, generally defined as the ability to buy and sell a particular asset without significantly affecting its price. According to the theory, a sharp decline in an asset's price can become self-sustaining and lead to a financial market crisis. Following a sharp decline in an asset's price, investors normally will buy the asset after they deem its price has dropped enough and help stabilize the market, but in times of crisis, investors are unable or unwilling to buy the asset. As the asset's price declines, more investors sell and push the price lower. At the extreme, the asset market's liquidity dries up and market gridlock takes hold. However, not all academics subscribe to this theory, but because the alternative theories are largely beyond the scope of our work, we only discuss them briefly.

Some studies we reviewed suggested that deleveraging through asset sales can lead to a downward asset spiral during times of market stress when market liquidity is low. Following a drop in an asset's price, one or more financial institutions may sell the asset. As noted above, certain financial institutions tend to adjust their balance sheets in a procyclical manner and, thus, may react in concert to a drop in an asset's price by selling the asset. When market liquidity is low, asset sales may cause further price declines. Under fair value accounting, financial institutions holding the asset will revalue their positions based on the asset's lower market value and record a loss that reduces their equity. For leveraged institutions holding the asset, the impact of their losses on capital will be magnified. To lower their leverage or risk, the institutions may sell more of their asset holdings, which can cause the asset's price to drop even more and induce another round of selling. In other words, when market liquidity is low, namely in times of market stress, asset sales establish lower market prices and result in financial institutions marking down their positions— potentially creating a reinforcing cycle of deleveraging. In the extreme, this downward asset spiral could cause the asset's price to be set below its fundamental value, or at a "fire sale" price.

Some studies we reviewed also suggested that deleveraging through asset sales could lead to a downward asset spiral when funding liquidity is low. In contrast to market liquidity, which is an asset-specific characteristic, funding liquidity generally refers to the availability of funds in the market that firms can borrow to meet their obligations. For example, financial institutions can increase their leverage by using secured or collateralized loans, such as repurchase agreements, to fund assets. Under such transactions, borrowers post securities with lenders to secure their loans. Lenders typically will not provide a loan for the full market value of the posted securities, with the difference called a margin or haircut. This deduction protects the lenders against default by the borrowers. When the prices of assets used to secure or collateralize loans decline significantly, borrowers may be required to post additional collateral, for example, if the value of the collateral falls below the loan amount or if a lender increased its haircuts.[33] Leveraged borrowers may find it difficult to post additional collateral, in part because declining asset prices also could result in losses that are large relative to their capital. If borrowers faced margin calls, they could be forced to sell some of their other assets to obtain the cash collateral. If the borrowers cannot meet their margin calls, the lenders may take possession of the assets and sell them. When market liquidity is low, such asset sales may cause the asset prices to drop more. If that occurred, other firms that have borrowed against the same assets could face margin calls to post more collateral, which could lead to another round of asset sales and subsequent price declines. Moreover, asset spirals stemming from reduced market or funding liquidity can reinforce each other.

Importantly, other theories that do not involve asset spirals caused by deleveraging through asset sales provide possible explanations for the sharp price declines in mortgage-related securities and other financial instruments. Moreover, as the crisis is complex, no single theory likely is to explain in full what occurred or necessarily rule out other explanations. Because such theories are largely beyond the scope of our work, we discuss them only in brief. First, given the default characteristics of the mortgages underlying their related securities and falling housing prices, the current valuations of such securities may reflect their true value, not "fire sale" prices. While there may have been some overreaction, this theory holds that low market prices may result from asset prices reverting to more reasonable values after a period of overvaluation. Second, the low prices of mortgage-related securities and other financial instruments may have resulted from the uncertainty surrounding their true value. This theory holds that investors may lack the information needed to distinguish between the good and bad securities and, as a result, discount the prices of the good securities.[34] In the extreme, investors may price the good securities far below their true value, leading to a collapse of the market. These two theories and the deleveraging hypothesis may provide some insight into how the financial crisis has unfolded and are not mutually exclusive. Nonetheless, at this juncture, it is difficult to determine whether a return to fundamentals, uncertainty, or forced asset sales played a larger causal role.

Studies Suggested That Deleveraging Could Have a Negative Effect on Economic Growth

In addition to deleveraging by selling assets, banks and broker-dealers can deleverage by restricting new lending as their own financial condition deteriorates, such as to preserve their capital and protect themselves against future losses. However, the studies we reviewed stated that this deleveraging strategy raises concerns because of the possibility it may slow economic growth.[35] In short, the concern is that banks, because of their leverage, will need to cut back their lending by a multiple of their credit losses to restore their balance sheets or capital-to-asset ratios. The contraction in bank lending can lead to a decline in consumption and investment spending, which reduces business and household incomes and negatively affects the real economy. Moreover, rapidly declining asset prices can inhibit the ability of borrowers to raise money in the securities markets.

One study suggested that the amount by which banks reduce their overall lending will be many times larger than their mortgage-related losses.[36] For example, the study estimated that if leveraged institutions suffered about $250 billion in mortgage-related losses, it would lead them to reduce their lending by about $1 trillion. However, these results should be interpreted with caution given that such estimates are inherently imprecise and subject to great uncertainty. Moreover, a portion of any reduction in bank lending could be due to reasons independent of the need to deleverage, such as a decline in the creditworthiness of borrowers, a tightening of previously lax lending standards, or the collapse of securitization markets.[37] In commenting on the study, a former Federal Reserve official noted that banks are important providers of credit but a contraction in their balance sheets would not necessarily choke off all lending.[38] Rather, he noted that a key factor in the current crisis is the sharp decline in securities issuances, and the decline has to be an important part of the story of why the current financial market turmoil is affecting economic activity. In summary, the Federal Reserve official said that the mortgage credit losses are a problem because they are hitting bank balance sheets at the same time that the securitization market is experiencing difficulties. As mentioned above, the securities markets have played an increasingly dominant role over banks in the financial intermediation process.

Regulators and Market Participants Had Mixed Views about the Effects of Deleveraging in the Current Crisis

Officials from federal financial regulators, two securities firms, a bank, and a credit rating agency whom we interviewed had mixed views about the effects of deleveraging by financial institutions in the current crisis. Nearly all of the officials told us that large banks and securities firms generally have sought to reduce their risk exposures since late 2007, partly in response to liquidity pressures. The institutions have used a number of strategies to deleverage, including raising new capital; curtailing certain lines of business based on a reassessment of their risk and return; and selling assets, including trading assets, consumer and commercial loans, and noncore businesses. Regulatory officials said that hedge funds and other asset managers, such as mutual funds, also have deleveraged by selling assets to meet redemptions or margin calls. According to officials at a securities firm, raising capital and selling financial assets was easier in the beginning of the crisis, but both became harder to do as the crisis continued. Regulatory and credit rating agency officials also said that financial institutions have faced challenges in selling mortgages and other loans that they planned to securitize, because the securitization markets essentially have shut down during the crisis.

The regulators and market participants we interviewed had mixed views on whether sales of financial assets contributed to a downward price spiral. Officials from one bank and the Federal Reserve staff said that due to the lack of market liquidity for some instruments and the unwillingness of many market participants to sell them, declines in prices that may be attributed to market-driven asset spirals generally resulted from the use of models to price assets in the absence of any sales. Federal Reserve staff also said that it is hard to attribute specific factors as a cause of an observed asset spiral because of the difficulty in disentangling the interacting factors that can cause financial asset prices to move down. In contrast, officials from two securities firms and a credit rating agency, and staff from SEC and OCC told us that asset spirals occurred in certain mortgage and other debt markets. The securities firm officials said that margin calls forced sales in illiquid markets and caused the spirals. Officials from one securities firm said that financial institutions, such as hedge funds, generally sought to sell first those financial assets that were hardest to finance, which eventually caused their markets to become illiquid. The absence of observable prices for such assets then caused their prices to deteriorate even more. According to the securities firm officials, firms that needed to sell assets to cover losses or meet margin calls helped to drive such asset sales. OCC staff attributed some of the downward price spirals to the loss of liquidity in the securitization markets. They said that traditional buyers of securitized assets became sellers, causing the securitization markets to become dislocated.

As suggested in an April 2008 testimony by the former president of the Federal Reserve Bank of New York, reduced funding liquidity may have resulted in a downward price spiral during the current crisis:

> Asset price declines—triggered by concern about the outlook for economic performance—led to a reduction in the willingness to bear risk and to margin calls. Borrowers needed to sell assets to meet the calls; some highly leveraged firms were unable to meet their obligations and their counterparties responded by liquidating the collateral they held. This put downward pressure on asset prices and increased price volatility. Dealers raised margins further to compensate for heightened volatility and reduced liquidity. This, in turn, put more pressure on other leveraged investors. A self- reinforcing downward spiral of higher haircuts forced sales, lower prices, higher volatility and still lower prices.[39]

Similarly, in its white paper on the Public-Private Investment Program, Treasury has indicated that deleveraging through asset sales has led to price spirals:

The resulting need to reduce risk triggered a wide-scale deleveraging in these markets and led to fire sales. As prices declined further, many traditional sources of capital exited these markets, causing declines in secondary market liquidity. As a result, we have been in a vicious cycle in which declining asset prices have triggered further deleveraging and reductions in market liquidity, which in turn have led to further price declines. While fundamentals have surely deteriorated over the past 18-24 months, there is evidence that current prices for some legacy assets embed substantial liquidity discounts.[40]

FDIC and OCC staff and officials from a credit rating agency told us that some banks have tightened their lending standards for certain types of loans, namely those with less-favorable risk-adjusted returns. Such loans include certain types of residential and commercial mortgages, leverage loans, and loans made to hedge funds. OCC staff said that some banks began to tighten their lending standards in 2007, meaning that they would not be making as many marginal loans, and such action corresponded with a decline in demand for loans. According to credit rating officials, banks essentially have set a target of slower growth for higher-risk loans that have performed poorly and deteriorated their loan portfolios. In addition, OCC and credit rating officials said that the largest banks rely heavily on their ability to securitize loans to help them make such loans. To that end, they said that the securitization markets need to open up and provide funding.

As we have discussed in our prior work, since the crisis began, federal regulators and authorities have undertaken a number of steps to facilitate financial intermediation by banks and the securities markets.[41] To help provide banks with funds to make loans, Treasury, working with the regulators, has used its authority under the act to inject capital into banks so that they would be stronger and more stable. Similarly, the Federal Reserve has reduced the target interest rate to close to zero and has implemented a number of programs designed to support the liquidity of financial institutions and foster improved conditions in financial markets. These programs include provision of short-term liquidity to banks and other financial institutions and the provision of liquidity directly to borrowers and investors in key credit markets. To support the functioning of the credit markets, the Federal Reserve also has purchased longer-term securities, including government-sponsored enterprise debt and mortgage-backed securities. In addition, FDIC has created the Temporary Liquidity Guarantee Program, in part to strengthen confidence and encourage liquidity in the banking system by guaranteeing newly issued senior unsecured debt of banks, thrifts, and certain holding companies.

REGULATORS LIMIT FINANCIAL INSTITUTIONS' USE OF LEVERAGE PRIMARILY THROUGH REGULATORY CAPITAL REQUIREMENTS

Federal financial regulators generally have imposed capital and other requirements on their regulated institutions as a way to limit excessive use of leverage and ensure the stability of the financial system and markets. Federal banking and thrift regulators have imposed minimum risk-based capital and non-risk-based leverage ratios on their regulated institutions. In addition, they supervise the capital adequacy of their regulated institutions through ongoing monitoring, including on-site examinations and off-site tools. Bank holding companies are subject to capital and leverage ratio requirements similar to those for banks.[42]

Thrift holding companies are not subject to such requirements; rather, capital levels of thrift holding companies are individually evaluated based on each company's risk profile. SEC primarily uses its net capital rule to limit the use of leverage by broker-dealers. Firms that had participated in SEC's now defunct CSE program calculated their risk-based capital ratios at the holding company level in a manner generally consistent with the method banks used.[43] Other financial institutions, such as hedge funds, use leverage but, unlike banks and broker-dealers, typically are not subject to regulatory capital requirements; instead, market discipline plays a primary role in limiting leverage. Finally, the Federal Reserve regulates the use of securities as collateral to finance security purchases, but federal financial regulators told us that such credit did not play a significant role in the buildup of leverage leading to the current crisis.

Federal Banking and Thrift Regulators Have Imposed Minimum Capital and Leverage Ratios on Their Regulated Institutions to Limit the Use of Leverage

Federal banking and thrift regulators (Federal Reserve, FDIC, OCC, and OTS) restrict the excessive use of leverage by their regulated financial institutions primarily through minimum risk-based capital requirements established under the Basel Accord and non-risk based leverage requirements. If a financial institution falls below certain capital requirements, regulators can impose certain restrictions, and must impose others, and thereby limit a financial institution's use of leverage. Under the capital requirements, banks and thrifts are required to meet two risk-based capital ratios, which are calculated by dividing their qualifying capital (numerator) by their risk-weighted assets (denominator).[44] Total capital consists of core capital, called Tier 1 capital, and supplementary capital, called Tier 2 capital.[45] Total risk-weighted assets are calculated using a process that assigns risk weights to the assets according to their credit and market risks. This process is broadly intended to assign higher risk weights and require banks to hold more capital for higher-risk assets. For example, cash held by a bank or thrift is assigned a risk weight of 0 percent for credit risk, meaning that the asset would not be counted in a bank's total risk-weighted assets and, thus, would not require the bank or thrift to hold any capital for that asset. OTC derivatives also are included in the calculation of total risk-weighted assets. Banks and thrifts are required to meet a minimum ratio of total capital to risk-weighted assets of 8 percent, with at least 4 percent taking the form of Tier 1 capital. However, regulators told us that they can recommend that their institutions hold capital in excess of the minimum requirements, if warranted (discussed in more detail below).

Banks and thrifts also are subject to minimum non-risk-based leverage standards, measured as a ratio of Tier 1 capital to total assets. The minimum leverage requirement to be adequately capitalized is between 3 and 4 percent, depending on the type of institution and a regulatory assessment of the strength of its management and controls.[46] Leverage ratios have been part of bank and thrift regulatory requirements since the 1980s, and regulators continued to use the leverage ratios after the introduction of risk-based capital requirements to provide a cushion against risks not explicitly covered in the risk-based capital requirements, such as operational weaknesses in internal policies, systems, and controls or model risk or related measurement risk. The greater level of capital required by the risk-based or leverage capital calculation is the binding overall minimum requirement on an institution.

Federal banking regulators are required to take increasingly severe actions as an institution's capital deteriorates under Prompt Corrective Action (PCA).[47] These rules apply to banks and thrifts but not to bank holding companies. Under PCA, regulators are to classify insured depository institutions into one of five capital categories based on their level of capital: well-capitalized, adequately capitalized, undercapitalized, significantly undercapitalized, and critically undercapitalized.[48] Institutions that fail to meet the requirements to be classified as well or adequately capitalized generally face several mandatory restrictions or requirements. Specifically, the regulator will require an undercapitalized institution to submit a capital restoration plan detailing how it is going to become adequately capitalized. Moreover, no insured institution may pay a dividend if it would be undercapitalized after the dividend. When an institution becomes significantly undercapitalized, regulators are required to take more forceful corrective measures, including requiring the sale of equity or debt, restricting otherwise allowable transactions with affiliates, or restricting the interest rates paid on deposits. After an institution becomes critically undercapitalized, regulators have 90 days to place the institution into receivership or conservatorship or to take other actions that would better prevent or reduce long-term losses to the insurance fund.[49]

Regulators Can Use Various Oversight Approaches to Monitor and Enforce Capital Adequacy

Federal bank and thrift regulators can supervise the capital adequacy of their regulated institutions by tracking the financial condition of their regulated entities through on-site examinations and continuous monitoring for the larger institutions.[50] According to Federal Reserve officials, the risk-based capital and leverage measures are relatively simple ratios and are not sufficient, alone, for assessing overall capital adequacy. In that regard, the supervisory process enables examiners to assess the capital adequacy of banks at a more detailed level. On-site examinations serve to evaluate the institution's overall risk exposure and focus on an institution's capital adequacy, asset quality, management and internal control procedures, earnings, liquidity, and sensitivity to market risk (CAMELS).[51] For example, the examination manual directs Federal Reserve examiners to evaluate the internal capital management processe s and assess the risk and composition of the assets held by banks. Similarly, OCC examiners told us that they focused on the capital levels of large banks in their examinations during the current crisis and raised concerns about certain banks' weak results from the stress testing of their capital adequacy.

Federal bank and thrift regulatory officials told us that they also can encourage their regulated institutions to hold more than the minimum required capital, if warranted. For example, if examiners find that an institution is exceeding its capital ratios but holding a large share of risky assets, the examiners could recommend that the bank enhance its capital. As stated in the Federal Reserve's examination manual, because risk-based capital does not take explicit account of the quality of individual asset portfolios or the range of other types of risks to which banks may be exposed, banks generally are expected to operate with capital positions above the minimum ratios. Moreover, banks with high levels of risk also are expected to maintain capital well above the minimum levels. According to OTS officials, under certain circumstances, OTS can require an institution to increase its capital ratio, whether through reducing its risk-weighted assets, boosting its capital, or both. For example, OTS could identify through its examinations that downgraded securities could be problematic for a firm. OTS can then require a troubled institution under its supervisory authority, through informal and formal actions, to in crease its capital ratio. Moreover, the charter application process for becoming a thrift institution can provide an opportunity to encourage institutions to increase their capital. Bank and thrift regulators also can use their enforcement process, if warranted, to require a bank or thrift to take action to address a capital-adequacy weakness.

Federal bank and thrift regulators told us that they also use off-site tools to monitor the capital adequacy of institutions. For example, examiners use Consolidated Reports of Condition and Income (Call Report) and Thrift Financial Report data to remotely assess the financial condition of banks and thrifts, respectively, and to plan the scope of on-site examinations.[52] Regulators also use computerized monitoring systems that use Call Report data to compute, for example, financial ratios, growth trends, and peer-group comparisons. OCC officials with whom we spoke said that they review Call Reports to ensure that banks are calculating their capital ratios correctly. FDIC officials also told us that they used the data on depository institutions to conduct informal analyses to assess the potential impact a credit event or other changes could have on banks' capital adequacy. They said that FDIC has performed such analyses on bank holdings of various types of mortgage-related securities.

In addition, federal bank and thrift regulators also can conduct targe ted reviews, such as those related to capital adequacy of their regulated entities. For example, in 2007, a horizontal study led by the Federal Reserve Bank of New York examined how large banks determined their economic capital, which banks use to help assess their capital adequacy and manage risk. Federal Reserve examiners told us that they typically do not conduct horizontal studies on leverage, because they cover the institutions' use of leverage when routinely supervising their institutions' capital adequacy. Federal Reserve officials told us supervisors believe that capital adequacy is better reviewed and evaluated through continuous monitoring processes that evaluate capital adequacy against the individual risks at a firm and compare capital and risk levels across a portfolio of institutions, rather than through the use of horizontal exams that would typically seek to review banks' processes.

Bank Holding C ompanies Are Subject to Capital and Leverage Ratio Requirements Similar to Those for Banks, but Thrift Holding Companies Are Not

Bank holding companies are subject to risk-based capital and leverage ratio requirements, which are similar to those applied to banks except for the lack of applicability of PCA and the increased flexibility affo rded to bank holding companies to use debt instruments in regulatory capital. The Federal Reserve requires that all bank holding companies with consolidated assets of $500 million or more meet risk-based capital requirements developed in accordance with the Basel Accord. In addition, it has required, with the other bank supervisors, revised capital adequacy rules to implement Basel II for the largest bank holding companies.[53] To be considered well-capitalized, a bank holding company with consolidated assets of $500 million or more generally must have a Tier 1 risk-based capital ratio of 4 percent, and a minimum total risk-based capital ratio of 8 percent, and a leverage ratio of at least 4 percent.[54]

According to OTS officials, thrift holding companies generally are not subject to minimum capital or leverage ratios because of their diversity. Rather, capital levels of thrift holding companies are individually evaluated based on each company's risk profile. OTS requires that thrift holding companies hold a "prudential" level of capital on a consolidated basis to support the risk profile of the holding company.[55] For its most complex firms, OTS requires a detailed capital calculation that includes an assessment of capital adequacy on a groupwide basis and identification of capital that might not be available to the holding company or its other subsidiaries, because it is required to be held by a specific entity for regulatory purposes. Under this system, OTS benchmarks thrift holding companies against peer institutions that face similar risks.

In supervising the capital adequacy of bank and thrift holding companies, the Federal Reserve and OTS are to focus on those business activities posing the greatest risk to holding companies and managements' processes for identifying, measuring, monitoring, and controlling those risks. The Federal Reserve's supervisory cycle for large complex bank holding companies generally begins with the development of a systematic risk-focused supervisory plan, which it then implements, and ends with a rating of the firm. The rating includes an assessment of holding companies' risk management and controls; financial condition, including capital adequacy; and impact on insured depositories.[56] In addition, the Federal Reserve requires that all bank holding companies serve as a source of financial and managerial strength to their subsidiary banks. Similarly, OTS applies the CORE (Capital, Organizational Structure, Risk Management, and Earnings) rating system for large complex thrift holding companies. CORE focuses on consolidated risks, internal controls, and capital adequacy rather than focusing solely on the holding company's impact on subsidiary thrifts. In reviewing capital adequacy, particularly in large, complex thrift holding companies, OTS considers the risks inherent in the enterprise's capital to absorb unexpected losses, support the level and composition of the parent company's and subsidiaries' debt, and support business plans and strategies.

The Federal Reserve and OTS have a range of formal and informal actions they can take to enforce their regulations for holding companies. Federal Reserve officials noted that the law provides explicit authority for any formal actions that may be warranted and incentives for bank holding companies to address concerns promptly or through less formal enforcement actions, such as corrective action resolutions adopted by the company's board of directors or memoranda of understanding in which the relevant Federal Reserve bank enters.[57] Similarly, OTS also has statutory authority to take enforcement actions against thrift holding companies and any subsidiaries of those companies.[58]

Both the Federal Reserve and OTS also monitor the capital adequacy of their respective regulated holding companies using off-site tools. For example, the Federal Reserve noted that it obtains financial information from bank holding companies in a uniform format through a variety of periodic regulatory reports and uses the data to conduct peer analysis, including a comparison of their capital adequacy ratios. Similarly, according to a June 2008 testimony by an OTS official, OTS in 2008 conducted an extensive review of capital levels at the thrift holding companies and found that savings and loan holding company peer group averages were strong.[59]

SEC Has Regulated the Use of Leverage by Broker- Dealers Primarily through Its Net Capital Rule

According to SEC staff, the agency regulates the use of leverage by registered broker-dealers primarily through the risk-based measures prescribed in its net capital and customer protection rules.[60] SEC adopted these rules pursuant to its broad authority to adopt rules and regulations regarding the financial responsibility of broker-dealers that it finds necessary in the public interest or for the protection of customers.[61]

Under the net capital rule, broker-dealers are required to maintain a minimum amount of net capital at all times. Net capital is computed in several steps. A broker-dealer's net worth (assets minus liabilities) is calculated using U.S. Generally Accepted Accounting Principles (GAAP). Certain subordinated liabilities are added back to GAAP equity because the net capital rule allows them to count toward capital, subject to certain conditions. Deductions are taken from GAAP equity for assets that are not readily convertible into cash, such as unsecured receivables and fixed assets. The net capital rule further requires prescribed percentage deductions from GAAP equity, called "haircuts." Haircuts provide a capital cushion to reflect an expectation about possible losses on proprietary securities and financial instruments held by a broker-dealer resulting from adverse events. The amount of the haircut on a position is a function of, among other things, the position's market risk liquidity. A haircut is taken on a broker-dealer's proprietary position because the proceeds received from selling assets during liquidation depend on the liquidity and market risk of the assets.

Under the net capital rule, a broker-dealer must at all times have net capital equal to the greater of two amounts: (1) a minimum amount based on the type of business activities conducted by the firm or (2) a financial ratio.[62] The broker-dealers must elect one of two financial ratios: the basic method (based on aggregate indebtness) or the alternative method (based on aggregate debit items). That is, broker-dealers must hold different minimum levels of capital based on the nature of their business and whether they handle customer funds or securities. According to SEC staff, most broker-dealers that carry customer accounts use the alternative method. Under this method, broker-dealers are required to have net capital equal to the greater of $250,000 or 2 percent of aggregate debit items, which generally are customer-related receivables, such as cash and securities owned by customers but held by their broker-dealers.[63] This amount serves to ensure that broker-dealers have sufficient capital to repay creditors and pay their liquidation expense if they fail.

According to SEC staff, the customer protection rule, a separate but related rule, requires broker-dealers to safeguard customer property, so that they can return such property if they failed.[64] The rule requires a broker-dealer to take certain steps to protect the credit balances and securities it holds for customers. Under the rule, a broker-dealer must, in essence, segregate customer funds and fully paid and excess margin securities held by the firm for the accounts of customers. The intent of the rule is to require a broker-dealer to hold customer assets in a manner that enables their prompt return in the event of an insolvency, which increases the ability of the firm to wind down in an orderly self-liquidation and thereby avoid the need for a proceeding under the Securities Investor Protection Act of 1970.[65]

SEC oversees U.S. broker-dealers but delegates some of its authority to oversee broker-dealers to one or more of the various self-regulatory organizations, including the Financial Industry Regulatory Authority (FINRA), an SRO that was established in 2007 through the consolidation of NASD and the member regulation, enforcement, and arbitration functions of the New York Stock Exchange (NYSE). SEC and the SROs conduct regularly scheduled target examinations that focus on the risk areas identified in their risk assessments of firms and on compliance with relevant capital and customer protection rules.[66] SEC's internal control risk-management examinations, which started in 1995, cover the top 15 wholesale and top 15 retail broker-dealers and a number of mid-sized broker-dealers with a large number of customer accounts. SEC conducts examinations every 3 years at the largest institutions, while the SROs conduct more frequent examinations of all broker-dealers. For instance, FINRA examines all broker-dealers that carry customer accounts at least once annually. According to SEC and FINRA, they receive financial and risk area information on a regular basis from all broker-dealers. In addition, the largest brokers and those of financial concern provide additional information through monitoring programs and regular meetings with the firms.

SEC Regulated the Use of Leverage by Selected Broker-Dealers under an Alternative Net Capital Rule from 2005 to 2008

From 2005 to September 2008, SEC implemented the voluntary CSE program, in which five broker-dealer holding companies had participated. In 2004, SEC adopted the program by amending its net capital rule to establish a voluntary, alternative method of computing net capital. A broker-dealer became a CSE by applying for an exemption from the net capital rule and, as a condition of the exemption, the broker-dealer holding company consented to consolidated supervision (if it was not already subject to such supervision). According to SEC staff, a broker-dealer electing this alternative method is subject to enhanced net capital, early warning, recordkeeping, reporting, liquidity, and certain other requirements, and must implement and document an internal risk management system. Under the new alternative net capital rule, CSE broker-dealers were permitted to use their internal mathematical risk measurement models, rather than SEC's haircut structure, to calculate their haircuts for the credit and market risk associated with their trading and investment positions. Expecting that firms would be able to lower their haircuts and, in turn, capital charges by using their internal risk models, SEC required as a safeguard that CSE broker-dealers maintain at least $500 million in net capital and at least $1 billion in tentative net capital (equity before haircut deductions). According to SEC staff, because of an early warning requirement set at $5 billion for tentative net capital, CSE broker-dealers effectively had to maintain a minimum of $5 billion in tentative net capital. If a firm fell below that level, it would need to notify SEC, which could require the firm to take remedial action. Recognizing that capital is not synonymous with liquidity, SEC also expected each CSE holding company to maintain a liquid portfolio of cash and highly liquid and highly rated debt instruments in an amount based on its liquidity risk management analysis, which includes stress tests that address, among other things, illiquid assets.[67]

In addition to consenting to consolidated regulation, the CSE holding companies agreed to calculate their capital ratio consistent with the Basel II capital standards. SEC expected CSE holding companies to maintain a risk-based capital ratio of not less than 10 percent. According to SEC staff, the 10-percent risk-based capital ratio was the threshold that constituted a well-capitalized institution under the Basel standards and was consistent with the threshold used by banking regulators, but it was not a regulatory requirement. The CSE holding companies were required to notify SEC if they breached or were likely to breach the 10-percent capital ratio. According to SEC staff, if it received such a notification, the staff would have required the CSE holding company to take remedial action. Moreover, SEC staff said that they received and monitored holding company capital calculations on a monthly basis. SEC staff also said that the CSE holding companies were holding capital above the amount needed to meet the 10-percent risk-based capital ratio during the current crisis, except for one institution that later restored its capital ratio.

The holding companies and their broker-dealers that participated in the CSE program were not subject to explicit non-risk based leverage limits before or after SEC created the program. According to SEC staff, the broker-dealers' ability to increase leverage was limited through the application of haircuts on their proprietary positions under the net capital rule. To the extent that the use of their internal models (instead of SEC's haircut structure) by the broker-dealers enabled them to reduce the amount of their haircuts, they could take on larger proprietary positions and increase their leverage. However, SEC staff told us that the broker-dealers generally did not take such action after joining the CSE program. The staff said that the primary sources of leverage for the broker-dealers were customer margin loans, repurchase agreements, and stock lending. According to the staff, these transactions were driven by customers and counterparties, marked daily, and secured by collateral—exposing the broker-dealers to little, if any, market risk. In addition, SEC did not seek to impose a non-risk based leverage limit on CSE holding companies, in part because such a leverage ratio treated all on-balance sheet assets as equally risky and created an incentive for firms to move exposures off-balance sheet. Officials at a former CSE told us that their firm's decision to become a CSE was to provide the firm with another way to measure its capital adequacy. They said the firm did not view the CSE program as a strategy to increase its leverage, although it was able to reduce its broker-dealer's haircuts. According to the officials, the firm's increase in leverage after becoming a CSE likely was driven by market factors and business opportunities. In our prior work on Long-Term Capital Management (a hedge fund), we analyzed the assets-to-equity ratios of four of the five broker-dealer holding companies that later became CSEs and found that three had ratios equal to or greater than 28-to-1 at fiscal year-end 1998, which was higher than their ratios at fiscal year-end 2006 before the crisis began (see figure 6).[68]

SEC's Division of Trading and Markets had responsibility for administering the CSE program. According to SEC staff, the CSE program was modeled on the Federal Reserve's holding company supervision program. SEC staff said that continuous supervision was usually conducted through regular monthly meetings on-site with CSE firm risk managers to monitor liquidity and funding and to review how market and credit risks are identified, quantified, and communicated to senior management and whether senior managers have approved of the risk exposures. Quarterly meetings were held with senior managers from treasury and internal audit. According to SEC staff, these regularly scheduled risk meetings were frequently supplemented by additional on-site meetings and off-site discussions throughout the month. SEC did not rate risk-management systems or use a detailed risk assessment processes to determine areas of highest risk. During the CSE program, SEC staff concentrated their efforts on market, credit, and liquidity risks, because the alternative net capital rule focused on these risks, and on operational risk because of the need to protect investors. Because only five broker-dealer holding companies were subject to SEC's consolidated supervision, SEC staff tailored certain reporting requirements and reviews to focus on activities that posed material risks for that firm. According to SEC staff, the CSE program allowed SEC to conduct reviews across the five firms to gain insights into business areas that were material by risk or balance sheet measures, rapidly growing, posed particular challenges in implementing the Basel regulatory risk- based capital regime, or had some combination of these characteristics. Such reviews resulted in four firms modifying their capital computations.

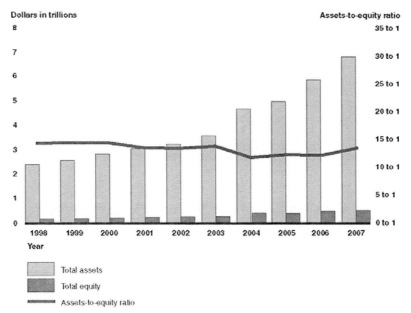

Source: GAO analysis of annual report and Federal Reserve Y-9C data for Bank of America, Citigroup, JPMorgan Chase, Wachovia, and Wells Fargo.

Figure 6. Ratio of Total Assets to Equity for Four Broker-Dealer Holding Companies, 1998 to 2007

In September 2008, the former SEC Chairman announced that the agency ended the CSE program. According to the SEC Chairman, the three investments banks formerly designated as CSEs are now part of a bank holding company structure and subject to supervision by the Federal Reserve. The chairman noted that SEC will continue to work closely with the Federal Reserve under a memorandum of understanding between the two agencies but will focus on its statutory obligation to regulate the broker-dealer subsidiaries of the bank holding companies, including the implementation of the alternative net capital computation by certain broker-dealers. While no institutions are subject to SEC oversight at the consolidated level under the CSE program, several broker-dealers within bank holding companies are still subject to the alternative net capital rule on a voluntary basis.[69]

Hedge Funds Generally Are Not Subject to Direct Regulations That Restrict Their Use of Leverage but Face Limitations through Market Discipline

Hedge funds have become important participants in the financial markets and many use leverage, such as borrowed funds and derivatives, in their trading strategies. They generally are structured and operated in a manner that enables them to qualify for exemptions from certain federal securities laws and regulations.[70] Because their investors are presumed to be sophisticated and therefore not require the full protection offered by the securities laws, hedge funds generally have not been subject to direct regulation. As a result, hedge funds typically are not subject to regulatory capital requirements or limited by regulation in their use of leverage. Instead, market discipline has the primary role, supplemented by indirect regulatory oversight of commercial banks and securities and futures firms, in constraining risk taking and leveraging by hedge fund managers (advisers).

Market participants (for example, investors, creditors, and counterparties) can impose market discipline by rewarding well-managed hedge funds and reducing their exposure to risky, poorly managed hedge funds. Hedge fund advisers use leverage, in addition to money invested into the fund by investors, to employ sophisticated investment strategies and techniques to generate returns. A number of large commercial banks and prime brokers bear and manage the credit and counterparty risks that hedge fund leverage creates. Typically, hedge funds seeking direct leverage can obtain funding either through margin financing from a prime broker or through the repurchase agreement markets. Exercising counterparty risk-management is the primary mechanism by which these types of financial institutions impose market discipline on hedge funds' use of leverage. The credit risk exposures between hedge funds and their creditors and counterparties arise primarily from trading and lending relationships, including various types of derivatives and securities transactions. Creditors and counterparties of large hedge funds use their own internal rating and credit or counterparty risk management processes and may require additional collateral from hedge funds as a buffer against increased risk exposure. As part of their due diligence, they typically request from hedge funds information such as capital and risk measures; periodic net asset valuation calculations; fees and redemption policy; and annual audited statements along with hedge fund managers' background and track record. Creditors and counterparties can establish credit terms partly based on the scope and depth of information that hedge funds are willing to provide, the willingness of the fund managers to answer questions during on-site visits, and the assessment of the hedge fund's risk exposure and capacity to manage risk. If approved, the hedge fund receives a credit rating and a line of credit. Some creditors and counterparties also can measure counterparty credit exposure on an ongoing basis through a credit system that is updated each day to determine current and potential exposures. As we reported in our earlier work, for market discipline to be effective, (1) investors, creditors, and counterparties must have access to, and act upon, sufficient and timely information to assess a fund's risk profile; (2) investors, creditors, and counterparties must have sound risk-management policies, procedures, and systems to evaluate and limit their credit risk exposures to hedge funds; and (3) creditors and counterparties must increase the costs or decrease the availability of credit to their hedge fund clients as the creditworthiness of the latter deteriorates.[71] Similar to other financial institutions, hedge funds also have had to deleverage. According to the 2008 Global Financial Stability Report by the International Monetary Fund, due to the current financial crisis, margin financing from prime brokers has been cut, and haircuts and fees on repurchase agreements have increased. The combination of these factors has caused average hedge fund leverage to fall to 1.4 times capital (from 1.7 times last year) according to market estimates.

Although hedge funds generally are not directly regulated, many advisers to hedge funds are subject to federal oversight. Under the existing regulatory structure, SEC and CFTC regulate those hedge fund advisers that are registered with them, and SEC, CFTC, as well as the federal bank regulators monitor hedge fund-related activities of other regulated entities, such as broker-dealers and commercial banks. As registered investment advisers, hedge fund advisers are subject to SEC examinations and reporting, record keeping, and disclosure requirements. Similarly, CFTC regulates those hedge fund advisers registered as commodity pool operators or commodity trading advisors.[72] CFTC has authorized the National Futures Association, an SRO, to conduct day-to-day monitoring of such registered entities. In addition, SEC, CFTC, and bank regulators use their existing authorities—to establish capital standards and reporting requirements, conduct risk-based examinations, and take enforcement actions—to oversee activities, including those involving hedge funds, of broker-dealers, futures commission merchants, and banks, respectively. As we recently reported, although none of the regulators we interviewed specifically monitored hedge fund activities on an ongoing basis, regulators generally have increased reviews—by such means as targeted examinations—of systems and policies to mitigate counterparty credit risk at the large regulated entities.[73]

Federal banking and securities regulators have established regulatory and supervisory structures to limit and oversee the use of leverage by financial institutions. However, as the financial crisis has unfolded and the regulatory oversight of troubled institutions has been scrutinized, concerns have been raised about the adequacy of such oversight in some areas. For example, in its material loss review on IndyMac Bank, the Treasury Inspector General (IG) found that OTS failed to take PCA action in a timely manner when IndyMac's capital adequacy classification first appeared to haven fallen below minimum standards.[74] In addition, the Treasury IG noted that OTS had given IndyMac satisfactory CAMELS ratings despite a number of concerns about IndyMac's capital levels, asset quality, management and liquidity during 2001 through 2007. Separately, a Federal Reserve official testified in March 2009 that the Federal Reserve has recognized that it needs to improve its communication of supervisory and regulatory policies, guidance, and expectations to those banks it regulates by frequently updating their rules and regulations and more quickly issuing guidance as new risks and concerns are identified.[75] As another example, in its audit of SEC's oversight of CSEs, the SEC IG found that the CSE program failed to effectively oversee these institutions for several reasons, including the lack of an effective mechanism for ensuring that these entities maintained sufficient capital.[76] The SEC IG made a number of recommendations to improve the CSE program. In commenting on the SEC IG report, management of SEC's Division of Trading and Markets stated that the report is fundamentally flawed in its processes, premises, analysis, and key findings and reaches inaccurate, unrealistic, and impracticable conclusions. Although the CSE program has ended, the former SEC Chairman stated in response to the IG report that the agency will look closely at the applicability of the recommendations to other areas of SEC's work.

The Federal Reserve Regulates the Use of Credit to Purchase Securities under Regulation T and U, but Regulators Said That Such Credit Did Not Play a Significant Role in the Buildup of Leverage

To increase their leverage, investors can post securities as collateral with broker-dealers, banks, and other lenders to obtain loans to finance security purchases. Historically, such lending has raised concerns that it diverted credit away from productive uses to speculation in the stock market and caused excessive fluctuations in stock prices. But the preponderance of academic evidence is that margin lending does not divert credit from productive uses and its regulation is not an effective tool for preventing stock market volatility. To prevent the excessive use of credit to purchase or trade securities, Section 7 of the Securities and Exchange Act of 1934 authorized the Federal Reserve System to regulate such loans.[77] Pursuant to that authority, the Federal Reserve has promulgated Regulations T, U, and X, which set the minimum amount of margin that customers must initially post when engaging in securities transactions on credit.[78] Regulation T applies to margin loans made by broker-dealers, Regulation U applies to margin loans made by banks and other lenders, and Regulation X applies to margin loans obtained by U.S. persons and certain related persons who obtain securities credit outside the United States to purchase U.S. securities, whose transactions are not explicitly covered by the other two regulations.[79] In effect, these regulations limit the extent to which customers can increase their leverage by using debt to finance their securities positions.

The Federal Reserve has raised and lowered the initial margin requirements for equity securities many times since enactment of the Securities Exchange Act of 1934. The highest margin requirement was 100 percent, adopted for about a year after the end of World War II. The lowest margin requirement was 40 percent and was in effect during the late 1930s and early 1940s. Otherwise, the initial margin requirement for equity securities has varied between 50 and 75 percent. The Federal Reserve has left the initial margin requirement at 50 percent since 1974.[80]

Federal Reserve, OCC, and SEC staff told us that credit extended under Regulation T and U generally did not play a significant role in the buildup of leverage before the current crisis. According to Federal Reserve staff, Regulation T and U cover only one of many sources of credit and market participants have many ways to obtain leverage not covered by the regulations. For example, the credit markets are international, and market participants can obtain credit overseas where Regulation T and U do not apply. Similarly, OCC staff said that the margin regulations largely have been made obsolete by market developments. Under Regulation T and U, margins are set at 50 percent for the initial purchase of equities, but large investors can obtain greater leverage using non-equity securities (such as government securities) as collateral and various types of derivatives.[81] Finally, SEC staff told us that hedge funds and other investors do not widely use equities for margin and, in turn, leverage purposes because of Regulation T's restrictions. The staff said that hedge funds and other market participants can use other financial instruments to increase their leverage, such as exchange-traded futures contracts. As shown in figure 7, the total margin debt (dollar value of securities purchased on margin) consistently increased from year-end 2002 to year-end 2007, but the amount of margin debt as a percentage of the total capitalization of NYSE and NASDAQ stock markets was less than 2 percent.[82]

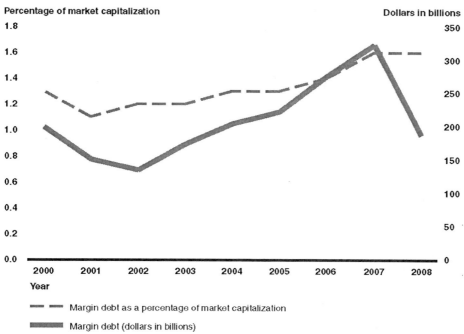

Source: GAO analysis of NYSE's margin debt data and the World Federation of Exchanges' market capitalization data.

Note: Margin debt as a percentage of the total stock market capitalization is overstated in the figure because the margin debt data include equity and non-equity securities but the market capitalization data include only equity securities.

Figure 7. Margin Debt and Margin Debt as a Percentage of the Total Capitalization of the NYSE and NASDAQ Stock Markets, 2000 through 2008

REGULATORS ARE CONSIDERING REFORMS TO ADDRESS LIMITATIONS THE CRISIS REVEALED IN REGULATORY FRAMEWORK FOR RESTRICTING LEVERAGE, BUT HAVE NOT REEVALUATED BASEL II IMPLEMENTATION

The financial crisis has revealed limitations in existing regulatory approaches that restrict leverage, and although regulators have proposed changes to improve the risk coverage of the regulatory capital framework, limit cyclical leverage trends and better address sources of systemic risk, they have not yet formally reevaluated U.S. Basel II implementation in considering needed reforms. First, regulatory capital measures did not always fully capture certain risks, particularly those associated with some mortgage-related securities held on and off balance sheets. As a result, a number of financial institutions did not hold capital commensurate with their risks and some lacked adequate capital or liquidity to withstand the crisis. Federal financial regulators are considering reforms to better align capital requirements with risk, but have not formally assessed the extent to which these reforms may address risk-evaluation concerns the crisis highlighted with respect to Basel II approaches. Such an assessment is critical to ensure that Basel II changes that would increase reliance on complex risk models and banks' own risk estimates do not exacerbate regulatory limitations revealed by the crisis. Second, the crisis illustrated how the existing regulatory framework might have contributed to cyclical leverage trends that potentially exacerbated the current crisis. For example, according to regulators, minimum regulatory capital requirements may not provide adequate incentives for banks to build loss- absorbing capital buffers in benign markets when it would be less expensive to do so. Finally, the financial crisis has illustrated the potential for financial market disruptions, not just firm failures, to be a source of systemic risk. With multiple regulators primarily responsible for individual markets or institutions, none of the financial regulators has clear responsibility to assess the potential effects of the buildup of systemwide leverage or the collective activities of the industry for the financial system. As a result, regulators may be limited in their ability to prevent or mitigate future financial crises.

Regulatory Capital Measures Did Not Fully Capture Certain Risks

While a key goal of the regulatory capital framework is to align capital requirements with risks, the financial crisis revealed that a number of large financial institutions did not hold capital commensurate with the full range of risks they faced. U.S. federal financial regulators and market observers have noted that the accuracy of risk-based regulatory capital measures depends on proper evaluation of firms' on and off-balance sheet risk exposures. However, according to regulators, before the crisis many large financial institutions and their regulators underestimated the actual and contingent risks associated with certain risk exposures. As a result, capital regulations permitted institutions to hold insufficient capital against those exposures, some of which became sources of large losses or liquidity pressures as market conditions deteriorated in 2007 and 2008. When severe stresses appeared, many large banks did not have sufficient capital to absorb losses and faced pressures to deleverage suddenly and in ways that collectively may have exacerbated market stresses.

Credit Risks

The limited risk-sensitivity of the Basel I framework allowed U.S. banks to increase certain credit risk exposures without making commensurate increases in their capital requirements.[83] Under the Basel I framework, banks apply one of five risk-weightings in calculating their risk-based capital requirements for loans, securities, certain off-balance sheet exposures, and other assets held in their banking books.[84] Because Basel I does not recognize differences in credit quality among assets in the same risk-weighted category, some banks may have faced incentives to take on high-risk, low-quality assets within each broad risk category.

U.S. regulators have noted that the risks associated with a variety of loan types increased in the years before the crisis due to a number of factors, including declining underwriting standards and weakening market discipline. For example, subprime and Alt-A mortgages originated in recent years have exhibited progressively higher rates of delinquency (see figure 8). However, as the risks of these loans increased, capital requirements did not increase accordingly. For example, under Basel I risk-weighting, a riskier loan reflecting declining underwriting standards could have received the same 50 percent risk-weighting as a higher quality mortgage loan. In particular, before the crisis, alternative mortgage products, such as interest-only and payment-option adjustable-rate mortgages, represented a growing share of mortgage originations as home prices increased nationally between 2003 and 2005.[85] Although mortgage statistics for these products reflected declining underwriting standards , Basel I rules did not require banks to hold additional capital for these loans relative to lower-risk, traditional mortgage loans in the same risk- weighting category. Larger-than-expected losses on loan portfolios depleted the regulatory capital of some large financial institutions, including two large thrift holding companies that ultimately failed. Through efforts to move certain large banks to the Basel II framework, U.S. federal financial regulators have sought to improve the risk-sensitivity of the risk-based capital framework.[86] However, FDIC officials told us that they are concerned that the advanced approaches of Basel II could require substantially less capital than Basel I. (For more detailed information about the Basel II framework, see app. IV.)

Trading Book Risks

The financial crisis has highlighted limitations associated with the use of internal models by financial institutions to calculate capital requirements for their trading book assets.[87] Under the Market Risk Amendment adopted in 1996, banks with significant trading assets used internal risk models to determine how much capital to hold against the market risk of their trading book assets. Banks widely use Value-at-Risk (VaR) models to help measure their market risk.[88] The capital rules require the use of VaR models as well as an additional capital requirement for specific risk. According to a report published by the Financial Services Authority, banks generally attributed low risk to their trading book positions based on the use of their models before the crisis and, thus, were subjected to relatively low regulatory capital charges for their trading positions.[89] However, since the onset of the crisis, several large banks have suffered, among other losses on trading book assets, billions of dollars in writedowns on "super senior," or highly rated CDOs. According to some regulators, losses on these financial instruments have been significantly higher than minimum capital charges implied by the institutions' internal risk models. That is, the risk models underestimated the institutions' risk exposures to CDOs. For some leveraged institutions, the size of these CDO positions were small relative to total assets, but the writedowns constituted a significant portion of total capital and led to a significant erosion of the institutions' regulatory capital. As discussed earlier, all else equal, a small decline in assets will result in a larger percentage decrease in capital for a leveraged institution.

U.S. and international regulators have identified problems in the way that some financial institutions applied internal risk models to determine capital requirements and noted that the crisis has raised fundamental questions about the inherent limitations of such models and the assumptions and inputs employed by some users. For example, banks' VaR models often relied on recent historical observation periods, rather than observations during periods of financial stress. An institution's reliance on short-term data from a period of high liquidity and low market volatility generally would have suggested that certain trading book assets carried low risks and required little capital. According to one international regulator, in the years leading up to the crisis, VaR measures may have suggested declining risk when, in fact, risks associated with certain mortgage-related securities and other trading book positions—and capital needs—were growing. However, even if longer time periods had been used, VaR models may not have identified the scale of risks associated with certain exposures because

VaR measures do not fully capture risks associated with low-probability, high-stress events. Moreover, as the crisis illustrated, VaR primarily measures the price volatility of assets but does not capture other risks associated with certain trading assets, including default risk. Although the Basel market risk framework directed institutions to hold capital against specific risks such as default risk, according to regulatory officials we spoke with, capital charges for specific risk did not adequately capture the default risk associated with certain exposures. Because of the inherent limitations of VaR models, financial institutions also are required to use stress tests to determine how much capital and liquidity might be needed to absorb losses in the event of a large shock to the system or a significant underestimation of the probability of large losses. According to the Basel Committee on Banking Supervision, institutions should test not only for events that could lower their profitability but also for rare but extreme scenarios that could threaten their solvency. However, according to regulatory officials, many firms did not test for sufficiently extreme scenarios, including scenarios that would render them insolvent.

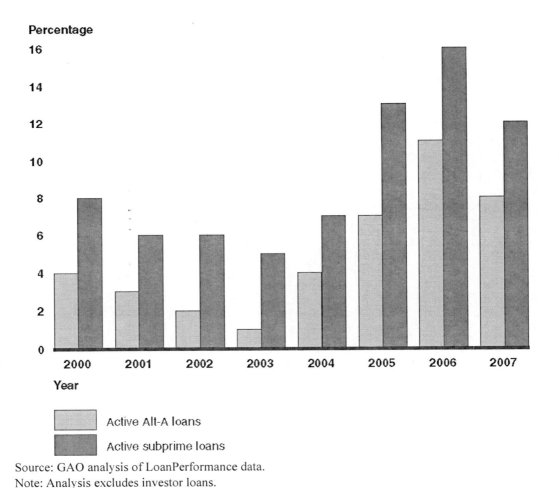

Source: GAO analysis of LoanPerformance data.
Note: Analysis excludes investor loans.

Figure 8. Foreclosures by Year of Origination—Alt-A and Subprime Loans for the Period 2000 to 2007

The crisis also revealed challenges with modeling the risks associated with relatively recent financial innovations. According to regulators, many market participants entered into new product lines without having sufficient data to properly measure the associated risks for determining capital needs. For example, the lack of historical performance data for CDOs presented challenges in estimating the potential value of these securities. In a March 2008 report, the Senior Supervisors Group—a body comprising senior financial supervisors from France, Germany, Switzerland, the United Kingdom, and the United States—reported that some financial institutions substituted price and other data associated with traditional corporate debt in their loss estimation models for similarly rated CDO debt, which did not have sufficient historical data.90 Furthermore, CDOs may lack an active and liquid market, as in the recent market turmoil, forcing participants to look for other sources of valuation information when market prices are not readily available. For instance, market participants often turned to internal models and other methods to value these products, which raised concerns about the consistency and accuracy of the resulting valuation information

Liquidity risks

In addition to capital required for credit and market risks, regulators direct financial institutions to consider whether additional capital should be held against risks that are not explicitly covered by minimum regulatory capital requirements.[91] Liquidity risk—the risk that a bank will be unable to meet its obligations when they come due, because of an inability to liquidate assets or obtain adequate funding—is one such risk. Prior to the crisis, most large financial institutions qualified as "well-capitalized," holding capital levels considered by regulators to exceed minimum requirements and provide some protection against risks such as liquidity risk. Regulators have noted that although strong capital positions can reduce the likelihood of liquidity pressures, capital alone is not a solution to inadequate liquidity. Many such "well-capitalized" institutions faced severe liquidity problems, underscoring the importance of liquidity risk management.

In particular, Bear Stearns, formerly a CSE, reported that it was in compliance with applicable rules with respect to capital and liquidity pools shortly before its failure, but SEC and Bear Stearns did not anticipate that certain sources of liquidity could rapidly disappear. According to SEC officials, Bear Stearns' failure was due to a run on liquidity, not capital. Shortly after Bear Stearns' failure, the then SEC Chairman noted that Bear Stearns failed in part when many lenders, concerned that the firm would suffer greater losses in the future, stopped providing funding to the firm, even on a fully-secured basis with high quality assets provided as collateral. SEC officials told us that neither they nor the broader regulatory community anticipated this development and that SEC had not directed CSEs to plan for the unavailability of secured funding in their contingent funding plans. SEC officials stated that no financial institution could survive without secured funding. Rumors about clients moving cash and security balances elsewhere and, more importantly, counterparties not transacting with Bear Stearns also placed strains on the firm's ability to obtain secured financing. Prior to these liquidity pressures, Bear Stearns reported that it held a pool of liquid assets well in excess of the SEC's required liquidity buffer, but this buffer quickly eroded as a growing number of lenders refused to rollover short- term funding. Bear Stearns faced the prospect of bankruptcy as it could not continue to meet its funding obligations. Although SEC officials have attributed Bear Stearns' failure to a liquidity crisis rather than capital inadequacy, these officials and market observers also stated that concerns about the strength of Bear Stearns' capital position—particularly given uncertainty about the potential for additional losses on its mortgage-backed securities—may have contributed to a crisis of confidence among its lenders, counterparties, and customers.

Before Bear Stearns' collapse in March 2008, the Senior Supervisors Group noted that many financial institutions underestimated their vulnerability to the prolonged disruption in market liquidity that began in the summer of 2007. In a March 2008 report, the group noted that many firms were forced to fund exposures that had not been anticipated in their contingency funding plans. Notably, the sudden sharp drop-off in demand for securitizations forced some firms to retain loans that they had "warehoused" to package as securitized products, intending to transfer their credit risk to another entity. As a result, many banks retained credit exposure to certain assets over a far longer time horizon than expected, increasing the risk that they would suffer losses on these assets. In a strained funding environment, many banks also had to provide larger amounts of funding than expected against certain unfunded lending commitments made prior to the crisis.

Off-Balance Sheet Risks

The financial crisis also has raised concerns about the management of and capital treatment for risks associated with certain off-balance sheet assets, including contingent liquidity and reputation risks. Many large financial institutions created SPEs to buy and hold mortgage-related securities and other assets that were previously on their balance sheets. For example, after new capital requirements were adopted in the late 1980s, some large banks began creating SPEs to hold assets against which they would have been required to hold more capital if the assets had been held in their institutions. SPEs also are known as off-balance sheet entities, because they generally are structured in such a way that their assets and liabilities are not required to be consolidated and reported as part of the overall balance sheet of the financial institution that created them. According to federal banking regulators, when a bank committed to provide contingent funding support to an SPE, it generally would have been required to hold a small amount of capital against such a commitment.[92] For some types of SPEs, such as structured investment vehicles, banks provided no such contingent commitments and were subject to no capital charge. Nevertheless, some institutions retained significant reputation risk associated with their structured investment vehicles, even if they were under no legal obligation to provide financial support.[93]

The market turmoil in 2007 revealed that many institutions and regulators underestimated the contingent liquidity risks and reputation risks associated with their SPEs.[94] In a 2008 report, the Senior Supervisors Group noted that some firms failed to price properly the risk that exposures to certain off-balance sheet vehicles might need to be funded on the balance sheet precisely when it became difficult or expensive to raise such funds externally. Some off-balance sheet entities were structured in a way that left them vulnerable to market disruptions. For example, some SPEs held long-term assets (for example, financial institution debt and CDOs) financed with short-term liabilities (such as commercial paper), exposing them to the risk that they would find it difficult or costly to renew their debt financing under less-favorable market conditions.

When the turmoil in the markets began in 2007, some banks had to finance the assets held by their SPEs when those SPEs were unable to refinance their expiring debt due to market concerns over the quality of the assets. In some cases, SPEs relied on financing commitments that banks had extended to them. In other cases, financial institutions supported troubled SPEs to protect their reputations with clients even when no legal requirement to do so existed. Some large banks brought SPE assets onto their balance sheets where they became subject to capital requirements (see figure 9). According to an official at the Federal Reserve, one large institution's decision to bring its structured investment vehicle assets onto the balance sheet did not have a significant, immediate impact on its capital ratio. Nevertheless, taking SPE assets onto their balance sheets required banks to hold capital against risk exposures that they previously had sought to transfer outside their institutions.

Market Developments Have Challenged the Regulatory System's Ability to Oversee the Capital Adequacy of Financial Institutions

While regulators have the authority to require banks to hold capital in excess of minimum capital requirements, the crisis highlighted challenges they face in identifying and responding to capital adequacy problems before market stresses appear.[95] In prior work on the financial regulatory structure, we have noted that the current U.S. financial regulatory system has relied on a fragmented and complex arrangement of federal and state regulators that has not kept pace with the major developments that have occurred in financial markets and products in recent decades (see figure 10).[96] The current system was not designed to adequately oversee today's large and interconnected financial institutions, the activities of which pose new risks to the institutions themselves as well as the risk that an event could affect the broader financial system (systemic risk). In addition, the increasingly critical role played by less-regulated entities, such as hedge funds, has further hindered the effectiveness of the financial regulatory system. Although many hedge fund advisors are now subject to some SEC oversight, some financial regulators and market participants remain concerned that hedge funds' activities can create systemic risk by threatening the soundness of other regulated entities and asset markets.

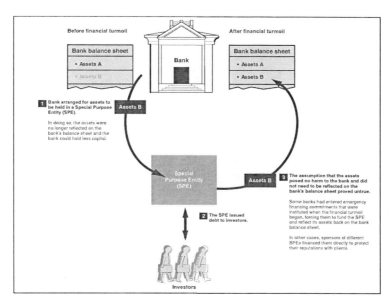

Source: GAO.

Figure 9. Example of an Off-Balance Sheet Entity

Developments in financial markets and products	Examples of how developments have challenged the regulatory system
Emergence of large, complex, globally active, interconnected financial conglomerates	Regulators sometimes lack sufficient authority, tools, or capabilities to oversee and mitigate risks.
	Identifying, preventing, mitigating, and resolving systemic crises has become more difficult.
Less-regulated entities have come to play increasingly critical roles in financial system	Nonbank lenders and a new private-label securitization market played significant roles in subprime mortgage crisis that led to broader market turmoil.
	Activities of hedge funds have posed systemic risks.
	Overreliance on credit ratings of mortgage-backed products contributed to the recent turmoil in financial markets.
	Financial institutions' use of off-balance sheet entities led to ineffective risk disclosure and exacerbated recent market instability.
New and complex products that pose challenges to financial stability and investor and consumer understanding of risks.	Complex structured finance products have made it difficult for institutions and their regulators to manage associated risks.
	Growth in complex and less-regulated over-the-counter derivatives markets have created systemic risks and revealed market infrastructure weaknesses.
	Investors have faced difficulty understanding complex investment products, either because they failed to seek out necessary information or were misled by improper sales practices.
	Consumers have faced difficulty understanding mortgages and credit cards with new and increasingly complicated features, due in part to limitations in consumer disclosures and financial literacy efforts.
	Accounting and auditing entities have faced challenges in trying to ensure that accounting and financial reporting requirements appropriately meet the needs of investors and other financial market participants.
Financial markets have become increasingly global in nature, and regulators have had to coordinate their efforts internationally.	Standard setters and regulators also face new challenges in dealing with global convergence of accounting and auditing standards.
	Fragmented U.S. regulatory structure has complicated some efforts to coordinate internationally with other regulators, such as negotiations on Basel II and certain insurance matters.

Sources: GAO (analysis); Art Explosion (images).

Figure 10. Key Developments and Resulting Challenges That Have Hindered the Effectiveness of the Financial Regulatory System

In prior work on regulatory oversight of risk management at selected large institutions, we found that oversight of institutions' risk-management systems before the crisis illustrated some limitations of the current regulatory system.[97] For example, regulators were not looking across groups of institutions to effectively identify risks to overall financial stability. In addition, primary, functional, and holding company regulators faced challenges aggregating certain risk exposures within large, complex financial institutions. According to one regulatory official, regulators faced difficulties understanding one large banks' subprime-related exposures, in part because these exposures were held in both the national bank and broker-dealer subsidiaries, each of which was overseen by a different primary or functional regulator. We found that regulators identified weaknesses in risk-management systems at the selected large, complex institutions before the crisis, but did not fully recognize the threats they posed and did not take forceful actions to address them until the crisis began.

Regulators Have Proposed Revisions to the Regulatory Capital Framework, but Have Not Yet Reevaluated Basel II Implementation in Light of Risk-Evaluation Concerns

Since the crisis began, U.S. federal financial regulators have worked together and with international regulators, such as through the Group of Twenty and the Basel Committee on Banking Supervision, in considering reforms that could increase the risk coverage of the regulatory capital framework.[98] U.S. and international regulators have proposed revisions to the Basel market risk framework to better ensure that institutions hold adequate levels of capital against trading book exposures.[99] Proposed revisions include applying higher capital requirements to resecuritizations such as CDOs and applying the same capital treatment to these securitizations whether on the bank's trading or banking book.[100] Regulators also have suggested raising the capital requirements that apply to certain off-balance sheet commitments. In June 2009, the Financial Accounting Standards Board published new accounting standards related to off-balance sheet entities, including a new rule that will require financial institutions to consolidate assets from certain SPEs.[101] In addition, regulators have issued recommendations related to improving risk management at institutions, including strengthening supervision of their VaR models and stress testing. As many institutions failed to anticipate the impact that liquidity pressures could have on their regulatory capital, regulators also have recommended ways to improve coordination of capital and liquidity planning. The current crisis demonstrated that risks such as liquidity and asset quality risks were increasing at institutions long before firms experienced losses that eroded capital. However, because capital can be a lagging indicator of problems that may threaten a firm's solvency, regulators have recommended that they and other market participants assess a broader range of risk indicators when assessing capital adequacy.

Although federal financial regulators have taken a number of steps to strengthen supervision of capital adequacy since the crisis began, they have not yet implemented proposals to increase the risk coverage of regulatory capital requirements. Among other actions, SEC staff are reviewing the liquidity of assets held by broker-dealers and considering whether capital charges for less liquid positions are appropriate, and the Federal Reserve has conducted stress tests to assess the capital adequacy of 19 banks under the Supervisory Capital Assessment Program and required 10 of the banks to raise capital to be better prepared to withstand a more adverse economic scenario. Federal financial regulators are continuing to work with international regulators in forums such as the Basel Committee on Banking Supervision, but have not formally revised capital requirements to address limitations revealed by the crisis or fully evaluated how some proposals would be implemented. For example, U.S. and international regulators have acknowledged the need to provide greater weight in determining capital adequacy to low-probability, high- loss events and are continuing to develop reforms to accomplish this goal. In its financial regulatory reform proposal released in June 2009, Treasury announced its intention to lead a working group of regulators and outside experts in conducting a reassessment of the existing regulatory capital framework for banks and bank holding companies and expressed support for the Basel Committee's ongoing efforts to reform the Basel II framework.[102]

In addition, the crisis highlighted some important concerns raised about the Basel II framework prior to the crisis, but federal financial regulators have not taken steps to formally reevaluate current U.S. plans to transition certain large financial institutions to Basel II. In our prior work on the U.S. Basel II transition, we noted that some regulators and market observers expressed concern about the ability of banks' models to adequately measure risks for regulatory capital purposes and the regulators' ability to oversee them. Although most U.S. banks have not yet implemented advanced risk-based approaches for credit risk, internal risk models applied by many U.S. firms before the crisis significantly underestimated risks and capital needs for trading book assets. Moreover, FDIC officials have indicated that capital requirements for most forms of credit risk under Basel II's advanced approaches will be substantially less than the Basel I requirements. Regulators already face resource constraints in hiring and retaining talent that are more binding than the resource constraints faced by the banks they regulate and this issue is likely to become more significant under Basel II. These resource constraints are a critical point because under Basel II regulators' judgment will likely play an increasingly important role in determining capital adequacy. In 2007, we recommended that regulators, at the end of the last transition period, reevaluate whether the advanced approaches of Basel II can and should be relied on to set appropriate capital requirements for the long term.[103] Federal financial regulators have proposed a study of banks' implementation of the advanced approaches after the second transitional year, but as a result of delays attributable in part to the financial crisis, it is unclear when this study will be completed. In 2008, we further recommended that regulators take steps jointly to plan for a study to determine if major changes need to be made to the advanced approaches or whether banks will be able to fully implement the current rule. We recommended that in their planning they consider, among other issues, the timing needs for the future evaluation of Basel II. Given the challenges regulators faced overseeing capital adequacy under Basel I, if regulators move forward with full implementation of Basel II before conducting such a reevaluation, changes to the regulatory capital framework may not address, and in some cases, possibly exacerbate limitations the crisis revealed in the regulatory framework. Federal Reserve officials with whom we spoke said that federal financial regulators are continuing to participate in international efforts to reevaluate the Basel II framework and expect the outcome of this work to influence U.S. Basel II implementation.

NONRISK-BASED CAPITAL REQUIREMENTS

In light of the risk-evaluation challenges revealed by the crisis, U.S. and international financial regulators and market observers have com mented on the potential benefits of supplementing risk-based capital measures with a nonriskbased capital requirement. While U.S. banks and bank holding companies were and continue to be subject to a minimum leverage ratio (Tier 1 Capital/Total Assets) and risk-based capital requirements, international banks based in industrialized countries generally were not subject to a minimum leverage requirement before and during the crisis. U.S. and international regulators have noted that the minimum leverage requirement can serve as an important backstop in the event that financial institutions quantify risks incorrectly, as many appear to have done in the years prior to the crisis. Moreover, the leverage ratio is easy to calculate and can be considered to cover areas that risk-based requirements do not currently address, such as interest rate risk and concentration risk. By limiting the total size of a firm's assets regardless of their associated risks, a minimum leverage requirement may serve to restrict the aggregate size of positions that might need to be simultaneously unwound during a crisis, thereby limiting the build-up of systemic risk. According to one regulatory official, subjecting institutions to both risk-based and minimum leverage requirements may reduce opportunities for regulatory arbitrage. However, the current crisis also illustrated limitations of the leverage ratio. For example, the U.S. leverage ratio requirement, as currently formulated, does not capture off-balance sheet exposures and, as a result, did not capture increasing risks associated with certain off-balance sheet vehicles. Furthermore, having a minimum leverage ratio in place did not safeguard against the failures and near-failures of some large financial institutions. Officials at some banks we spoke with noted that imposing a leverage ratio requirement conflicts with the purpose of moving to a conceptually more risk-sensitive capital allocation framework. Some bank officials expressed concern that the leverage ratio may, in some cases, provide disincentives for banks to hold low-risk assets on the balance sheet. However, according to the Federal Reserve, this disincentive does not present a regulatory capital problem from a prudential perspective so long as appropriate risk-based capital charges are levied against all assets and risk exposures that are retained by a bank. In a March 12, 2009, press release, the Basel Committee announced, among other things, its plan to improve the risk coverage of the capital framework and introduce a non-risk based supplementary measure.

Regulatory Capital Framework May Not Have Provided Adequate Incentives to Counteract Cyclical Leverage Trends and Regulators Are Considering Reforms to Limit Procyclicality

According to U.S. and international financial regulators, the tendency for leverage to move procyclically—increasing in strong markets and decreasing when market conditions deteriorate—can amplify business cycle fluctuations and exacerbate financial instability. As discussed earlier in this report, heightened systemwide leverage can increase the vulnerability of the financial system to a crisis, and when stresses appear, simultaneous efforts by institutions to deleverage may have adverse impacts on the markets and real economy. U.S. and international regulators, through forums such as the Financial Stability Forum and the Basel Committee on Banking Supervision, have expressed concern that the financial regulatory framework did not provide adequate incentives for firms to mitigate their procyclical use of leverage. For example, according to regulators, many financial institutions did not increase regulatory capital and other loss-absorbing buffers during the market upswing, when it would have been easier and less costly to do so.[104] Moreover, when the crisis began, rather than drawing down capital buffers in a controlled manner, these institutions faced regulatory requirements and market pressures to increase them. Although procyclicality may be inherent in banking to some extent, regulators have noted that elements of the regulatory framework may act as contributing factors.

Several interacting factors, including risk-measurement limitations, accounting rules, and market discipline can cause capital buffers to fall during a market expansion and rise during a contraction. With respect to risk-measurement limitations, the more procyclical the measurements of risk used to calculate regulatory capital requirements are, the more likely that these requirements will contribute to procyclical leverage trends. For example, U.S. and international regulators have noted that VaR measures of market risk tended to move procyclically before and during the crisis, particularly to the extent that banks relied on near-horizon estimates of quantitative inputs such as short-term volatility. In the years preceding the crisis, the internal risk models relying on such near-horizon estimates generally indicated that market risks were low, allowing banks to hold relatively small amounts of capital against trading book assets. Conversely, when measured risk spiked during the crisis, firms' models directed them to increase capital, when it was significantly more costly and difficult to do so. To the extent that risk measures are procyclical, the use of fair value accounting, which requires banks to periodically revalue trading book positions, also may contribute to procyclical leverage trends.[105] For example, when the fair value of super senior CDOs decreased suddenly, the associated writedowns taken in accordance with fair value accounting resulted in significant deductions to regulatory capital at some firms. Conversely, FDIC officials told us that attention should be given to whether regulatory rules motivated financial institutions to overvalue these illiquid instruments during the years leading up to the crisis. Finally, independent of regulatory requirements, market forces can influence the size of regulatory capital buffers through the market cycle. For example, banks consider the expectations of counterparties and credit rating agencies when deciding how much capital to hold.

U.S. and international financial regulators have acknowledged that limiting procyclical leverage trends is critical to improving the systemwide focus of the regulatory framework and have taken steps to assess possible reforms.[106] In addition to changes proposed to expand coverage of trading book risks, U.S. and international regulators have suggested revising the Basel market risk framework to reduce reliance on cyclical VaR-based capital estimates. For example, the Basel Committee has proposed requiring banks to calculate a stressed VaR (in addition to the existing VaR requirement) based on historical data from a period of financial distress relevant to the firm's portfolio. While most U.S. banks have not fully implemented Basel II approaches for modeling capital needs for credit risks, U.S. financial regulators noted before the crisis that elements of the U.S. implementation of Basel II, including use of through-the-cycle measures of risk and stress testing practices, would help to moderate the cyclicality of capital requirements.[107] However, federal financial regulators identified weaknesses with the stress testing practices of some large banks. In prior work, we recommended that federal financial regulators clarify the criteria that would be used for determining an appropriate average level of required capital and appropriate cyclical variation in minimum capital.[108] Although U.S. and international regulators have made progress in developing proposals to limit procyclical leverage trends, federal financial regulators have not formally incorporated such criteria into the regulatory framework..

Beyond limiting procyclicality arising from risk-measurement practic es, U.S. and international regulators have acknowledged that additional measures may be needed to ensure that firms build adequate buffers during strong economic conditions and that they can draw down these buffers during periods of stress. Regulators have proposed implementing countercyclical buffers, such as through explicit adjustments to increase minimum capital requirements during a market expansion and reduce them in a contraction, but have acknowledged some challenges in designing and implementing such measures. For example, regulators would need to assess the appropriate balance of discretionary and non-discretionary measures in achieving adjustment of capital requirements throughout the cycle.

One regulatory official told us that regulators face challenges identifying market troughs and, as a result, may find it difficult to adjust minimum capital requirements appropriately throughout the cycle. For example, uncertainty about the timing of an economic recovery may make it difficult in practice to reduce minimum capital requirements in a downturn. Furthermore, even if minimum regulatory capital requirements adjust appropriately, some procyclicality in buffers may be unavoidable as institutions respond to market expectations. As an example, an institution might face pressures from credit rating agencies and other market participants to reduce leverage as market strains appear, despite facing a lower minimum regulatory capital requirement. Finally, any such changes will need to incorporate ways to promote greater international consistency while reflecting differences in national economic cycles.

Financial Regulatory System Does Not Provid Sufficient Attention to Systemic Risk

In our prior work, we have noted that a regulatory system should focus on e risk to the financial system, not just institutions.[109] The financial crisis h as highlighted the potential for financial market disruptions, not just firm failures, to be a source of systemic risk. Ensuring the solvency of individual institutions may not be sufficient to protect the stability of the financial system, in part because deleveraging by institutions could have negative spillover effects. During economic weakness or market stress, an individual institution's efforts to protect its own safety and soundness (by reducing lending, selling assets, or raising collateral requirements) can cause stress for other market participants and contribute to a financial crisis. With multiple regulators primarily responsible for individual markets or institutions, none of the financial regulators is tasked with assessing the risks posed by the systemwide buildup of leverage and sudden deleveraging that may result from the collective activities of many institutions. Without a single entity responsible for assessing threats to the overall financial system, regulators may be limited in their ability to prevent or mitigate future crises.

U.S. regulators have recognized that regulators often focus on the financial condition of individual institutions and not on the financial stability of the financial system. In an August 2008 speech, the Federal Reserve Chairman stated that U.S. regulation and supervision focuses, at least informally, on some systemwide elements but outlined some more ambitious approaches to systemwide regulation.[110] Examples included (1) developing a more fully integrated overview of the entire financial system, partly because the system has become less-bank centered; and (2) conducting stress tests fo r a range of firms and markets, in part to provide insight into how a sharp change in asset prices might affect not only a particular institution but also impair liquidity in key markets. Regulators also have recommended that financial regulators monitor systemwide measures of leverage and measures of liquidity to enhance supervision of risks through the cycle. However, as the Federal Reserve Chairman has noted, the more comprehensive the regulatory approach, the more technically demanding and costly it would be for regulators and affected institutions.

Table 1. Comparison of Various Regulatory Reform Proposals to Address Systemic Risk

Proposal	How proposal addresses systemic risk
Treasury Financial Regulatory Reform Proposal (2009)	• Calls for creation of a Financial Services Oversight Council (FSOC) to oversee systemic risk across institutions, products, and markets. FSOC would have eight members, including the Treasury Secretary and the Chairmen of the Federal Reserve, CFTC, FDIC, and SEC. FSOC would replace the President's Working Group on Financial Markets and have a permanent, full-time staff.
	• Calls for stricter and more conservative regulatory capital, liquidity, and risk management requirements for all financial firms that are found to pose a threat to the U.S. economy's financial stability based on their size, leverage, and interconnectedness.
	• FSOC would identify such financial firms as Tier 1 Financial Holding Companies and hese firms all would be subject to consolid t ated supervision by the Federal Reserve.
FDIC Chairman	• Suggests creation of a systemic risk council (SRC) to oversee systemic risk across institutions, products, and markets. Treasury, FDIC, and the Federal Reserve, among others, would hold positions on SRC.
	• SRC would be responsible for setting capital and other standards designed to provide incentives to reduce or eliminate potential systemic risks.
	• SRC could have authority to overrule or force actions on behalf of other regulatory entities and would have authority to demand better information from systemically important entities.
Federal Reserve Chairman	• Calls for designation of an organization to oversee systemic risk across institutions, products, and markets.
	• Calls for strengthening regulatory standards for governance, risk management, capital, and liquidity.
	• Authority would look broadly at systemic risks, beyond the institution level to connections between institutions and other gaps in the current system.
SEC Chairman	• Calls for maintaining an independent capital markets regulator that focuses on investor protection and complements the role of any systemic risk regulator, in order to provide a more effective financial oversight regime.
	• Favors concept of a new "systemic risk council" comprised of the Treasury Department, Federal Reserve, FDIC, and SEC to monitor large institutions against financial threats and ensure sufficient capital levels and risk management.
	• Calls for bringing all OTC derivatives and hedge funds within a regulatory framework.
Group of Thirty	• Advocates consolidated supervision of all systemically important financial institutions.
	• Strengthens regulatory standards for risk management, capital, and liquidity.
	• Increases regulation and transparency of OTC derivatives markets.
Congressional Oversight Panel	• Calls for designation of an organization to oversee systemic risk across institutions, products, and markets.
	• Acknowledges the need for regulatory improvements regarding financial institution capital and liquidity.
	• Increases regulation and transparency of OTC derivatives markets.
Treasury Blueprint (2008)	• Designates an organization—the Federal Reserve—to have broad authority to oversee systemic risk across institutions, products, and markets.
	• Regulator would collect, analyze, and disclose information on systemically important issues and could examine institutions and generally take corrective actions to address problems.
	• Regulator could provide liquidity in systemic situations.

Source: GAO analysis of regulatory reform proposals.

Finally, creating a new body or designating one or more existing regulators with the responsibility to oversee systemic risk could serve to address a significant gap in the current U.S. regulatory system. Various groups, such as the Department of the Treasury, the Group of Thirty, and the Congressional Oversight Panel have put forth proposals for addressing systemic risk. Our analysis of these proposals found that each generally addresses systemic risk issues similarly by calling for a specific organization to be tasked with the responsibility of overseeing systemic risk in the financial system, but not all provided detail on which entity should perform this role or how it would interact with other existing regulators (see table 1).

For such an entity to be effective, it would likely need to have the independent ability to collect information, conduct examinations, and compel corrective actions across all institutions, products, and markets that could be a source of systemic risk. Such a regulator could assess the systemic risks that arise within and across financial institutions, within specific financial markets, across the nation, and globally. However, policymakers should consider that a potential disadvantage of providing an agency or agencies with such broad responsibility for overseeing financial entities could be that it may imply new or increased official government support or endorsement, such as a government guarantee, of such activities, and thus encourage greater risk taking by these financial institutions and investors. To address such concerns, some have proposed that entities designated as systemically important could correspondingly have increased requirements for capital adequacy or leverage limitations to offset the advantages that they may gain from implied government support. For example, in its recent proposal for financial regulatory reform, Treasury called for higher regulatory capital and other requirements for all financial firms found to pose a threat to financial stability based on their size, leverage, and interconnectedness to the financial system.

CONCLUSIONS

The causes of the current financial crisis remain subject to debate and additional research. Nevertheless, some researchers and regulators have suggested that the buildup of leverage before the financial crisis and subsequent disorderly deleveraging have compounded the current financial crisis. In particular, some studies suggested that the efforts taken by financial institutions to deleverage by selling financial assets could lead to a downward price spiral in times of market stress and exacerbate a financial crisis. However, alternative theories provide possible explanations; for example, the drop in asset prices may reflect prices reverting to more reasonable levels after a period of overvaluation or it may reflect uncertainty surrounding the true value of the assets. In addition, deleveraging by restricting new lending could slow economic growth and thereby contribute to a financial crisis.

The federal regulatory capital framework can serve an important role in restricting the buildup of leverage at individual institutions and across the financial system and thereby reduce the potential for a disorderly deleveraging process. However, the crisis has revealed limitations in the framework's ability to restrict leverage and to mitigate crises. Federal financial regulators have proposed a number of changes to improve the risk coverage of the regulatory capital framework, but they continue to face challenges in identifying and responding to capital adequacy problems before unexpected losses are incurred. These challenges will take on greater significance as regulators consider changes under Basel II that would increase reliance on complex risk models for determining capital needs, placing even greater demands on regulators' judgment in assessing capital adequacy. Although advanced modeling approaches offer the potential to align capital requirements more closely with risks, the crisis has underscored the potential for uncritical application of these models to miss or understate significant risks, especially when underlying data are limited. Indeed, concerns that advanced approaches could result in unsafe reductions in risk-based capital requirements influenced decisions by U.S. regulators to retain the leverage ratio requirement and to slowly phase in Basel II over several years. In prior work on the U.S. transition to Basel II for certain large financial institutions, we recommended that regulators, at the end of the last transition period, reevaluate whether the advanced approaches of Basel II can and should be relied on to set appropriate regulatory capital requirements in the long term. U.S. regulators plan to conduct an evaluation of the advanced approaches at the end of the second transitional year, but the timing of the completion of this study is uncertain. Without a timely reevaluation, regulators may not have the information needed to ensure that reforms to the regulatory capital framework adequately address the lessons learned from the crisis.

A principal lesson of the crisis is that an approach to supervision that focuses narrowly on individual institutions can miss broader problems that are accumulating in the financial system. In that regard, regulators need to focus on systemwide risks to and weaknesses in the financial system—not just on individual institutions. Although federal regulators have taken steps to focus on systemwide issues, no regulator has clear responsibility for monitoring and assessing the potential effects of a buildup in leverage in the financial system or a sudden deleveraging when financial market conditions deteriorate. However, leverage has been a source of problems in past financial market crises, such as the 1998 market disruptions involving Long-Term Capital Management. After that crisis, regulators recognized not only the need for better measures of leverage but also the difficulties in measuring leverage. Given the potential role leverage played in the current crisis, regulators clearly need to identify ways in which to measure and monitor systemwide leverage to determine whether their existing framework is adequately limiting the use of leverage and resulting in unacceptably high levels of systemic risk. In addition, research and experience have helped to provide insights on market, regulatory, and other factors that can reinforce the tendency for leverage to move procyclically and amplify business cycle fluctuations and exacerbate financial instability. Although regulators are taking action to address elements of the regulatory framework that may act as contributing factors, each regulator's authority to address the issue is limited to the institutions it supervises. To that end, without a systemwide focus, regulators may be limited in their ability to prevent or mitigate future crises.

MATTER FOR CONGRESSIONAL CONSIDERATION

As Congress considers assigning a single regulator, a group of regulators, or a newly created entity with responsibility for overseeing systemically important firms, products, or activities to enhance the systemwide focus of the financial regulatory system, Congress may wish to consider the merits of tasking this systemic regulator with:

- identifying ways to measure and monitor systemwide leverage and
- evaluating options to limit procyclical leverage trends.

RECOMMENDATION FOR EXECUTIVE ACTION

The current financial crisis has shown that risk models, as applied by many financial institutions and overseen by their regulators, could significantly underestimate the capital needed to absorb potential losses. Given that the Basel II approach would increase reliance on complex risk models for determining a financial institution's capital needs and place greater demands on regulators' judgment in assessing capital adequacy, we recommend that the heads of the Federal Reserve, FDIC, OCC, and OTS apply lessons learned from the current crisis and assess the extent to which Basel II reforms proposed by U.S. and international regulators may address risk evaluation and regulatory oversight concerns associated with advanced modeling approaches. As part of this assessment, the regulators should determine whether consideration of more fundamental changes under a new Basel regime is warranted.

AGENCY COMMENTS AND OUR EVALUATION

We provided the heads of the Federal Reserve, FDIC, OCC, OTS, SEC, and Treasury with a draft of this report for their review and comment. We received written comments from the Federal Reserve, FDIC, OCC, and SEC. These comments are summarized below and reprinted in appendixes V through VIII. We did not receive written comments from OTS and Treasury. Except for Treasury, the agencies also provided technical comments that we incorporated in the report where appropriate.

The Federal Reserve commented that high levels of leverage throughout the global financial system contributed significantly to the current financial crisis. It agreed that the recent crisis has uncovered opportunities to improve the risk sensitivity of the Basel I- and Basel II-based risk-based capital standards and noted that its staff is involved in current international efforts to strengthen minimum capital requirements. The Federal Reserve concurred with our recommendation for a more fundamental review of the Basel II capital framework, including risk evaluation and regulatory oversight concerns associated with the advanced approaches.

FDIC commented that the excessive use of leverage during the buildup to the crisis made individual firms and the financial system more vulnerable to shocks and reduced the regulators' ability to intervene before problems cascaded. FDIC also agreed with our recommendation and noted that it, along with other U.S. banking agencies, is working with the Basel Committee to develop proposals to address regulatory concerns discussed in our report. To the extent such proposals do not address the concerns, FDIC noted that it will consider the matter as part of the interagency review of Basel II that the agencies committed by regulation to undertake and will propose suitable remedies, if needed.

OCC agreed that recent events have highlighted certain weaknesses in its regulatory capital framework (both Basel I-based and Basel II) and noted that it is in the process of making modifications to address such weaknesses. It commented that Basel II lays a strong foundation for addressing supervisory challenges and remains committed to scrutinizing and improving the framework. With respect to our recommendation, OCC reiterated that it, along with the other banking agencies, will develop more formal plans to study the implementation of Basel II after a firmer picture of banks' implementation progress develops.

Finally, SEC staff commented that our recommendation is a valuable contribution and will take it into consideration in its recommendations to the SEC Commission. The staff also commented that SEC rules, including the broker-dealer net capital rule, largely conform to our conclusion that regulators need to identify ways in which to monitor and measure systemwide leverage to determine whether their existing framework is adequately limiting the use of leverage. Finally, the staff noted that SEC, along with other financial regulators, should build on and strengthen approaches that have worked, while taking lessons from what has not worked in order to be better prepared for future crises.

We are sending copies of this report to the Congressional Oversight Panel and interested congressional parties, the Chairman of the Board of Governors of the Federal Reserve System, the Chairman of FDIC, the Comptroller of the Currency, the Director of OTS, the Chairman of SEC, and the Secretary of the Treasury. In addition, the report will be available at no charge on GAO's Web site at http://www.gao.gov.

If you or your staff have any questions regarding this report, please contact me at (202) 512-5837 or williamso@gao.gov. Contact points for our Offices of Congressional Relations and Public Affairs may be found on the last page of this report. GAO staff who made major contributions to this report are listed in appendix X.

Orice Williams Brown
Director, Financial Markets
and Community Investment

List of Congressional Committees

The Honorable Christopher J. Dodd
Chairman
The Honorable Richard C. Shelby
Ranking Member
Committee on Banking, Housing, and Urban Affairs
United States Senate

The Honorable Barney Frank
Chairman
The Honorable Spencer Bachus
Ranking Member
Committee on Financial Services
House of Representatives

APPENDIX I: SCOPE AND METHODOLOGY

To assess the way in which the leveraging and deleveraging by financial institutions has contributed to the current financial crisis, we reviewed and summarized academic and other studies that included analysis of deleveraging as a potential mechanism for propagating a market disruption. Based on our searches of research databases (EconLit, Google Scholar, and the Social Science Research Network), we identified 15 studies, which included published and working papers that were released between 2008 and 2009. (See the bibliography for the studies included in our literature review.) Given our mandate, our literature search and review focused narrowly on deleveraging by financial institutions, although other economic mechanisms might have played a role in propagating the disruptions in the subprime mortgage markets to other financial markets. Based on our selection criteria, we determined that the 15 studies were sufficient for our purposes. Nonetheless, these studies do not provide definitive findings about the role of deleveraging relative to other mechanisms, and we relied on our interpretation and reasoning to develop insights from the studies reviewed. To obtain information on the ways that financial institutions increased their leverage before the crisis and deleveraged during the crisis and effects such activities had, we interviewed officials from two securities firms that used to participate in SEC's now defunct Consolidated Supervised Entity Program (CSE), a large bank, and a credit rating agency. We also interviewed staff from the Board of Governors of the Federal Reserve System (Federal Reserve), Federal Reserve Bank of New York, Federal Deposit Insurance Corporation (FDIC), Office of the Comptroller of the Currency (OCC), Office of Thrift Supervision (OTC), and Securities and Exchange Commission (SEC) for the same purposes.

To describe regulations that federal financial regulators have adopted to try to limit the use of leverage by financial institutions and federal oversight of the institutions' compliance with the regulations, we reviewed and analyzed relevant laws and regulations, and other regulatory guidance and materials, related to the federal oversight of the use of leverage by financial institutions. For example, we reviewed examination manuals and capital adequacy guidelines for banks and bank holding companies used by their respective federal bank regulators. In addition, we reviewed SEC's net capital guidelines for broker-dealers. We also reviewed the extensive body of work that GAO has completed on the regulation of banks, securities firms, hedge funds, and other financial institutions. In addition, we interviewed staff from the Federal Reserve, FDIC, OCC, OTS, and SEC about the primary regulations their agencies have adopted to limit the use of leverage by their regulated financial institutions and their regulatory framework for overseeing the capital adequacy of their institutions. To obtain more detailed information, we interviewed Federal Reserve Bank of New York and OCC examiners responsible for supervising a bank holding company and two national banks, respectively. We also interviewed officials from two securities firms and one bank to obtain information on the effect federal regulations had on their use of leverage. Finally, to gain insights on the extent to which federal financial regulators used their regulatory tools to limit the use of leverage, we also reviewed testimonies provided by officials of federal financial regulatory agencies as well as reports by the offices of inspector general at the Department of the Treasury and SEC.

To identify and analyze limitations in the regulatory framework used to restrict leverage and changes that regulators and others have proposed to address such limitations, we reviewed and analyzed relevant reports, studies, and public statements issued by U.S. and international financial regulators. Specifically, to identify potential limitations in the regulatory capital framework, we reviewed analyses and recommendations published by regulators through working groups such as the President's Working Group on Financial Markets,[111] the Basel Committee on Banking Supervision,[112] the Financial Stability Forum,[113] and the Senior Supervisors' Group.[114] To obtain perspectives on limitations revealed by the crisis and regulatory efforts to address these limitations, we also spoke with officials from the federal financial regulators and market participants (two securities firms, a large bank, and a credit rating agency) discussed above. Finally, we reviewed prior GAO work on the need to modernize the financial regulatory system and the U.S. transition to Basel II for certain large financial institutions.

For our three objectives, we collected and analyzed data for descriptive purposes. For example, to identify leverage trends, we collected and analyzed publicly available financial data on selected financial institutions, including large broker-dealer and bank holding companies, and industrywide data, including the Federal Reserve's Flow of Funds data and Bureau of Economic Analysis's gross domestic product data. To illustrate trends in margin debt, we used margin debt data from the New York Stock Exchange and market capitalization data from the World Federation of Exchanges. To describe foreclosure trends, we collected and analyzed LoanPerformance's foreclosure data on certain types of mortgages. We assessed the reliability of the data and found they were sufficiently reliable for our purposes.

We conducted this performance audit from February 2009 and July 2009 in accordance with generally accepted government auditing standards. Those standards require that we plan and perform the audit to obtain sufficient, appropriate evidence to provide a reasonable basis for our findings and conclusions based on our audit objectives. We believe that the evidence obtained provides a reasonable basis for our findings and conclusions based on our audit objectives.

APPENDIX II: BRIEFING TO CONGRESSIONAL STAFF

Draft

Briefing to Staff of the Senate Committee on Banking, Housing and Urban Affairs

Mandated Report on Leveraging and Deleveraging by Financial Institutions and the Current Financial Crisis Preliminary Findings
May 27, 2009

Briefing to Staff of the House Committee on Financial Services

Mandated Report on Leveraging and Deleveraging by Financial Institutions and the Current Financial Crisis Preliminary Findings
May 27, 2009

Briefing to Staff of the Congressional Oversight Panel

Mandated Report on Leveraging and Deleveraging by Financial Institutions and the Current Financial Crisis Preliminary Findings
May 27, 2009

Briefing Outline

- Objectives
- Scope and Methodology
- Background
- Summary
- Leverage Increased before the Crisis, and Research Suggests That Subsequent Deleveraging Could Have Contributed to the Crisis
- Financial Regulators Seek to Limit Financial Institutions' Use of Leverage Primarily through Varied Regulatory Capital Requirements
- Crisis Revealed Limitations in Regulatory Framework for Restricting Leverage, and Regulators Are Considering Reforms to Improve Rules and Oversight

Objectives

- Objectives
  - How have the leveraging and deleveraging by financial institutions contributed to the current financial crisis, according to primarily academic and other studies?
  - What regulations have federal financial regulators adopted to try to limit the use of leverage by financial institutions, and how do the regulators oversee the institutions' compliance with the regulations?
  - What, if any, limitations has the current financial crisis revealed about the regulatory framework used to restrict leverage, and what changes have regulators and others proposed to address these limitations?

Scope and Methodology

- To accomplish our objectives, we
  - reviewed and analyzed academic and other studies assessing the economic mechanisms that possibly helped the mortgage-related losses spread to other markets and expand into the current financial crisis;
  - analyzed publicly available financial data for selected financial institutions and industrywide data, including the Board of Governors of the Federal Reserve System's (Federal Reserve) Flow of Funds data, to identify leverage trends;

- reviewed and analyzed relevant laws and regulations, and other regulatory guidance and materials, related to the federal oversight of the use of leverage by financial institutions;
- interviewed federal financial regulators and market participants, including officials from a bank, two securities firms, and a credit rating agency;
- reviewed and analyzed studies identifying challenges associated with the regulation and oversight of the use leverage by financial institutions and proposals to address such challenges; and
- reviewed prior GAO work on the financial regulatory system.

Background

- The financial services industry comprises a broad range of financial institutions.
- In the United States, large parts of the financial services industry are regulated under a complex system of multiple federal and state regulators and self-regulatory organizations that operate largely along functional lines.
  - Bank supervisors include the Federal Reserve, Federal Deposit Insurance Corporation (FDIC), Office of the Comptroller of the Currency (OCC), and Office of Thrift Supervision (OTS).
  - Other functional supervisors include the Securities and Exchange Commission (SEC), self-regulatory organizations, and state insurance regulators.
  - Consolidated supervisors are the Federal Reserve and OTS.
- Leverage can be defined and measured in numerous ways.
  - One broad definition is the ratio between some measure of risk and capital.
  - A simple measure of balance sheet leverage is the ratio of total assets to equity, but this measure treats all assets as equally risky.
  - A risk-based leverage measure, as used by regulators, is the ratio of capital to risk-weighted assets.
- Many financial institutions use leverage to expand their ability to invest or trade in financial assets and to increase their return on equity.
- Financial institutions can increase their leverage, or their risk exposure relative to capital, in a number of ways. For example, they can use borrowed funds, rather than capital, to finance an asset or enter into derivatives contracts.

Summary

- Studies we reviewed suggested that leverage increased before the current crisis and deleveraging by financial institutions could have contributed to the current crisis in two ways. Specifically, deleveraging through (1) sales of financial assets during times of market stress could lead to downward price spirals for such assets and (2) the restriction of new lending could slow economic growth. However, these studies do not provide definitive findings.
- For financial institutions subject to regulation, federal financial regulators primarily limit the use of leverage by such institutions through varied regulatory capital

requirements. In addition, regulators can oversee the capital adequacy of their regulated institutions through ongoing monitoring, which includes on-site examinations and off-site tools. However, other entities such as hedge funds generally are not subject to regulation that directly restricts their leverage; instead, market discipline plays the primary role in constraining risk taking and leveraging by hedge funds.

- The financial crisis has revealed limitations in existing regulatory approaches used to restrict leverage. According to regulators, the regulatory capital framework did not ensure that institutions held capital commensurate with their risks and did not provide adequate incentives for institutions to build prudential buffers during the market upswing. When the crisis began, many institutions lacked the capital needed to absorb losses and faced pressure to deleverage. Regulators have called for reforms to improve the risk coverage of the regulatory capital framework and the systemwide focus of the financial regulatory system.

Figures 1 and 2 show the changes in balance sheet leverage in aggregate for five large broker-dealer and bank holding companies, respectively, from 2002 to 2007.

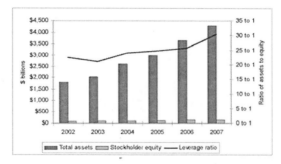

Source: GAO analysis of annual report data for Bear Stearns, Goldman Sachs, Lehman Brothers, Morgan Stanley, and Merrill Lynch.

Figure 1. Assets-to-Equity Ratio for Five Large U.S. Broker-Dealer Holding Companies, 2002 to 2007

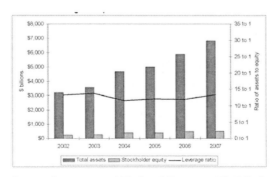

Source: GAO analysis of annual report and Federal Reserve Y- 9C data for Bank of America, Citigroup, JP Morgan Chase, Wachovia, and Wells Fargo.

Figure 2. Assets-to-Equity Ratio for Five Large U.S. Bank Holding Companies, 2002 to 2007

Leveraging and Deleveraging Could Have Contributed to the Crisis

- Leverage within the financial sector increased before the financial crisis began around mid-2007, and financial institutions have attempted to deleverage since the crisis began.
  - Since no single measure of leverage exists, the studies we reviewed generally identified sources that aided in the build up of leverage before the crisis. These sources included the use of repurchase agreements, special purpose entities, and over-the-counter derivatives, such as credit default swaps.
  - Studies we reviewed found that banks have tended to manage their leverage in a procyclical manner—increasing their leverage when prices rise and decreasing their leverage when prices fall.
  - Despite generally reducing their exposure to subprime mortgages through securitization, some banks ended up with large exposures to such mortgages relative to their capital. For example, some banks held mortgage-related securities for trading or investment purpose; some were holding mortgages or mortgage-related securities that they planned to securitize but could not do so after the crisis began, and some brought onto their balance sheets mortgage-related securities held by structured investment vehicles.
  - Following the onset of the financial crisis, banks and financial institutions have attempted to deleverage in a number of ways, including raising equity and selling assets.
- Some studies suggested that deleveraging through asset sales could lead to downward spirals in asset prices under certain circumstances and contribute to a crisis.
  - In theory, a sharp decline in an asset's price can become self-sustaining and lead to a financial market crisis, because financial intermediation has moved into markets and away from institutions. But not all academics subscribe to this theory.
  - Studies we reviewed suggested that deleveraging through asset sales can lead to a downward asset spiral during times of market stress when market liquidity is low.
  - Studies we reviewed also suggested that deleveraging through asset sales could lead to a downward asset spiral when funding liquidity, or the ease with which firms can obtain funding, is low.
- Alternative theories also may help to explain the recent decline in asset prices.
- Studies suggested that deleveraging by restricting new lending could have a negative effect on economic growth.
  - The concern is that banks will need to cut back their lending to restore their balance sheets, leading to a decline in consumption and investment spending, which reduces business and household incomes and negatively affects the real economy.
  - A former Federal Reserve official noted that banks are important providers of credit, but a key factor in the current crisis is the sharp decline in securities issuance, which has to be an important part of why the current financial market

turmoil is affecting economic activity. The official said that the mortgage credit losses are a problem because they are hitting bank balance sheets at the same time that the securitization market is experiencing difficulties.
- Regulators and market participants that we interviewed had mixed views about the effects of deleveraging in the current crisis.
  - Some regulators and market participants said that asset sales generally have not led to downward price spirals, but others said that asset sales of a broad range of debt instruments have led to such spirals.
  - Regulators and market participants told us that some banks have tightened their lending standards for some types of loans, such as ones that have less favorable risk-adjusted returns or have been performing poorly. Federal bank examiners told us that the tightening of lending standards corresponded with a decline in loan demand.
  - Federal bank examiners told us that large banks rely on their ability to securitize loans to facilitate their ability to make such loans and, thus the inability to securitize loans has impaired their ability to make loans.
  - Since the crisis began, federal regulators and other authorities have facilitated financial intermediation by banks and the securities markets.

Federal Financial Regulatory Oversight of Use of Leverage by Financial Institutions

- Federal banking and thrift regulators (Federal Reserve, FDIC, OCC and OTS) try to restrict the use of leverage by their regulated financial institutions primarily through minimum risk-based capital and leverage requirements.
  - Banks and thrifts are required to meet two minimum risk-based capital ratios. However, regulators told us that they can require an institution to meet more than the minimum requirements if, for example, the institution has concentrated positions or a high risk profile.
  - Regulators impose minimum leverage ratios on banks and thrifts to provide a cushion against risks not explicitly covered in the risk-based capital requirements (such as for operational weaknesses in internal policies, systems, and controls).
  - Regulators are required to classify institutions based on their level of capital and take increasingly severe actions, known as prompt corrective action, as an institution's capital deteriorates.
- Federal bank and thrift regulators oversee the capital adequacy of their regulated institutions through ongoing monitoring, which includes on-site examinations and off-site tools.
  - Examiners evaluate the institution's overall risk exposure with particular emphasis on what is known as CAMELS—the adequacy of its capital, and asset quality, the quality of its management and internal control procedures, the strength of its earnings, the adequacy of its liquidity, and its sensitivity to market risk.

- Regulators can also use off-site tools to monitor the capital adequacy of institutions such as by remotely assessing the financial condition of their regulated institutions and plan the scope of on-site examinations.
- Regulators also can conduct targeted reviews, such as those related to capital adequacy of their regulated entities.
- Although bank holding companies are subject to similar capital and leverage ratio requirements as banks, thrift holding companies are not subject to such requirements.
    - Bank holding companies are subject to risk-based capital and leverage ratio requirements, which are similar to those applied to banks.
    - In contrast, OTS requires that thrift holding companies hold a "prudential" level of capital on a consolidated basis to support the risk profile of the company.
    - To supervise the capital adequacy of bank and thrift holding companies, the Federal Reserve and OTS, respectively, focus on those business activities posing the greatest risk to holding companies and managements' processes for identifying, measuring, monitoring, and controlling those risks.
    - The Federal Reserve and OTS have a range of formal and informal actions they can take to enforce their regulations for holding companies and they also monitor the capital adequacy of their respective regulated holding companies by obtaining uniform information from their holding companies and conducting peer analysis.
- SEC regulated the use of leverage by broker-dealers participating in SEC's Consolidated Supervised Entity (CSE) program under an alternative net capital rule from 2005 to 2008.
    - Under the alternative net capital rule, CSE broker-dealers were required to hold minimum levels of net capital (i.e., net liquid assets) but permitted to use their own internal models to calculate their haircuts for the credit and market risk associated with their trading and investment positions. SEC required as a safeguard that they maintain at least $500 million in net capital and at least $1 billion in tentative net capital (equity before haircut deductions). SEC staff said that CSE broker-dealers, in effect, had to maintain a minimum of $5 billion in tentative net capital or face remedial action.
    - The CSE holding companies calculated their risk-based capital ratio consistent with the method banks used, were expected to maintain a risk-based capital ratio of no less than 10 percent, and had to notify SEC if they breached or were likely to breach this ratio.
    - SEC also expected each CSE holding company to maintain a liquid portfolio of cash and highly liquid and highly rated debt instruments in an amount based on its liquidity risk management analysis.
    - SEC's Division of Trading and Markets had responsibility for administering the CSE program, and SEC's continuous supervision of CSEs usually was conducted off site.
- Other entities, such as hedge funds, have become important financial market participants, and many use leverage. However, they generally are not subject to regulation that directly restricts their use of leverage but may face limitations through market discipline.

- Although hedge funds generally are not subject to regulatory capital requirements, SEC and the Commodity Futures Trading Commission (CFTC) regulate some hedge fund advisers and subject them to disclosure requirements.
- Large banks and prime brokers bear the credit and counterparty risks that hedge fund leverage creates. They may seek to impose market discipline on hedge funds primarily by exercising counterparty risk management through due diligence, monitoring, and requiring additional collateral to secure existing exposures and provide a buffer against future exposures.
- SEC, CFTC, and bank regulators also use their authority to establish capital standards and reporting requirements, conduct risk-based examinations, and take enforcement actions to oversee activities of their regulated institutions acting as creditors and counterparties to hedge funds.
- The Federal Reserve limits investors' use of credit to purchase securities under Regulation T and U, but regulators told us such credit did not play a significant role in the buildup of leverage because market participants can obtain credit elsewhere where these regulations do not apply.

Crisis Revealed Limitations in Regulatory Framework for Restricting Leverage

The existing regulatory capital framework did not fully capture certain risks.

- A key goal of the regulatory capital framework is to align capital requirements with risks.
- However, according to regulators, many large financial institutions and their regulators underestimated capital needs for certain risk exposures.

  - **Credit risks** – The limited risk-sensitivity of the Basel I framework allowed banks to increase certain credit risk exposures without making commensurate increases in their capital requirements.

  - **Trading book risks** – Internal risk models, as applied by some large banks, underestimated the market risk and capital needs for certain trading assets.

  - **Liquidity risks** – Many institutions underestimated their vulnerability to a prolonged disruption in market liquidity.

  - **Off-balance sheet exposures** – Some large banks held no capital against the risk that certain special purpose entity (SPE) assets could have to be brought back on the bank's balance sheet if these entities experienced difficulties.

- The crisis illustrated challenges with increasing reliance on internal risk models for calculating capital requirements.

- Through forums such as the President's Working Group on Financial Markets and the Financial Stability Forum, U.S. and foreign regulators have called for changes to better align capital requirements with risks.

The regulatory framework may contribute to procyclical leverage trends.

- According to regulators, the tendency for leverage to move procyclically—increasing in strong markets and decreasing when market conditions deteriorate—can amplify business cycle fluctuations and exacerbate financial instability.
- U.S. regulators have expressed concern that capital requirements did not provide adequate incentives to increase loss-absorbing capital buffers during the market upswing, when it would have been less costly to do so.
- According to regulators, several interacting factors can cause capital buffers to fall during a market expansion and rise during a contraction. These factors include:
  - limitations in risk measurement,
  - accounting rules, and
  - market discipline.

The current regulatory framework does not adequately address systemic risk.
- The regulatory system focuses on the solvency of individual institutions, but more attention to other sources of systemic risk is needed.
- For example, during a period of market stress, an individual institution's efforts to protect its safety and soundness can cause stress for other market participants and heighten systemic risk.
- Regulatory officials have acknowledged the need to improve the systemwide focus of the financial regulatory system and suggested changes include:
  - taking steps to limit the contribution of the regulatory framework to procyclicality;
  - use of sector-level leverage ratios and systemwide stress tests; and
  - creation of a systemic regulator.

Appendix III: Transition to Basel II Has Been Driven by Limitations of Basel I and Advances in Risk Management at Large

(Information in this appendix is based solely on a GAO report issued in early 2007.[115] Thus, the information does not capture any of the events that have transpired since the current financial crisis began.)

When established internationally in 1988, Basel I represented a major step forward in linking capital to risks taken by banking organizations, strengthening banks' capital positions, and reducing competitive inequality among international banks. Regulatory officials have noted that Basel I continues to be an adequate capital framework for most banks, but its limitations make it increasingly inadequate for the largest and most internationally active banks. As implemented in the United States, Basel I consists of five broad credit risk categories, or risk weights (table 2).[116] Banks must hold total capital equal to at least 8 percent of the total value of their risk-weighted assets and tier 1 capital of at least 4 percent. All assets are assigned a risk weight according to the credit risk of the obligor and the nature of any qualifying collateral or guarantee, where relevant. Off-balance sheet items, such as credit derivatives and loan commitments, are converted into credit equivalent amounts and also assigned risk weights. The risk categories are broadly intended to assign higher risk weights to—and require banks to hold more capital for—higher risk assets.

However, Basel I's risk-weighting approach does not measure an asset's level of risk with a high degree of accuracy, and the few broad categories available do not adequately distinguish among assets within a category that have varying levels of risk. For example, although commercial loans can vary widely in their levels of credit risk, Basel I assigns the same 100 percent risk weight to all these loans. Such limitations create incentives for banks to engage in regulatory capital arbitrage—behavior in which banks structure their activities to take advantage of limitations in the regulatory capital framework. By doing so, banks may be able to increase their risk exposure without making a commensurate increase in their capital requirements.

In addition, Basel I recognizes the important role of credit risk mitigation activities only to a limited extent. By reducing the credit risk of banks' exposures, techniques such as the use of collateral, guarantees, and credit derivatives play a significant role in sound risk management. However, many of these techniques are not recognized for regulatory capital purposes. For example, the U.S. Basel I framework recognizes collateral and guarantees in only a limited range of cases.[117] It does not recognize many other forms of collateral and guarantees, such as investment grade corporate debt securities as collateral or guarantees by externally rated corporate entities. As a result, regulators have indicated that Basel II should provide for a better recognition of credit risk mitigation techniques than Basel I.

Table 2. U.S. Basel I Credit risk Categories

Major assets	Risk weight
Cash: claims on or guaranteed by central banks of Organization for Economic Cooperation and Development countries; claims on or guaranteed by Organization for Economic Cooperation and Development central governments and U.S. government agencies. The zero weight reflects the lack of credit risk associated with such positions.	0%
Claims on banks in Organization for Economic Cooperation and Development countries, obligations of government-sponsored enterprises, or cash items in the process of collection.	20%
Most one-to-four family residential mortgages; certain privately issued mortgage-backed securities and municipal revenue bonds.	50%
Represents the presumed bulk of the assets of commercial banks. It includes commercial loans, claims on non-Organization for Economic Cooperation and Development central governments, real assets, certain one-to-four family residential mortgages not meeting prudent underwriting standards, and some multifamily residential mortgages.	100%
Asset-backed and mortgage-backed securities and other on-balance sheet positions in asset securitizations that are rated one category below investment grade.	200%

Source: GAO analysis of federal regulations. See, e.g., 12 C.F.R. Part 3, App. A (OCC).

Furthermore, Basel I does not address all major risks faced by banking organizations, resulting in required capital that may not fully address the entirety of banks' risk profiles. Basel I originally focused on credit risk, a major source of risk for most banks, and was amended in 1996 to include market risk from trading activity. However, banks face many other significant risks—including interest rate, operational, liquidity, reputational, and strategic risks—which could cause unexpected losses for which banks should hold capital. For example, many banks have assumed increased operational risk profiles in recent years, and at some banks operational risk is the dominant risk.[118] Because minimum required capital under Basel I does not depend directly on these other types of risks, U.S. regulators use the supervisory review process to ensure that each bank holds capital above these minimums, at a level that is commensurate with its entire risk profile. In recognition of Basel I's limited risk focus, Basel II aims for a more comprehensive approach by adding an explicit capital charge for operational risk and by using supervisory review (already a part of U.S. regulators' practices) to address all other risks.

Banks are developing new types of financial transactions that do not fit well into the risk weights and credit conversion factors in the current standards. For example, there has been significant growth in securitization activity, which banks engaged in partly as regulatory arbitrage opportunities.[119] To respond to emerging risks associated with the growth in derivatives, securitization, and other off-balance sheet transactions, federal regulators have amended the risk-based capital framework numerous times since implementing Basel I in 1992. Some of these revisions have been international efforts, while others are specific to the United States. For example, in 1996, the United States and other Basel Committee members adopted the Market Risk Amendment, which requires capital for market risk exposures arising from banks' trading activities.[120] By contrast, federal regulators amended the U.S. framework in 2001 to better address risk for asset securitizations.[121] These changes, while consistent with early proposals of Basel II, were not adopted by other countries at the time. The finalized international Basel II accord, which other countries are now adopting, incorporates many of these changes.

Despite these amendments to the current framework, the simple risk-weighting approach of Basel I has not kept pace with more advanced risk measurement approaches at large banking organizations. By the late 1990s, some large banking organizations had begun developing economic capital models, which use quantitative methods to estimate the amount of capital required to support various elements of an organization's risks. Banks use economic capital models as tools to inform their management activities, including measuring risk-adjusted performance, setting pricing and limits on loans and other products, and allocating capital among various business lines and risks. Economic capital models measure risks by estimating the probability of potential losses over a specified period and up to a defined confidence level using historical loss data. This method has the potential for more meaningful risk measurement than the current regulatory framework, which differentiates risk only to a limited extent, mostly based on asset type rather than on an asset's underlying risk characteristics. Recognizing the potential of such advanced risk measurement techniques to inform the regulatory capital framework, Basel II introduces "advanced approaches" that share a conceptual framework that is similar to banks' economic capital models. With these advanced approaches, regulators aim not only to increase the risk sensitivity of regulatory measures of risk but also to encourage the advancement of banks' internal risk management practices.

Although the advanced approaches of Basel II aim to more closely align regulatory and economic capital, the two differ in significant ways, including in their fundamental purpose, scope, and consideration of certain assumptions. Given these differences, regulatory and economic capital are not intended to be equivalent. Instead, some regulators expect that the systems and processes that a bank uses for regulatory capital purposes should be consistent with those used for internal risk management purposes. Regulatory and economic capital approaches both share a similar objective: to relate potential losses to a bank's capital in order to ensure it can continue to operate. However, economic capital is defined by bank management for internal business purposes, without regard for the external risks the bank's performance poses on the banking system or broader economy. By contrast, regulatory capital requirements must set standards for solvency that support the safety and soundness of the overall banking system. In addition, while the precise definition and measurement of economic capital can differ across banks, regulatory capital is designed to apply consistent standards and definitions to all banks. Economic capital also typically includes a benefit from portfolio diversification, while the calculation of credit risk in Basel II fails to reflect differences in diversification benefits across banks and over time. Also, certain key assumptions may differ, such as the time horizon, confidence level or solvency standard, and data definitions. For example, the probability of default can be measured at a point in time (for economic capital) or as a long-run average measured through the economic cycle (for Basel II). Moreover, economic capital models may explicitly measure a broader range of risks, while regulatory capital as proposed in Basel II will explicitly measure only credit, operational, and where relevant, market risks.

APPENDIX IV: THREE PILLARS OF BASEL II

Basel II aims for a more comprehensive approach to addressing risks, based on three pillars: (1) minimum capital requirements, (2) supervisory review, and (3) market discipline in the form of increased public disclosure.

Pillar 1: Minimum Capital Requirements

Pillar 1 of the advanced approaches rule features explicit minimum capital requirements, designed to ensure bank solvency by providing a prudent level of capital against unexpected losses for credit, operational, and market risk. The advanced approaches, which are the only measurement approaches available to and required for core banks in the United States, will make capital requirements depend in part on a bank's own assessment, based on historical data, of the risks to which it is exposed.

Credit Risk
Under the advanced internal ratings-based approach, banks must establish risk rating and segmentation systems to distinguish risk levels of their wholesale (most exposures to companies and governments) and retail (most exposures to individuals and small businesses) exposures, respectively. Banks use the results of these rating systems to estimate several risk

parameters that are inputs to supervisory formulas. Figure 11 illustrates how credit risk will be calculated under the Basel II advanced internal ratings-based approach. Banks must first classify their assets into exposure categories and subcategories defined by regulators: for wholesale exposures those subcategories are high-volatility commercial real estate and other wholesale; for retail exposures those subcategories are residential mortgages, qualifying revolving exposures (e.g., credit cards), and other retail. Banks then estimate the following risk parameters, or inputs: the probability a credit exposure will default (probability of default or PD), the expected size of the exposure at the time of default (exposure at default or EAD), economic losses in the event of default (loss given default or LGD) in "downturn" (recession) conditions, and, for wholesale exposures, the maturity of the exposure (M). In order to estimate these inputs, banks must have systems for classifying and rating their exposures as well as a data management and maintenance system. The conceptual foundation of this process is that a statistical approach, based on historical data, will provide a more appropriate measure of risk and capital than a simple categorization of asset types, which does not differentiate precisely between risks. Regulators provide a formula for each exposure category that determines the required capital on the basis of these inputs. If all the assumptions in the supervisory formula were correct, the resulting capital requirement would exceed a bank's credit losses in a given year with 99.9 percent probability. That is, credit losses at the bank would exceed the capital requirement with a 1 in 1,000 chance in a given year, which could result in insolvency if the bank only held capital equal to the minimum requirement.

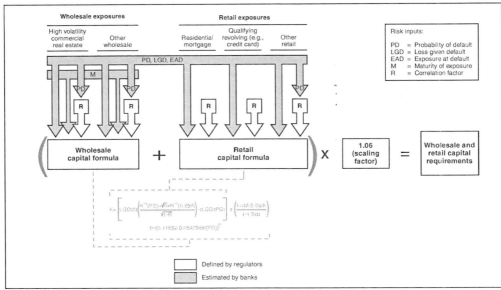

Source: GAO analysis of information from the advanced approaches rule.
Notes: This figure focuses on wholesale and retail nondefaulted exposures, an important component of the total credit risk calculation. The total credit risk capital requirement also covers defaulted wholesale and retail exposures, as well as risk from securitizations and equity exposures. A bank's qualifying capital is also adjusted, depending on whether its eligible credit reserves exceed or fall below its expected credit losses.

Figure 11. Computation of Wholesale and Retail Capital Requirements under the Advanced Internal Ratings-based Approach for Credit Risk

Banks may incorporate some credit risk mitigation, including guarantees, collateral, or derivatives, into their estimates of PD or LGD to reflect their efforts to hedge against unexpected losses.

Operational Risk

To determine minimum required capital for operational risk, banks will use their own quantitative models of operational risk that incorporate elements required in the advanced approaches rule. To qualify to use the advanced measurement approaches for operational risk, a bank must have operational risk management processes, data and assessment systems, and quantification systems. The elements that banks must incorporate into their operational risk data and assessment system are internal operational loss event data, external operational loss event data, results of scenario analysis, and assessments of the bank's business environment and internal controls. Banks meeting the advanced measurement approaches' qualifying criteria would use their internal operational risk quantification system to calculate the risk-based capital requirement for operational risk, subject to a solvency standard specified by regulators, to produce a capital buffer for operational risk designed to be exceeded only once in a thousand years.

Market Risk

Regulators have allowed certain banks to use their internal models to determine required capital for market risk since 1996 (known as the market risk amendment or MRA). Under the MRA, a bank's internal models are used to estimate the 99th percentile of the bank's market risk loss distribution over a 10-business-day horizon, in other words a solvency standard designed to exceed trading losses for 99 out of 100 10-businessday intervals. The bank's market risk capital requirement is based on this estimate, generally multiplied by a factor of three. The agencies implemented this multiplication factor to provide a prudential buffer for market volatility and modeling error. The OCC, Federal Reserve, and FDIC are proposing modifications to the market risk rules, to include modifications to the MRA developed by the Basel Committee, in a separate notice of proposed rulemaking issued concurrently with the proposal for credit and operational risk. OTS is proposing its own market risk rule, including the proposed modifications, as a part of that separate notice of proposed rulemaking.

In previous work, regulatory officials generally said that changes to the rules for determining capital adequacy for market risk were relatively modest and not a significant overhaul. The regulators have described the objectives of the new market risk rule as including enhancing the sensitivity of required capital to risks not adequately captured in the current methodologies of the rule and enhancing the modeling requirements consistent with advances in risk management since the implementation of the MRA. In particular, the rule contains an incremental default risk capital requirement to reflect the growth in traded credit products, such as credit default swaps, that carry some default risk as well as market risk. The Basel Committee currently is in the process of finalizing more far-reaching modifications to the MRA to address issues highlighted by the financial crisis.

Pillar 2: Supervisory Review

The Pillar 2 framework for supervisory review is intended to ensure that banks have adequate capital to support all risks, including those not addressed in Pillar 1, and to encourage banks to develop and use better risk management practices. Banks adopting Basel II must have a rigorous process of assessing capital adequacy that includes strong board and senior management oversight, comprehensive assessment of risks, rigorous stress testing and validation programs, and independent review and oversight. In addition, Pillar 2 requires supervisors to review and evaluate banks' internal capital adequacy assessments and monitor compliance with regulatory capital requirements. Under Pillar 2, supervisors must conduct initial and ongoing qualification of banks for compliance with minimum capital calculations and disclosure requirements. Regulators must evaluate banks against established criteria for their (1) risk rating and segmentation system, (2) quantification process, (3) ongoing validation, (4) data management and maintenance, and (5) oversight and control mechanisms. Regulators are to assess a bank's implementation plan, planning and governance process, and parallel run, and ongoing performance. Under Pillar 2, regulators should also assess and address risks not captured by Pillar 1 such as credit concentration risk, interest rate risk, and liquidity risk.

Pillar 3: Market Discipline in the Form of Increased Disclosure

Pillar 3 is designed to encourage market discipline by requiring banks to disclose additional information and allowing market participants to more fully evaluate the institutions' risk profiles and capital adequacy. Such disclosure is particularly appropriate given that Pillar I allows banks more discretion in determining capital requirements through greater reliance on internal methodologies. Banks would be required to publicly disclose both quantitative and qualitative information on a quarterly and annual basis, respectively. For example, such information would include a bank's risk- based capital ratios and their capital components, aggregated information underlying the calculation of their risk-weighted assets, and the bank's risk assessment processes. In addition, federal regulators will collect, on a confidential basis, more detailed data supporting the capital calculations. Federal regulators would use this additional data, among other purposes, to assess the reasonableness and accuracy of a bank's minimum capital requirements and to understand the causes behind changes in a bank's risk-based capital requirements. Federal regulators have developed detailed reporting schedules to collect both public and confidential disclosure information.

APPENDIX V: COMMENTS FROM THE BOARD OF GOVERNORS OF THE FEDERAL RESERVE SYSTEM

**BOARD OF GOVERNORS
OF THE
FEDERAL RESERVE SYSTEM
WASHINGTON, D. C. 20551**

DANIEL K. TARULLO
MEMBER OF THE BOARD

July 13, 2009

Ms. Orice Williams
Director, Financial Markets and Community Investment
U.S. General Accountability Office
Washington, DC 20548

Dear Ms. Williams,

The Federal Reserve appreciates the opportunity to review and comment on the GAO's report entitled "Financial Crisis Highlights Need to Improve Oversight of Leverage at Financial Institutions and Across the System" (GAO-09-739) (Report). High levels of leverage throughout the global financial system ranging from consumer and homeowner indebtedness, to the leverage embedded in various types of financial products, to the capital structures of many financial institutions, along with a number of other factors, contributed significantly to the current financial crisis. The Report provides a thorough review of the academic literature and other studies in its endeavor to isolate the role of leverage and de-leveraging in the crisis. It also provides an important view into the various regulatory capital regimes underlying the trends in leverage at both commercial and investment banking organizations and an assessment of those regimes moving forward.

The Federal Reserve supports the Report's analysis of the limits of the Basel I-based risk-based capital standards to appropriately measure and allocate capital against the risks undertaken by banking organizations. The Federal Reserve also agrees that the recent crisis has revealed problems in both the U.S. Basel I- and Basel II-based risk-based capital standards. Federal Reserve staff is significantly involved in current international efforts to strengthen minimum capital requirements in areas where many banks have experienced losses including those related to securitizations, counterparty credit risk exposures, and trading book exposures. Changes to the trading book framework include proposals to better capture the credit risk of trading activities and incorporate a new stressed value-at-risk (VaR) requirement that is expected to help dampen the cyclicality of risk-based capital requirements. The Federal Reserve concurs with the Report's recommendation for a more fundamental review of the Basel II capital framework.

The Federal Reserve supports the Report's observation that the current regulatory capital framework may not have provided adequate incentives to counteract

E-mail: Daniel.Tarullo@frb.gov • Telephone: (202) 452-3735 • Facsimile: (202) 736 1960

Ms. Orice Williams
Page 2

cyclical leverage trends. As the Report notes, international and U.S. supervisors have efforts currently underway to explore countercyclical capital buffers, strengthen loan loss provisioning practices, and undertake concrete steps to dampen excessive capital volatility over the cycle. The Federal Reserve believes the financial system would benefit from a more explicitly macroprudential approach to financial regulation in addition to the current microprudential approach. Such an approach should include monitoring of system-wide leverage and identifying options to limit procyclical leverage trends.

The Federal Reserve believes that, as part of a broad agenda to address systemic risks, Congress should consider establishing a robust framework for consolidated supervision of all systemically important financial firms. Firms whose failure would pose a systemic risk must be subject to especially close supervisory oversight of risk-taking, risk management, and financial condition, and be held to high capital and liquidity standards.

Federal Reserve staff has separately provided GAO staff with technical and correcting comments on the draft report. We hope these comments were helpful.

Thank you for your efforts on this important matter. The Federal Reserve appreciates the professionalism of, and the careful analysis performed by, the GAO review team.

Sincerely,

Daniel K. Tarullo

APPENDIX VI: COMMENTS FROM THE FEDERAL DEPOSIT INSURANCE CORPORATION

Federal Deposit Insurance Corporation
550 17th Street NW, Washington, D.C. 20429-9990

Office of the Chairman

July 9, 2009

Ms. Orice M. Williams
Director, Financial Markets and Community Investment
United States Government Accountability Office
441 G Street, NW
Washington, D.C. 20548

Dear Ms. Williams:

The Federal Deposit Insurance Corporation (FDIC) appreciates the opportunity to comment on the draft report *Financial Markets Regulation: Financial Crisis Highlights Need to Improve Oversight of Leverage at Financial Institutions and Across System* (GAO-09-739) (Report) that the Government Accountability Office (GAO) submitted to the FDIC on June 22, 2009. The Report addresses how leverage and de-leveraging may have contributed to the financial crisis, existing regulations and supervisory approaches to limit leverage, and limitations the crisis has revealed in these regulatory approaches. This letter represents our overall reaction to the Report; additional technical comments have been provided by our staff.

Excessive use of leverage during the buildup to the crisis made individual firms and our financial system more vulnerable to shocks, and reduced the regulators' ability to intervene before problems cascaded. The Report's emphasis on the importance of regulatory mechanisms to constrain leverage in the financial system is entirely appropriate.

We strongly endorse the Report's recommendation that the regulators undertake a fundamental review of Basel II to assess whether that new framework would adequately address concerns about the use of banks' internal models for determining regulatory capital requirements. In addition to requiring insufficient capital as revealed by the crisis, the advanced approaches of Basel II embody a degree of regulatory deference to banks that is concerning. Accordingly, while the Report cites the locus of regulatory capital authority over systemically important financial firms as a matter for Congressional consideration, attention also needs to be given to ensuring that regulatory authorities are used strongly and as intended.

The FDIC and the other U.S. banking agencies are working with the Basel Committee to develop proposals to increase the level and quality of capital in the banking system, reduce the pro-cyclicality of capital regulation, improve the risk-capture of the Basel framework, and introduce a non-risk based (leverage) capital ratio internationally to supplement the risk-based capital requirements. It is anticipated these proposals would be developed by the end of this year for subsequent comment and implementation. Whether these Basel Committee proposals and their ultimate form of implementation will address the fundamental concerns about Basel II raised in the Report remains to be seen. The FDIC will consider this matter as part of the interagency review of Basel II that the agencies committed by regulation to undertake, and will propose suitable remedies if needed.

July 9, 2009

In conclusion, we would like to commend the GAO's review team for producing a thoughtful and comprehensive report.

Sincerely,

Sheila C. Bair
Chairman

APPENDIX VII: COMMENTS FROM THE OFFICE OF THE COMPTROLLER OF THE CURRENCY

Comptroller of the Currency
Administrator of National Banks

Washington, DC 20219

July 10, 2009

Ms. Orice M. Williams Brown
Director, Financial Markets and Community Investment
United States Government Accountability Office
Washington, DC 20548

Dear Ms. Brown:

We have received and reviewed your draft report titled "Financial Markets Regulation: Financial Crisis Highlights Need to Improve Oversight of Leverage at Financial Institutions and Across System." Your report responds to a Congressional mandate to study the role of leverage in the current financial crisis and federal oversight of leverage. The report examines the extent to which leverage and the sudden deleveraging of financial institutions was a factor driving the current financial crisis.

The study considers the effectiveness of the regulatory capital framework during the crisis and finds:

> The financial crisis has revealed limitations in existing regulatory approaches that serve to restrict leverage....Furthermore, the crisis highlighted past concerns about the approach to be taken under Basel II, a new risk-based capital framework based on an international accord, such as the ability of banks' models to adequately measure risks for regulatory capital purposes and the regulators' ability to oversee them.[1]

To address this issue, the study recommends that "regulators should assess the extent to which Basel II reforms may address risk evaluation and regulatory oversight concerns associated with advanced modeling approaches used for capital adequacy purposes."[2]

The OCC agrees that recent events have highlighted certain weaknesses in our regulatory capital framework – both Basel I-based and Basel II – and we are in the process of making modifications to address them. During the course of the development of the Basel II framework, and consistent with the evolution of our current Basel I-based regulatory capital regime, we have consistently maintained that the Basel II framework will need refinement and adjustment over time. To this end, in January 2009, the Basel Committee on Banking Supervision (BCBS)

---

[1] GAO Report to Congressional Committees *Financial Crisis Highlights Need to Improve Oversight of Leverage at Financial Institutions and Across System (GAO-09-739), July 2009*, Pages 6-7.
[2] GAO Report, Page 8.

proposed amendments to strengthen the Basel II framework.[3] The proposals primarily target the framework's ability to measure and assess appropriate capital for the risks in banks' trading books and complex securitization exposures. To prevent a recurrence of the dramatic increase in leverage that contributed to the recent losses from trading activities, the proposals include an incremental capital charge to augment the existing Value at Risk (VaR) capital charge. Supervisory enhancements to the securitization framework include additional guidance for complex derivative structures known as ReRemics. This guidance will facilitate the continuance of healthy secondary market activity, while dampening the growth in more risky segments. Prior to finalizing these revisions and enhancements, the Basel Committee expects to undertake a detailed impact analysis to ensure a better understanding of the level of minimum required capital generated by the Basel II framework.

We continue to believe that Basel II lays a strong foundation for addressing the supervisory challenges posed by an increasingly complex, sophisticated, and global financial environment. However, we remain committed to scrutinizing and improving the framework. As stated in our previous response to the GAO's study[4] on Basel II implementation:

> To ensure the effectiveness of Basel II in meeting supervisory needs, the banking agencies are committed to conducting a study of the advanced approaches implementation to determine if there are any material deficiencies in the framework. The banking agencies will develop more formal plans for the interagency study after a firmer picture of banks' implementation progress develops.[5]

We appreciate the opportunity to comment on the draft report.

Sincerely,

John C. Dugan
Comptroller of the Currency

---

[3] The Basel Committee on Banking Supervision Consultative Document *Proposed enhancements to the Basel II framework (January 2009)*, The Basel Committee on Banking Supervision Consultative Document *Guidelines for computing capital for incremental risk in the trading book (January 2009)*, and The Basel Committee on Banking Supervision Consultative Document *Revisions to the Basel II market risk framework (January 2009)*.
[4] *Risk-Based Capital: New Basel II Rules Reduced Certain Competitive Concerns, but Bank Regulators Should Address Remaining Uncertainties (GAO-08-953, September 2008)*.
[5] Interagency response to GAO-08-953, December 2008.

Appendix VIII: Comments from the Securities and Exchange Commission

UNITED STATES
SECURITIES AND EXCHANGE COMMISSION
WASHINGTON, D.C. 20549

DIVISION OF
TRADING AND MARKETS

July 17, 2009

Ms. Orice M. Williams Brown
Director, Financial Markets and Community Investment
United States Government Accountability Office
Washington, DC 20548

Dear Ms. Williams Brown:

We have received and reviewed the draft GAO report "Financial Markets Regulation: Financial Crisis Highlights Need to Improve Oversight of Leverage at Financial Institutions and Across System" (GAO-09-739) (the "GAO Report"). We are pleased to have this opportunity to comment on the report as well as the issue of leverage in financial institutions.

The GAO Report has recommended that federal financial regulators need to assess the extent to which Basel II's reforms proposed by U.S. and international regulators may address risk evaluation and regulatory oversight concerns associated with advanced modeling approaches. As part of this assessment, the GAO Report states that regulators should determine whether consideration of more fundamental changes under a new Basel regime is warranted. We believe these are valuable contributions to the regulatory framework and will take them into consideration in our recommendations to the Commission. The GAO Report also states that regulators "clearly need to identify ways in which to measure and monitor systemwide leverage to determine whether their existing framework is adequately limiting the use of leverage and resulting in unacceptably high levels of systemic risk." We believe our rules, which are described in more detail below, conform in large measure to your suggestions.

Broker-dealer Net Capital Rule

The importance of maintaining high levels of liquidity has been the underlying premise of the Commission's net capital rule since it was adopted in 1975, and the Commission continued to emphasize liquidity when creating the Consolidated Supervised Entity or "CSE" program. Whereas commercial banks may use insured deposits to fund their businesses and have access to the Federal Reserve as a backstop liquidity provider, the CSE broker-dealers were prohibited under Commission rules from financing their investment bank activities with customer funds or securities held in a broker-dealer. The Commission was not authorized to provide a liquidity backstop to CSE broker-dealers or CSE holding companies.

The Commission action in 2004 to adopt rules establishing the CSE Program that permitted a broker-dealer to use an alternate method to compute net capital has been mischaracterized by some commenters as being a major contributor to the current crisis, or

Ms. Orice M. Williams Brown
Page 2

alternately, as having allowed broker-dealers to increase their leverage. Since August 2008, these commenters have suggested that the 2004 amendments removed a "12-to-1" leverage restriction that had prevented broker-dealers from taking on debt that exceeded more than twelve times their capital and, as a consequence, the Commission allowed these firms to increase their debt-to-capital ratios. These commenters point to the 2004 amendments as a significant factor leading to the demise of Bear Stearns. However, in fact, the 2004 amendments did not alter the leverage limits in the broker-dealer net capital rule.

The net capital rule requires a broker-dealer to undertake two calculations: (1) a computation of the minimum amount of net capital the broker-dealer must maintain; and (2) a computation of the actual amount of net capital held by the broker-dealer. The "12-to-1" restriction is part of the first computation, and it was not changed by the 2004 amendments. The greatest changes effected by the 2004 amendments were to the second computation of actual net capital.

Under the net capital rule, a broker-dealer calculates its actual net capital amount by starting with net worth computed according to generally accepted accounting principles and then adding to that amount qualifying subordinated loans. Next, the broker-dealer deducts from that amount illiquid assets such as fixed assets, goodwill, real estate, most unsecured receivables, and certain other assets. This leaves the broker-dealer with what is known as "tentative net capital," which generally consists of liquid securities positions and cash. A broker-dealer's tentative net capital represents the amount of liquid assets that exceed all liabilities of the broker-dealer. The final step in calculating net capital is to take percentage deductions (haircuts) from the securities positions. The percentage deductions are prescribed in the rule and are based on, among other things, the type of security, e.g., debt or equity, the type of issuer, e.g., US government or public company, the availability of a ready market to trade the security, and, if a debt security, the time to maturity and credit rating. The amount left after deducting the haircuts from the securities positions is the broker-dealer's net capital. This actual amount of net capital needs to be equal to or greater than the required minimum.

The 2004 amendments permitted the CSE broker-dealers to reduce the value of the securities positions (the last step in computing actual net capital) using statistical value-at-risk (VaR) models rather than the prescribed percentage deductions in the net capital rule. This is how commercial banks — under the Basel Accord — had been computing market risk charges for trading positions since 1997.

Because the CSE broker-dealers were permitted to use modeling techniques to compute market and credit risk deductions, the Commission imposed a requirement that they file an early warning notice if their tentative net capital fell below $5 billion. This became their effective minimum tentative net capital requirement. The $5 billion minimum amount was comparable to the amount of tentative net capital the broker-dealers maintained prior to the 2004 amendments. The early warning requirement was designed to ensure that the use of models to compute haircuts would not substantially change the amount of tentative net capital actually maintained by the broker-dealers. The levels of tentative net capital in the broker-dealer subsidiaries remained relatively stable after they began operating under the 2004 amendments, and, in some cases, increased significantly.

Ms. Orice M. Williams Brown
Page 3

CSE Program

In 2004, the Commission adopted two regimes to fill a statutory gap —there is no provision in the law that requires investment bank holding companies to be supervised on a consolidated basis at the holding company level. One regime, the Supervised Investment Bank Holding Company ("SIBHC") program, provided group-wide supervision of holding companies that include broker-dealers based on the specific statutory authority in the Gramm-Leach-Bliley Act concerning voluntary consolidated supervision of investment bank holding companies. However, the Commission's authority under the SIBHC program is severely limited because holding companies that owned a subsidiary that was an insured depository institution were ineligible under the statute for this program. The other regime, the CSE program, provided for voluntary consolidated supervision based on the Commission's authority over the regulated broker-dealer. The CSE program permitted certain broker-dealers to utilize an alternate net capital computation provided the broker-dealer's holding company submitted to consolidated oversight.

Each CSE holding company was required, among other things, to compute on a monthly basis its group-wide capital in accordance with the Basel standards, and was expected to maintain an overall Basel capital ratio at the consolidated level of not less than the Federal Reserve Bank's 10% "well-capitalized" standard for bank holding companies. CSEs were also required to file an "early warning" notice with the Commission in the event that certain minimum thresholds, including the 10% capital ratio, were breached or were likely to be breached.

Each CSE holding company was required to provide the Commission, on a periodic basis, with extensive information regarding its capital and risk exposures, including market risk, credit risk, and liquidity risk. For the first time, the Commission had the ability to examine the activities of a CSE holding company that took place outside the U.S. registered broker-dealer subsidiary. This allowed Commission staff to get a direct view of the risk taking (and corresponding risk management controls) of the entire enterprise.

Thus, the Commission did not eliminate or relax any requirements at the holding company level because previously there had been no requirements. In fact, through the creation and implementation of the CSE program, the Commission increased regulatory standards applicable to the CSE holding companies.

Importance of Liquidity Risk

CSE holding companies relied on the ongoing secured and unsecured credit markets for funding, rather than broker-dealer customer deposits; therefore liquidity and liquidity risk management were of critical importance. In particular, the Commission's rules required CSE holding companies to maintain funding procedures designed to ensure that the holding company had sufficient stand-alone liquidity to withstand the complete loss of all short term sources of unsecured funding for at least one year. In addition, with respect to secured funding, these procedures incorporated a stress test that estimated what a prudent lender would lend on an asset under stressed market conditions, e.g., a haircut. Another premise of this liquidity risk

Ms. Orice M. Williams Brown
Page 4

management planning was that assets held in a regulated entity could not be used to resolve financial weaknesses elsewhere in the holding company structure. The assumption was that during a stress event, including a tightening of market liquidity, regulators in the U.S. and relevant foreign jurisdictions would not permit a withdrawal of capital from regulated entities. Therefore, each CSE holding company was required to maintain a substantial "liquidity pool" comprised of unencumbered highly liquid assets, such as U.S. Treasuries, that could be moved to any subsidiary experiencing financial stress.

The CSE program required stress testing and substantial liquidity pools at the holding company to allow firms to continue to operate normally in stressed market environments. But what neither the CSE regulatory approach nor most existing regulatory models had taken into account was the possibility that secured funding could become unavailable, even for high-quality collateral such as U.S. Treasury and agency securities. The existing models for both commercial and investment banks are premised on the expectation that secured funding would be available in any market environment, albeit perhaps on less favorable terms than normal. Thus, one lesson from the Commission's oversight of CSEs — Bear Stearns in particular — is that no parent company liquidity pool can withstand a "run on the bank." Supervisors simply did not anticipate that a run-on-the-bank was indeed a real possibility for a well-capitalized securities firm with high quality assets to fund.

Recent events in the capital markets and the broader economy have presented significant challenges that are rightly the subject of review, notwithstanding the financial regulatory system's long record of accomplishment. The Commission, along with other financial regulators, should build on and strengthen approaches that have worked, while taking lessons from what has not worked in order to be better prepared for future crises.

Thank you again for the opportunity to provide comments to the GAO as it prepares its final draft of the report.

Sincerely,

Michael A. Macchiaroli
Associate Director
Division of Trading and Markets

APPENDIX IX: LETTER FROM THE FEDERAL RESERVE REGARDING ITS AUTHORITY TO REGULATE LEVERAGE AND SET MARGIN REQUIREMENTS

BOARD OF GOVERNORS
OF THE
FEDERAL RESERVE SYSTEM
WASHINGTON, D. C. 20551

SCOTT G. ALVAREZ
GENERAL COUNSEL

May 26, 2009

Susan D. Sawtelle, Esq.
Managing Associate General Counsel
United States Government Accountability Office
441 G Street, NW
Washington, DC 20548

Dear. Ms. Sawtelle:

This is in response to your letter dated April 2, 2009, requesting information about the Board's authority to monitor and regulate leverage among financial institutions and to set margin requirements.

<u>Limiting leverage of financial institutions supervised by the Board</u>

The Board has general statutory authority to limit leverage among institutions that it supervises, including state member banks and bank holding companies, under the Federal Reserve Act, the Federal Deposit Insurance Act, the Bank Holding Company Act, and the International Lending Standards Act.[1] The Board also has specific statutory authority to evaluate and regulate the capital adequacy of supervised institutions.[2]

Through its capital adequacy guidelines, the Board has limited the leverage of state member banks and bank holding companies by requiring them to meet a minimum "leverage ratio" and two minimum risk-based capital ratios, the "tier 1 risk-based capital ratio" and the "total risk-based capital ratio."[3]

---

[1] See 12 U.S.C. 329; 12 U.S.C. 1831o; 12 U.S.C. 1844(b); 12 U.S.C. 3907, 3909.

[2] 12 U.S.C. 1844(b); 12 U.S.C. 3907, 3909.

[3] See 12 CFR part 208, subpart D and Appendices A and B; 12 CFR part 225, Appendices A and D.

- 2 -

Leverage ratio. The leverage ratio is a ratio of an institution's core capital ("tier 1 capital")[4] to average total consolidated assets.[5] The purpose of the leverage ratio is to provide a simple measure of an institution's tangible capital to assets. State member banks generally must meet a minimum leverage ratio of 4 percent.[6] Bank holding companies with consolidated assets of $500 million or more generally also must meet a minimum leverage ratio of 4 percent.[7]

Risk-based capital ratios. The tier 1 risk-based capital ratio is a ratio of an institution's tier 1 capital to its risk-weighted assets[8] (including certain off-balance sheet exposures). The total risk-based capital ratio is a ratio of total capital (tier 1 capital plus tier 2 capital)[9] to risk-weighted assets.[10] The purpose of the

---

[4] Tier 1 capital is defined in the Board's capital adequacy guidelines. Generally, it consists of voting common stock, certain types of preferred stock, limited amounts of trust preferred securities, and certain minority interests. 12 CFR parts 208 and 225, Appendix A, section II.A.1.

[5] See 12 CFR part 208, Appendix B; 12 CFR part 225, Appendix D.

[6] 12 CFR 208.43; 12 CFR part 208, Appendix B, section II.a. The Board has established a minimum leverage ratio of 3 percent for state member banks with a composite rating of "1."

[7] 12 CFR part 225, Appendix D, section II.a. The Board has established a minimum leverage ratio of 3 percent for bank holding companies with a composite rating of "1," and for bank holding companies that have implemented the Board's market risk rule. See infra, n. 8. In addition, bank holding companies with consolidated assets of less than $500 million are subject to similar restrictions on leverage under the Board's Small Bank Holding Company Policy Statement. See 12 CFR part 225, Appendix C.

[8] Risk-weighted assets are calculated under the Board's capital adequacy guidelines. See 12 CFR part 208, Appendices A and F (state member banks); 12 CFR part 225, Appendices A and G (bank holding companies). State member banks and bank holding companies whose trading activity equals or exceeds 10 percent or more of total assets or $1 billion also must calculate their exposure to market risk under the Board's market risk rule. See 12 CFR parts 208 and 225, Appendix E.

[9] Tier 2 capital is defined in the Board's capital adequacy guidelines and generally consists of allowances for loan and leases losses, subordinated debt, perpetual preferred stock and trust preferred securities that cannot be included in tier 1 capital. 12 CFR parts 208 and 225, Appendix A, section II.A.2.

risk-based capital ratios is to provide risk-sensitive measures of state member banks and bank holding companies' capital adequacy. All state member banks and bank holding companies with consolidated assets of $500 million or more generally must meet a minimum tier 1 risk-based capital ratio of 4 percent and a minimum total risk-based capital ratio of 8 percent.[11]

While the leverage and risk-based ratios establish minimum capital requirements for state member banks and bank holding companies, the Board generally expects such institutions to operate well above these minimum ratios and in all cases, hold capital commensurate with the level and nature of the risks to which they are exposed.[12] Where an institution's capital is deemed inadequate in light of its risk profile, the Board has the authority to issue a capital directive against it to require it to improve its capital position.[13] Through these requirements and its authority over capital levels of supervised institutions, the Board is able to monitor and limit the leverage of state member banks and bank holding companies.

Limiting leverage through securities margin authority

The Board also has authority to establish some limits on the leverage of market participants where the credit is used for the purpose of purchasing securities. The Board's securities margin authority is found in section 7 of the Securities Exchange Act of 1934 ("SEA").[14] Section 7(a) authorizes the Board to limit the amount of credit that may be extended and maintained on securities (other than exempted securities and security futures products). It also contains a statutory initial margin requirement. Section 7(b) authorizes the Board to raise or lower the margin requirements contained in section 7(a). The Board has adopted three margin regulations pursuant to section 7 of the SEA, each described below. These regulations apply to specific types of credits and specific types of transactions.

---

[10] See 12 CFR part 208, Appendices, A, E, and F; 12 CFR part 225, Appendices A, E, and G.

[11] 12 CFR parts 208 and 225, Appendix A, section IV.A. See supra, n. 7.

[12] 12 CFR parts 208 and 225, Appendix A, section I.

[13] 12 U.S.C. 1818(i); 12 U.S.C. 1831o; 12 U.S.C. 1844(b); 12 U.S.C. 3907(b)(2); 12 CFR part 263, subpart E.

[14] 15 U.S.C. 78g. Section 7 of the SEA only covers financial products that are "securities" under the SEA. Other financial products and derivatives are not within the Board's SEA authority.

- 4 -

<u>Regulation T</u>, "Credit by Brokers and Dealers," regulates extensions of credit by brokers and dealers for the purpose of purchasing securities.[15] In addition to establishing initial margin requirements for purchases and short sales of securities, it establishes payment periods for margin and cash transactions. It also contains exceptions for credit to certain broker-dealers, arbitrage transactions and loans to employee stock option plans. Specific authority for Regulation T is found in section 7(c) of the SEA.

<u>Regulation U</u>, "Credit by Banks or Persons Other Than Brokers or Dealers for the Purpose of Purchasing or Carrying Margin Stock," applies the Board's margin requirements to United States lenders other than those covered by Regulation T.[16] Nonbank lenders who extend securities credit above certain dollar thresholds must register with the Federal Reserve and file annual reports on this activity. Bank and nonbank lenders are generally subject to the same requirements. Specific authority for this regulation is found in section 7(d) of the SEA. Regulation U covers equity securities only, as section 7(d) exempts loans by a bank on a security other than an equity security.

<u>Regulation X</u>, "Borrowers of Securities Credit," applies margin requirements to United States persons and certain related persons who obtain securities credit outside the United States to purchase United States securities.[17] It also imposes liability on borrowers who obtain credit within the United States by willfully causing a violation of Regulation T or Regulation U. Regulation X implements section 7(f) of the SEA.

The Board has raised and lowered the initial margin requirements many times since enactment of the SEA. The highest margin requirement was 100 percent, adopted for about a year after the end of World War II. The lowest margin requirement was 40 percent and was in effect during the late 1930s and early 1940s. Otherwise, the initial margin requirement has varied between 50 and 75 percent. The Board has left the initial margin requirement at 50 percent since 1974.

Although section 7 of the SEA gives the Board the authority to adopt initial and maintenance margins, the Board has chosen to adopt only initial margin requirements. Broker-dealers, however, are required to join the Financial Industry

---

[15] 12 CFR part 220.

[16] 12 CFR part 221.

[17] 12 CFR part 224.

- 5 -

Regulatory Authority and are therefore subject to its maintenance margin requirements.[18]

Limiting leverage through monetary policy

The Federal Reserve, acting through the Federal Open Market Committee, also can use monetary policy to affect indirectly the amount of leverage in the financial system.[19] By raising interest rates, the Federal Reserve reduces the money supply and raises the cost of credit, thereby reducing the amount of leverage available in the U.S. financial system. Similarly, by lowering interest rates, the Federal Reserve increases the money supply and reduces the cost of credit, thereby allowing the amount of leverage available in the U.S. financial system to increase.

We hope this information is helpful. If you have additional questions regarding the Board's authority to establish capital requirements, please contact April C. Snyder, Counsel, at (202) 452-3099, and Benjamin W. McDonough, Senior Attorney, at (202) 452-2036. If you have any questions regarding the Board's margin rules (Regulations T, U, and X), please contact Scott Holz, Senior Counsel, at (202) 452-2966.

Sincerely,

[signature]

---

[18] See New York Stock Exchange Rule 431 and National Association of Securities Dealers Rule 2520.

[19] 12 U.S.C. 263.

APPENDIX X: GAO CONTACT AND STAFF ACKNOWLEDGMENTS

GAO Contact

Orice Williams Brown (202) 512-8678 or williamso@gao.gov

Staff Acknowledgments

In addition to the contacts named above, Karen Tremba (Assistant Director); Lawrence Evans, Jr.; John Fisher; Marc Molino; Timothy Mooney; Akiko Ohnuma; Linda Rego; Barbara Roesmann; John Treanor; and Richard Tsuhara made significant contributions to this report.

BIBLIOGRAPHY

Acharya, V. & Schnabl. P. (2009). How Banks Played the Leverage "Game"?" in Acharya, V. and Richardson, M. (Eds.). *Restoring Financial Stability: How to Repair a Failed System*. John Wiley and Sons. Chapter 2.

Adrian, Tobias, & Hyun Song Shin. (2008). "Liquidity, Financial Cycles and Monetary Policy." *Current Issues in Economics and Finance*. Federal Reserve Bank of New York. Vol. 14, No. 1, January/February.

Baily, Martin N., Robert E. Litan, & Matthew S. Johnson. (2008). "The Origins of the Financial Crisis." *Fixing Finance Series*-Paper 3. Washington, D.C.: The Brookings Institution. November.

Blundell-Wignall. (2008). "The Subprime Crisis: Size, Deleveraging and Some Policy Options." *Financial Market Trends*. Organization for Economic Cooperation and Development.

Brunnermeier, Markus K. "Deciphering the (2007-08). Liquidity and Credit Crunch." *Journal of Economic Perspectives. 23*, No. 1. 2009. 77-100.

Buiter, Willem H.(2008). "Lessons from the North Atlantic Financial Crisis." (2008) Paper prepared for presentation at the conference "*The Role of Money Markets*" jointly organized by Columbia Business School and the Federal Reserve Bank of New York on May 29-30, (May).

Cohen, Ben, and Eli Remolona. "*The Unfolding Turmoil of (2007–2008): Lessons and Responses*." Proceedings of a Conference, Sydney, Australia, Reserve Bank of Australia, Sydney.

Devlin, Will, & Huw McKay. (2008) "The Macroeconomic Implications of Financial 'Deleveraging'." *Economic Roundup*. Issue 4.

Frank, Nathaniel, Brenda Gonzalez-Hermosillo, & Heiko Hesse. (2007). "Transmission of Liquidity Shocks: Evidence from the Subprime Crisis." *International Monetary Fund Working Paper WP/08/200*. August 2008.

Gorton, Gary B. (2008). "*The Panic of (2007)*." Paper prepared for Federal Reserve Bank of Kansas City, Jackson Hole Conference, August. October 4.

Greenlaw, David, Jan Hatzius, Kashyap, Anil K. & Hyun Song Shin. "*Leveraged Losses: Lessons from the Mortgage Meltdown.*" U.S. Monetary Policy Forum Report No. 2. Rosenberg Institute, Brandeis International Business School and Initiative on Global Markets, University of Chicago Graduate School of Business. 2008.

International Monetary Fund. "Financial Stress and Deleveraging: Macrofinancial Implications and Policy." Global Financial Stability Report. Washington, D.C.: October 2008.

Kashyap, Anil K., Raghuram G. Rajan, & Jeremy C. Stein. (2008). "*Rethinking Capital Regulation.*" Paper prepared for Federal Reserve Bank of Kansas City symposium on "Maintaining Stability in a Changing Financial System." Jackson Hole, Wyoming. August 2 1-23, 2008. September.

Khandani, Amir E., & Andrew W. Lo. (2008)."*What Happened to the Quants in August 2007?: Evidence from Factors and Transactions Data.* Working paper. October 23.

Tobias Adrian & Hyun Song Shin. (2008). "*Liquidity and Financial Contagion.*" Banque de France. Financial Stability Review. Special issue on liquidity. No. 11. February.

Related GAO Products

Troubled Asset Relief Program: March 2009 Status of Efforts to Address Transparency and Accountability Issues. GAO-09-504. Washington, D.C.: March 31, 2009.

Financial Regulation: Review of Regulators' Oversight of Risk Management Systems at a Limited Number of Large, Complex Financial Institutions. GAO-09-499T. Washington, DC.: March 18, 2009.

Financial Regulation: A Framework for Crafting and Assessing Proposals to Modernize the Outdated U.S. Financial Regulatory System. GAO-09-216. Washington, D.C.: January 8, 2009.

Risk-Based Capital: New Basel II Rules Reduce Certain Competitive Concerns, but Bank Regulators Should Address Remaining Uncertainties. GAO-08-953. Washington, D.C.: September 12, 2008.

Hedge Funds: Regulators and Market Participants Are Taking Steps to Strengthen Market Discipline, but Continued Attention Is Needed. GAO-08-200. Washington, D.C.: January 24, 2008.

Financial Market Regulation: Agencies Engaged in Consolidated Supervision Can Strengthen Performance Measurement and Collaboration. GAO-07-154. Washington, D.C.: March 15, 2007.

Deposit Insurance: Assessment of Regulators' Use of Prompt Corrective Action Provisions and FDIC's New Deposit Insurance Program. GAO-07-242. Washington, D.C.: February 15, 2007.

Risk-Based Capital: Bank Regulators Need to Improve Transparency and Overcome Impediments to Finalizing the Proposed Basel II Framework. GAO-07-253. Washington, D.C.: February 15, 2007.

Long-Term Capital Management: Regulators Need to Focus Greater Attention on Systemic Risk. GAO/GGD-00-3. Washington, D.C.: October 29, 1999.

GAO's Mission

The Government Accountability Office, the audit, evaluation, and investigative arm of Congress, exists to support Congress in meeting its constitutional responsibilities and to help improve the performance and accountability of the federal government for the American people. GAO examines the use of public funds; evaluates federal programs and policies; and provides analyses, recommendations, and other assistance to help Congress make informed oversight, policy, and funding decisions. GAO's commitment to good government is reflected in its core values of accountability, integrity, and reliability.

End Notes

[1] Derivatives are financial products whose value is determined from an underlying reference rate (interest rates, foreign currency exchange rates); an index (that reflects the collective value of various financial products); or an asset (stocks, bonds, and commodities). Derivatives can be traded through central locations, called exchanges, where buyers and sellers, or their representatives, meet to determine prices; or privately negotiated by the parties off the exchanges or over the counter (OTC).

[2] Capital generally is defined as a firm's long-term source of funding, contributed largely by a firm's equity stockholders and its own returns in the form of retained earnings. One important function of capital is to absorb losses.

[3] Pub. L. No. 110-343, div. A, 122 Stat. 3765 (2008), codified at 12 U.S.C. §§ 5201 et seq.

[4] Section 102 of the act, 12 U.S.C. § 5212, authorizes Treasury to guarantee troubled assets originated or issued prior to March 14, 2008, including mortgage-backed securities.

[5] Section 117 of the act, 12 U.S.C. § 5227.

[6] In a May 26, 2009, letter, the Federal Reserve outlined its authority to monitor and regulate leverage and to set margin requirements (see app. IX).

[7] For example, see GAO, *Troubled Asset Relief Program: March 2009 Status of Efforts to Address Transparency and Accountability Issues*, GAO-09-504 (Washington, D.C.: Mar. 31, 2009).

[8] Under its CSE program, SEC supervised five broker-dealer holding companies—Bear Stearns, Lehman Brothers, Merrill Lynch, Goldman Sachs, and Morgan Stanley—on a consolidated basis. Following the sale of Bear Stearns to JPMorgan Chase, the Lehman Brothers bankruptcy filing, and the sale of Merrill Lynch to Bank of America, the remaining CSEs opted to become bank holding companies subject to Federal Reserve oversight. SEC terminated the CSE program in September 2008 but continues to oversee these firms' registered broker-dealer subsidiaries.

[9] See GAO, *Financial Regulation: A Framework for Crafting and Assessing Proposals to Modernize the Outdated U.S. Financial Regulatory System*, GAO-09-216 (Washington, D.C.: Jan. 8, 2009).

[10] For more detailed information about bank and financial holding companies, see GAO, *Financial Market Regulation: Agencies Engaged in Consolidated Supervision Can Strengthen Performance Measurement and Collaboration*, GAO-07-154 (Washington, D.C.: Mar. 15, 2007).

[11] For a more detailed discussion of the regulatory structure, see GAO-07-154 and GAO-09-216.

[12] As discussed below, SEC used to oversee certain broker-dealer holding companies on a consolidated basis.

[13] The Basel Committee on Banking Supervision (Basel Committee) seeks to improve the quality of banking supervision worldwide, in part by developing broad supervisory standards. The Basel Committee consists of central bank and regulatory officials from Argentina, Australia, Belgium, Brazil, Canada, China, France, Germany, Hong Kong SAR, India, Indonesia, Italy, Japan, Korea, Luxembourg, Mexico, the Netherlands, Russia, Saudi Arabia, Singapore, South Africa, Spain, Sweden, Switzerland, Turkey, the United Kingdom, and the United States. The Basel Committee's supervisory standards are also often adopted by nonmember countries.

[14] According to OTS staff, OTS did not adopt the capital requirements for trading book market risk.

[15] GAO, *Risk-Based Capital: New Basel II Rules Reduced Certain Competitive Concerns, but Bank Regulators Should Address Remaining Uncertainties*, GAO-08-953 (Washington, D.C.: Sept. 12, 2008).

[16] See, for example, Mark Jickling, Causes of the Financial Crisis, Congressional Research Service, R40173 (Washington, D.C.: Jan. 29, 2009).

[17] Our review of the literature included primarily academic studies analyzing the events surrounding the current financial crisis. Because the crisis began around mid-2007, we limited the scope of our literature search to studies issued after June 2007. These studies include published papers and working papers.

[18] See, for example, Financial Services Authority, *The Turner Review: A Regulatory Response to the Global Banking Crisis* (London: March 2009); Willem H. Buiter, "Lessons from the North Atlantic Financial Crisis," paper prepared for presentation at the conference "The Role of Money Markets," jointly organized by Columbia Business School and the Federal Reserve Bank of New York on May 29-30, 2008 (May 2008); Martin Neil Baily, Robert E. Litan, and Matthew S. Johnson, "The Origins of the Financial Crisis," *Fixing Finance Series*-Paper 3, (Washington, D.C.: The Brookings Institution, November 2008); and Ben Cohen and Eli Remolona, "The Unfolding Turmoil of 2007–2008: Lessons and Responses," Proceedings of a Conference, Sydney, Australia, Reserve Bank of Australia, Sydney.

[19] Under a repurchase agreement, a borrower generally acquires funds by selling securities to a lender and agreeing to repurchase the securities after a specified time at a given price. Such a transaction is called a repurchase agreement when viewed from the perspective of the borrower, and a reverse repurchase agreement from the point of view of the lender.

[20] For example, a market observer commented that Lehman Brothers' failure stemmed partly from the firm's high level of leverage and use of short-term debt. According to the market observer, Lehman Brothers used short-term debt to finance more than 50 percent of its assets at the beginning of the crisis, which is a profitable strategy in a low interest rate environment but increases the risk of "runs" similar to the ones a bank faces when it is rumored to be insolvent. Any doubt about the solvency of the borrower makes short-term lenders reluctant about renewing their lending.

[21] See, for example, Acharya, V. and P. Schnabl, How Banks Played the Leverage "Game"? in Acharya, V., Richardson, M. (Eds.) *Restoring Financial Stability: How to Repair a Failed System*, John Wiley and Sons (chap. 2) (2009).

[22] For a discussion of embedded leverage in CDOs, see The Joint Forum, Credit Risk Transfer, Basel Committee on Banking Supervision (Basel, Switzerland: October 2004).

[23] We use the term "securities firms" generally to refer to the holding companies of broker-dealers.

[24] See, for example, Adrian, Tobias, and Hyun Song Shin, "Liquidity, Financial Cycles and Monetary Policy," *Current Issues in Economics and Finance*, Federal Reserve Bank of New York, vol. 14, no. 1, January/February 2008.

[25] Fair value accounting, also called "mark-to-market," is a way to measure assets and liabilities that appear on a company's balance sheet and income statement. Measuring companies' assets and liabilities at fair value may affect their income statement. For more detailed information, see SEC's Office of Chief Accountant and Division of Corporate Finance, "Report and Recommendations Pursuant to Section 133 of the Emergency Economic Stabilization Act of 2008: Study on Mark-To-Market Accounting" (Washington, D.C.: Dec. 30, 2008).

[26] The 30-to-1 ratio of assets to equity is not unprecedented. In 1998, four of the five broker-dealer holding companies had assets-to-equity ratio equal to or greater than 30 to 1.

[27] See, for example, David Greenlaw, Jan Hatzius, Anil K. Kashyap, and Hyun Song Shin, "Leveraged Losses: Lessons from the Mortgage Meltdown," paper for the U.S. Monetary Policy Forum (2008).

[28] Meredith Whitney, Kaimon Chung, and Joseph Mack, "No Bad Bank Please," Oppenheimer Equity Research Industry Update, Financial Institutions (New York: Jan. 29, 2009).

[29] Sovereign wealth funds generally are pools of government funds invested in assets in other countries.

[30] See, for example, Markus K. Brunnermeier, "Deciphering the 2007-08 Liquidity and Credit Crunch," *Journal of Economic Perspectives* 23, no. 1 (2009), pp. 77-100; Greenlaw et al. (2008); and Anil K., Kashyap, Raghuram G. Rajan, and Jeremy C. Stein, "Rethinking Capital Regulation," paper prepared for Federal Reserve Bank of Kansas City symposium on "Maintaining Stability in a Changing Financial System," Jackson Hole, Wyoming, August 21- 23, 2008 (September 2008).

[31] Darryll Hendricks, John Kambhu, and Patricia Mosser, "Systemic Risk and the Financial System, Appendix B: Background Paper," *Federal Reserve Bank of New York Economic Policy Review* (November 2007).

[32] A full analysis of the role played by banks in financial intermediation would need to consider the share of credit intermediated or securitized by affiliates, subsidiaries, and sponsored investment vehicles of bank holding companies and financial holding companies.

[33] In addition to increases in haircuts, other factors can cause liquidity stress. For example, financial institutions negotiate margins on OTC derivatives to protect themselves from the risk of counterparty default. Changes in the value of OTC derivatives can result in margin calls and result in liquidity stress.

[34] The seminal paper on this issue is Akerlof, George A., "The Market for 'Lemons': Quality Uncertainty and the Market Mechanism," *Quarterly Journal of Economics*, 84(3), pp. 488- 500, 1970.

[35] See, for example, Devlin, Will, and Huw McKay, The Macroeconomic Implications of Financial "Deleveraging," Economic Roundup, Issue 4, 2008; Greenlaw et al. (2008); and Kashyup et al. (2008). Devlin and Hew (2008) note that there is a large and growing body of empirical evidence to suggest that shocks to a bank capital-to-asset ratios that lead to a contraction in the availability of credit within an economy can have large and long-lasting economic effects.

[36] Greenlaw et al. (2008).

[37] On the other hand, any decline in lending may be partially offset by the Troubled Asset Relief Program, the Term Asset-Backed Securities Loan Facility, or other monetary and fiscal policies designed to mitigate the effects of the financial crisis.

[38] Frederic S. Mishkin, Governor of the Board of the Federal Reserve System, Speech on "Leveraged Losses: Lessons from the Mortgage Meltdown," at the U.S. Monetary Policy Forum (New York, N.Y.: Feb. 29, 2008).

[39] Timothy F. Geithner, "Actions by the New York Fed in Response to Liquidity Pressures in Financial Markets," Testimony before the U.S. Senate Committee on Banking, Housing and Urban Affairs (Washington, D.C.: Apr. 3, 2008).

[40] Treasury, Public-Private Investment Program, $500 Billion to $1 Trillion Plan to Purchase Legacy Assets, White Paper.

[41] See, for example, GAO-09-504.

[42] Bank holding companies are permitted to include certain debt instruments in regulatory capital that are impermissible for insured banks and, as discussed below, are not subject to statutory Prompt Corrective Action.

[43] Under its CSE program, SEC supervised broker-dealer holding companies—Bear Stearns, Lehman Brothers, Merrill Lynch, Goldman Sachs, and Morgan Stanley—on a consolidated basis. Following the sale of Bear Stearns to JPMorgan Chase, the Lehman Brothers bankruptcy filing, and the sale of Merrill Lynch to Bank of America, the remaining CSEs opted to become bank holding companies subject to Federal Reserve oversight. SEC terminated the CSE program in September 2008 but continues to oversee these firms' registered broker-dealer subsidiaries.

[44] The Prompt Corrective Action regulations and the key regulatory capital requirements for banks and thrifts are outlined in 12 C.F.R. pts. 3, 6 (OCC); 208 (FRB); 325 (FDIC) and 565, 567 (OTS).

[45] Regulations limit what may be included in Tier 1 and Tier 2 capital. Tier 1 capital can include common stockholders' equity, noncumulative perpetual preferred stock, and minority equity investments in consolidated subsidiaries. For example, see 12 C.F.R. pt. 325, app. A (I)(A)(1). The remainder of a bank's total capital also can consist of tier 2 capital which can include items such as general loan and lease loss allowances (up to a maximum of 1.25 percent of risk-weighted assets), cumulative preferred stock, certain hybrid (debt/equity) instruments, and subordinated debt with a maturity of 5 years or more. For example, see 12 C.F.R. pt. 325, app. A(I)(A)(2).

[46] Banks holding the highest supervisory rating have a minimum leverage ratio of 3 percent; all other banks must meet a leverage ratio of at least 4 percent. Bank holding companies that have adopted the Market Risk Amendment or hold the highest supervisory rating are subject to a 3 percent minimum leverage ratio; all other bank holding companies must meet a 4 percent minimum leverage ratio. According to FDIC officials, in practice, a bank with a 3 to 4 percent leverage ratio would be less than well capitalized for Prompt Corrective Action purposes (discussed below) and would be highly unlikely to be assigned the highest supervisory rating.

[47] 12 U.S.C. § 1831o. The Federal Deposit Insurance Act, as amended by the Federal Deposit Insurance Corporation Improvement Act of 1991, requires federal regulators to take specific action against banks and thrifts that have capital levels below minimum standards.

[48] Regulators use three different capital measures to determine an institution's capital category: (1) a total risk-based capital measure, (2) a Tier 1 risk-based capital measure, and (3) a leverage (or non-risk-based) capital measure. For additional information, see GAO, *Deposit Insurance: Assessment of Regulators' Use of Prompt Corrective Action Provisions and FDIC's New Deposit Insurance Program*, GAO-07-242 (Washington, D.C.: Feb. 15, 2007).

[49] Any determination to take other action in lieu of receivership or conservatorship for a critically undercapitalized institution is effective for no more than 90 days. After the 90-day period, the regulator must place the institution in receivership or conservatorship or make a new determination to take other action. Each new determination is subject to the same 90-day restriction. If the institution is critically undercapitalized, on average, during the calendar quarter beginning 270 days after the date on which the institution first became critically undercapitalized, the regulator is required to appoint a receiver for the institution. Section 38 contains an exception to this requirement, if, among other things, the regulator and chair of the FDIC Board of Directors both certify that the institution is viable and not expected to fail.

[50] Banks usually are examined at least once during each 12-month period and more frequently if they have serious problems. In addition, well-capitalized banks with total assets of less than $250 million can be examined on an 18-month cycle.

[51] At each examination, examiners assign a supervisory CAMELS rating, which assesses six components of an institution's financial health: capital, asset quality, management, earnings, liquidity, and sensitivity to market risk. An institution's CAMELS rating is known directly only by the institution's senior management and appropriate regulatory staff. Regulators never publicly release CAMELS ratings, even on a lagged basis.

[52] All FDIC-insured banks and savings institutions that are supervised by FDIC, OCC, or the Federal Reserve must submit quarterly Consolidated Reports on Condition and Income (Call Reports), which contain a variety of financial information, including capital amounts. FDIC-insured thrifts supervised by OTS must file similar reports, called Thrift Financial Reports.

[53] On December 7, 2007, the banking regulatory agencies issued a final rule entitled "Risk- Based Capital Standards: Advanced Capital Adequacy Framework – Basel II." 72 Fed. Reg. 69288 (Dec. 7, 2007). In addition to this final rule, the agencies issued a proposed revision to the market risk capital rule. 71 Fed. Reg. 55958 (Sept. 25, 2006).

[54] Well-capitalized for bank holding companies does not have the same meaning as in a PCA context; it is used in the application process.

[55] Under the Homeowners' Loan Act of 1933, as amended, companies that own or control a savings association are subject to supervision by OTS. 12 U.S.C. § 1467a.

[56] Each bank holding company is assigned a composite rating (C) based on an evaluation and rating of its managerial and financial condition and an assessment of future potential risk to its subsidiary depository institution(s). The main components of the rating system represent: Risk Management (R); Financial Condition (F); and potential Impact (I) of the parent company and nondepository subsidiaries on the subsidiary depository institution(s). The Impact rating focuses on downside risk—that is, on the likelihood of significant negative impact on the subsidiary depository institutions. A fourth component rating, Depository Institution (D), will generally mirror the primary regulator's assessment of the subsidiary depository institution(s).

[57] The Federal Reserve's formal enforcement powers for bank holding companies and their nonbank subsidiaries are set forth at 12 U.S.C. § 1818(b)(3).

[58] See 12 U.S.C. § 1467a(g), (i) and 12 U.S.C. § 1818(b)(9).

[59] Senior Deputy Director and Chief Operating Officer, Scott M. Polakoff, before the Subcommittee on Securities, Insurance, and Investment, Committee on Banking, Housing, and Urban Affairs, U.S. Senate (Washington, D.C.: June 19, 2008).

[60] SEC has broad authority to adopt rules and regulations regarding the financial responsibility of broker-dealers that it finds are necessary or appropriate in the public interest or for the protection of investors and, pursuant to that authority, adopted the net capital rule (17 C.F.R. § 240.15c3-1) and related rules. 40 Fed. Reg. 29795, 29799 (July 16, 1975). Specifically, the SEC determined that the net capital rule was necessary and appropriate to provide safeguards with respect to the financial responsibility and related practices of brokers or dealers; to eliminate illiquid and impermanent capital; and to assure investors that their funds and securities are protected against financial instability and operational weaknesses of brokers or dealers. *Id*. See also 17 C.F.R. 240.15c3-3.

[61] 15 U.S.C. § 78o(c)(3).

[62] CFTC imposes capital requirements on futures commission merchants, which are similar to broker-dealers but act as intermediaries in commodity futures transactions. Some firms are registered as both a broker-dealer and futures commission merchant and must comply with both SEC's and CFTC's regulations.

[63] In comparison, under the basic method, broker-dealers must have net capital equal to at least 6 2/3 percent of their aggregate indebtedness. The 6-2/3 percent requirement implies that broker-dealers must have at least $1 of net capital for every $15 of its indebtedness (that is, a leverage constraint). Most small broker-dealers typically use the basic method because of the nature of their business.

[64] See 17 C.F.R. § 240. 15c3-3.

[65] Pub. L. No. 91-598, 84 Stat. 1636, codified at 15 U.S.C. §§ 78aaa-78lll.

[66] As part of its oversight, SEC also evaluates the quality of FINRA oversight in enforcing its members' compliance through oversight inspections of FINRA and inspections of broker- dealers. SEC also directly assesses broker-dealer compliance with federal securities laws through special and cause examinations.

[67] To assess the adequacy of both capital and liquid assets, SEC staff takes a scenario-based approach. A key premise of the scenario analysis is that during a liquidity stress event, the holding company would not receive additional unsecured funding.

[68] GAO, *Long-Term Capital Management: Regulators Need to Focus Greater Attention on Systemic Risk*, GAO/GGD-00-3 (Washington, D.C.: Oct. 29, 1999). The report did not present the assets-to-equity ratio for Bear Stearns, but its ratio also was above 28 to 1 in 1998.

[69] Bear Stearns was acquired by JPMorgan Chase, Lehman Brothers failed, Merrill Lynch was acquired by Bank of America, and Goldman Sachs and Morgan Stanley have become bank holding companies.

[70] Although there is no statutory definition of "hedge fund," the term commonly is used to describe pooled investment vehicles directed by professional managers that often engage in active trading of various types of assets, such as securities and derivatives and are structured and operated in a manner that enables the fund and its advisers to qualify for exemptions from certain federal securities laws and regulations that apply to other investment pools, such as mutual funds.

[71] See GAO, *Hedge Funds: Regulators and Market Participants Are Taking Steps to Strengthen Market Discipline, but Continued Attention Is Needed*, GAO-08-200 (Washington, D.C.: Jan. 24, 2008).

[72] Except as may otherwise be provided by law, a commodity pool operator (CPO) is an individual or organization that operates an enterprise, and, in connection therewith, solicits or receives funds, securities or property from third parties, for the purpose of trading in any commodity for future delivery on a contract market or derivatives execution facility. 7 U.S.C. § 1a(5). A commodity trading advisor (CTA) is, except as otherwise provided by law, any person who, for compensation or profit, (1) directly or indirectly advises others on the

advisability of buying or selling any contract of sale of a commodity for future delivery, commodity options or certain leverage transactions contracts, or (2) as part of a regular business, issues analyses or reports concerning the activities in clause (1). 7 U.S.C. § 1a(6). In addition to statutory exclusions to the definition of CPO and CTA, CFTC has promulgated regulations setting forth additional criteria under which a person may be excluded from the definition of CPO or CTA. *See* 17 C.F.R. §§ 4.5 and 4.6 (2007).

[73] See GAO-08-200.

[74] Office of Inspector General, Department of the Treasury, *Safety and Soundness: Material Loss Review of IndyMac Bank, FSB,* OIG-09-032 (Washington, D.C.: Feb. 26, 2009).

[75] Roger T. Cole, Director, Division of Banking Supervision and Regulation, before the Subcommittee on Securities, Insurance, and Investment, Committee on Banking, Housing, and Urban Affairs, U.S. Senate (Washington, D.C.: Mar. 18, 2009).

[76] Office of Inspector General, U.S. Securities and Exchange Commission, *SEC's Oversight of Bear Stearns and Related Entities: The Consolidated Supervised Entity Program,* 446- A (Washington, D.C.: Sept. 25, 2008).

[77] Ch. 404, § 7, 48 Stat. 881 (June 6, 1934) *codified at* 15 U.S.C. § 78g.

[78] Margin rules also have been established by U.S. securities self-regulatory organizations, such as NYSE Rule 431 and NASD Rule 2520, which limit the extension of credit by member broker-dealers. While FINRA is establishing new FINRA rules, the old rules continue to be effective until replaced by an applicable new FINRA rule.

[79] Regulation X, 12 C.F.R pt. 224, generally applies to U.S. citizens borrowing from non-U.S. lenders. Regulation X extends to borrowers the provisions of Regulations T and U for the purpose of purchasing or carrying securities. In that regard, our discussion focuses on Regulations T and U, 12 C.F.R. pts. 220 and 221.

[80] Although section 7 of the Securities Exchange Act gives the Federal Reserve the authority to adopt initial and maintenance margins, the Federal Reserve has chosen to adopt only initial margin requirements. Broker-dealers, however, are required to join the Financial Industry Regulatory Authority and are therefore subject to its maintenance margin requirements. See New York Stock Exchange Rule 431 and National Association of Securities Dealers Rule 2520.

[81] Under regulation T, broker-dealers may accept exempted and margin securities as collateral for loans used to purchase securities. Exempted securities include government and municipal securities. Margin securities comprise a broad range of equity and non- equity, or debt, securities. The Federal Reserve has set the initial margin requirement for equity securities at 50 percent of their market value. In contrast, non-equity securities (e.g., corporate bonds, mortgage-related securities, and repurchase agreements on non-equity securities) and exempt securities are subject to a "good faith" margin requirement. Good faith margin means that a broker-dealer may extend credit on a particular security in any amount consistent with sound credit judgment.

[82] Even though the total amount of margin debt decreased significantly from December 2007 to December 2008, the total margin debt as a percentage of total market capitalization did not decline, because the total market capitalization also declined significantly during this period.

[83] With the exception of broker-dealer holding companies participating in the SEC's CSE program, U.S. banks operated under the Basel I regulatory capital framework prior to the crisis.

[84] Assets held in the banking book generally include assets that are not actively traded and intended to be held for longer periods than trading portfolio assets. See appendix III for information about how assets are assigned to risk-weighting categories under Basel I.

[85] Before the crisis, to purchase homes borrowers might not be able to afford with a conventional fixed-rate mortgage, an increasing number of borrowers turned to alternative mortgage products, which offer comparatively lower and more flexible monthly mortgage payments for an initial period. Interest-only and payment option adjustable rate mortgages allow borrowers to defer repayment of principal and possibly part of the interest for the first few years of the mortgage. For more about the risks associated with alternative mortgage products, see GAO, *Alternative Mortgage Products: Impact on Defaults Remains Unclear, but Disclosure of Risks to Borrowers Could Be Improved,* GAO-06-1021 (Washington, D.C.: Sept. 19, 2006*)*.

[86] For more about the U.S. efforts to transition large banks to the Basel II framework, see GAO, *Risk-Based Capital: Bank Regulators Need to Improve Transparency and Overcome Impediments to Finalizing the Proposed Basel II Framework,* GAO-07-253 (Washington, D.C.: Feb. 15, 2007).

[87] Trading book assets generally include securities that the bank holds in its trading portfolio and trades frequently. Trading book assets also can include securities that institutions intend to hold until maturity. For example, a security may be booked in the trading book because the derivative position used to hedge its return is in the trading book.

[88] VaR is a statistical measure of the potential loss in the fair value of a portfolio due to adverse movements in underlying risk factors. The measure is an estimate of the expected loss that an institution is unlikely to exceed in a given period with a particular degree of confidence. Specific risk means changes in the market value of specific positions due to factors other than broad market movements and includes such risks as the credit risk of an instrument's issuer.

[89] See the Financial Services Authority, *The Turner Review: A Regulatory Response to the Global Banking Crisis* (London: March 2009). The Financial Services Authority is the United Kingdom's financial regulator.

[90] See Senior Supervisors Group, *Observations on Risk Management Practices during the Recent Market Turbulence* (New York: Mar. 6, 2008).

[91] Risk-based regulatory capital ratios measure credit risk, market risk, and (under Basel II) operational risk. Risks not measured under pillar I include liquidity risk, concentration risk, reputational risk, and strategic risk.

[92] Contingent funding support includes liquidity facilities and credit enhancements. Liquidity facilities are the assurance of a loan or guarantee of financial support to back up an off-balance sheet entity. Credit enhancements are defined as a contractual arrangement in which a bank retains or assumes a securitization exposure and, in substance, provides some degree of added protection to the parties to the transaction.

[93] Reputation risk is the potential for financial loss associated with negative publicity regarding an institution's business practices and subsequent decline in customers, costly litigation, or revenue reductions.

[94] Contingent liquidity risk refers to the risk that a bank would have to satisfy contractual or non-contractual obligations contingent upon certain events taking place.

[95] 12 U.S.C. §1831o(c)(1)(B)(i).

[96] See GAO-09-216.

[97] GAO, *Financial Regulation: Review of Regulators' Oversight of Risk Management Systems at a Limited Number of Large, Complex Financial Institutions*, GAO-09-499T (Washington, D.C.: Mar. 18, 2009).

[98] In April 2009, the Group of Twenty, which represents the world's leading and largest emerging economies, met in London to discuss the international response to the global financial crisis.

[99] In January 2009, the Basel Committee on Banking Supervision proposed revisions to the Basel II market risk framework.

[100] The Basel Committee on Banking Supervision has defined a resecuritization exposure as a securitization exposure where one or more of the underlying exposures is a securitization exposure.

[101] Statement 166 eliminates the exemption from consolidation for certain SPEs. A second new standard, Statement 167, requires ongoing reassessments of whether consolidation is appropriate for assets held by certain off-balance sheet entities. These new standards will impact financial institution balance sheets beginning in 2010.

[102] Department of the Treasury, *Financial Regulatory Reform: A New Foundation* (Washington, D.C.: June 2009).

[103] GAO-07-253.

[104] Other regulatory loss-absorbing buffers include loan loss provisions and margin and collateral requirements. Provisions for loan losses allow banks to recognize income statement losses for expected loan portfolio losses before they occur. Current accounting rules require recognition of a loan loss provision only when a loan impairment event takes place or events occur that are likely to result in future non-payment of a loan. Some observers have commented that earlier provisioning for loan losses may help to reduce the magnitude of financial losses that hit the income statement and deplete regulatory capital when market conditions deteriorate. To address the potential contribution of these other buffers to procyclicality, domestic and international regulators have proposed changes in a Financial Stability Forum report: *Report of the Financial Stability Forum on Addressing Procyclicality in the Financial System* (Basel, Switzerland: April 2009).

[105] The financial crisis has highlighted challenges associated with balancing the goals of providing sufficient financial disclosures for investors and maintaining financial stability. The Financial Accounting Standards Board recently revised fair value accounting rules to allow firms to distinguish between losses arising from the underlying creditworthiness of assets and losses arising from market conditions.

[106] See GAO-09-216. GAO included systemwide focus as one of nine elements in a proposed framework for evaluating financial regulatory reforms. Systemwide focus refers to having mechanisms to identify, monitor, and manage risks to the financial system regardless of the source of the risk or the institutions in which it is created.

[107] 72 Fed. Reg. 69288, 69393 (Dec. 7, 2007).

[108] GAO-07-253.

[109] GAO-09-216.

[110] Federal Reserve Chairman Ben S. Bernanke, Opening Remarks at Kansas City Federal Reserve's Bank 2008 Symposium on Maintaining Stability in a Changing Financial System (August 2008).

[111] The President's Working Group on Financial Markets was established by Executive Order No. 12631, 53 Fed. Reg. 9421 (Mar. 18, 1988). The Secretary of the Treasury chairs the group, the other members of which are the chairpersons of the Federal Reserve, SEC, and Commodity Futures Trading Commission. The group was formed to enhance the integrity, efficiency, orderliness, and competitiveness of the U.S. financial markets and maintain investor confidence in those markets.

[112] The Basel Committee on Banking Supervision (Basel Committee) seeks to improve the quality of banking supervision worldwide, in part by developing broad supervisory standards. The Basel Committee consists of central bank and regulatory officials from Argentina, Australia, Belgium, Brazil, Canada, China, France, Germany, Hong Kong SAR, India, Indonesia, Italy, Japan, Korea, Luxembourg, Mexico, the Netherlands, Russia, Saudi Arabia, Singapore, South Africa, Spain, Sweden, Switzerland, Turkey, the United Kingdom, and the United States. The Basel Committee's supervisory standards are also often adopted by nonmember countries.

[113] The Financial Stability Forum comprises national financial authorities (central banks, supervisory authorities, and finance ministries) from the G7 countries, Australia, Hong Kong, Netherlands, Singapore, and Switzerland, as well as international financial institutions, international regulatory and supervisory groupings, committees of central bank experts and the European Central Bank. In April 2009, the Financial Stability Forum was re-established as the Financial Stability Board, with a broadened mandate to promote financial stability.

[114] The Senior Supervisors Group is composed of eight supervisory agencies: France's Banking Commission, Germany's Federal Financial Supervisory Authority, the Swiss Federal Banking Commission, the Financial Services Authority, the Federal Reserve, the Federal Reserve Bank of New York, OCC, and SEC.

[115] See GAO, *Risk Based Capital: Bank Regulators Need to Improve Transparency and Overcome Impediments to Finalizing Basel II Framework*, GAO-07-253 (Washington, D.C.: Feb. 15, 2007).

[116] In addition to the risk weights in table 2, a dollar-for-dollar capital charge applies for certain recourse obligations. See 66 Fed. Reg. 59614, 59620 (Nov. 29, 2001).

[117] As implemented in the United States, Basel I assigns reduced risk weights to exposures collateralized by cash on deposit; securities issued or guaranteed by central governments of Organization for Economic Cooperation and Development countries, U.S. government agencies, and U.S. government-sponsored enterprises; and securities issued by multilateral lending institutions. Basel I also has limited recognition of guarantees, such as those made by Organization for Economic Cooperation and Development countries, central governments, and certain other entities. See 12 C.F.R. Part 3 (OCC); 12 C.F.R. Parts 208 and 225 (Federal Reserve); 12 C.F.R. Part 325 (FDIC); and 12 C.F.R. Part 567 (OTS).

[118] The Basel Committee defines operational risk as the risk of loss resulting from inadequate or failed internal processes, people, and systems or from external events, including legal risks, but excluding strategic and reputational risk. Examples of operational risks include fraud, legal settlements, systems failures, and business disruptions.

[119] Securitization is the process of pooling debt obligations and dividing that pool into portions (called tranches) that can be sold as securities in the secondary market. Banks can use securitization for regulatory arbitrage purposes by, for example, selling high-quality tranches of pooled credit exposures to third-party investors, while retaining a disproportionate amount of the lower-quality tranches and therefore, the underlying credit risk.

[120] 61 Fed. Reg. 47358 (Sept. 6, 1996).

[121] 66 Fed. Reg. 59614 (Nov. 29, 2001).

In: Who Regulates Whom: U.S. Finanial Oversight
Editor: Milton H. Lazarus

ISBN: 978-1-60876-981-0
© 2010 Nova Science Publishers, Inc.

Chapter 8

WHO REGULATES WHOM? AN OVERVIEW OF U.S. FINANCIAL SUPERVISION

Mark Jickling and Edward V. Murphy

SUMMARY

Federal financial regulation in the United States has evolved through a series of piecemeal responses to developments and crises in financial markets. This report provides an overview of current U.S. financial regulation: which agencies are responsible for which institutions and markets, and what kinds of authority they have.

Banking regulation is largely based on a quid pro quo that was adopted in response to widespread bank failures. The federal government provides a safety net for some banking operations and in return the banks accept federal regulation of their operations, including the amount of risk they may incur. For example, federal deposit insurance reduces customers' incentive to withdraw their funds at the first sign of trouble. In return for federal deposit insurance, bank regulators can order a stop to "unsafe and unsound" banking practices and can take prompt corrective action with troubled banks, including closing the institution. There are five federal bank regulators, each supervising different (and often overlapping) sets of depository institutions.

Federal securities regulation is based on the principle of disclosure, rather than direct regulation. Firms that sell securities to the public must register with the Securities and Exchange Commission (SEC), but the agency has no authority to prevent excessive risk taking. SEC registration in no way implies that an investment is safe, only that the risks have been fully disclosed. The SEC also registers several classes of securities market participants and firms, but relies more on industry self-regulation than do the banking agencies. Derivatives trading is supervised by the Commodity Futures Trading Commission (CFTC), which oversees trading on the futures exchanges, which have self-regulatory responsibilities as well. There is also a large over-the-counter (off-exchange) derivatives market that is largely unregulated.

The Federal Housing Finance Agency (FHFA) oversees a group of government-sponsored enterprises (GSEs)—public/private hybrid firms that seek both to earn profits and to further the policy objectives set out in their statutory charters. Two GSEs, Fannie Mae and Freddie Mac, were placed in conservatorship by the FHFA in September 2008 after losses in mortgage asset portfolios made them effectively insolvent. A number of financial markets are unregulated, including some of the largest. No federal agency has jurisdiction over trading in foreign exchange or U.S. Treasury securities; nonbank lenders fall outside the regulatory umbrella; and hedge funds, private equity firms, and venture capital investors are largely unregulated (although their transactions in securities and derivatives markets may be).

The United States has never attempted a wholesale reformation of the entire regulatory system comparable to the 1986 "Big Bang" in the UK, which reorganized regulatory agencies across industry lines and sought to implement a consistent philosophy of regulation. In the wake of the current financial turmoil, however, such a reevaluation is possible, and a number of broad restructuring proposals have already come forward.

In the 111th Congress, S. 566, "Financial Product Safety Commission Act of 2009," introduced by Senator Durbin, would create a federal financial regulator whose sole focus is the safety of consumer financial products.

This report does not attempt to analyze the strengths and weaknesses of the U.S. regulatory system. Rather, it provides a description of the current system, to aid in the evaluation of reform proposals. It will be updated as warranted by market events.

INTRODUCTION

Historically, the major changes in financial regulation in the United States have come in response to crisis. Thus, one could have predicted that the turmoil beginning in 2007 would lead to calls for reform. A number of studies and reports have already proposed broad changes to the division of supervisory authority among the various federal agencies and in the tools and authorities available to individual regulators.[1] This report provides a basis for evaluating and comparing such proposals by setting out the basic structure of federal financial regulation as it stood at the beginning of the 111th Congress.

Few would argue that regulatory failure was solely to blame for the current crisis, but it is widely considered to have played a part. In February 2009, Treasury Secretary Timothy Geithner summed up two key problem areas:

> Our financial system operated with large gaps in meaningful oversight, and without sufficient constraints to limit risk. Even institutions that were overseen by our complicated, overlapping system of multiple regulators put themselves in a position of extreme vulnerability. These failures helped lay the foundation for the worst economic crisis in generations.[2]

In this analysis, regulation failed to maintain financial stability at the systemic level because there were gaps in regulatory jurisdiction and because even overlapping jurisdictions—where institutions were subject to more than one regulator—could not ensure the soundness of regulated financial firms. In addition, limits on risk-taking were insufficient. Regulators have a number of risk-reduction tools at their disposal, but the chief one is capital regulation—standards that require firms to maintain capital cushions to protect themselves against unexpected losses.

To create a context for what follows, this report begins with basic analysis of systemic risk and capital regulation. The first section briefly discusses regulatory jurisdiction and systemic risk, and includes a chart listing the major regulators and the types of institutions they supervise. The chart also indicates certain emergency authorities available to the regulators, including those that relate to systemic financial disturbances. The second section focuses on capital requirements and how standards are set by bank, securities, and futures regulators.

The next section provides a brief overview of each of the federal financial regulatory agencies. Because the current crisis is likely to provoke a serious reconsideration of the levels of capital that financial firms should be required to maintain as a cushion against insolvency, the capital standards that each agency applies to various classes of financial firms are also set out.

Finally, the report discusses of several major areas of financial markets that are not subject to any federal regulation.

FINANCIAL CRISES, REGULATORY JURISDICTION, AND SYSTEMIC RISK

The United States has experienced several financial panics and economic disruptions in its history. Reactions to financial disruptions have resulted in a complex regulatory framework, in which some agencies have overlapping jurisdictions, and where there may be some regulatory gaps. With each new crisis, including the current one, there are calls to address perceived gaps and weaknesses in the regulatory system. Financial disruptions can originate from at least three sources:

- *failures within the financial system itself*, such as a breakdown in the ability of banks and other financial intermediaries to process their obligations to one another in a timely and efficient manner;
- *demands on the financial system from other sectors of the economy*, such as unexpected pressure on banks to honor their obligations to depositors and investors more quickly than they can accumulate liquid assets; and
- *weakness in real economic sectors*, such as an unexpected drop in the capacity of firms and consumers to repay bank loans.

Processes within the Financial Sector

Financial disruptions can manifest themselves within the financial sector itself (represented in the **Figure 1** by the numeral 1). For example, banks may have trouble processing checks and other third-party claims, or loans to other banks. Because the willingness and ability of market participants to extend loans and make trades often depends on trust that others will honor their obligations to them in a timely manner, disruptions in interbank lending markets, clearinghouses, and trading exchanges can disrupt financial flows to the wider economy.[3] The Panic of 1857 may represent an instance in which interbank markets failed and contributed to a wider recession— subsequent reforms sought to redress problems within the financial sector itself. Prior to the Civil War, the debts of state-chartered banks circulated as currency. A clearinghouse system was required to process these state bank notes, which often traded at a discount vis-a-vis each other, similar to the way that international currencies today have exchange rates. The value of a state bank note often depended on the perceived safety and soundness of the banks that issued the note. Private inter-bank clearinghouse systems, such as New England's Suffolk Bank, coordinated the processing of bank claims. The Panic of 1857 was a financial crisis in which the value of state bank notes became uncertain and the wider economy suffered a recession. The Suffolk Bank failed in 1858. Partially in response to this crisis, the United States established a single national currency, coordinated through a system of federally chartered banks. The safety and soundness of these banks is regulated by the Office of the Comptroller of the Currency (OCC), established in 1863.

These three types of problems are illustrated in the **Figure 1** and discussion below.

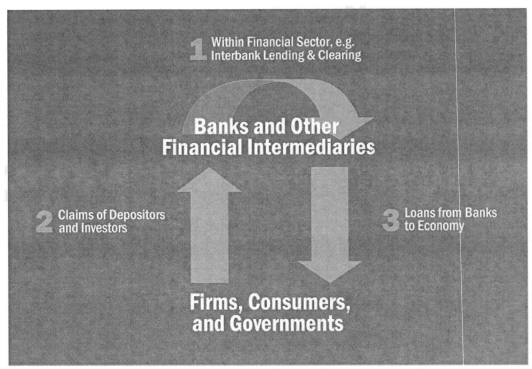

Source: CRS.

Figure 1. Where Financial Disruptions Arise

Honoring Claims of Depositors and Investors

Financial disruptions can result from problems between banks and their sources of funding, whether investors or depositors (indicated by the numeral 2 in the **Figure 1**). Banks and other financial intermediaries often have a timing mismatch: the value of their assets may only be recoverable over a long period of time, but their liabilities may be subject to immediate repayment. Banks plan for this duration mismatch using a variety of risk-management techniques, but at the end of the day, there are limits to their ability to accommodate changes in investor/depositor behavior. If investors or depositors demand repayment too quickly, a bank may be forced to sell its less liquid assets at a steep discount to meet immediate obligations. The resulting losses, or the fear of such losses, can damage the financial system and cut off credit to the wider economy.

The Panic of 1907 may represent an instance in which banks were unprepared for changes in the behavior of investors and depositors. In 1907, the seasonal increase in demand for currency coincided with disruptions in the New York money market caused by a commodities speculator. F.A. Heinze had used funds from the Mercantile National Bank, which was subject to OCC supervision, in a failed attempt to corner the copper market. Fearing bank insolvency, depositors began a series of runs on institutions believed to be associated with Heinze, including the New York Knickerbocker Bank. During the ensuing liquidity crisis, the swamped OCC staff's response time for currency deliveries slowed down even as demand for money increased. National banks turned to a variety of substitutes for national currency, including the financial resources of investor J.P. Morgan. Partially as a response to this crisis, the United States established a system of federally regulated bank reserves. The Federal Reserve was created in 1914.

Table 1. Systemic Crises and the Creation of Financial Regulators

Systemic Event	Perceived Problem	Solution	New Regulator	Year Created
Panic of 1857	Failure of Private Clearing houses that Processed State Bank Notes (circulated as currency)	Create Single National Currency Through System of Federally Chartered and Regulated Banks	Office of the Comptroller of the Currency (OCC)	1863
Panic of 1907	Series of Runs on Banks and Financial Trusts with Inadequate Reserves	Create Lender of Last Resort with Power to Regulate a National System of Bank Reserves	Federal Reserve	1913
Great Depression	Series of Runs on Banks by Small Depositors who Feared Full Value of Deposits Would Not be Honored	Create Limited Deposit Insurance to Maintain Depositor Confidence and Prevent Bank Runs	Federal Deposit Insurance Corporation (FDIC)	1933
	Sharp Decline in Stock Prices along with Widespread Belief that Some Investors had an Information Advantage Reduced Confidence in Securities Markets	Restore Confidence in Securities Markets by Standardizing Disclosures and Requiring Regular Reporting	Securities and Exchange Commission (SEC)	1934

Source: CRS.

The Great Depression may represent another episode in which banks were unprepared for changes in depositor behavior. Rising unemployment both increased the need for households to withdraw their savings deposits and reduced the flow of funds into banks through loan repayment. Fear that banks would not be able to honor their commitments to depositors caused a series of bank runs in 1931 and 1933, which forced banks to sell assets at steep discounts. To reduce the likelihood of future bank runs, Congress established a federal insurance program for bank deposits: the Federal Deposit Insurance Corporation (FDIC) was created in 1933.

Performance of Loans from Banks to the Economy

Financial disruptions can also result from worse-than-expected performance of loans from banks to households, businesses, and governments, indicated by the numeral 3 in the figure above. Banks and other financial intermediaries do not expect all loans to be repaid on time and in full; rather, there is always some allowance for loan losses. When loan losses rise above expectations, however, banks become less capitalized. To avoid an undercapitalized system, the OCC and other regulators with safety and soundness authority require subject institutions to prepare for some loan losses. In addition, they examine subject institutions' loan portfolios to assess the overall prudence of lending behavior and attempt to prevent overly risky lending.

During the 2001-2005 housing boom, large volumes of mortgage lending were conducted through non-bank institutions, which were not subject to the prudential lending standards of the bank regulators. Many large banks bought mortgage-backed securities based on such loans—or assumed the equivalent risk exposure through off-balance sheet financing arrangements or derivatives contracts—and have since suffered unexpected losses and become undercapitalized. Some believe that the current crisis is evidence of a regulatory gap, and have called for the establishment of a new systemic risk regulator with authority to oversee all financial institutions and firms that could trigger a systemic disruption.

Thus, new proposals to create a regulator exclusively concerned with systemic risk repeat the pattern that has characterized the development of U.S. financial regulation. The term "systemic risk" does not have a single, agreed-upon definition. Some define systemic risk as the risk an institution faces that it cannot diversify against. In other circumstances, systemic risk is defined as the risk that the linkages between institutions may affect the financial system as a whole, through a dynamic sometimes referred to as contagion. These definitions are compatible in some cases; for example, the linkages between financial institutions could prevent any single lender from effectively protecting itself from problems that emerge in the system as a whole.

The two definitions do not always apply to the same circumstances. Particular institutions in some sectors might face risks that are not diversifiable and that arise from sources other than the financial system. Similarly, linkages between institutions can create aggregate risks that individual institutions could hedge against if they chose to do so, but there is no assurance that the institutions would. In fact, another way to think about systemic risk is that it arises because all market participants have incentives to limit their own risk-taking to prevent loss of the own capital, but no participant will willingly limit its risk-taking—the source of its profitability—to reduce the possibility of a systemic disruption.

Table 2. Federal Financial Regulators and Who They Supervise

Regulatory Agency	Institutions Regulated	Emergency/Systemic Risk Powers	Other Notable Authority
Federal Reserve	Bank holding companies,[a] financial holding companies, state banks that are members of the Federal Reserve System, U.S. branches of foreign banks, foreign branches of U.S. banks	Lender of last resort to member banks (through discount window lending). In "unusual and exigent circumstances" the Fed may lend to "any individual, partnership, or corporation ... "	The Fed issues consumer protection regulations under various federal laws, including the Truth-in-Lending Act
Office of the Comptroller of the Currency (OCC)	National banks, U.S. federal branches of foreign banks		
Office of Thrift Supervision (OTS)	Federally chartered and insured thrift institutions, savings and loan holding companies		
National Credit Union Administration (NCUA)	Federally-chartered or insured credit unions	Serves as a liquidity lender to credit unions experiencing liquidity shortfalls through the Central Liquidity Facility	Operates a deposit insurance fund for credit unions, the National Credit Union Share Insurance Fund (NCUSIF)
Securities and Exchange Commission (SEC)	Securities exchanges, brokers, and dealers; mutual funds; investment advisers. Registers corporate securities sold to the public	May unilaterally close markets or suspend trading strategies for limited periods	Authorized to set financial accounting standards which all publicly traded firms must use
Commodity Futures Trading Commission (CFTC)	Futures exchanges, brokers, pool operators, advisers	May suspend trading, order liquidation of positions, or raise margins in emergencies.	
Federal Housing Finance Agency (FHFA)	Fannie Mae, Freddie Mac, and the Federal Home Loan Banks	Acting as conservator (since Sept. 2008) for Fannie and Freddie	

Source: CRS.

Notes: For more detail on banking regulation, see the chart "Banking Institutions and Their Regulators," http://www.newyorkfed.org/publications.

a. See Appendix A.

Asset bubbles represent one form of systemic risk. In good times, loans are less likely to default; therefore, it might make sense for any individual bank to increase its leverage and reduce its capital reserves. However, overly easy lending and reduced capital reserves in good times can lead to a bubble in the price of assets financed with loans, such as farms or houses (even tulip bulbs). When the bubble eventually deflates, simultaneous deterioration of banks' balance sheets can result.

Over the years, the financial regulatory system has been modified to address various sources of financial instability and evolving concepts of systemic risk. Not all federal financial regulators have authority to address systemic risk, and no single regulator has jurisdiction over all the financial institutions and markets that may become sources of systemic risk.

Table 2 below sets out the current federal financial regulatory structure: the agencies and the financial institutions they regulate. Supplemental material—charts that illustrate the differences between banks, bank holding companies, and financial holding companies—appears in **Appendix A**.

CAPITAL REQUIREMENTS

As a general accounting concept, capital means the equity of a business—the amount by which its assets exceed its liabilities.[4] The more capital a firm has, the greater its capacity to absorb losses and remain solvent. Financial regulators require the institutions they supervise to maintain specified minimum levels of capital—defined in various ways—in order to reduce the number of failing firms and to minimize losses to investors, customers, and taxpayers when failures do occur. Capital requirements represent a cost to businesses because they restrict the amount of funds that may be loaned or invested in the markets. Thus, there is a perpetual tension: firms structure their portfolios to reduce the amount of capital they must hold, while regulators continually modify capital standards to prevent excessive risk-taking.

In U.S. banking regulation, capital standards are based on the Basel Accords, an international framework developed under the auspices of the Bank for International Settlements.[5] The guiding principle of the Basel standards is that capital requirements should be risk-based. The riskier an asset, the more capital a bank should hold against possible losses. The Basel Accords provide two broad methodologies for calculating risk-based capital: (1) a standardized approach to credit risk determinations, based on external risk assessments (such as bond ratings), and (2) an alternative approach that relies on banks' internal risk models and rating systems. Adoption of the latter method—set out in the 2004 Basel II framework—in the United States has been slow, and thus far is limited to a few large banks.[6]

Table 3 shows how the standardized approach works in assessing the amount of capital to be held against credit risk in various types of financial instruments. The Basel Accords call for a basic capital requirement of 8% of the value of an asset; the risk-weighting then determines what percentage of that 8% baseline will apply to a given asset. For example, if the risk-weighting is 0%, no capital must be held (i.e., 8% X 0% = 0). A risk weighting of 100% means that the full 8% requirement applies. Assets weighted above 100% require that a multiple of the 8% capital requirement be held.

Federal banking regulators use the Basel Accords as the basis for their capital requirements. **Table 4** sets out the specific standards imposed by each.

Table 3. The Basel Accords: Risk Weightings for Selected Financial Assets Under the Standardized Approach (percentages of the 8% baseline capital requirement)

Asset	AAA to AA-	A+ to A-	BBB+ to BBB-	BB+ to B-	Below B-	Unrated
Sovereign Debt	0%	20%	50%	100%	150%	100%
Bank Debt	20%	50%	50%	100%	150%	100%
Corporate Debt	20%	50%	100%	NA	150% (below BB-)	100%
Assets not Assigned Ratings by Standard & Poor's or other Credit Rating Agencies						
Residential Mortgages	35%					
Commercial Real Estate	100%					
Past Due Loans	100%-150% (depending on specific provisions made to cover loan losses)					
Securitization Tranches rated between BB+ and BB- 350%						

Source: Basel Committee on Banking Supervision, *International Convergence of Capital Measurement and Capital Standards*, BIS, November 2005, pp. 15-22.

The SEC's net capital rule, set out in 17 CFR 240.15c3-1, imposes an "Aggregate Indebtedness Standard." No broker/dealer shall permit its aggregate indebtedness to all other persons to exceed 1500% of its net capital (or 800% of its net capital for 12 months after commencing business as a broker or dealer). The 1500% (or 15-to-1) ratio of debt to liquid capital, is arithmetically equivalent to a 6 % capital requirement.

Ta Non-Bank Capital Requirements

The SEC's Net Capital Rule

The SEC's net capital rule, set out in 17 CFR 240.15c3-1, imposes an "Aggregate Indebtedness Standard." No broker/dealer shall permit its aggregate indebtedness to all other persons to exceed 1500% of its net capital (or 800% of its net capital for 12 months after commencing business as a broker or dealer). The 1500% (or 15-to-1) ratio of debt to liquid capital, is arithmetically equivalent to a 6⅔ % capital requirement.

To calculate liquid capital, SEC rules require that securities and other assets be given a "haircut" from their current market values (or face value, in the case of bonds), to cover the risk that the asset's value might decline before it could be sold. The haircut concept is essentially the same as the standardized risk weights in the Basel Accords. The riskier the asset, the greater the haircut. For example, U.S. Treasury securities might have a haircut of zero to 1%; municipal securities, 7%; corporate bonds, 15%; common stock, 20%; and certain assets, such as unsecured receivables or securities for which no ready market exists, receive a haircut of 100%. As discussed below, the intent of the net capital rule is not the same as that of banking capital requirements, because the SEC is not a safety and soundness regulator. The net capital rule is meant to ensure that brokerages cease operations while they still have assets to meet their customers' claims.

ble 4. Capital Standards for Federally Regulated Depository Institutions

Agency	Capital Standard	Source
OCC	Minimum risk-based capital ratio of 8%. (The ratio measures bank capital against assets, with asset values risk-weighted, or adjusted on a scale of riskiness.)	12 CFR § 3.6 ("Minimum capital ratios")
	In addition, banks must maintain Tier 1 capital in an amount equal to at least 3.0% of adjusted total assets. (A simple definition of Tier 1 capital is stockholders' equity, or the net worth of the institution.) The 3% total assets leverage ratio applies to the most highly rated banks, which are expected to have well-diversified risks, including no undue interest rate risk exposure; excellent control systems; good earnings; high asset quality; high liquidity; and well managed on-and off-balance sheet activities; and in general b be considered strong banking organizations, with a rating of 1 under CAMELS rating system of banks. For other banks, the minimum Tier 1 leverage ratio is 4%.	
FDIC	The FDIC requires institutions to maintain the same minimum leverage capital requirements (ratio of Tier 1 capital to assets) as the OCC, that is, 3% for the most highly-rated institutions and 4% for others.	12 CFR § 325.3, ("Minimum leverage capital requirement")
Federal Reserve	State banks that are members of the Federal Reserve System must meet an 8% risk-weighted capital standard, of which at least 4% must be Tier 1 capital (3% for strong banking institutions rated "1" under the CAMELS rating system of banks).	12 CFR § 208.4, Regulation H ("Membership of State Banking Institutions in the Federal Reserve System") and 12 CFR § 204.9 (Reserve requirements)
	In addition, the Fed establishes levels of reserves that depository institutions are required to maintain for the purpose of facilitating the implementation of monetary policy by the Federal Reserve System. Reserves consist of vault cash (currency) or deposits at the nearest regional Federal Reserve branch, held against the bank's deposit liabilities, primarily checking, saving, and time deposits (CDs). The size of these reserves places a ceiling on the amount of deposits that financial institutions can have outstanding, and ties deposit liabilities to the amount of assets (loans) these institutions can acquire.	
OTS	Risk-based capital must be at least 8% of risk-weighted assets. Federal statute requires that OTS capital regulations be no less stringent than the OCC's. Tangible capital must exceed 1.5% of adjusted total assets. The leverage ratio (Tier 1 capital to assets) must be 4% of adjusted total assets (3% for thrifts with a composite CAMELS rating of 1).	12 CFR §567
NCUA	Credit unions must maintain a risk-based net worth of 7%, as a minimum to be considered well-capitalized.	NCUA Regulations (Section 702, Subpart A)

Source: CRS.

a. Tier 1 capital or core capital means the sum of common stockholders' equity, noncumulative perpetual preferred stock, and minority interests in consolidated subsidiaries, minus all intangible assets, minus identified losses, minus investments in certain financial subsidiaries, and minus the amount of the total adjusted carrying value of nonfinancial equity investments that is subject to a deduction from Tier 1 capital.

b. See Appendix B.

CFTC Capital Requirements

Futures commission merchants (or FCMs, the futures equivalent of a securities broker/dealer) are subject to adjusted net capital requirements. Authority to enforce the capital rules is delegated by the CFTC to the National Futures Association (NFA), a self-regulatory organization created by Congress.

Each NFA Member that is required to be registered with the CFTC as a Futures Commission Merchant (Member FCM) must maintain "Adjusted Net Capital" (as defined in CFTC Regulation 1.17) equal to or in excess of the greatest of:

(i) $500,000;
(ii) For Member FCMs with less than $2,000,000 in Adjusted Net Capital, $6,000 for each remote location operated;
(iii) For Member FCMs with less than $2,000,000 in Adjusted Net Capital, $3,000 for each associated person;
(iv) For securities brokers and dealers, the amount of net capital specified by SEC regulations;
(v) 8% of domestic and foreign domiciled customer and 4% of non-customer (excluding proprietary) risk maintenance margin/performance bond requirements for all domestic and foreign futures and options on futures contracts excluding the risk margin associated with naked long option positions;
(vi) For Member FCMs with an affiliate that engages in foreign exchange (FX) transactions and that is authorized to engage in those transactions solely by virtue of its affiliation with a registered FCM, $7,500,000; or
(vii) For Member FCMs that are counterparties to FX options, $5,000,000, except that FX Dealer Members must meet the higher requirement in Financial Requirements Section 11.[7]

Federal Housing Finance Agency

FHFA is authorized to set capital classification standards for the Federal Home Loan Banks, Fannie Mae, and Freddie Mac that reflect the differences in operations between the banks and the latter two gocerbment-sponsored enterprises.[8] The law defines several capital classifications, and prescribes regulatory actions to be taken as a GSE's condition worsens.

FHFA may downgrade the capital classification of a regulated entity (1) whose conduct could rapidly deplete core or total capital, or (in the case of Fannie or Freddie) whose mortgage assets have declined significantly in value, (2) which is determined (after notice and opportunity for a hearing) to be in an unsafe or unsound condition, or (3) which is engaging in an unsafe or unsound practice.

No growth in total assets is permitted for an *undercapitalized* GSE, unless (1) FHFA has accepted the GSE's capital restoration plan, (2) an increase in assets is consistent with the plan, and (3) the ratio of both total capital to assets and tangible equity to assets is increasing. An undercapitalized entity is subject to heightened scrutiny and supervision.

If a regulated entity is *significantly undercapitalized*, FHFA must take one or more of the following actions: new election of Directors, dismissal of Directors and/or executives, and hiring of qualified executive officers, or other actions. Without prior written approval, executives of a significantly undercapitalized regulated entity may not receive bonuses or pay raises. In addition, FHFA may appoint a receiver or conservator for several specified causes related to financial difficulty and/or violations of law or regulation.

When a GSE becomes *critically undercapitalized*, mandatory receivership or conservatorship provisions apply. For example, FHFA must appoint itself as the receiver if a regulated entity's assets are (and have been for 60 days) less than its obligations to its creditors, or if the regulated entity has (for 60 days) not been generally paying its debts as they come due. The FHFA appointed itself conservator for both Fannie and Freddie in September 2008, before either GSE had failed to make timely payments on debt obligations.

THE FEDERAL FINANCIAL REGULATORS

Banking Regulators

Banking regulation in United States has evolved over time into a system of multiple regulators with overlapping jurisdictions. There is a dual banking system, in which each depository institution is subject to regulation by its chartering authority: state or federal. In addition, because virtually all depository institutions are federally insured, they are subject to at least one federal primary regulator, i.e., the federal authority responsible for examining the institution for safety and soundness and for ensuring its compliance with federal banking laws. The primary federal regulator of national banks is their chartering authority, the Office of the Comptroller of the Currency (OCC). The primary federal regulator of state-chartered banks that are members of the Federal Reserve System is the Board of Governors of the Federal Reserve System. State- chartered banks that are not members of the Federal Reserve System have the FDIC as their primary federal regulator. Thrifts (both state- or federally-chartered) have the Office of Thrift Supervision as their primary federal regulator. All of these, because their deposits are covered by FDIC deposit insurance, are also subject to FDIC's regulatory authority. Credit unions–federallychartered or federally-insured–are regulated by the National Credit Union Administration. Federal consumer protection laws, many of which are implemented under rules issued by the Board of Governors of the Federal Reserve System, are enforced upon depository institutions by their primary federal regulator.

In general, lenders are expected to be prudent when extending loans. Each loan creates risk for the lender. The overall portfolio of loans extended or held by a lender, in relation to other assets and liabilities, affects that institution's stability. The relationship of lenders to each other, and to wider financial markets, affects the financial system's stability. The nature of these risks can vary between industry sectors, including commercial loans, farm loans, and consumer loans. Safety and soundness regulation encompasses the characteristics of (1) each loan; (2) the balance sheet of each institution; and (3) the risks in the system as a whole.

Each loan has a variety of risk characteristics of concern to lenders and their regulators. Some of these risk characteristics can be estimated at the time the loan is issued. Credit risk, for example, is the risk that the borrower will fail to repay the principal of the loan as promised. Rising interest rates create another risk because the shorter-term interest rates that the lender often pays for its funds rise (e.g., deposit or CD rates) while the longer-term interest rates that the lender will receive from fixed-rate borrowers remain unchanged. Falling interest rates are not riskless either: fixed-rate borrowers may choose to repay loans early, reducing the lender's expected future cash flow. Federal financial regulators take into account expected default rates, prepayment rates, interest-rate exposure, and other risks when examining the loans issued by covered lenders.

Each lender's balance sheet can reduce or enhance the risks of the individual loans that make it up. A lender with many loans exposed to prepayment risk when interest rates fall, for example, could compensate by acquiring some assets that rise in value when interest rates fall. One example of a compensating asset would be an interest-rate derivative contract. Lenders are required to keep capital in reserve against the possibility of a drop in value of loan portfolios or other risky assets. Federal financial regulators take into account compensating assets, risk-based capital requirements, and other prudential standards when examining the balance sheets of covered lenders.

When regulators determine that a bank is taking excessive risks, or engaging in unsafe and unsound practices, they have a number of powerful tools at their disposal to reduce risk to the institution (and ultimately to the federal deposit insurance fund). They can require banks to reduce specified lending or financing practices, dispose of certain assets, and order banks to take steps to restore sound balance sheets. Banks have no alternative but to comply, since regulators have life-or-death options, such as withdrawing deposit insurance or seizing the bank outright.

The five federal banking agencies are briefly discussed below.

Office of the Comptroller of the Currency

The Office of the Comptroller of the Currency (OCC) was created in 1863 as part of the Department of Treasury to supervise federally chartered banks ("national" banks) and to replace the circulation of state bank notes with a single national currency (Chapter 106, 13 STAT. 99). The OCC regulates a wide variety of financial functions, but only for federally chartered banks. The head of the OCC, the Comptroller, is also a member of the board of the FDIC and a director of the Neighborhood Reinvestment Corporation. The OCC has examination powers to enforce its responsibilities for the safety and soundness of nationally chartered banks. The OCC has strong enforcement powers, including the ability to issue cease and desist orders and revoke federal bank charters.

In addition to institution-level examinations, the OCC oversees systemic risk among nationally chartered banks. The OCC's use of the term systemic risk is more consistent with the linkages definition than the undiversifiable risk definition. One example of OCC systemic concerns is the regular survey of credit underwriting practices. This survey compares underwriting standards over time and assesses whether OCC examiners believe the credit risk of nationally chartered bank portfolios is rising or falling. In addition, the OCC publishes regular reports on the derivatives activities of U.S. commercial banks.

Federal Deposit Insurance Corporation

The Federal Deposit Insurance Corporation (FDIC) was created in 1933 to provide assurance to small depositors that they would not lose their savings if their bank failed (P.L. 74-305, 49 Stat. 684). The FDIC is an independent agency that insures deposits, examines and supervises financial institutions, and manages receiverships, assuming and disposing of the assets of failed banks. The FDIC manages the deposit insurance fund, which consists of risk-based assessments levied on depository institutions. The fund is used for various purposes, primarily for resolving failed or failing institutions. The FDIC has broad jurisdiction because nearly all banks and thrifts, whether federally or state-chartered, carry FDIC insurance.

Deposit insurance reform was enacted in 2006 (P.L. 109-173, 119 STAT. 3601), including raising the coverage limit for retirement accounts to $250,000 and indexing both its limit and the general deposit insurance coverage ceiling to inflation. The reform act made changes to the risk-based assessment system to determine the payments of individual institutions. Within a range set by the reform act, the FDIC uses notice and comment rulemaking to set the designated reserve ratio (DRR) that supports the Deposit Insurance Fund (DIF). The FDIC uses its power to examine individual institutions and to issue regulations for all insured depository institutions to monitor and enforce safety and soundness.

In 2008, as the financial crisis worsened, Congress enacted a temporary increase in the deposit insurance ceiling from $100,000 to $250,000 for most accounts.[9] Using emergency authority it received under the Federal Deposit Insurance Corporation Improvement Act of 1991 (FDICIA, P.L. 102-242),[10] the FDIC made a determination of systemic risk in October 2008 and announced that it would temporarily guarantee (1) newly issued senior unsecured debt of banks, thrifts, and certain holding companies, and (2) non-interest bearing deposit transaction accounts (e.g., business checking accounts), regardless of dollar amount.[11]

The Federal Reserve

The Board of Governors of the Federal Reserve System was established in 1913 to provide stability in the banking sector through the regulation of bank reserves (P.L. 63-43, 38 STAT. 251). The System consists of the Board of Governors in Washington and 12 regional reserve banks. In addition to its authority to conduct national monetary policy, the Federal Reserve has safety and soundness examination authority for a variety of lending institutions including bank holding companies; U.S. branches of foreign banks; and state-chartered banks that are members of the federal reserve system. Under the Gramm-Leach-Bliley Act (GLBA, P.L. 106-102), the Fed serves as the umbrella regulator for financial holding companies, which are defined as conglomerates that are permitted to engage in a broad array of financially related activities.

In addition to institution-level examinations of covered lenders, the Federal Reserve oversees systemic risk. This role has come about not entirely through deliberate policy choices, but partly by default, as a result of the Fed's position as lender of last resort and its consequent ability to inject capital or liquidity into troubled institutions. The Federal Reserve's standard response to a financial crisis has been to announce that it stood ready to provide liquidity to the system. This announcement worked well until 2007: a range of crises—the Penn Central bankruptcy, the stock market crash of 1987, the junk bond collapse, sovereign debt crises, the Asian crises of 1997- 1998, the dot.com crash, and the 9/11 attacks—were quickly brought under control without systemic consequences. In 2007, however, the Fed's liquidity provision failed to restore stability. As a result, the Fed's role as the primary systemic risk regulator will be closely scrutinized.

Office of Thrift Supervision

The Office of Thrift Supervision (OTS), created in 1989 during the savings and loan crisis (P.L. 101-73, 103 STAT. 183), is the successor institution to the Federal Savings and Loan Insurance Corporation (FSLIC), created in 1934 and administered by the old Federal Home Loan Bank Board. The OTS has the responsibility of monitoring the safety and soundness of federal savings associations and their holding companies. The OTS also supervises federally insured state savings associations. The OTS is part of the Treasury Department but is primarily funded by assessments on covered institutions. The primary business model of most thrifts is accepting deposits and offering home loans, but thrifts offer many other financial services.

There are three main advantages for firms to choose a federal thrift charter. First, a federal thrift charter shields the institution from some state regulations, because federal banking law can preempt state law.[12] Second, a federal thrift charter permits the institution to open branches nationwide under a single regulator, while state-chartered thrifts must comply with multiple state regulators. Third, a federal thrift charter and its holding company are regulated by the same regulator, but a federal bank charter may split regulation of the institution (OCC) from regulation of its holding company (FRB). Thus, a number of diversified financial institutions that are not primarily savings and loans have come under the supervision of OTS as "thrift holding companies," including Lehman Brothers, AIG, and Morgan Stanley.

OTS was created in response to the savings and loan crisis of the late 1980s. That crisis was characterized by an increase in the number of bad loans coincident with inflation, rising costs of deposits, and significantly declining collateral values, primarily in commercial real estate. The magnitude of the losses threatened to overwhelm the deposit insurance funds in the FSLIC. In 1989 Congress enacted the Financial Institutions Reform, Recovery, and Enforcement Act of 1989 (FIRREA, P.L. 101-73), which reorganized thrift regulation and created OTS. FIRREA also created the Resolution Trust Corporation (RTC), charged with sorting out which thrifts could be successfully reorganized or merged with others and which were beyond help. The RTC paid deposit insurance claims and liquidated the assets of failed thrifts.

National Credit Union Administration

The National Credit Union Administration (NCUA), originally part of the Farm Credit Administration, became an independent agency in 1970 (P.L. 91-206, 84 STAT. 49). The NCUA regulates all federal credit unions and those state credit unions that elect to be federally insured. It administers a Central Liquidity Facility, which is the credit union lender of last resort, and the National Credit Union Share Insurance Fund, which insures credit union deposits. Credit unions are member-owned financial cooperatives, and must be not-for-profit institutions. As such, they receive preferential tax treatment compared to mid-sized banks.

Non-Bank Financial Regulators

Securities and Exchange Commission

The Securities and Exchange Commission (SEC) was created as an independent agency in 1934 to enforce newly-written federal securities laws (P.L. 73-291, 48 Stat. 881). The SEC is not primarily concerned with ensuring the safety and soundness of the firms it regulates, but rather with maintaining fair and orderly markets and protecting investors from fraud. This distinction largely arises from the absence of government guarantees for securities investors comparable to deposit insurance. The SEC does not have the authority to limit risks taken by non-bank financial institutions, nor the ability to prop up a failing firm. Two types of firms come under the SEC's jurisdiction: (1) all corporations that sell securities to the public, and (2) securities broker/dealers and other securities markets intermediaries.

Firms that sell securities—stocks and bonds—to the public are required to register with the SEC. Registration entails the publication of detailed information about the firm, its management, the intended uses for the funds raised through the sale of securities, and the risks to investors. The initial registration disclosures must be kept current through the filing of periodic financial statements: annual and quarterly reports (as well as special reports when there is a material change in the firm's financial condition or prospects).

Beyond these disclosure requirements, and certain other rules that apply to corporate governance, the SEC does not have any direct regulatory control over publicly traded firms. Bank regulators are expected to identify unsafe and unsound banking practices in the institutions they supervise, and have power to intervene and prevent banks from taking excessive risks. The SEC has no comparable authority; the securities laws simply require that risks be disclosed to investors. Registration with the SEC, in other words, is in no sense a guarantee that a security is a good or safe investment.

To enable investors to make informed investment choices, the SEC has statutory authority over financial accounting standards. All publicly traded firms are required to use generally accepted accounting principles (GAAP), which are formulated by the Financial Accounting Standards Board (FASB), the American Institute of Certified Public Accountants (AICPA), and the SEC itself.

Besides publicly traded corporations, a number of securities market participants are also required to register with the SEC (or with one of the industry self-regulatory organizations that the SEC oversees). These include stock exchanges, securities brokerages (and numerous classes of their personnel), mutual funds, auditors, investment advisers, and others. To maintain their registered status, all these entities must comply with rules meant to protect public investors, prevent fraud, and promote fair and orderly markets. The area of SEC supervision most analogous to banking regulation is broker/dealer regulation. Several provisions of law and regulation protect brokerage customers from losses arising from brokerage firm failure. The Securities Investor Protection Corporation (SIPC), created by Congress in 1970, operates an insurance scheme funded by assessments on broker/dealers (and with a backup line of credit with the U.S. Treasury). SIPC guarantees customer accounts up to $500,000 for losses arising from brokerage failure or fraud (but not market losses). Unlike the FDIC, however, SIPC does not examine broker/dealers and has no regulatory powers.

Since 1975, the SEC has enforced a net capital rule applicable to all registered broker/dealers. The rule requires broker/dealers to maintain an excess of capital above mere solvency, to ensure that a failing firm stops trading while it still has assets to meet customer claims. Net capital levels are calculated in a manner similar to the risk-based capital requirements under the Basel Accords, but the SEC has its own set of risk weightings, which it calls haircuts. The riskier the asset, the greater the haircut.

While the net capital rule appears to be very close in its effects to the banking agencies' risk- based capital requirements, there are significant differences. The SEC has no authority to intervene in a broker/dealer's business if it takes excessive risks that might cause net capital to drop below the required level. Rather, the net capital rule is often described as a liquidation rule—not meant to prevent failures but to minimize the impact on customers. Moreover, the SEC has no authority comparable to the banking regulators' prompt corrective action powers: it cannot preemptively seize a troubled broker/dealer or compel it to merge with a sound firm.

The differences between bank and securities regulation with respect to safety and soundness came into sharp focus with the collapse of Bear Stearns, one of the five largest investment banks, in March 2008.[13] The SEC monitored Bear Stearns' financial condition until shortly before the collapse (which was precipitated by the refusal of other market participants to extend short-term credit), and believed that the firm had sufficient levels of capital and liquidity. When bankruptcy suddenly loomed, it was the Federal Reserve that stepped in to broker the sale of Bear Stearns to JP Morgan Chase by agreeing to purchase $30 billion of "toxic" Bear Stearns assets.

The Bear Stearns situation highlighted several apparent anomalies in the U.S. regulatory structure. The SEC lacked safety and soundness powers over the institutions it supervised, while the Fed was forced to commit funds to an investment bank over which it had no regulatory jurisdiction. The anomaly became even more pronounced when the Fed subsequently established a lending facility to provide short-term credit to other investment banks.[14]

The Bear Stearns collapse showed the inability of the SEC to respond to a brokerage failure with systemic risk implications. There is more to the story, however, than the differences between bank regulation and the SEC's net capital rule. In 2004, the SEC devised a voluntary supervisory scheme for the largest investment banks, called the Consolidated Supervised Entities (CSE) program.[15] The CSE firms were all registered broker/dealers, but were also large holding companies with extensive operations carried on outside the broker/dealer unit. Thus, the SEC had no capital requirement that applied to the entire investment bank. Under CSE, this was to change: as a substitute for the net capital rule, the firms agreed to abide by the Basel risk-based standard, and maintain that level of capital *at the holding company level*. On a voluntary basis, the firms agreed to grant the SEC the authority to examine and monitor their compliance, above and beyond the SEC's explicit statutory authority.[16]

Whatever the intent of the CSE program, it did not succeed in preventing excessive risk-taking by the participants.[17] By the end of September 2008, all five CSE investment banks had either failed (Lehman Brothers), merged to prevent failure (Merrill Lynch and Bear Stearns), or applied for bank holding company status (Morgan Stanley and Goldman Sachs).[18] On September 26, 2008, SEC Chairman Cox announced the end of the CSE program, declaring that "[t]he last six months have made it abundantly clear that voluntary regulation does not work. When Congress passed the Gramm-Leach-Bliley Act, it created a significant regulatory gap by failing to give to the SEC or any agency the authority to regulate large investment bank holding companies."[19]

Commodity Futures Trading Commission

The Commodity Futures Trading Commission (CFTC) was created in 1974 to regulate commodities futures and options markets, which at the time were poised to expand beyond their traditional base in agricultural commodities to encompass contracts based on financial variables such as interest rates and stock indexes. The CFTC's mission is to prevent excessive speculation, manipulation of commodity prices, and fraud. Like the SEC, the CFTC oversees industry self- regulatory organizations (SROs)—the futures exchanges and the National Futures Association— and requires the registration of a range of industry firms and personnel, including futures commission merchants (brokers), floor traders, commodity pool operators, and commodity trading advisers.

Like the SEC, the CFTC does not directly regulate the safety and soundness of individual firms. Nevertheless, its oversight can have important consequences for the ability of market participants to manage financial risk. Futures, options, and derivatives can have a systemic impact.

Some argue that the CFTC's ability to respond to systemic crises is limited because a large part of the derivatives market is exempt from its jurisdiction. Derivatives contracts may be traded in an unregulated over-the-counter (OTC) market, so long as no small investors are allowed to trade. OTC derivatives are some of the largest financial markets in the world, and many OTC market participants also trade on the CFTC-regulated futures exchanges, but the CFTC does not receive regular reports about price, volume, and size of positions in the OTC markets.

Federal Housing Finance Agency

The Federal Housing Finance Agency (FHFA) was created in 2008 by the Housing and Economic Recovery Act of 2008 (P.L. 110-289) to consolidate and strengthen regulation of a group of housing finance-related government-sponsored enterprises (GSEs): Fannie Mae, Freddie Mac, and the Federal Home Loan Banks.[20] The FHFA succeeded the Office of Federal Housing Enterprise Oversight (OFHEO) and the Federal Housing Finance Board (FHFB).

The impetus to create the FHFA came from concerns about risk—including systemic risk— arising from the rapid growth of the GSEs, particularly Fannie and Freddie. These two GSEs were profit-seeking, shareholder-owned corporations that took advantage of their government- sponsored status to accumulate undiversified investment portfolios of over $1.5 trillion, consisting almost exclusively of home mortgages (and securities and derivatives based on those mortgages).

The FHFA was given enhanced safety and soundness powers resembling those of the federal bank regulators. These powers included the ability to set capital standards, to order the enterprises to cease any activity or divest any asset that posed a threat to financial soundness, and to replace management and assume control of the firms if they became seriously undercapitalized.

The FHFA's first action was to place both Fannie and Freddie in conservatorship.[21] Fannie and Freddie continue to operate, under an agreement with the U.S. Treasury. The Treasury will provide capital to the two firms, by means of preferred stock purchases, to ensure that each remains solvent. In return, the government assumed a 79.9% equity ownership position in the firms.

Regulatory Umbrella Groups

The need for coordination and data sharing among regulators has led to the formation of innumerable interagency task forces to study particular market episodes and make recommendations to Congress. Two interagency organizations have attained permanent status.

Federal Financial Institution Examinations Council

The Federal Financial Institutions Examination Council (FFIEC) was created by legislation[22] in 1979 as a formal interagency body to coordinate federal regulation of lending institutions. Through the FFIEC, the federal banking regulators issue a single set of reporting forms for covered institutions. The FFIEC also attempts to harmonize auditing principles and supervisory decisions. The FFIEC is made up of the Federal Reserve, OCC, FDIC, OTS, and NCUA, each of which employs examiners to enforce safety and soundness regulations for lending institutions.

- Federal financial institution examiners evaluate the risks of covered institutions. The specific safety and soundness concerns common to the FFIEC agencies can be found in the handbooks employed by examiners to monitor lenders. Each subject area of the handbook can be updated separately. Examples of safety and soundness subject areas include important indicators of risk, such as capital adequacy, asset quality, liquidity, and sensitivity to market risk.

President's Working Group on Financial Markets

The President's Working Group on Financial Markets (PWG) was created by President Reagan through executive order in 1988.[23] The PWG includes the Secretary of the Treasury and the Chairmen of the Federal Reserve, the SEC, and the CFTC. It is not a formal agency subject to congressional oversight, although each member is subject to Senate confirmation at the time of appointment.

The impetus for the creation of the PWG was the stock market crash of October 1987, and specifically the role that the stock index futures markets (under CFTC jurisdiction) had played in creating panic in the stock market (regulated by SEC). Studies conducted by the SEC, the CFTC, a blue-ribbon panel appointed by the President (the Presidential Task Force on Market Mechanisms, or Brady Commission), and the stock and futures exchanges reached strikingly different conclusions; the task of the PWG was to study the studies and issue a further report.

The PWG was not dissolved, but continued to provide interagency coordination and information sharing, and to study entities and products that raised intermarket regulatory issues, such as hedge funds and OTC derivatives. In March 2008, at the direction of President Bush, the PWG issued a policy statement on the ongoing financial crisis.[24]

UNREGULATED MARKETS AND INSTITUTIONS

Although federal financial statutes and regulations fill many volumes, not all participants in the financial system are regulated. In some cases, unregulated (or self-regulated) markets appear to work very well, but disruptions or major frauds in these markets are likely to bring calls for increased government supervision. The dynamic nature of financial markets is a perennial challenge to regulatory structure design, because a market that appears insignificant at the time a law is written may grow into a potential threat to systemic stability in a few years. The following are some of the major unregulated markets and institutions.

Foreign Exchange Markets

Buying and selling currencies is essential to foreign trade, and the exchange rate determined by traders has major implications for a country's macroeconomic policy. The market is one of the largest in the world, with daily turnover in excess of $3 trillion.[25] Nevertheless, no U.S. agency has regulatory authority over the foreign exchange market.

Trading in currencies takes place between large global banks, central banks, hedge funds and other currency speculators, commercial firms involved in imports and exports, fund managers, and retail brokers. There is no centralized marketplace, but rather a number of proprietary electronic platforms that have largely supplanted the traditional telephone broker market.

Despite the fact that extreme volatility in exchange rates for a number of European and Asian currencies in the 1990s was often blamed on currency speculators, neither U.S. nor foreign regulators have moved towards regulating the market.

U.S. Treasury Securities

The secondary, or resale, market for Treasury securities is largely unregulated. Like the foreign exchange market, there is no central exchange, but there are a number of proprietary, computer-based transaction systems. Treasury securities were exempted from SEC regulation by the original securities laws of the 1930s. In 1993, following a successful corner of a Treasury bond auction by Salomon Brothers, Congress passed the Government Securities Act Amendments (P.L. 103-202), which required brokers and dealers that were not already registered with the SEC to register as government securities dealers. (Existing broker/dealer registrants were simply required to notify the SEC that they were in the government securities business.) Nevertheless, the government securities market remains much more lightly regulated than the corporate securities markets.

The primary market in Treasury securities, where new debt instruments are sold to fund government operations, is also relatively unregulated. A principal channel for the distribution of new Treasuries is a group of firms called primary dealers, who purchase securities at auction for their own accounts and for their customers. The primary dealers are 19 commercial and investment banks, both foreign and domestic. The primary dealer list is maintained by the Federal Reserve Bank of New York, which conducts auctions for the Treasury, but its relationship to the dealers is commercial, rather than regulatory.[26] The New York Fed does, however, collect certain data about primary dealers' transactions in government securities.

In March 2008, as part of its multifaceted attempt to supply liquidity to the financial system, the Federal Reserve established a Primary Dealer Credit Facility, to make short-term loans against a variety of collateral (including asset-backed and mortgage-backed securities) to the primary dealers.[27] This step attracted attention because the primary dealer group included investment banking firms over which the Fed had no regulatory authority.

OTC Derivatives

As noted above, the Commodity Exchange Act contains exemptions from CFTC regulation for derivative contracts and markets where all traders are "eligible contract participants," that is, not small businesses or retail investors. About two-thirds of OTC derivatives are contracts linked to interest rates; foreign exchange and credit derivatives each account for about 9%; and contracts linked to physical commodity and stock prices account for about 2% each.[28]

Whether the unregulated status of OTC derivatives constitutes a troublesome regulatory gap has been debated in Congress and among the regulators. One view has been that there is no government interest in regulating these markets, since all participants are sophisticated and able to manage the risks. Another is that derivatives contracts make up an invisible web of financial obligations and exposures, and that the failure of a large derivatives dealer could trigger cascading losses throughout the global system.

A case that is likely to shape debate is that of AIG, whose insurance operations are regulated by New York state, but whose large derivatives trading business—the firm was a leader in the credit default swap market[29]—was not regulated (although, technically, the firm was a thrift holding company under OTS supervision). Massive losses in credit default swaps forced the Fed and Treasury to craft an ad hoc rescue of AIG, which involves over $150 billion in loans and guarantees.[30]

Legislation in the 111th Congress (H.R. 977) would require reporting of OTC derivatives trades to the CFTC, require centralized clearing of OTC contracts, restrict participation in the credit default swap market, and direct the CFTC to consider limits on the size of speculative positions.

Private Securities Markets

The securities laws mandate registration of and extensive disclosures by public securities issuers, but also provide for private sales of securities, which are not subject to disclosure requirements.

Private placements of securities may only be offered to limited numbers of "accredited investors" who meet certain asset tests. (Most purchasers are life insurers and other institutional investors.) There are also restrictions on the resale of private securities.

The size of the private placement market is subject to considerable variation from year to year, but at times the value of securities sold privately exceeds what is sold into the public market. In recent decades, venture capitalists and private equity firms have come to play important roles in corporate finance. The former typically purchase interests in private firms, which may be sold later to the public, while the latter often purchase all the stock of publicly traded companies and take them private.

Nonbank Lenders

During the housing boom of the early 2000s, substantial volumes of mortgages were written not by chartered depository institutions, but by nonbank lenders with access to credit from Wall Street firms involved in the securitization of mortgages. These lenders were not subject to safety and soundness regulation, although they were required to comply with the Federal Reserve's Truth in Lending Act consumer protection regulations. Many view these lenders as having been instrumental in the relaxation of credit standards, leading to what many now regard as the unsustainable housing price bubble that triggered the current crisis.[31]

Hundreds of these nonbank mortgage lenders failed in 2007 and 2008, as delinquency rates on their subprime and other non-traditional mortgages soared. Potential reforms of securitization and the non-bank lending channel are now under consideration.[32]

Hedge Funds

Hedge funds are pools of managed money that structure themselves to fit into exemptions in the federal securities laws—in effect, they are unregulated mutual funds. By limiting the number of investors, and restricting access to wealthy investors who meet specified asset tests, hedge funds avoid regulation by the SEC.[33] Since there are no reporting requirements, the size of the hedge fund universe can only be estimated, but before losses in 2008, it was commonly stated that hedge funds had about $2 trillion of investor funds under management.

Hedge funds have shown their potential for causing systemic disturbances. The case of Long Term Capital Management (LTCM) is one example of the Federal Reserve arranging for reorganization of an institution believed to pose systemic risk if it failed. Another hedge fund debacle—the failure of the Amaranth fund—is said to have caused significant fluctuations in the price of natural gas.[34] It is noteworthy, however, that hedge fund failures do not appear to have played a major role in the development of the current financial crisis. Some have argued that they may actually have played a stabilizing role, by absorbing losses that would otherwise have accrued to regulated financial institutions. But this judgment is regarded by others as premature; the crisis continues to unfold.

APPENDIX A. FORMS OF BANKING ORGANIZATIONS

The structure of banks can be complex. Currently, the regulator of a particular activity of a bank or its subsidiary in part depends on the activity of the subsidiary or its charter, as described above. The following flow charts provide simplified representations of various bank structures. In some cases, the umbrella bank and its subsidiaries may have different regulators.

Figure A-1. National Bank

Figure A-2. National Bank and Subsidiaries

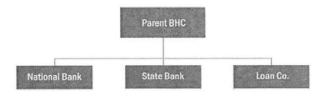

Figure A-3. Bank Holding Company

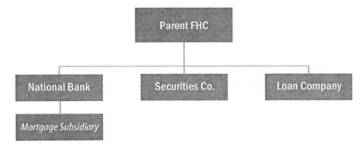

Figure A-4. Financial Holding Company

APPENDIX B. BANK RATINGS: UFIRS AND CAMELS

Federal bank regulators conduct confidential assessments of covered banks. The Federal Financial Institutions Examination Council (FFIEC) helps coordinate the ratings system used by bank examiners so that there is some consistency to the examinations, although the ratings do take into account differences in bank size, sophistication, complexity of activities, and risk profile. The FFIEC adopted the Uniform Financial Institutions Rating System (UFIRS) in 1979. The system was revised in 1996 and is often referred to as the CAMELS rating system. CAMELS stands for **C**apital adequacy, **A**sset quality, **M**anagement, **E**arnings, **L**iquidity, and **S**ensitivity to market risk. A description of the CAMELS system is found in the Comptrollers Handbook: Bank Supervision Process, provided by the OCC.[35] Market factors can affect more than one category in the CAMELS ratings.

Capital Adequacy

This component assesses the level of capital held by the institution in relation to the risks that it takes. Capital adequacy can be affected by a number of factors, including changes in credit risk, market risk, and the institution's financial condition. Increases in problem assets would require increased capital. Capital adequacy is also supposed to reflect risks even if they are technically off of the bank's balance sheet.

Asset Quality

Asset quality refers to existing and potential credit risk associated with a the bank's portfolio. Like capital adequacy, this component is supposed to reflect risk even if it is not technically on the bank's balance sheet. Asset quality can include changes in loan default rates, investment performance, exposure to counterparty risk, and all other risks that may affect the value or marketability of an institution's assets.

Management Capability

The governance of the bank, including management and board of directors, is assessed in relation to the nature and scope of the bank's activities. This rating is affected by the level and quality of management oversight. It also includes legal compliance, responsiveness to auditor recommendations, and similar issues.

Earnings Quantity and Quality

The rating of a bank's earnings takes into account current earnings and the sustainability of future earnings. Earnings that rely on favorable tax effects and nonrecurring events receive lower ratings. Similarly, inadequate controls for expenses can reduce the rating for earnings. Difficulties in forecasting and managing risks can also reduce the earnings rating.

Liquidity

Liquidity includes the ability of a bank to meet its expected funding needs. For a given institution size and complexity, this factor assesses the ability of the firm to fulfill its financial obligations in a timely manner. Liquidity refers to the ability to meet short-term funding needs without incurring excessive losses, which might occur if assets had to be sold at a steep discount in a time-pressure situation (or "fire sale"). Liquidity also includes assessments of specific financial categories, such as the trend and stability of deposits, and the expected ability to securitize and sell pools of assets.

Sensitivity to Market Risk

Market risk includes potential changes in the prices of financial assets, such as movements in interest rates, foreign exchange rates, commodity prices, and stock prices. The nature and scope of a bank's activities can affect the markets that it is exposed to; therefore, market risk is closely related to the other CAMELS factors. This rating takes into account management's ability to identify and manage the risks that can arise from the bank's trading activities in financial markets. It also takes into account interest rate risk from nontrading positions, such as any duration mismatch in loans held to maturity.

APPENDIX C. ACRONYMS

AICPA	American Institute of Certified Public Accountants
CAMELS	Capital Adequacy, Asset Quality, Management, Liquidity, Sensitivity to Market Risk
CFTC	Commodity Futures Trading Commission
CSE	Consolidated Supervised Entities
EESA	Emergency Economic Stabilization Act
FASB	Financial Accounting Standards Board
FDIC	Federal Deposit Insurance Corporation
FFIEC	Federal Financial Institution Examination Council
FHFA	Federal Housing Finance Agency
FHFB	Federal Housing Finance Board
FRB	Federal Reserve Board
FSLIC	Federal Savings and Loan Insurance Corporation
GAAP	Generally Accepted Accounting Principles
GSE	Government-Sponsored Enterprise
NCUA	National Credit Union Administration
OCC	Office of the Comptroller of the Currency

OFHEO	Office of Federal Housing Enterprise Oversight
OTS	Office of Thrift Supervision
PWG	President's Working Group on Capital Markets
SEC	Securities and Exchange Commission
SIPC	Securities Investor Protection Corporation
SRO	Self Regulatory Organization
UFIRS	Uniform Financial Institutions Rating System

Appendix D. Glossary of Terms

This glossary has been compiled from several earlier CRS reports, from the CFTC and SIFMA websites, and from other sources.

Affiliate—A corporate relationship of control. Two companies are affiliated when one owns all or a large part of another, or when both are controlled by a third (holding) company (see subsidiary). All subsidiaries are affiliates, but affiliates that are less than 50% controlled are usually not treated as subsidiaries.

Agency relationship—A business relationship of two parties in which one represents the other in transactions with third parties. The agent negotiates on behalf of the party actually at risk, who is known as the "principal." A commission goes to the agent who does not take on the risk of the transaction; the profit or loss goes to the principal.

Asset-backed security—A bond that represents a share in a pool of debt obligations or other assets. The holder is entitled to some part of the repayment flows from the underlying debt. (See "securitization.")

Bank holding company—A business incorporated under state law, which controls through equity ownership ("holds") one or more banks and, often, other affiliates in financial services as allowed by its regulator, the Federal Reserve. On the federal level, these businesses are regulated through the Bank Holding Company Act.

Bank Holding Company Act—The federal statute under which the Federal Reserve regulates bank holding companies and financial holding companies (FHC). Besides the permissible financial activities enumerated in the Gramm-Leach-Bliley Act (P.L. 106-102), the law provides a mechanism between the Federal Reserve and the Department of the Treasury to decide what is an appropriate new financial activity for FHCs.

Blue sky laws—State statutes that govern the offering and selling of securities.

Broker/dealer—An individual or firm that buys and sells securities for itself as well as for customers. Broker/dealers are registered with the Securities and Exchange Commission.

Bubble—Self-reinforcing process in which the price of an asset exceeds its fundamental value for a sustained period, often followed by a rapid price decline. Speculative bubbles are usually associated with a "bandwagon" effect in which speculators rush to buy the commodity (in the case of futures, "to take positions") before the price trend ends, and an even greater rush to sell the commodity (unwind positions) when prices reverse.

Capital requirements—Capital is the owners' stake in an enterprise. It is a critical line of defense when losses occur, both in banking and nonbanking enterprises. Capital requirements help assure that losses that might occur will accrue to the institution incurring them. In the case of banking institutions experiencing problems, capital also serves as a buffer against losses to the federal deposit insurance funds.

Charter conversion—Banking institutions may, with the approval of their regulators, switch their corporate form between: commercial bank or savings institution, National or State charter, and to stockholder ownership from depositor ownership. Various regulatory conditions may encourage switching.

Clearing Organization—An entity through which futures and other derivative transactions are cleared and settled. A clearing organization may be a division or affiliate of a particular exchange, or a freestanding entity. Also called a clearing house, multilateral clearing organization, or clearing association.

Collateralized debt obligation (CDO)—A bond created by the securitization of a pool of asset- backed securities.

Collateralized mortgage obligation (CMO)—A multiclass bond backed by a pool of mortgage pass-through securities or mortgage loans.

Commercial bank—A deposit-taking institution that can make commercial loans, accept checking accounts, and whose deposits are insured by the Federal Deposit Insurance Corporation. National banks are chartered by the Office of the Comptroller of the Currency; state banks, by the individual states.

Commodity Futures Modernization Act of 2000 (CFMA, P.L. 106-554, 114 Stat. 2763)— overhauled the Commodity Exchange Act to create a flexible structure for the regulation of futures and options trading, and established a broad statutory exemption from regulation for OTC derivatives.

Community financial institution—As provided for in the Gramm-Leach-Bliley Act, a member of the Federal Home Loan Bank System whose deposits are insured under the Federal Deposit Insurance Act and which has assets of less than $500 million (calculated according to provisions in the law, and in succeeding years to be adjusted for inflation). Such institutions may become members without meeting requirements with regard to the percentage of total assets that must be in residential mortgage loans and may borrow from the Federal Home Loan Banks for small business and agriculture.

Conservatorship—When an insolvent financial institution is reorganized by a regulator with the intent to restoring it to an ongoing business.

Counterparty—The opposite party in a bilateral agreement, contract, or transaction, such as a swap.

Credit Default Swap (CDS)—A tradeable contract in which one party agrees to pay another if a third party experiences a credit event, such as default on a debt obligation, bankruptcy, or credit rating downgrade.

Credit Risk—The risk that a borrower will fail to repay a loan in full, or that a derivatives counterparty will default.

Credit union—A nonprofit financial cooperative of individuals with one or more common bonds (such as employment, labor union membership, or residence in the same neighborhood). May be state or nationally chartered. Credit unions accept deposits of members' savings and transaction balances in the form of share accounts, pay dividends (interest) on them out of earnings, and primarily provide consumer credit to members. The federal regulator for credit unions is the National Credit Union Administration.

Dealer—An individual or financial firm engaged in the purchase and sale of securities and commodities such as metals, foreign exchange, etc., for its own account and at its own risk as principal (see broker). Commercial banks are typically limited to acting as dealers in specified high-quality debt obligations, such as those of the federal government.

Depository institution—Customarily refers to commercial banks, savings institutions, and credit unions, since traditionally the greater part of their funding has been in the form of deposits. Deposits are a customer's funds placed with an institution according to agreed on terms and conditions and represent a credit to the depositor.

Derivatives—Financial contracts whose value is linked to the price of an underlying commodity or financial variable (such as an interest rate, currency price, or stock index). Ownership of a derivative does not require the holder to actually buy or sell the underlying interest. Derivatives are used by hedgers, who seek to shift risk to others, and speculators, who can profit if they can successfully forecast price trends. Examples include futures contracts, options, and swaps.

Discount window—Figurative term for the Federal Reserve facility for extending credit directly to eligible depository institutions. It may be used to relieve temporary cash shortages at banks and other depository institutions. Borrowers are expected to have tried to borrow elsewhere first and must provide collateral as security for loans. The term derives from the practice whereby bankers would come to a Reserve Bank teller window to obtain credit in the early days of the Federal Reserve System.

Dual banking system—The phrase refers to the fact that banks may be either federally or state- chartered. In the case of state-chartered banks, the state is the primary regulator; for national banks, the Office of the Comptroller of the Currency is the primary regulator.

Electronic fund transfer (EFT) systems—A variety of systems and technologies for transferring funds electronically rather than by paper check.

Exchange—A central marketplace with established rules and regulations where buyers and sellers meet to trade futures and options contracts or securities.

Federal Home Loan Banks—Twelve regional member-owned federally sponsored organizations that extend credit to their member banking institutions, largely to finance mortgages made to homeowners. The 12 FHLBs make up a single government-sponsored enterprise.

Federal safety net—A broad term referring to protection of banking institutions through deposit insurance, discount window credit, other lender of last resort support, and certain forms of regulations to reduce risk. Commercial and industrial companies generally lack any of these cushions against loss.

Financial businesses—In discussions about financial services modernization, usually refers to commercial banks and savings institutions, securities firms, and insurance companies and agents, as contrasted with commercial and industrial firms.

Financial holding company—A holding company form authorized by the Gramm-Leach-Bliley Act that goes beyond the limits a of bank holding company. It can control one or more banks, securities firms, and insurance companies as permitted by law and/or regulation.

Financial institution—An enterprise that uses its funds chiefly to purchase financial assets such as loans and debt securities, as opposed to tangible property. Financial institutions are differentiated by the manner in which they invest their funds: in loans, bonds, stocks, or some combination; as well as by their sources of funds. Depository financial institutions are differentiated in that they may accept deposits which are federally insured against loss to the depositor. Nondepository financial institutions such as life and property/casualty insurance companies, pension funds, and mutual funds obtain funds through other types of receipts, whose values may fluctuate with market conditions.

Financial subsidiary—Under the Gramm-Leach-Bliley Act, both national and state-chartered banks are authorized to form financial subsidiaries to engage in activities that would not otherwise be permitted within the bank itself, subject to certain limits. Besides the permissible financial activities enumerated in P.L. 106-102, the law provides a mechanism between the U.S. Department of the Treasury and the Federal Reserve to decide what is an appropriate new financial activity for a financial subsidiary.

Firewalls—Barriers to the flow of capital, information, management, and other resources among business units owned by a common entity. In case of financial distress of one operation ("fire"), the "walls" are intended to prevent the spread of loss to the other units—especially to banking units. Example: losses in a securities subsidiary of a holding company could not be covered by any of the holding company's bank subsidiaries.

Foreign bank—Banks and their holding companies headquartered in other countries may have a variety of financial operations in the United States: U.S.-chartered subsidiary banks, agencies, branches, and representative offices. Their primary federal regulator is the Federal Reserve, under the International Banking Act of 1978 as amended. States and the Office of the Comptroller of the Currency may also regulate them.

Functional regulation—Regulatory arrangements based on activity ("function") rather than organizational structure. The Gramm-Leach-Bliley Act called for more functional regulation than in the past.

Glass-Steagall Act—Part of the Banking Act of 1933; divided the commercial and investment banking industries. The Gramm-Leach-Bliley Act repealed two sections of the act dealing with the relationship between banks and securities firms.

Government-sponsored enterprise (GSE)—GSEs are private companies with government charters. Government sponsorship typically gives them a funding advantage over purely private competitors, while their charters restrict the kinds of businesses they may conduct.

Gramm-Leach-Bliley Act of 1999—P.L. 106-102, also known as the Financial Services Modernization Act, authorized increased affiliations between banks, securities firms, and insurers. Permitted the establishment of financial holding companies, under the regulation of the Federal Reserve. Also addressed privacy protection for consumers' financial data.

Haircut—In computing the value of assets for purposes of capital, segregation, or margin requirements, a percentage reduction from the stated value (e.g., book value or market value) to account for possible declines in value that may occur before assets can be liquidated.

Hedge funds—Hedge funds are essentially unregulated mutual funds. They are pools of invested money that buy and sell stocks and bonds and many other assets, including precious metals, commodities, foreign currencies, and derivatives (contracts whose prices are derived from those of other financial instruments). Hedge funds are limited to qualified investors with high net worth.

Hedging—Investing with the intention of reducing the impact of adverse movements in interest rates, commodities, or securities prices. Typically, the hedging instrument gains value as the hedged item loses value, and vice versa.

Insolvent—A firm whose liabilities exceed its assets.

Institutional regulation—Regulation that is institution-specific as contrasted with activity- specific (see functional regulation).

Investment bank—A financial intermediary, active in the securities business. Investment banking functions include underwriting (marketing newly registered securities to individual or institutional investors), counseling regarding merger and acquisition proposals, brokerage services, advice on corporate financing, and proprietary trading.

Investment bank holding company—A holding company for securities firms authorized under the Gramm-Leach-Bliley Act. Such holding companies are subject to regulation by the Securities and Exchange Commission.

Issuer—A person or entity (including a company or bank) that offers securities for sale. The issuing of securities, where the proceeds accrue to the issuer, is distinct from the secondary, or resale, market, where securities are traded among investors.

Lender of last resort—Governmental lender that acts as the ultimate source of credit in the financial system. In the United States, the Federal Reserve has this role.

Leverage—The ability to control large dollar amounts of a commodity or security with a comparatively small amount of capital. Leverage can be obtained through borrowing or the use of derivatives.

Limited-purpose bank—Although generally commercial firms may not conduct a banking business, some exceptions exist. Examples: Nonbank banks are banks that either accept deposits or make commercial loans but cannot do both. Such banks grew up through a loophole in law which was closed by the Competitive Equality Banking Act of 1987 (CEBA). Credit card banks conduct credit card operations. Industrial loan companies in a few states may offer restricted banking services.

Liquidity—The ability to trade an asset quickly without significantly affecting its price, or the condition of a market with many buyers and sellers present. Also, the ability of a person or firm to access credit markets.

Liquidity risk—The possibility that the market for normally-liquid assets will suddenly dry up, leaving firms unable to convert assets into cash. Also, the risk that other firms will refuse to extend credit on any terms to a firm that is perceived as distressed.

Market risk—The risk that the price of a tradeable security or asset will decline, resulting in a loss to the holder.

Merchant banker—A European style investment banker concentrating on corporate deals, in which it may invest its own funds.

Money market mutual fund (MMF)—A form of mutual fund that pools funds of individuals and other investors for investment in high-grade, short-term debt and bank deposits paying market rates of return. Examples of these money market instruments include U.S. Treasury bills, certificates of deposit, and commercial paper. In addition to the investment features, most MMFs offer check-writing redemption features.

Moral hazard—The tendency of people to take more risks once another party has agreed to provide protection. Regulatory interventions to bail out failing firms are often said to create moral hazard, on the assumption that others will expect to be saved from their mistakes, too.

Mortgage-backed security (MBS)—A bond backed by a pool of mortgage loans. The bondholders receive a share of the interest and principal payments on the underlying mortgages. The cash flows may be divided among different classes of bonds, called tranches.

Mutual fund—An investing company that pools the funds of individuals and other investors, and uses them to purchase large amounts of debt or equity obligations of businesses and sometimes debt obligations of governments. The owners of the mutual fund hold proportional shares in the entire pool of securities in which a fund invests. Owners pay taxes on their distributions from a fund; the mutual fund itself is not normally subject to federal or state income taxation.

Naked option—The sale of a call or put option without holding an equal and opposite position in the underlying instrument.

Operational risk—The possibility that a financial institution will suffer losses from a failure to process transactions properly, from accounting mistakes, from rogue traders or other forms of insider fraud, or from other causes arising inside the institution.

Over-the-counter (OTC)—Trading that does not occur on a centralized exchange or trading facility. OTC transactions can occur electronically or over the telephone.

Ponzi Scheme—Named after Charles Ponzi, a man with a remarkable criminal career in the early 20th century, the term has been used to describe pyramid arrangements whereby an enterprise makes payments to investors from the proceeds of a later investment rather than from profits of the underlying business venture, as the investors expected, and gives investors the impression that a legitimate profit-making business or investment opportunity exists, where in fact it is a mere fiction.

Receivership—When an insolvent financial institution is taken over with the intent to liquidate its assets.

Resolution Trust Corporation (RTC) - The agency set up to resolve savings and loans declared failed beginning in 1989. Between 1989 and mid-1995, the Resolution Trust Corporation closed or otherwise resolved 747 thrifts with total assets of $394 billion.

Savings association—A savings and loan association, mutual savings bank, or federal savings bank, whose primary function has traditionally been to encourage personal saving (thrift) and home buying through mortgage lending. In recent years, such institutions' charters have been expanded to allow them to provide commercial loans and a broader range of consumer financial services. The federal regulator for most savings associations is the Office of Thrift Supervision. Also known as savings and loans, thrifts, and mutual savings banks.

Securities Investor Protection Corporation (SIPC)—A private nonprofit membership corporation set up under federal law to provide financial protection for the customers of failed brokers and/or dealers. SIPC is a liquidator; it has no supervisory or regulatory responsibilities for its members, nor is it authorized to bail out or in other ways assist a failing firm.

Securitization—The process of transforming a cash flow, typically from debt repayments, into a new marketable security. Holders of the securitized instrument receive interest and principal payments as the underlying loans are repaid. Types of loans that are frequently securitized are home mortgages, credit card receivables, student loans, small business loans, and car loans.

Self-regulatory organizations (SROs)—National securities or futures exchanges, national securities or futures associations, clearing agencies and the Municipal Securities Rulemaking Board are all authorized to make and enforce rules governing market participants. The respective federal regulatory agency has authority in connection with SROs and may require them to adopt or modify their rules. Examples of SROs in the securities industry include the Financial Industry Regulatory Authority (FINRA), and the New York Stock Exchange.

Special-purpose entities (SPEs)—Also referred to as off–balance-sheet arrangements, SPEs are legal entities created to perform a specific financial function or transaction. They isolate financial risk from the sponsoring institution and provide less-expensive financing. The assets, liabilities, and cash flows of an SPE do not appear on the sponsoring institution's books.

Speculation—a venture or undertaking of an enterprising nature, especially one involving considerable financial risk on the chance of unusual profit.

State regulation—Under the dual system of bank regulation, states as well as the federal government may charter, regulate, and supervise depository institutions. States are the primary regulators in the insurance field. States also have authority over securities companies, mortgage lending companies, personal finance companies, and other types of companies offering financial services.

Structured debt—Debt that has been customized for the buyer, often by incorporating complex derivatives.

Subordinated debt—Debt over which senior debt takes priority. In the event of bankruptcy, subordinated debtholders receive payment only after senior debt claims are paid in full.

Subsidiary—A company whose controlling shares are owned 50% or more by another ("parent") corporation. Like companies with less than 50% ownership, it is an affiliate of the controlling company. A subsidiary is usually consolidated for regulatory and reporting purposes with its parent.

Systemic Risk—The term "systemic risk" does not have a single, agreed-upon definition. Some define systemic risk as the risk an institution faces that it cannot diversify against. In other circumstances, systemic risk is defined as the risk that the linkages between institutions may affect the financial system as a whole, through a dynamic sometimes referred to as contagion.

Thrift holding company—Also known as a savings and loan holding company, a business that controls one or more savings associations. These holding companies are regulated under the Home Owners' Loan Act by the Office of Thrift Supervision.

Too-big-to-fail doctrine—an implicit regulatory policy holding that very large financial institutions must be rescued by the government, because their failure would destabilize the entire financial system. (See "moral hazard.")

Umbrella supervision—The term applied to comprehensive regulation of a holding company and its parts by one or more holding company regulator(s).

Underwriter—For securities markets, see investment bankers. For insurance, underwriters are the life, health and property-casualty companies that receive premiums and pay off losses and other risks as they occur. The underwriters bear the risks of losses and expenses exceeding receipts.

Unitary thrift holding company (UTHC)—A holding company that owns a single thrift institution. A distinction between UTHCs and other thrift holding companies has been that a UTHC could be involved in any lines of business, whereas the others have been restricted to certain activities primarily financial in nature. The Gramm-Leach-Bliley Act limits the commercial activities and affiliations of new UTHCs.

Universal bank—An organizational model typical of some foreign countries whereby a bank can exist as an operating enterprise and own directly a variety of other businesses (See Subsidiary). It contrasts with the banking model typical in the United States where the parent holding company owns several different businesses, all structurally separate (See "affiliate."). In practice, the two approaches are not exclusive.

ACKNOWLEDGMENTS

The authors gratefully acknowledge helpful comments from our colleagues Walter Eubanks, Marc Labonte, and Maureen Murphy.

End Notes

[1] See, e.g., U.S. Treasury, *Blueprint for a Modernized Financial Regulatory Structure*, March 2008. http://www.treas.gov/press/releases/reports/Blueprint.pdf; Group of Thirty, *Financial Reform: A Framework for Financial Stability,* January 2009. http://www.group30.org/pubs/recommendations.pdf; Congressional Oversight Panel, *Special Report on Regulatory Reform,* January 2009. http://cop.senate.gov/documents/cop-012909-reportregulatoryreform.pdf; and Government Accountability Office, *Financial Regulation: A Framework for Crafting and Assessing Proposals to Modernize the Outdated U.S. Financial Regulatory System,* GAO-09-310T, January 14, 2009.

[2] Remarks by Treasury Secretary Timothy Geithner Introducing the Financial Stability Plan, February 10, 2009. http://www.ustreas.gov/press/releases/tg18.htm

[3] Examples of potential disruptions that markets appear to have handled with relative resilience include the stock market crash of 1987, during which the stock ticker "ran late," and more recent concern that the trading technology for credit default swaps might not be able to process the volume of obligations if a large institution such as Fannie Mae or Freddie Mac suffered a credit event. Currently, the Federal Reserve oversees a

domestic interbank clearing system for banks while the CFTC and the SEC oversee trading exchanges for commodities and securities respectively.

[4] Regulatory uses of "capital" include more specific definitions and classifications.

[5] See CRS Report RL3 3278, *The Basel Accords: The Implementation of II and the Modification of I*, by Walter W. Eubanks.

[6] See CRS Report RL34485, *Basel II in the United States: Progress Toward a Workable Framework*, by Walter W. Eubanks.

[7] National Futures Association, *NFA Manual/Rules*, Section 7001.
http://www.nfa.futures.org/nfaManual/manualFinancial.asp#fins1

[8] See Sections 1142 and 1143 of the Housing and Economic Recovery Act of 2008, P.L. 110-289.

[9] Section 135 of the Emergency Economic Stabilization Act of 2008 (EESA, P.L. 110-343).

[10] FDICIA created a new section 13(c)(4) of the Federal Deposit Insurance Act, 12 USC § 1823(c)(4)(G).

[11] "FDIC Announces Plan to Free Up Bank Liquidity," Press Release, October 14, 2008. http://www.fdic.gov/news/news/press/2008/pr08100.html

[12] The scope of federal preemption has been the subject of recent court decisions. See CRS Report RS22485, *Watters v. Wachovia Bank, N.A.*, by M. Maureen Murphy.

[13] See CRS Report RL34420, *Bear Stearns: Crisis and "Rescue" for a Major Provider of Mortgage-Related Products*, by Gary Shorter.

[14] See CRS Report RL34427, *Financial Turmoil: Federal Reserve Policy Responses*, by Marc Labonte.

[15] SEC, "Holding Company Supervision Program Description: Consolidated Supervised Entities ("CSEs")," http://www.sec.gov/divisions/marketreg/hcsupervision.htm.

[16] The Market Reform Act of 1990 permits the SEC to collect certain financial information from unregulated affiliates of broker/dealers, under the Broker-Dealer Risk Assessment Program.

[17] Some argue that CSE allowed the investment banks to hold less capital and increase their leverage. For two views on this issue, see Stephen Labaton, "Agency's '04 Rule Let Banks Pile Up New Debt, and Risk," New York Times, October 3, 2008, p. A1, and: Testimony of SEC Chairman Christopher Cox, House Oversight and Government Reform Committee, October 23, 2008. (Response to question from Rep. Christopher Shays.)

[18] By becoming bank holding companies, Morgan Stanley and Goldman Sachs placed themselves under Federal Reserve regulation, presumably to signal to the markets that their financial condition was being monitored.

[19] SEC, "Chairman Cox Announces End of Consolidated Supervised Entities Program," Press Release 2008-230.

[20] For more on GSEs and their regulation, see CRS Reports CRS Report RS21724, *GSE Regulatory Reform: Frequently Asked Questions*, by N. Eric Weiss, and CRS Report RS21663, *Government-Sponsored Enterprises(GSEs): An Institutional Overview*, by Kevin R. Kosar.

[21] See CRS Report RS22950, *Fannie Mae and Freddie Mac in Conservatorship*, by Mark Jickling.

[22] P.L. 95-630, 92 STAT. 3641.

[23] Executive Order 12631, March 18, 1988, 53 FR 9421.

[24] President's Working Group on Financial Markets, "Policy Statement on Financial Market Developments," March 2008, http://www.ustreas.gov/press/releases/reports/pwgpolicystatemktturmoil_03122008.pdf.

[25] Bank for International Settlements, *Triennial Central Bank Survey: Foreign exchange and derivatives market activity*, December 2007, p. 1. http://www.bis.org/publ/rpfxf07t.pdf

[26] http://www.newyorkfed.org/aboutthefed/fedpoint/fed02.html.

[27] Federal Reserve Bank of New York, "Federal Reserve Announces Establishment of Primary Dealer Credit Facility," Press Release, March 16, 2008.
http://www.newyorkfed.org/newsevents/news/markets/2008/rp080316.html.

[28] Bank for International Settlements, *Quarterly Review*, December 2008, p. A103.
http://www.bis.org/publ/qtrpdf/r_qt0812.htm.

[29] See CRS Report RS22932, *Credit Default Swaps: Frequently Asked Questions*, by Edward V. Murphy.

[30] CRS Report RL34427, *Financial Turmoil: Federal Reserve Policy Responses*, by Marc Labonte, p. 16.

[31] Weakening underwriting standards are just one of many explanations for the housing bubble, including unsustainable capital flows that may have been due to a global savings glut or monetary policies that may have been too expansionary for too long.

[32] See CRS Report RS22722, *Securitization and Federal Regulation of Mortgages for Safety and Soundness*, by Edward V. Murphy.

[33] See CRS Report 94-511, *Hedge Funds: Should They Be Regulated?*, by Mark Jickling.

[34] United States Senate, Permanent Subcommittee on Investigations of the Committee on Homeland Security and Governmental Affairs, *Staff Report: Excessive Speculation in the Natural Gas Market*, June 25, 2007.

[35] The Comptrollers handbooks are occasionally updated. The most recent handbook for the Bank Supervision Process is dated September 2007 and can be found at http://www.occ.gov/handbook/banksup.pdf.

CHAPTER SOURCES

The following chapters have been previously published:

Chapter 1 – This is an edited, excerpted and augmented edition of a United States Congressional Research Service publication, Report Order Code R40613, dated May 29, 2009.

Chapter 2 – This is an edited, excerpted and augmented edition of a United States publication, Report Order Code R40696, dated July 17, 2009.

Chapter 3 – This is an edited, excerpted and augmented edition of a United States Department of the Treasury publication, dated 2009.

Chapter 4 – These remarks were delivered as Statement of Orice M. Williams, Director, Financial Markets and Community Investment, before the Subcommittee on Capital Markets, Insurance and Government Sponsored Enterprises, U.S. House of Representatives, dated May 7, 2009. Government Accountability Office (GAO), Publication GAO-09-677T.

Chapter 5 – This is an edited, excerpted and augmented edition of a United States publication, Report Order Code R40417, dated March 6, 2009.

Chapter 6 – This is an edited, excerpted and augmented edition of a United States Government Accountability Office (GAO), Report to Congressional Committees. Publication GAO-09-739, dated July 2009.

Chapter 7 – This is an edited, excerpted and augmented edition of a United States publication, Report Order Code R40249, dated March 16, 2009.

Index

9

9/11, 244

A

academics, xii, 38, 117, 135, 157, 196
accountability, x, xi, 13, 15, 25, 36, 37, 39, 40, 41, 43, 50, 52, 57, 58, 60, 83, 84, 85, 88, 90, 97, 100, 102, 105, 124, 224
accounting, 44, 49, 61, 106, 111, 112, 140, 155, 158, 181, 183, 200, 225, 229, 237, 238, 246, 262
accounting standards, 44, 49, 61, 111, 112, 181, 237, 246
achievement, 140
adjustment, 184
administrators, 136, 139
adverse event, 166
age, 29, 64
agriculture, 257
alternatives, 101, 132
amortization, 94
annual review, 11
antitrust, 19
appetite, 63
arbitrage, 39, 50, 63, 65, 84, 85, 183, 201, 202, 230
arbitration, 32, 90, 99, 167
Argentina, 224, 229
Asia, 129
assessment, 67, 111, 144, 149, 162, 165, 170, 174, 189, 203, 205, 206, 227, 244
assessment procedures, 111
assumptions, viii, 2, 10, 14, 15, 154, 175, 203, 204
attacks, 244
Attorney General, viii, 2, 10, 11, 19, 20, 84, 87
auditing, 117, 147, 192, 249
Australia, 222, 224, 225, 229, 230
authors, 264
automation, 101
availability, 26, 28, 38, 50, 54, 63, 71, 137, 154, 155, 158, 170, 225
awareness, 30, 94, 132

B

background, xiii, 135, 155, 170
bail, 261, 262
bank failure, vii, xiii, 107, 137, 231
bankers, 152, 258
bankruptcy, viii, 1, 3, 8, 18, 41, 102, 103, 177, 224, 226, 244, 247, 258, 263
barriers, 16, 29
BBB, 18, 239
behavior, 10, 19, 102, 123, 131, 137, 139, 155, 201, 235, 236
Belgium, 224, 229
benchmarks, 129, 165
benign, 7, 149, 174
bias, 6, 129
Big Bang, xiv, 232
binding, 43, 47, 60, 100, 149, 163, 182
blame, 96, 232
blind spot, 66
board members, 100
bond market, 2
bondholders, 262
bonding, 128
bonds, vii, viii, 1, 2, 3, 9, 71, 74, 118, 122, 128, 129, 137, 201, 224, 228, 239, 246, 258, 259, 260, 262
borrowers, 28, 39, 40, 72, 73, 83, 95, 96, 97, 117, 136, 137, 148, 158, 159, 161, 228, 242
borrowing, 66, 130, 228, 261
branching, 44, 63, 64
Brazil, 224, 229

breaches, 150
breakdown, 72, 73, 233
buffer, 170, 177, 199, 205, 257
burn, 19
business cycle, 61, 139, 183, 188, 200
business environment, 205
business model, 2, 6, 14, 15, 17, 245
buyer, 4, 263

C

calibration, 58
Canada, 5, 224, 229
capital flows, 265
capital markets, 9, 61, 98, 155, 186
capital mobility, 136
cartel, 16
cash flow, 44, 61, 243, 262, 263
categorization, 204
category b, 201
central bank, 20, 80, 135, 138, 201, 224, 229, 230, 250
certificates of deposit, 261
China, 224, 229
circulation, 20, 243
City, 18, 222, 223, 225, 229
civil rights, 87, 88
Civil War, 234
clarity, 10, 92
classes, xiv, 18, 231, 233, 246, 262
classification, 54, 171, 241
clients, 17, 47, 73, 99, 117, 122, 123, 132, 133, 170, 177, 179
closure, 107
collaboration, 106
collateral, 19, 61, 82, 99, 122, 123, 139, 140, 147, 148, 158, 160, 162, 168, 170, 172, 177, 185, 199, 201, 205, 228, 229, 245, 251, 258
colleges, 48, 106, 107, 108
commerce, 44, 56, 64, 66, 90
commercial bank, 53, 63, 64, 65, 66, 82, 170, 171, 201, 243, 257, 258, 259
commodity, xii, 19, 67, 77, 79, 115, 116, 117, 118, 171, 227, 248, 251, 255, 257, 258, 261
commodity futures, xii, 115, 116, 227
commodity markets, 117
communication, 100, 171
community, xii, 38, 42, 63, 84, 87, 88, 89, 90, 97, 105, 177
compensation, 17, 20, 27, 43, 45, 49, 59, 60, 73, 74, 95, 98, 100, 110, 227

compensation package, 43, 60, 100
competition, 4, 6, 13, 16, 17, 19, 27, 28, 59, 62, 69, 78, 84, 95, 96
competitive advantage, 33, 65
competitiveness, 20, 71, 125, 229
competitors, 29, 260
complement, 136
complexity, ix, 6, 16, 20, 28, 35, 55, 93, 94, 111, 123, 254, 255
compliance, xiii, 27, 49, 67, 83, 84, 87, 88, 89, 90, 97, 111, 113, 124, 125, 143, 146, 167, 177, 191, 193, 206, 227, 242, 247, 254
components, xii, 115, 144, 206, 226, 227
composition, 58, 71, 163, 165
computation, 120, 169
computing, 167, 260
concentration, 16, 64, 68, 119, 182, 206, 229
confidence, x, 6, 15, 30, 36, 41, 60, 82, 83, 84, 95, 104, 125, 138, 161, 178, 202, 203, 228, 229
conflict, viii, 2, 5, 7, 11, 17, 27, 28, 88, 95, 99
conflict of interest, viii, 2, 5, 7, 11, 17, 95, 99
congressional hearings, 4
consensus, 42, 105
consent, 4, 25, 96
consolidation, 167, 229
consultants, 60
consulting, 7, 14, 57, 103, 125
consumer protection, ix, xi, 24, 25, 26, 27, 28, 29, 30, 35, 37, 40, 41, 46, 47, 57, 59, 64, 70, 83, 84, 85, 86, 87, 88, 89, 90, 96, 100, 237, 242, 252
consumption, 159, 196
contingency, 82, 108, 178
continuity, 107
control, ix, 35, 44, 56, 64, 103, 104, 109, 150, 155, 163, 167, 197, 206, 227, 240, 244, 246, 248, 256, 259, 261
convergence, 112
conversion, 71, 202, 257
copper, 235
corporate finance, 252
corporate governance, 246
corporations, vii, viii, 1, 2, 28, 48, 104, 246, 248
correlation, 122
correlations, 6
costs, 26, 28, 30, 31, 39, 47, 51, 58, 59, 69, 86, 88, 91, 92, 93, 94, 95, 98, 101, 102, 104, 136, 137, 139, 150, 170, 245
counsel, 60
counseling, 260
Court of Appeals, 125

covering, 20, 76, 125
credit market, 6, 18, 145, 161, 172, 261
Credit Rating Agency Reform Act, 4, 5
creditors, 3, 56, 65, 67, 110, 115, 116, 117, 118, 120, 122, 123, 129, 148, 166, 170, 199, 242
creditworthiness, vii, viii, 1, 2, 3, 8, 9, 28, 159, 170, 229
crime, 30
crisis management, xi, 37, 48, 107, 108
criticism, 6, 19
culture, 28, 84, 100
currency, 19, 29, 130, 224, 234, 235, 240, 243, 250, 258
current prices, 161
customers, xiii, 17, 64, 65, 98, 99, 104, 107, 150, 166, 168, 172, 178, 229, 231, 238, 240, 246, 247, 251, 256, 262

D

danger, 76, 103
data collection, 89
data processing, 25
database, 14, 18, 74
death, 243
debts, 95, 234, 242
decisions, 5, 15, 19, 25, 26, 27, 29, 37, 74, 85, 90, 92, 93, 95, 98, 100, 101, 121, 124, 154, 188, 224, 249, 265
deduction, 101, 158, 240
defense, 87, 257
defined benefit pension, 125, 133
definition, 4, 8, 29, 31, 32, 39, 48, 49, 50, 66, 105, 106, 109, 194, 203, 227, 228, 236, 240, 243, 263
delinquency, 174, 252
delivery, 227
demographic characteristics, 137
Department of Justice, 46, 86, 87, 100
deposits, 66, 107, 136, 137, 138, 163, 236, 240, 242, 243, 245, 255, 257, 258, 259, 261
detection, 18, 27, 131
deterrence, 131
differentiation, 113
directors, viii, 2, 13, 14, 68, 165, 254
discipline, ix, 35, 116, 119, 122, 123, 170
discrimination, 25, 85, 97
dislocation, 6
distress, 41, 102, 139
distribution, 39, 72, 205, 250
District of Columbia, 125
diversification, 64, 75, 118, 135, 203

diversity, 57, 88, 165
division, 19, 84, 125, 232, 257
dominance, 19
draft, 17, 111, 149, 189
drawing, 68, 141, 183
duration, 70, 73, 235, 255
duties, 27, 29, 30, 31, 32, 47, 57, 94, 95, 98, 121

E

early warning, 135, 136, 167
earnings, 145, 163, 197, 226, 240, 254, 258
East Asia, 128
economic activity, 139, 159, 197
economic crisis, 232
economic cycle, 185, 203
economic efficiency, 70
economic growth, 35, 54, 130, 139, 144, 147, 159, 187, 194, 196
economic performance, 160
economics, 11, 16, 29, 140
election, 241
electronic trade, 74, 77
e-mail, 9, 19, 20
employees, 25, 31, 60, 101, 104, 128
employment, 47, 101, 258
end-users, 77
energy, 4, 79
environment, 91, 139, 178, 225
Equal Credit Opportunity Act, 26, 86
equality, 109, 110
equities, 172
equity market, 18
erosion, 138, 175
estimating, 177, 202
ethics, 5
European Central Bank, 230
European Commission, 15
European style, 261
European Union, viii, 2, 14, 70
evolution, 39, 50
examinations, 51, 54, 57, 62, 67, 81, 87, 116, 118, 119, 120, 131, 144, 148, 161, 163, 164, 167, 171, 187, 195, 197, 198, 199, 227, 243, 244, 254
exchange rate, 224, 234, 250
exclusion, 8, 99
execution, 77, 96, 137, 227
Executive Order, 17, 125, 229, 265
exercise, 53, 71, 87, 104, 112, 116, 118, 123
expertise, 15, 19, 41, 45, 69, 84, 102, 118, 122
exports, 250

exposure, 39, 55, 72, 82, 111, 121, 122, 129, 131, 146, 151, 155, 157, 163, 170, 178, 194, 196, 197, 201, 204, 229, 236, 240, 243, 254
externalities, 55

F

Fair Housing Act, 87
fairness, xi, 25, 29, 37, 41, 47, 83, 90, 97, 98
faith, 92, 95, 228
family, 25, 68, 71, 201
farms, 238
fear, 92, 235
federal law, 27, 30, 46, 88, 116, 118, 121, 237, 262
Federal Reserve Board, 41, 43, 52, 57, 93, 102, 103, 104, 105, 135, 255
Federal Reserve regulations, 84
feedback, 12
fiduciary responsibilities, 122
finance, ix, xiii, 6, 7, 10, 11, 12, 13, 14, 17, 19, 33, 35, 64, 71, 75, 89, 104, 131, 135, 136, 148, 151, 160, 162, 172, 178, 194, 225, 230, 248, 259, 263
financial difficulty, 242
financial distress, xiii, 55, 56, 116, 119, 123, 135, 136, 140, 184, 259
financial instability, 183, 188, 200, 227, 238
financial intermediaries, ix, 28, 35, 41, 47, 83, 94, 95, 98, 155, 233, 235, 236
financial oversight, x, 36, 186
financial regulation, vii, x, xii, xiii, 36, 38, 51, 231, 232, 236
financial resources, 28, 82, 235
financial sector, xi, 37, 40, 60, 69, 72, 85, 144, 147, 155, 196, 233
Financial Services Authority, 30, 175, 225, 228, 230
financial shocks, 28
financial soundness, 248
financial stability, x, xiii, 36, 41, 42, 43, 44, 48, 51, 52, 53, 54, 55, 56, 57, 67, 68, 70, 96, 102, 103, 108, 109, 132, 135, 136, 144, 180, 185, 186, 187, 229, 230, 232
financial support, 178, 229
financing, 49, 62, 65, 110, 111, 117, 124, 153, 170, 177, 178, 236, 243, 260, 263
firewalls, 62
First Amendment, 7, 8, 9, 20
flexibility, 164
flight, 69
flood, 69
fluctuations, 172, 183, 188, 200, 252
focusing, ix, 24, 25, 97, 111, 165

forecasting, 255
foreclosure, 28, 90, 192
foreign banks, 44, 62, 110, 237, 244
foreign exchange, vii, xiv, 130, 232, 241, 250, 251, 255, 258
foreign exchange market, 130, 250
foreign firms, 109
fragility, 63
France, 177, 223, 224, 229, 230
franchise, 13
fraud, 7, 8, 18, 20, 30, 40, 45, 75, 76, 77, 83, 90, 97, 117, 122, 131, 132, 230, 246, 248, 262
freedom, 8, 128
FSB, 48, 49, 106, 107, 108, 109, 110, 111, 112, 228
fuel, 154
funding, ix, 24, 25, 30, 38, 41, 46, 50, 53, 59, 68, 85, 89, 102, 124, 136, 138, 139, 150, 155, 158, 160, 161, 168, 170, 177, 178, 196, 224, 227, 229, 235, 255, 258, 260

G

G7 countries, 230
GDP, 145, 153, 154
Generally Accepted Accounting Principles, 73, 112, 145, 166, 255
Germany, 177, 224, 229, 230
global markets, 131
goals, 25, 48, 71, 76, 88, 90, 106, 110, 118, 128, 139, 229
governance, 43, 57, 103, 186, 206, 254
government intervention, 29, 129
government securities, 5, 172, 250, 251
grades, vii, viii, 1, 2, 3
grants, 86
Great Depression, viii, ix, 23, 24, 35, 63, 235, 236
gross domestic product, 145, 154, 192
groups, 117, 122, 180, 187
growth, 4, 15, 39, 40, 41, 55, 67, 72, 75, 77, 83, 84, 89, 91, 123, 131, 133, 137, 155, 161, 164, 202, 205, 241, 248
guidance, xii, 26, 31, 49, 56, 85, 87, 110, 111, 115, 116, 118, 121, 122, 140, 147, 171, 191, 194
guidelines, 25, 43, 49, 59, 106, 108, 110, 116, 117, 124, 139, 191
guilty, 14

H

harm, 31, 38, 50, 101
harmonization, 78, 79

health, 145, 226, 264
hedging, 73, 260
higher quality, 175
hiring, 182, 241
historical reason, 40, 83
holding company, ix, x, 36, 41, 44, 59, 60, 65, 66, 71, 102, 150, 162, 165, 166, 167, 168, 169, 180, 191, 198, 227, 245, 247, 251, 256, 259, 261, 264
home ownership, 71
homeowners, 259
Hong Kong, 224, 229, 230
hopes, 28
host, 108
House, ix, 4, 16, 18, 19, 23, 24, 32, 95, 133, 190, 192, 265, 267
household income, 159, 196
households, 30, 33, 38, 50, 53, 69, 96, 97, 101, 132, 139, 157, 236
housing, ix, 5, 6, 10, 14, 17, 20, 35, 38, 49, 63, 71, 139, 141, 152, 154, 155, 158, 236, 248, 252, 265
human resources, 62
hybrid, vii, xiv, 96, 226, 232
hypothesis, 159

I

identification, 42, 47, 51, 53, 91, 109, 165
illiquid asset, 167
images, 145, 180
IMF, 107, 111
immunity, 91
implementation, 5, 49, 80, 110, 111, 139, 144, 149, 169, 173, 182, 184, 190, 205, 206, 240
imports, 250
incentives, 15, 43, 49, 53, 54, 56, 59, 60, 73, 74, 90, 94, 95, 101, 110, 149, 154, 165, 174, 183, 186, 195, 200, 201, 236
income, 33, 39, 72, 73, 90, 93, 97, 101, 102, 125, 136, 139, 140, 225, 229, 262
income distribution, 33
income tax, 101, 262
increased competition, 15
independence, 11, 60, 85
indexing, 244
India, 224, 229
indication, 27
indicators, 55, 136, 181, 249
indices, 18
Indonesia, 224, 229
industrialized countries, 182
inefficiency, 69

inequality, 200
inertia, 101
inflation, 244, 245, 257
information exchange, 108, 110, 111
information sharing, 42, 51, 106, 107, 113, 249
infrastructure, 39, 40, 72, 80, 82, 84
injury, iv, 27
innovation, ix, x, 24, 25, 26, 29, 36, 39, 41, 69, 72, 75, 78, 83, 84, 85, 92, 93, 136, 137, 138, 152
insight, 159, 186
inspections, 120, 227
instability, 79, 119, 123, 130
instruments, 6, 17, 39, 40, 49, 58, 72, 76, 77, 78, 79, 109, 111, 122, 123, 130, 138, 145, 146, 147, 154, 155, 157, 158, 160, 164, 166, 167, 172, 175, 184, 197, 198, 226, 238, 250, 260, 261
integration, 55, 70
integrity, x, 7, 11, 15, 19, 36, 45, 74, 77, 79, 124, 125, 224, 229
interaction, 120
interbank market, 234
interdependence, 7
interest rates, 93, 94, 129, 130, 139, 150, 154, 163, 224, 242, 243, 248, 251, 255, 260
intermediaries, 47, 78, 86, 89, 91, 93, 95, 98, 116, 119, 123, 227, 246
internal controls, 150, 165, 205
internal processes, 230
international financial institutions, 230
International Monetary Fund, 107, 170, 222, 223
international standards, 49, 78, 80, 106, 110, 112, 140
internet, 93
investment bank, viii, xii, 2, 10, 11, 20, 39, 50, 52, 53, 64, 65, 66, 67, 104, 117, 123, 125, 127, 131, 247, 251, 260, 261, 264, 265
isolation, 20, 57
Italy, 111, 224, 229

J

Japan, 5, 224, 229
jobs, 15, 69
journalists, 7, 8, 20
judgment, 96, 112, 182, 188, 189, 228, 252
jurisdiction, vii, xiv, 30, 31, 40, 46, 52, 78, 83, 84, 85, 86, 87, 88, 90, 97, 99, 232, 233, 238, 244, 246, 247, 248, 249
justification, 66, 125, 131

K

Korea, 224, 229

L

labor, 258
lack of confidence, 6
land, 84
language, 21, 30, 132
laws, 1, 4, 5, 8, 18, 26, 27, 28, 46, 47, 65, 76, 77, 78, 79, 84, 86, 87, 88, 96, 97, 98, 99, 100, 115, 116, 117, 140, 143, 146, 170, 191, 194, 227, 242, 246, 250, 251, 252, 256
leadership, 42, 47, 84, 100, 105
leakage, 102
legislation, ix, 4, 5, 17, 23, 24, 25, 32, 42, 43, 45, 48, 52, 53, 60, 63, 69, 70, 80, 81, 86, 90, 91, 99, 104, 132, 138
legislative proposals, ix, 23, 24
lender of last resort, 244, 245, 259
licenses, 14, 16
life span, 129
lifetime, 102
likelihood, 6, 7, 20, 75, 101, 177, 227, 236
limitation, 63, 139
line, 49, 56, 61, 87, 110, 125, 170, 246, 257
liquid assets, 137, 177, 198, 227, 233, 235, 261
liquidate, 129, 150, 177, 262
literacy, 90
litigation, 8, 78, 84, 150, 229
local government, 53
low risk, 151, 175
lower prices, 160

M

macroeconomic policy, 250
maintenance, 108, 204, 206, 228, 241
mandates, xiii, 91, 128
manipulation, 45, 75, 76, 77, 130, 248
market capitalization, 173, 192, 228
market discipline, xii, 39, 40, 72, 73, 115, 116, 117, 118, 122, 123, 124, 125, 132, 144, 148, 162, 170, 174, 183, 195, 198, 199, 200, 203, 206
market failure, 10
market share, 19
marketability, 254
marketing, 77, 92, 260
marketplace, 70, 90, 91, 94, 101, 250, 259

measurement, 5, 10, 111, 129, 163, 167, 183, 184, 200, 202, 203, 205
measures, ix, xii, 10, 35, 40, 45, 46, 59, 68, 74, 75, 76, 83, 86, 87, 90, 94, 97, 101, 106, 113, 115, 117, 144, 148, 152, 163, 166, 169, 170, 173, 174, 175, 182, 184, 186, 188, 202, 226, 240
membership, 42, 47, 51, 63, 69, 108, 258, 262
metals, 128, 258, 260
Mexico, 224, 229
minority, 226, 240
missions, 51, 76, 77, 84
model, 2, 3, 11, 12, 17, 18, 19, 29, 71, 92, 94, 106, 112, 136, 138, 162, 264
modeling, 7, 20, 143, 149, 177, 184, 188, 189, 205
models, viii, xi, 2, 3, 7, 10, 12, 14, 15, 19, 28, 37, 129, 144, 149, 154, 160, 167, 168, 174, 175, 177, 181, 182, 184, 188, 189, 198, 199, 202, 203, 205, 238
modernization, 259
monetary policy, 59, 80, 240, 244
money, xii, 3, 18, 25, 30, 49, 58, 68, 69, 110, 111, 125, 127, 128, 130, 132, 148, 159, 170, 235, 252, 260, 261
money laundering, 49, 69, 110, 111
moral hazard, 103, 130, 261, 264
mortality, 129
mortality rate, 129
mortgage-backed securities, viii, 1, 2, 5, 6, 9, 10, 11, 15, 19, 58, 74, 155, 161, 201, 224, 236, 251
multiplication, 205

N

nation, ix, 35, 38, 39, 50, 69, 72, 187
natural gas, 252
negotiating, 122
negotiation, 90
Netherlands, 224, 229, 230
New England, 234
New York, iv
New York Stock Exchange, 145, 167, 192, 228, 263
newspapers, 8
North America, 106
Norway, 141

O

Obama Administration, v, viii, ix, 23, 24, 31, 132
objectives, vii, viii, ix, x, xiii, xiv, 17, 23, 24, 26, 30, 36, 45, 75, 76, 77, 79, 80, 81, 86, 97, 118, 143, 146, 147, 192, 193, 205, 232
objectivity, 7

obligation, 150, 169, 178, 257, 258
observations, 7, 16, 175
oil, xii, 127
oligopoly, 6
opacity, 94
operator, 227
Operators, 78
order, xiii, 14, 26, 41, 53, 55, 57, 60, 67, 71, 73, 81, 87, 93, 96, 101, 102, 111, 118, 125, 145, 186, 190, 203, 204, 231, 237, 238, 243, 248, 249
Organization for Economic Cooperation and Development, 201, 222, 230
ownership, 119, 125, 147, 249, 256, 257, 263

P

parameters, 204
Parliament, 21
partnership, 104, 237
payroll, 101
PCA, 145, 163, 164, 171, 227
peer group, 166
peer review, 49, 110, 111
penalties, 47, 90, 91, 93, 94, 95, 150
pension plans, xii, 115, 117, 118, 121, 122, 125
percentile, 205
perceptions, 96, 130
permit, 66, 67, 78, 93, 110, 121, 239
planning, 55, 108, 181, 182, 206
police, 77
policy choice, 244
policy makers, 41, 83, 84, 107
pools, x, 10, 11, 36, 39, 44, 50, 67, 110, 117, 123, 128, 132, 177, 225, 227, 252, 255, 260, 261, 262
poor, 76
population, 132
portfolio, vii, 1, 18, 118, 121, 124, 129, 164, 167, 184, 198, 203, 228, 229, 242, 254
portfolio investment, 118
portfolios, xiv, 39, 71, 72, 73, 80, 130, 131, 136, 137, 152, 153, 155, 161, 163, 175, 232, 236, 238, 243, 248
power, 19, 60, 61, 64, 97, 104, 122, 244, 246
premiums, 95, 150, 264
president, 15, 16, 17, 135, 160
pressure, 116, 118, 130, 160, 195, 233, 255
prevention, 27, 42, 105
prices, ix, 6, 7, 35, 38, 49, 77, 136, 139, 144, 147, 150, 153, 155, 157, 158, 159, 160, 161, 175, 177, 186, 187, 196, 224, 248, 255, 257, 260
privacy, 90, 260

private firms, 252
private investment, 62, 67
private sector, 63, 116, 118, 119, 120, 124
probability, 6, 151, 176, 181, 202, 203, 204
probe, 19
producers, 70
product market, 40, 83
production, 73, 87
profit, 9, 28, 71, 128, 130, 131, 136, 227, 245, 248, 256, 258, 262, 263
profit margin, 71
profitability, 31, 140, 176, 237
profits, vii, ix, xiv, 19, 28, 29, 33, 35, 128, 139, 232, 262
program, 19, 44, 66, 67, 84, 120, 124, 125, 148, 162, 167, 168, 169, 171, 198, 224, 226, 228, 236, 247
protocol, 16
psychology, 29
public debt, 104
public interest, 4, 5, 166, 227
public policy, 15, 17, 45, 71, 75, 77, 129
public sector, 121
publishers, 8

R

race, 6, 42, 105
range, 25, 41, 44, 46, 55, 56, 57, 61, 65, 78, 80, 83, 86, 87, 89, 90, 100, 117, 128, 129, 145, 150, 155, 157, 163, 165, 174, 181, 186, 194, 197, 198, 201, 203, 228, 244, 248, 262
rating agencies, vii, viii, 1, 2, 4, 8, 9, 11, 13, 14, 15, 16, 18, 19, 20, 74, 75
ratings, vii, viii, 1, 2, 3, 4, 5, 6, 7, 8, 9, 10, 11, 12, 13, 14, 15, 16, 17, 18, 19, 20, 40, 45, 72, 73, 74, 75, 112, 113, 171, 203, 226, 238, 254, 255
real assets, 201
real estate, 25, 30, 33, 204, 245
real time, 131
real-time basis, 92
reason, 40, 57, 81, 83, 130
reasoning, 8, 20, 154, 191
recession, ix, 35, 101, 204, 234
recognition, 4, 59, 61, 73, 112, 117, 201, 202, 229, 230
recovery, x, 36, 185
refining, 48, 105
reforms, viii, x, xi, xii, 2, 10, 11, 13, 14, 15, 23, 24, 36, 37, 38, 41, 42, 83, 105, 108, 143, 144, 148, 149, 173, 181, 184, 188, 189, 195, 229, 234, 252

regulatory framework, xii, 27, 28, 38, 40, 44, 63, 65, 68, 69, 72, 83, 98, 144, 146, 147, 149, 174, 182, 183, 184, 186, 188, 191, 193, 200, 202, 233
regulatory oversight, xii, 115, 117, 143, 144, 148, 149, 170, 171, 180, 189
regulatory requirements, 162, 183, 184
relationship, 6, 39, 72, 74, 98, 242, 251, 256, 260
relaxation, 73, 252
reliability, 6, 7, 16, 124, 147, 192, 224
repair, 90
reputation, 150, 178
Requirements, 55, 161, 164, 182, 193, 203, 205, 217, 238, 239, 241
resale, 250, 252, 261
reserves, 61, 130, 204, 235, 238, 240, 244
resilience, ix, 35, 64, 265
resolution, 39, 41, 47, 48, 50, 51, 56, 89, 102, 103, 104, 107, 108
resource allocation, 17
resources, 39, 41, 42, 46, 53, 60, 69, 72, 78, 83, 84, 89, 90, 97, 116, 259
response time, 235
responsiveness, 254
restructuring, xi, xiv, 37, 48, 108, 232
retail, 65, 98, 99, 101, 167, 203, 204, 250, 251
retained earnings, 140, 224
retention, 73, 74
retirement, 47, 60, 101, 102, 244
returns, 71, 78, 101, 116, 117, 118, 121, 122, 129, 148, 161, 170, 197, 224
revenue, 4, 6, 9, 14, 19, 20, 150, 201, 229
rewards, x, 36, 128
risk assessment, 167, 169, 206, 238
risk factors, 228
risk profile, 44, 55, 56, 68, 96, 148, 162, 165, 170, 197, 198, 202, 206, 254
risk-taking, 60, 232, 236, 238, 247
Russia, 129, 224, 229

S

sales, 86, 99, 125, 130, 144, 147, 157, 158, 160, 161, 194, 196, 197, 251
sanctions, 14, 47, 99
Sarbanes-Oxley Act, 4
satisfaction, 104
Saudi Arabia, 224, 229
savings, ix, xi, 3, 26, 27, 35, 37, 46, 47, 85, 86, 95, 101, 102, 136, 145, 153, 166, 226, 227, 236, 237, 243, 245, 257, 258, 259, 262, 264, 265
savings banks, 262

search, 128, 129, 191, 224
searches, 191
Secretary of the Treasury, 41, 42, 48, 51, 102, 104,
Securities Exchange Act, 3, 4, 18, 66, 125, 172, 228
security, 9, 12, 13, 15, 17, 19, 47, 78, 90, 92, 101, 102, 119, 148, 162, 172, 177, 228, 246, 256, 258, 261, 262, 263
segregation, 260
selectivity, 19
self-interest, 29
self-regulation, xiv, 132, 231
Senate, 4, 18, 25, 133, 190, 192, 226, 227, 228, 249, 265
sensitivity, 145, 163, 174, 175, 189, 197, 199, 202, 205, 226, 249
separation, ix, 24, 25, 66
service provider, 89, 94, 118, 123
severe stress, 55, 174
severity, 75, 155
shape, 153, 251
shareholder value, 43, 49, 59, 110
shareholders, 60, 68, 71, 100, 128
shares, 14, 125, 262, 263
sharing, 48, 107, 249
shock, 79, 94, 176
short run, 139
short-term liabilities, 178
Singapore, 224, 229, 230
smoothing, 120
software, 3
solvency, 71, 130, 149, 153, 176, 181, 185, 200, 203, 205, 225, 247
South Africa, 224, 229
SPA, 86
space, 15
Spain, 224, 229
spectrum, vii, viii, 1, 2
speculation, xi, xii, 37, 127, 131, 139, 172, 248
speech, 8, 9, 20, 120, 140, 186
speed, 2
spillover effects, 107, 149, 185
stability, ix, xiii, 35, 39, 41, 45, 50, 52, 58, 60, 69, 71, 80, 81, 83, 84, 102, 103, 135, 146, 148, 149, 161, 185, 242, 244, 250, 255
standard of living, 28
standardization, 45, 48, 74, 106
state borders, 64
state laws, 27, 88
state regulators, 89, 150, 179, 194, 245
statistics, viii, 2, 5, 12, 89, 175

statutes, 3, 6, 28, 46, 77, 78, 79, 86, 87, 88, 89, 90, 96, 250, 256
steel, xii, 127
stock, 17, 33, 116, 117, 118, 121, 128, 130, 140, 150, 168, 172, 173, 226, 239, 240, 244, 246, 248, 249, 251, 252, 255, 258, 265
stock exchange, 246
stock markets, 128, 172
stock price, 140, 150, 172, 251, 255
strain, 67, 116, 119
strategies, xii, 101, 117, 121, 123, 127, 128, 130, 131, 146, 151, 157, 160, 165, 170, 237
strength, 45, 55, 71, 79, 82, 162, 165, 177, 197
stress, x, xiii, 36, 41, 55, 71, 79, 105, 116, 118, 120, 135, 139, 144, 158, 163, 167, 175, 181, 184, 185, 186, 187, 194, 196, 200, 206, 225, 227
strictures, x, 36
structuring, 5, 10
subpoena, 87, 97
subprime loans, 15, 20, 95, 96, 137, 152
subscribers, 5, 8
subsidy, 44, 61, 66
substitutes, 96, 235
summer, 153, 178
supervisor, 44, 46, 52, 53, 55, 56, 57, 59, 66, 85, 88, 97, 125
supervisors, 39, 56, 57, 59, 62, 63, 70, 72, 87, 88, 107, 110, 138, 150, 152, 164, 177, 194, 206
supply, 251
Supreme Court, 8, 9, 20
surveillance, 12
susceptibility, 45, 68
sustainability, 254
sustainable growth, 85
Sweden, 224, 229
switching, 257
Switzerland, 177, 224, 225, 229, 230
symbols, 13, 14

T

talent, 182
targets, 97
tax incentive, 101
telecommunications, 4
telephone, 250, 262
tension, 238
terrorism, 69
threat, x, 17, 36, 42, 43, 44, 51, 52, 53, 54, 67, 68, 76, 109, 131, 132, 185, 187, 248, 250
threats, xiii, 52, 56, 57, 84, 135, 180, 185, 186

threshold, 44, 67, 73, 101, 110, 120, 132, 168
thresholds, 54, 107, 125, 139
thrifts, 27, 40, 62, 63, 83, 144, 148, 150, 157, 161, 162, 163, 164, 165, 197, 226, 240, 244, 245, 262
time deposits, 240
time frame, 5
time periods, 175
time-frame, 69
timing, 92, 97, 182, 185, 188, 235
tracking, 89, 163
trade, 33, 67, 77, 78, 117, 119, 123, 132, 151, 172, 194, 248, 250, 258, 259, 261
trading partners, 130
tranches, 18, 19, 39, 72, 75, 155, 230, 262
transformation, 67
transition, 63, 182, 188, 192, 228
transition period, 182, 188
transparency, ix, x, xi, 11, 13, 14, 15, 16, 18, 25, 35, 36, 37, 40, 41, 44, 45, 47, 49, 60, 61, 72, 73, 74, 75, 76, 77, 79, 83, 90, 91, 94, 97, 100, 112, 113, 116, 118, 122, 138, 186
trial, 90
trust, xi, 30, 37, 44, 64, 66, 74, 95, 98, 100, 234
trustworthiness, 95
turbulence, 7
Turkey, 224, 229
turnover, 250

U

U.S. Department of the Treasury, 259
U.S. economy, 185
U.S. Treasury, vii, xiv, 232, 239, 246, 249, 250, 261, 264
UK, xiv, 232
uncertainty, 4, 17, 75, 88, 130, 153, 158, 159, 178, 185, 187
unemployment, ix, 35, 137, 236
uniform, 74, 131, 140, 141, 165, 198
unions, xi, 25, 26, 38, 63, 237, 240, 242, 245, 258
United Kingdom, 30, 177, 224, 228, 229
universe, 128, 252
updating, 92, 171

V

validation, 206
variables, 120, 129, 248
vehicles, xii, 54, 58, 59, 62, 69, 75, 115, 121, 178, 183, 196, 225, 227
vein, 16

velocity, 10
venture capital, vii, xiii, xiv, 44, 67, 127, 132, 133, 232, 252
venue, 99
voice, 16, 70, 100
volatility, xii, 75, 117, 121, 127, 130, 131, 160, 172, 175, 184, 204, 205, 250
vulnerability, 68, 135, 137, 178, 183, 199, 232

W

weakness, 79, 164, 185, 233
wealth, 125, 157, 225
web, 31, 133, 251
websites, 256
welfare, 29
wholesale, xiv, 167, 203, 204, 232
wind, 71, 167
workers, 65, 101
working groups, 192
workplace, 101
World Bank, 107
World War I, 172
worry, 130
writing, 83, 84, 87, 261